Perception, Common Sense, and Science

James W. Cornman

New Haven and London   Yale University Press

1975

Designed by John O. C. McCrillis.
and set in Times Roman type.
Printed in the United States of America by
The Murray Printing Co., Forge Village, Mass.

Published in Great Britain, Europe, and Africa by
Yale University Press, Ltd., London.
Distributed in Latin America by Kaiman & Polon,
Inc., New York City; in India by UBS Publishers'
Distributors Pvt., Ltd., Delhi; in Japan by
John Weatherhill, Inc., Tokyo.

Acknowledgment is gratefully made to the following
journals and publishers for permission to use material
by James W. Cornman:

"A Reconstruction of Berkeley: Minds and Physical
Objects as Theoretical Entities," *Ratio* 13 (1971):
76–87.
"Can Eddington's 'Two' Tables be Identical?"
Australasian Journal of Philosophy 52 (1974): 22–38.
"Craig's Theorem, Ramsey-Sentences, and Scientific
Instrumentalism," *Synthèse* 25 (1972): 82–128.
"On Direct Perception," *The Review of Metaphysics* 26
(1972): 38–56.
"Theoretical Phenomenalism," *Nous* 7 (1973): 120–28.
"Theoretical Terms, Berkeleyan Notion, and Minds,"
in C.M. Turbayne, ed., *Berkeley's Principles: Text and
Commentaries* (New York: Bobbs-Merrill, 1970),
pp. 161–81.

To

Debbie Cornman   Diane Cornman
Julie Cornman   Libby Cornman

for the happiness they have brought me

Contents

the nervous system, 228; Second Objection: Dependence of
seeing "real" color on which conditions are optimal, 230;
Third Objection: Perception by other creatures versus human
perception, 233; Fourth Objection: Microscopes and the color
of blood, 236; Fifth Objection: Atomic constituents and
continuous color, 240; Sixth Objection: No one property of
objects correlates with one color, 241; Seventh Objection: The
time-gap argument against naive realism, 243; Conclusion about
naive realism, 246

Preface

This book completes one phase of the task I began in *Metaphysics, Reference, and Language* (New Haven: Yale University Press, 1966), where I argued for a certain view of metaphysical problems. I claimed that these problems are external to the linguistic frameworks of the terms used to formulate them, because they concern the nature of what is referred to by some of these terms. As I shall clarify somewhat in chapter 1, a resolution of such a problem requires examination of competing, purported descriptions of those referents—for example, a common-sense description, a phenomenalistic description, and a purely scientific description of what there is. Such an examination would require a philosopher to take a position that not only is independent of all of the various competing linguistic frameworks, but also allows him to compare what there is with what the various descriptions say there is. But, I argued, such an external stance is unobtainable, and so a philosopher's best hope is to look for internal, linguistic clues to the external, metaphysical problems.

Throughout *Metaphysics, Reference, and Language*, my prime example of a metaphysical problem was the mind-body problem, and I used it primarily to illustrate my thesis about metaphysical problems. In *Materialism and Sensations* (New Haven: Yale University Press, 1971), however, I delved more deeply into this particular metaphysical problem by examining in detail reasons for or against the thesis that each sensation is identical with—perhaps, nothing but—some brain state. By the end of that examination I reached three conclusions relevant to the present book. The first is that, contrary to my first impressions, much can be done to eliminate many of the competing resolutions of an external problem without relying on any thesis about which linguistic features are internal clues to external problems. The second, which confirms the first, is that there is at most one plausible materialistic solution to the mind–body problem, namely, what I called "adverbial" materialism because of its adverbial view of sense experience. It proposes, for example, that people sense red-ly rather than that they sense red sense-data when they perceive something red in the appropriate conditions.

The third conclusion is that the adverbial materialistic theory is plausible, given the evidence that I examined in *Materialism and Sensations*, but much evidence was not yet considered. Of particular importance was whether this materialistic view of adverbial states of sensing conjoins plausibly with any of the most reasonable metaphysical theories of perception and the physical world. Surely, what these theories require of sensations in perception provides an independent test of any conclusion about the mind–body problem that is based on considerations other than perception. It was, in part, to provide this independent test that I wrote the present book about our perception of and the nature of the world around us. I apply this test to adverbial materialism in the Appendix after my conclusion about which metaphysical theory of perception and the external world is most reasonable.

Of course, the conclusion of the present book is not used merely to test previous conclusions. I also use it, with the past conclusions, to arrive at a plausible metaphysical view of man, the world around him, and his relationship to it when he perceives it. That is, I argue in the Appendix, that my past examination of the mind–body problem, and my present examination of perception and the external world provide some reason to think that one particular metaphysical thesis of this sort is more reasonable than its competitors.

The present book completes one phase of what I began in *Metaphysics, Reference, and Language* in the sense that it completes my consideration of the purely metaphysical issues that are directly relevant to the external problem I first considered in that book. But, as emphasized in the concluding chapter of the present book, there are other phases of the task that remain untouched. Some of these seem relevant to any resolution of the metaphysical problem of man, the world, and his perception of the world. That is, there are nonmetaphysical issues that may count for or against certain of the competing resolutions of a metaphysical problem. For example, problems concerning empirical knowledge, and others raised by human action and moral responsibility are thought to be relevant to such metaphysical problems. Thus, although with this book I have completed one phase of my task, I am faced with others I have only just begun.

I have received two important sorts of help in writing this book. One is extensive philosophical discussion with and criticism by others. Rather than thank here those who have helped, I acknowledge my debt to them at the appropriate places in the text. The other aid is the long, uninterrupted periods of time made available by two grants. I wish to thank here the American Council of Learned Societies for a fellowship, 1970–71, and the National Science Foundation for grant GS-28550.

University of Pennsylvania   JAMES W. CORNMAN
October 1974

Introduction

Most people, including many philosophers, behave and talk as if they are direct realists when they are involved in and reacting to their environment and their perception of it rather than theorizing about it. Indeed, it might be claimed, they act as if they are what are called "naive" realists. When not theorizing or thinking about theories of perception and the world we supposedly perceive, most of us seem to believe that there is a world of physical objects that exist and have certain properties independently of being perceived. And, when we perceive these objects, we believe we are immediately acquainted with them and some of these properties. Thus many people act and talk as if they believe we directly perceive flowers, velvet material, perfume, wine, phonograph records, and also their sizes, shapes, weights, colors, textures, odors, tastes, and sounds. When we think or theorize about perception, however, especially when we consider the facts of perceptual relativity and hallucinations, and scientific claims about the causation of perceptual experiences and the finite speed of light, many of us tend to espouse quite a different view of both perception and the external world. We theorize that we perceptually experience the effect of a quite complicated causal process which begins when some physical object either directly or indirectly affects some sense organ, and ends with a sensory experience. In certain cases, such as some involving distant stars, the causal process takes so long to occur that the object supposedly perceived does not exist at the time the relevant perceptual experience occurs. Not only does this bit of theorizing tempt many people to conclude that physical objects are at most perceived indirectly, but also that the objects lack many of those properties, such as color and odor, we so often behave as if they have. Both the external world and our perception of it seem to be quite different on this theory from the more usual, perhaps naive, views of them.

It is when we have such an apparently sharp conflict between two views of what there is, that a philosophical problem clearly arises. This is especially true when common-sense beliefs seem to

1

conflict with conclusions drawn from scientific claims. Further-more, it is predictable, when such a philosophical problem arises, that philosophers will tend to gravitate towards extreme positions. In this case, those who value science highly tend to become scientific realists of the sorts that rule out even a chance of a reconciliation with common sense. Others say that science is merely a method and not a metaphysics, and so it has no ontological consequences that would threaten the supremacy of common sense. Unlike these philosophers, I feel pulled in both directions. It is hard for me to doubt that I directly see broad expanses of color spread out on the surfaces of most familiar objects around me, and I find strong initial plausibility in the view that the scientific method uncovers the discrete, unobservable particles that constitute physical objects.

It is natural that someone in such a situation should attempt to bring about a reconciliation. This is what I shall try to do in this book by carefully examining the issues involved and then using the results to argue for the thesis that we directly perceive sensuous-ly colored physical objects which are constituted of discrete unobservable particles postulated by scientific theories. In par-ticular, I shall try to do this by defending a carefully laid out argument which concludes that this form of direct realism, which I shall call "compatible common-sense realism," is more reasonable than its most plausible competitors. One of these, for example, is a form of phenomenalism derived from Berkeley's theory, which I call "theoretical" phenomenalism because it construes physical objects as theoretical constructions out of sensa. This distinguishes it from the analytical phenomenalism of A. J. Ayer. Another is a form of indirect realism derived from the scientific realism of Wilfrid Sellars with its postulation of sensa as constituents of perceptual experiences.

I have talked rather blythely above about direct realism, indirect realism, direct perception, and indirect perception. I have also claimed my first aim is to clarify the issues involved in the conflicting views of perception and the external world. But, by using notorious-ly vague and ambiguous terms, such as 'directly perceive,' have I ruined my chances, even before I begin, to clarify anything at all? If J. L. Austin is right, I am doomed from the start. He says:

> Philosophers, it is said, 'are not, for the most part, prepared

to admit that such objects as pins or cigarettes are ever directly perceived.' Now of course what brings us up short here is the word 'directly'—a great favourite among philosophers, but actually one of the less conspicuous snakes in the linguistic grass. We have here, in fact a typical case of a word, which already has a very special use, being gradually stretched without caution or definition or any limit, until it becomes, first perhaps obscurely metaphorical, but ultimately meaning-less.[1]

Austin is surely right in claiming that 'directly perceive' is not only an important term for philosophers, but also that it has been neither used with caution, nor clearly defined. He is wrong, I hope to show, to conclude that it has become ultimately meaningless in the works of these philosophers. One way to show this is to provide a definition for it, and then show how the term so defined can be used to help understand important philosophical positions more clearly.

Defining 'directly perceive' is made hard enough by the confused and vague ways philosophers have used the term, but it is made even more difficult by the fact that it is used quite differently by different philosophers. Two philosophers whose philosophy depends upon a clear understanding of direct perception are Berkeley and Russell. Consider what they say that is relevant to an understanding of their uses of the term. Berkeley, through Philonous, asks Hylas, "Are those things only perceived by the senses which are perceived immediately? Or may those things properly be said to be 'sensible' which are perceived mediately, or not without the intervention of others?"[2] Russell, in speaking of knowledge by acquaintance, says that "we have *acquaintance* with anything of which we are directly aware, without the intermediary of any process of inference or any knowledge of truths. Thus in the presence of my table I am acquainted with the sense-data that make up the appearance of my table."[3] Another quite common interpretation is given by Norman Malcolm who states

---

[1] J. L. Austin, *Sense and Sensibilia* (New York: Oxford University Press, 1964), p. 15.

[2] G. Berkeley, *Principles, Dialogues, and Philosophical Correspondence*, C. M. Turbayne, ed. (New York: Bobbs-Merrill, 1965), p. 111.

[3] B. Russell, *The Problems of Philosophy* (New York, Oxford University Press: 1959), p. 45.

the definition, "*A directly* perceives *x* if and only if *A*'s assertion that he perceives *x* could not be mistaken."[4]

These three statements are interestingly different concerning the degree to which they construe 'directly perceive' as a term describing a factual perceptual relationship between a perceiver and an object, and the degree to which they construe it as an epistemological term. In this quotation, Berkeley considers a thing to be immediately or directly perceived when it is perceived without the perception of some intermediary thing. On this construal 'directly perceive' seems to have no epistemological component. For Russell, however, not only must the object of which we are directly aware be given or presented to the perceiver without any intervening object, but it also seems that we must have noninferential knowledge about it, knowledge not mediated by any other knowledge or premises. Russell, then, adds an epistemological feature to the Berkeleyan purely factual interpretation. Malcolm's construal, on the other hand, is almost completely epistemological, for it implies little about the factual relationship someone has to an object when he directly perceives it.

I find it important to try to define a purely factual or nonepistemic sense of 'directly perceive' in order to see whether the crucial distinctions among direct realists, indirect realists, such as Locke, and phenomenalists, such as Berkeley, can be made so they have no epistemic consequences. My claim is that the differences are essentially factual, and, if you like, metaphysical. They are, as I shall briefly argue in the conclusion, epistemologically neutral.

To give initial plausibility to this claim, consider the thesis that something is directly perceivable in an epistemological sense if and only if it is directly perceivable in something like the factual sense expressed in the preceding quotation from Berkeley. Both halves of this equivalence are questionable. It has been plausibly argued that sense-data are causal, but not epistemological, intermediaries in perception, and, consequently, that there is direct, noninferential knowledge of physical objects despite the causal intermediary.[5] It has also been claimed that conclusions about physical objects are to be justified using premises about objectless,

---

[4] N. Malcolm, *Knowledge and Certainty: Essays and Lectures* (Englewood Cliffs, New Jersey: Prentice-Hall, 1963), p. 89.

[5] See A. M. Quinton, "The Problem of Perception", *Mind* (1955): 28–51.

adverbial sensing events rather than premises about sense-data.[6] That is, the epistemologically basic empirical premises would not consider sensory experience to be events of perceivers experiencing phenomenal objects, such as red sense-data. Instead, sensory experience would be viewed as events of perceivers being in states of sensing in various ways, such as objectless states of sensing red-ly, or, in other words, red-sensing. It follows from the preceding claim that, despite there being no intermediary objects, the perceptual knowledge of physical objects is indirect, inferential, and, it would seem, less than certain. These examples illustrate that it is far from clear what relationships there are between the epistemological and factual senses of 'directly perceive.' This point is reinforced by noting that directly perceiving in Malcolm's epistemological sense is clearly compatible with indirectly or mediately perceiving in the preceding Berkeleyan, purely factual sense. The converse is also true.

Definition of a Nonepistemic Sense of 'Directly Perceive'

My present aim is to produce a justifiable definition of a nonepistemic sense of 'directly perceive.' To do so, we need some conditions of adequacy. The most important condition is that it must enable us to specify clearly some of the crucial differences among direct realism, indirect realism, and phenomenalism. One consequence of this is that no adequate definition should logically entail that only phenomenal individuals, such as sensory ideas, sense-data, percepts, and pictorial images, are directly perceived. Whether these phenomenal objects, which I shall call "sensa," or physical objects, or other things are directly perceived is to be decided by the requirements of scientific and philosophical theories of perception and the physical world rather than by definition. Thus a definition of the technical term 'sensum' should also leave this question open. The following rough characterization meets this condition. A sensum is a phenomenal individual, that is, an individual that exists when and only when experienced and that has among its properties at least one phenomenal property.

---

[6] For such a claim, see R. M. Chisholm, *Perceiving* (Ithaca, New York: Cornell University Press, 1957), Chap. 5. I shall discuss the adverbial sensing theory in Chapter 2. See also Chisholm, *Theory of Knowledge* (Englewood Cliffs, N. J.: Prentice-Hall, 1966), Chap. 6.

By 'phenomenal property' I mean, roughly, a nonphysical property something has when and only when it is experienced to have that property.[7]

On the preceding definition 'sensum' covers a wide variety of individuals. For example, someone accepts sensa as characterized here if he holds that there are Lockean simple ideas, A. J. Ayer's sense-data, Russell's percepts, what Firth seems to mean by 'ostensible physical objects,' or what various people call "mental images," including after-images, dream images, hallucinatory apparitions, and memory images.[8] I wish to use 'sensum' in this very broad way because my primary interest here is the issue of whether we directly perceive physical objects, or whether our perception of them involves direct perception of phenomenal individuals. For this purpose, as we shall see, there is no need to assume or consider any particular species of phenomenal individual. Furthermore, by using this generic sense we can avoid the seemingly endless debates about which sorts of phenomenal individuals should be accepted.

Another condition of adequacy is that if indirect realism is true, then sensa and only sensa are directly perceivable, but that if a Berkeleyan phenomenalism is true, then sensa and things constituted of sensa, that is, physical objects, are directly perceivable. This is not to say that for Berkeley physical objects are directly perceived in an epistemic sense, but only that things such as a cherry (which, as Philonous says, "is nothing but a congeries of sensible impressions, or ideas perceived by various senses"[9]) are perceived, as Berkeley says, without intermediaries. Indeed, one central problem in formulating the definition will be to explicate in what sense direct realists and Berkeleyan phenomenalists rule out these intermediaries which indirect realists propose.

In defining 'directly perceive' we are specifying one species of

---

[7] For a definition of 'physical property,' see my *Materialism and Sensations* (New Haven: Yale Unviersity Press, 1971), p. 12.

[8] A. J. Ayer discusses sense-data in many places, for example, in *The Problem of Knowledge* (Baltimore: Penguin Books, 1956), pp. 84–112. R. Firth discusses ostensible physical objects in "Sense-Data and the Percept Theory," reprinted in *Perceiving, Sensing, and Knowing*, R. Swartz, ed. (Garden City, N. Y.: Anchor Books, 1965), pp. 204–70. J. J. Gibson assumes mental images in, for example, "On the Relation between Hallucination and Perception," *Leonardo* (1970): 425–27.

[9] Berkeley, pp. 195–96.

perceiving which is to be contrasted with indirectly perceiving. I am not, then, interested in defining 'perceive' and so will rely on a rather intuitive grasp of it at this point. Nevertheless, it is worth pointing out here that, as I shall use 'perceive' throughout the book, both physical objects and "perceptual" sensa (that is, any sensa that constitute perceptual experiences) are perceived. So percepts would be perceived, but not pains. And I shall use 'observe' so that only physical objects are observed, and 'sense' so that at most sensa are sensed. I shall also use 'experience' as a genus term for all modes of awareness, including observing and sensing. Furthermore, my use of 'perceive' will become clearer as different theories of perception are discussed and evaluated throughout the book. We can begin the search for a definition of 'directly perceive' by an initial attempt to uncover the relevant sort of intermediary:

S directly perceives p at time $t =$ $_{df}$.
   (1) S perceives p at t, and
   (2) it is false that S would perceive p at t only if at t he were to experience something different from p.

I might note that if we were to settle on the preceding attempt with a denial as its second condition, and were to define 'indirectly perceive' using (1) and the undenied conditional of (2), then we might agree with Austin that "the notion of perceiving indirectly wears the trousers—'directly' takes whatever sense it has from the contrast with its opposite,"[10] because we would understand (2) in terms of its undenied conditional. However, as we shall see, this will not be true of the definition that finally evolves.

Obviously this first attempt will not do. Although it would allow us to derive that anything seen only by means of seeing its effect on something else is not seen directly, it will not allow the claim of a direct realist that in seeing John's face, but no other part of John, we are directly seeing John. And it will not allow the Berkeleyan claim that we directly see a cherry by directly seeing one of the sensory ideas that compose it. A similar problem is that sometimes we see parades by seeing only some of their members, and so the preceding definition would not allow direct perception of parades.

[10] Austin, p. 15.

Perceptual Intermediaries and Constituents

The problem for the preceding definition is that constituents of things, whether parts or members, are not the sort of intermediaries that entail indirect perception of what they constitute. Let us amend condition (2) as follows:

> (2a) It is false that S would perceive p at t only if at t he were to experience something x which is different from p and is not a constituent (either a part or member) of p.

This definition does not require indirect perception of Berkeleyan cherries seen by means of sense-data, people seen by means of their faces, and parades seen by means of their members. There are, however, counterexamples. Let p be a brick which at time t is a constituent of a wall, x. Then, contrary to a direct realist who would claim we usually see both brick walls and the bricks in them directly, the revised definition would require that the brick is seen indirectly. Someone would see this brick at t only if he were to see the wall, which is not a constituent of the brick, because in seeing the brick at t he is thereby seeing the wall, although not all of the wall. This is also true in any case of seeing John's face and thereby seeing John, seeing members of a parade and thereby seeing the parade, and for a Berkeleyan, seeing sensa that constitute a cherry. Given (2a), we would have to conclude that John's face, members of parades, and sensa that constitute Berkeleyan physical objects are indirectly perceived.

The problem again involves constituents and intermediaries. In this case, however, we must allow x to have p as a constituent. We can now try:

> (2b) It is false that S would perceive p at t only if at t he were to experience something x, which is different from p and which neither is a constituent of p nor has p as a constituent.

This version avoids all the previous objections, but there is another which refutes it. Consider seeing at t a ship model inside a tinted but transparent bottle. We would not see the model at t if we did not perceive the bottle which is neither a constituent of the model nor has the model as a constituent. Thus, according to (2b) and contrary to direct realism, we would indirectly perceive the model.

Indirect Perception and Causal Intermediaries

We have, I believe, gone as far as we can go to avoid counter-examples without considering that for an indirect realist sensa are causal intermediaries. As Locke says, "Whatsoever the mind perceives *in itself*, or is the immediate object of perception, thought, or understanding, that I call *idea*; and the power to produce any idea in our mind, I call *quality* of the subject wherein that power is."[11] He goes on to say that because qualities such as shape "may be perceived at a distance by the sight, it is evident some singly imperceptible bodies must come from them to the eyes, and thereby convey to the brain some motion; which produces these ideas which we have of them in us."[12] J. Eccles, a contemporary physiologist, has a view which differs from Locke's primarily in containing a more detailed scientific description of the physiology of perception. He says:

> With perception the sequence of events is that some stimulus to a sense organ causes the discharge of impulses along afferent nerve fibers to the brain, which, after various synaptic relays, eventually evoke specific spatio-temporal patterns of impulses in the neuronal network of the cerebral cortex. The transmission from sense organ to cerebral cortex is by a coded pattern of nerve impulses that is quite unlike the original stimulus to that organism and the spatio-temporal pattern of neuronal activity that is evoked in the cerebral cortex would be again different. Yet, as a consequence of these cerebral patterns of activity, I experience sensations.[13]

We can eliminate the problem raised by the ship model by specifying that the sort of intermediary which indirect perception requires is one which we are caused to experience because of stimulation of a sense organ by a stimulus object, either directly by the object itself or indirectly through stimulus from the object. We

[11] J. Locke, *An Essay Concerning Human Understanding,* Book II, Chap. 8, sec. 8.
[12] Ibid., Book II, Chap. 8, sec. 12.
[13] J. Eccles, *The Brain and the Unity of Conscious Experience* (Cambridge, England: Cambridge University Press, 1965), pp. 17–18.

can incorporate this into our definition as follows:

(2c) It is false that S would perceive p at t only if at t he were to experience something x which is different from p, which neither is a constituent of p nor has p as a constituent, and which S experiences at t because of the stimulation of a sense organ of S by p.

I find, however, that once we refer to a causal relation in the definition we can drop the subjunctive mood without ill effect. Because the conjunction resulting from putting the denied hypothetical in the indicative mood contains (1) as a conjunct, we can simplify (2c) to:

(2d) Nothing experienced by S at t which is different from p, and which neither is a constituent of p, nor has p as a constituent, is experienced by S at t because of the stimulation of a sense organ of S by p.

Given this indicative version we can symbolize it to facilitate testing for counterexamples:

(2e) $(x)[(Esxt) \cdot x \neq p \cdot \sim Cxp \cdot \sim Cpx) \supset \sim Ssxtp]$.

Here $Esxt = S$ experiences x at t, $Cxp = x$ is constituent of p, and $Ssxtp = S$ experiences x at t because of p stimulating a sense organ of S. However, once we see how $Ssxtp$ is interpreted we also can see that it entails $Esxt$. Consequently, (2e) is equivalent to:

(2f) $(x)[(x \neq p \cdot \sim Cxp \cdot \sim Cpx) \supset \sim Ssxtp]$.

We can see that (2f) avoids all the preceding problems. A direct realist who uses this definition will not be refuted by seeing John by seeing his face, seeing a parade by seeing some of its members, seeing a wall by seeing a brick in it, or seeing a ship model in a bottle. And a Berkeleyan phenomenalist can use the definition without having to conclude that he experiences certain sensa indirectly because he would experience them only if he were to perceive the cherry of which they are constituents. There are still, however, at least five objections that must be considered before we move on.

TWO MORE OBJECTIONS: ELECTRON TRACES AND PERSONS IN COATS

The first two objections are quite similar and can be dispelled without further amendment, but others will force additional revisions. The first objection is that this definition requires a direct realist to draw the mistaken conclusion that an electron passing through a cloud chamber is directly perceived, but its bubble trail is indirectly perceived. The point is that the trail is the stimulus object that results in someone perceiving the electron. Indeed, one electron is not a stimulus object at all, because the stimulus that affects our eyes is transmitted from the bubble trail rather than the electron. This objection can be refuted as follows. While an electron would be directly perceived *if* it were perceived at all (that is, if the first condition were met) and while the bubble trail would be indirectly perceived *if* the electron were experienced (that is, if the denial of the second condition were met) neither antecedent is true and the mistaken claim is not derivable. A solitary electron is neither a stimulus object nor something experienced because of stimulus transmitted from a stimulus object, and so it is neither perceived nor experienced in the relevant way. This is not to deny that there is a sense in which it is true that someone perceives that an electron passed through the cloud chamber, or even that there is a sense in which a scientist might claim to see the electron as it passed through the chamber.[14] But whatever these senses might be, they are not those relevant to the notions of direct and indirect perception we are trying to elucidate.

The second objection can be handled in a similar way. I look out a window and catch a glimpse of John going by completely covered from head to toe in a huge, long coat. The problem here is that it seems we must draw the mistaken conclusion that I directly perceive John but not his coat, because the coat is the stimulus object which results in my seeing John, but he is not something which transmits any stimulus to me at all. The issue, as in the preceding objection, is whether I perceive or experience John in the relevant way in addition to his huge coat. Two opposing views about this are expressed by Descartes and Chisholm, who says:

Descartes remarks, in the second of his *Meditations*, that if he

---

[14] For more detail, see my *Materialism and Sensations*, pp. 64–69.

were to look into the street where men are walking by, "the
terms of ordinary language" might mislead him into saying
that he sees men. "Nevertheless what do I see from this window
except hats and cloaks which might cover automata? But I
judge that they are men, and thus I comprehend, solely by the
faculty of judgment which resides in my mind, that which I
believed I saw with my eyes." But why not say that he sees men
who are wearing hats and cloaks? Descartes' reasoning,
apparently, is this: he does not see faces (let us suppose), and
he does not see what is covered by the hats or the cloaks; hence
(he concludes) he sees only hats and cloaks, not people
wearing hats and cloaks. And if he were to continue with this
reasoning, he might be led to say, even more strictly, that he
does not see the hats or the cloaks. For he does not see the inside of hats and cloaks; he does not see the sides which face
away from him; nor does he see all of the threads on those sides
which do face him. Hence, by reasoning similar to the above,
he might conclude that what he sees are at best certain *parts*
of the surfaces of the outer parts of one of the sides of the hats
and of the cloaks. The next step in this reasoning would be to
conclude: "Indeed, there is no part even of the outer surfaces
which I see; for with respect to any such part, there is, surely,
some part of *it* which I do not see. What I see, therefore,
cannot be a part of any physical things."[15]

My claim is that Descartes is right, and he can justify his claim
without accepting the reasoning Chisholm imputes to him. If the
bottle containing the ship model is painted black and if we have a
can, rather than a glass jar of peas, then although it is true that
someone sees a bottle with a ship inside, and sees a can of peas, he
sees neither the model nor the peas. There is nothing special about
people in this regard. While we say that we see a man in a coat, when
no part of his body is visible, rather than that we see a coat with a
man inside, it is clearly the latter which is correct. That is, it is
correct unless we should accept Chisholm's intimation that
Descartes' reasoning leads to the clearly mistaken conclusion that
we never perceive physical objects. But we can avoid this conclusion
by supplying Descartes with a different premise from the one

---

[15] Chisholm, p. 154.

Chisholm attributes to him. If Descartes' view required the premise:

P1 If S sees p then S sees all constituents of p,

then the unacceptable conclusion could be derived. But Descartes' claim needs only:

P2 If S sees p and p has constituents, then S sees *some* constituent of p.

While the converse of P2 is false, unless restricted to parts which are not detached, P2 seems quite acceptable.[16] Given P2 and that no part of John, the ship model or a pea in the can is visible, it follows that neither John, the model, nor any pea is seen. And, since it is clear that they are not experienced in a way relevant to the definition, we can reject this objection. Furthermore, since it is clear that some part of John's coat is seen, P2 cannot be used to begin the slide to the conclusion that no physical object is seen. Both Descartes' claim and the definition of 'directly perceive' with (2f) avoid the second problem. But (2f) faces three more serious problems.

Three Last Problems: Reflections and Apparitions

The first problem concerns seeing a murky pond with a tree reflected in it. Although we might agree that the tree is indirectly perceived in some sense, the pond would be directly perceived given direct realism. But, if (2f) were correct, then the pond would be indirectly perceived because the tree is experienced as a result of stimulation of a sense organ of the perceiver by the pond. In order to avoid this problem, we must specify that a direct realist cannot allow the experience of certain sensa to occur in perception. Thus we should amend (2f) to include reference to sensa:

$$(2g)\ (x)[(Sx \cdot x \neq p \cdot \sim Cxp \cdot \sim Cpx) \supset \sim Ssxtp].$$

Here $Sx = x$ is a sensum. With (2g), experiencing the tree when perceiving the pond does not commit a direct realist to indirect perception of the pond.

The second and third problems require further revisions. The

---

[16] Cf. Chisholm, p. 155.

second arises because it is possible that certain stimulations of
sense organs result in someone experiencing a sensum which is a
feeling of fright or pleasure, or perhaps even an hallucinatory
apparition or an image of a past occurrence. For example, one
result of witnessing a gory automobile accident might be a nauseous
feeling or a vivid image of a previously witnessed accident.[17]
Clearly, a direct realist would not want to be committed to claiming
that if such a feeling or image is caused, the accident is indirectly
perceived, but (2g) would yield that result. The third problem
arises by considering that sometimes a person sees a room that is
empty, but a figure appears to be in the room because some drugs
cause him to hallucinate. It is possible that the person's total perceptual experience while he is perceiving the room consists in his
sensing in some way regarding the room, but also being in some
relationship to a sensum which is an apparition of a figure in the
room. Given condition (2g), this experience that includes a sensing
event and also a sensum would lead to the mistaken conclusion that
the person indirectly perceives the room.

In order to handle these problems, we must somehow delimit
those sensa which would count against direct perception. We can
do this by distinguishing between a person's total perceptual
experience at one time and his perceptual experience of the object p.
While a direct realist can allow that some sensa are constituents of
the total experience, he cannot allow that a person's perceptual
experience of p consists in the person experiencing any one or
indeed any group of sensa. Let us, then, make our last amendments,
so that we get:

$$(2h) \ (x)\{[(Sx \ v \ Gx) \cdot x \neq p \cdot \sim Cxp \cdot \sim Cpx] \supset \ \sim Psptx\}.$$

The new terms are $Gx = x$ is a group of sensa, and $Psptx = S$'s
perceptual experience of p at t consists in S experiencing x at t. This
final version allows perceivers to perceive directly something, p,
even if sensa, such as images and apparitions, are experienced when
p is perceived and regardless of what may have caused the perceiver
to experience those sensa. It also has the advantage of eliminating
all reference to causation of experiences and stimulation of sense
organs. While the preceding attempt did not entail that there are

[17] Ibid., pp. 146–49, for Chisholm's attempt to handle a similar problem for his definition
of 'appear.'

such entities, its denial, which would be required for indirect perception, would have had such consequences. All else being equal, a definition which does not entail specific causal claims and assumptions about stimuli is to be preferred.

DIRECT REALISM, INDIRECT REALISM, AND BERKELEYAN PHENOMENALISM

We are almost ready to distinguish among direct realism, indirect realism, Berkeleyan phenomenalism, and other metaphysical theories of perception and the external world, but we must first define two more terms. The first is 'indirectly perceive,' which we can easily define by saying that S indirectly perceives p at t just in case condition (1) and the denial of (2h) are true. The second needed is 'directly perceivable', because the basic differences among the three views do not concern what we actually perceive, but rather what we are able to perceive. Furthermore, it is clear that the issues do not concern merely whether something is directly perceivable, but whether physical objects are directly perceivable. It is clear also that we are concerned with what is directly perceivable by normal perceivers in conditions normal for their perception. That things are not perceivable in certain abnormal conditions, and that everything may be perceivable by an all-perfect deity are not relevant to the differences we are trying to elucidate. With these points in mind, we can use the following definition:

> Some p's are directly perceivable $=$ $_{df}$. There are situations in which some p would be directly perceived by a normal observer when conditions are normal for perception.

The preceding definitions can be used to help distinguish the basic differences among the first three philosophical theses. I shall do this by trying to isolate the minimum claim about which each one of the three differs from the other two. I do this to allow as many varieties of each position as possible and to discover whether any of the theories entail any epistemological claims. Historically, epistemological and factual strands have been confusingly intertwined in discussions of these three positions. It is my claim that all three theses can be understood more clearly and defended or attacked more decisively once these strands are sharply distinguished. We can begin by distinguishing indirect realism from direct realism and Berkeleyan phenomenalism. According to the latter two:

(1) Some physical objects are directly perceivable.

Indirect realists deny this. For an indirect realist, if a physical object, p, should be perceived by someone, S, then S's perceptual experience of p would consist of S experiencing some sensum or group of sensa which is different from p, is neither a constituent of p, nor has p as a constituent. Thus, according to indirect realists:

(2) All physical objects which are perceivable are indirectly perceivable.

Here we have the kind of view of perception found classically in Locke and today, it seems, in Sellars' view of "the scientific image."[18] Of course, their views have important differences, as we shall see in Chapter 7, but they specify varieties of indirect realism rather than totally distinct kinds of realism. One major disagreement concerns how we are to justify claims about the properties that external objects have when we directly perceive only sensa. While both agree that the external world is as science says it is, Sellars does not justify this thesis by basing it on Locke's claim that some, but only some, sensa resemble the properties of external objects. Locke's attempt fails because there is no way, given his epistemological theory, that he can verify the resemblance claim by observation. If, however, some sort of indirect justification can be given to Sellars' two claims that science explains best and whatever explains best describes best, then by comparing properties of sensa with the properties that science assigns to external objects, Locke's resemblance claim may turn out to be justified after all. Of course, that claim would not be the basis for knowledge of the external world as it is for Locke.

Indirect realists and Berkeleyan phenomenalists make a common claim that is denied by direct realists:

(3) Whenever a physical object is perceived a sensum is directly perceived.

[18] For a discussion of Sellars' views on sensa, see Chapter 7; my "Sellars, Scientific Realism, and Sensa", *Review of Metaphysics* (1970): 417–51; and *Materialism and Sensations*, Chap. 7.

For direct realists, the perceptual experience of a physical object involved in perception of the object does not include sensa as constituents. It is worth noting that while a direct realist denies that sensa are constituents of perceptual experience of physical objects, he need not state that no sensa are directly experienced when physical objects are perceived. As we have seen, direct realism is compatible with the existence of afterimages, memory images, pains, and other feelings which someone might directly experience when perceiving a physical object. Furthermore, direct realism is not committed to three features generally attributed to one of its most naive species: physical objects have all those properties they are normally perceived as having; these properties are normally unaffected by changes in perceivers and conditions of perception; and perceiving an object consists in being perceptually acquainted with it. Another species of direct realism contains a causal thesis for which objectless adverbial sensing events, such as red-sensings, are caused rather than events with red sensa as constituents.[19] On this theory there would be no experienced intermediaries, and no physical objects need have any of those properties they are perceived to have. Such a version of direct realism is consistent with a Sellarsian and Lockean view of the external world. It differs essentially from these positions by its conception of persons, their states, and the entities that they directly perceive.

Indirect and direct realists hold one thing in common, which is necessary for realism and sufficient to refute Berkeleyan phenomenalism:

(4) Some physical objects do not have sensa as constituents.

Notice that a realist need not make the stronger claim that no physical objects have sensa as constituents. Realism is compatible with the existence of sensa and the claim that they are identical with parts of brains. For such a view, brains would have sensa as constituents. A realist would, of course, maintain that no physical objects have only individual sensa as constituents. A Berkeleyan would certainly agree that many physical objects have constituents which are not individual sensa. For example, human bodies have

19 See Chisholm, pp. 142–51, for an analysis of '*S* perceives *x*' that refers to the causation of adverbial sensings.

brains as constituents and no brain is one sensum. However, a Berkeleyan, but not a realist, would claim that each physical object not only has sensa as constituents, but also is identical with some group of sensa. Of course, explicating the sense in which physical objects are constituted of sensa is a difficult task that lies ahead of us. The attempt to use the linguistic thesis of analytical phenomenalism fails, as I hope to show in Chapter 3. Physical objects seem not to be logical constructs out of sensa. However the question whether they might be construed as theoretical constructs remains open. Indeed, in Chapter 5 I shall attempt to defend theoretical phenomenalism—the thesis that physical objects are theoretical constructs—against Sellars' objections.

If we conjoin the claim that each physical object is identical with some group of sensa with the claim that no group of sensa exists when not perceived, then we can derive what would be another crucial difference between realism and phenomenalism: no physical objects exist when not perceived. However, as we shall see in Chapter 5, there is a way a Berkeleyan can interpret existence claims about physical objects so that he could consistently accept that some physical objects exist even when not perceived by any perceiver at all.

ELIMINATIVE PHENOMENALISM AND KANTIAN REALISM

Thus far I have concentrated upon the Berkeleyan version of phenomenalism, but this is not enough for our purposes because we are also interested in the general theory of metaphysical phenomenalism and species of it that differ from the Berkeleyan kind. Since all versions of phenomenalism accept (3), and would accept (2) and the denial of (1) only if there should be no physical objects, the one place for a specific difference concerns:

(5) There are physical objects.

I shall call the species of phenomenalism that denies (5), "eliminative" phenomenalism, and delineate two subspecies according to whether or not they accept the following thesis about physical object terms:

(6) Some physical object terms are referring terms.

We shall consider a version of eliminative phenomenalism that denies (6), and two that accept (6). I shall call the former "instru-mentalistic" phenomenalism, because it construes all physical object terms as theoretical terms and all theoretical terms as nonreferring, inferring devices. One of the versions that accepts (6) agrees that physical object terms are theoretical terms, but claims they are referring terms that fail to denote anything, because, like 'ether' and 'phlogiston,' there is no explanatory need to postulate referents for them. I shall call this theory the "postulation elimin-ation" theory.

The second version of eliminative phenomenalism that accepts (6) states not only that physical object terms are referring terms, but also that there are entities they denote, namely, sensa. In this it agrees with Berkeleyan phenomenalism, but the disagreement comes in the claim that any physical object description that implies there are physical objects is false because there are no physical objects. According to this theory the status of physical object terms is like that of 'Zeus's thunderbolts.' Although there are entities denoted by 'Zeus's thunderbolts,' namely, discharges of static electricity in the atmosphere, there are no Zeus's thunder-bolts. Just as there is no explanatory or descriptive need for 'Zeus's thunderbolts,' so also, for this theory, there is no such need for physical-object terms. I shall call this the " 'physical object' elimina-tion" theory.[20]

One thesis common to these versions of eliminative phenomenal-ism is that no group of sensa is identical with a physical object. And since if this Berkeleyan use of sensa is abandoned there may well be no reason for a phenomenalist to prefer a sensum theory to an objectless sensing theory, we should distinguish two sub-species of each version of eliminative phenomenalism. They differ according to whether they accept:

(7) There are sensa, for example, red sensa,

or

(8) There are objectless sensings, for example, red-sensings.

---

[20] These three versions of eliminative phenomenalism correspond to three versions of eliminative materialism I discuss in *Materialism and Sensations*, Chaps. 4 and 5. They correspond respectively to Rylean behaviorism, the postulation elimination theory, and the 'sensation' elimination theory. Berkeleyan phenomenalism corresponds to reductive materialism, discussed in Part I.

The latter claim has the quite counterintuitive consequence that there are no objects to be perceived, either directly or indirectly. There are only perceivers who sense in various ways.

It may seem at this point that we have multiplied distinctions well beyond necessity, but we need to make one more before moving on. Given only the preceding eight statements we cannot distinguish Kant's realistic theory, which he calls "transcendental idealism," from phenomenalism.[21] Thus there is still a difference between realists and phenomenalists we have not captured. Indeed, depending on what Kant means by 'transcendentally ideal,' and whether he is a sensum or a sensing theorist, he would agree either with a Berkeleyan phenomenalist or with certain of the varieties of eliminative phenomenalism about the first eight statements above. According to Kant, physical objects which constitute the phenomenal world are nothing but appearances, and so they are transcendentally ideal. He may have meant by this that they are nothing but sensa as a Berkeleyan claims, or that they really do not exist at all as an eliminative theorist claims. On the latter construal of Kant, physical objects are the objects that, contrary to fact, would exist if any objects correspond to the intersubjective conceptual framework with which we respond, indeed must respond, to the sense impressions (whether sensa or sensings) caused by things-in-themselves. On all three interpretations, then, a Kantian would deny (4), either because all physical objects would be merely sensa or because none would exist. In this he would agree with the phenomenalists and disagree with the other realists. How, then, does he differ from all phenomenalists? What makes him a realist? According to Kant, what he calls "idealism," and what I have called "phenomenalism,"

> consists in the assertion that there are none but thinking beings, all other things which we think are preceived in intuition, being nothing but representations in the thinking beings, to which no object external to them in fact corresponds. I, on the contrary, say that things as objects of our senses existing outside us are given, but we know nothing of what they may be

[21] For a claim that Kant's theory is extremely similar to Berkeley's phenomenalism, see C. Turbayne, "Kant's Refutation of Dogmatic Idealism," *Philosophical Quarterly*, 5 (1955): 225–44. M. Wilson, "Kant and 'the Dogmatic Idealism of Berkeley'," *Journal of the History of Ideas*, 9 (1971): 459–75, replies to this.

in themselves, knowing only their appearances, that is, the representations which they cause in us by affecting our senses. Consequently I grant by all means that there are bodies without us, that is, things which, though quite unknown to us as to what they are in themselves, we yet know the representations which their influence on our sensibility procures us. These representations we call "bodies," a term signifying merely the appearance of the thing which is unknown to us, but not therefore less actual. Can this be termed idealism? It is the very contrary.[22]

The preceding quotation not only shows Kant's view that physical objects, that is, "bodies," are nothing but appearances, it also pinpoints his difference from phenomenalists as concerning the existence of objects that are neither perceivers nor sensa. These are the things-in-themselves about which we know only that they correspond in some way to those sensory experiences that they cause perceivers to have. Consequently, the various Kantian theories have a thesis about "external" objects in common with all realists but with no phenomenalists, namely:

(9) There are external objects, that is, objects (perhaps unknowable) which are not perceivers, which exist independently of any (finite) perceiver, and which generally would not be affected by being perceived.

It is because the imperceptable things-in-themselves, satisfy (9) that Kant is a realist. More specifically, he holds one version of what I shall call "nondirect" realism, because, by denying perception of external objects, he thereby denies direct perception of them.

With the preliminary definitions and distinctions completed, the primary task remaining, the task of the rest of the book, is to construct, explain, clarify, and defend the argument I shall use to justify what I have called compatible common-sense realism. This theory, which will be developed later in the book, accepts only (1), (4), (5), (6), (8), and (9) of the preceding statements. Because of this, it is one species of direct realism. It also states that physical objects have many of those sensuous properties, such as color, we tend to believe they have when we respond to our environment,

---

[22] I. Kant, *Prolegomena to Any Future Metaphysics*, L. W. Beck, ed. (Indianapolis and New York: Bobbs-Merrill, 1950), Remark II to §13, p. 36.

and they also have those constituents and causal relations we tend to ascribe to them when scientifically theorizing about them. It is because of this I call it a "compatible" version of direct realism. Justifying such a position is obviously a huge task, especially once we see the wide variety of opposing theories, including two varieties of indirect realism, and three major versions and several subspecies of phenomenalism and Kantian realism. My general procedure will be to try to find the most reasonable opposing realistic theories and the most reasonable versions of phenomenalism, and to argue that it is more reasonable to accept compatible common-sense realism than any of these others. In order to begin to see the details of this procedure, let us turn to Chapter 1 in which I shall lay out and explain the argument I shall use.

1 An Argument for Compatible Common-Sense Realism

My purpose is to justify a particular metaphysical theory. This immediately raises the question of whether there is any way to provide grounds for choosing such a theory instead of its alternatives. And if there is such a way, will the theory it selects be shown to be reasonable enough to make it acceptable? These two questions are extremely difficult to answer because there are no easily recognizable and usable canons of evidence or principles of reason available in the area of metaphysics. As I have briefly summarized in the Preface, my explanation of this difficulty is that metaphysical problems are external in a sense that precludes solution. Nevertheless, I have argued that there is a way in which internal clues to external problems might be provided in such a manner that one proposed resolution of each metaphysical problem might be shown to be the most reasonable. This approach requires the assumption of an hypothesis about which available linguistic features of terms are sufficient for the terms being referring expressions, and which features are sufficient for their not being referring terms. Then those resolutions of metaphysical problems that violate the assumed conditions for either referring or nonreferring would be eliminated. Ideally, only one resolution would be left unscathed for each problem, and it would, thereby, be shown to be the most reasonable. If this ideal is obtained for a wide variety of metaphysical problems, given the assumption, then both the reference hypothesis and the resolutions it specifies would be justified.

There are two problems about this procedure which have worried me. First, it may well be that two or more different assumed hypotheses about reference which specify different resolutions are equally effective, and second, that no assumption will single out just one resolution for each of a large number of problems. If either problem is insolvable, then what Quine calls the "inscrutability of ontology" results.[1] Of course, the first problem might

---

[1] I have discussed theories of reference and the inscrutability of ontology in more detail in "Reference and Ontology: Inscrutable but not Relative," *The Monist* (July, 1975).

be considerably alleviated by applying various additional, generally accepted tests to those competing reference hypotheses that survive the preceding basic test for these hypotheses. Some of these tests as applied to an assumption about reference are that, *ceteris paribus*, it is more reasonable to choose the hypothesis that assumes the least number of untestable hypotheses and the fewest kinds of empirically unnecessary entities, that is simplest to apply, and that accords most closely with our ordinary beliefs about which terms are and which terms are not referring terms. Of course, such tests still might not resolve the first problem. If this is so, then it may be that the best we can do is to argue that one assumption about reference and its set of resolutions are as reasonable as any other, and so it is not unreasonable to accept them. But this rather weak justification, which assumes that the second problem is avoided, would be even more drastically weakened without a solution to the second problem. Furthermore, the additional tests applied to the assumed referring hypothesis do not help alleviate the second problem. While they provide ways to eliminate alternative reference assumptions, they do not help us refine any particular assumption so that it specifies just one resolution for each of a large number of metaphysical problems. However, these tests are species of those used to evaluate assumptions of many different sorts. Thus it may be that the direct application of the appropriate versions of the tests to competing metaphysical theories will result in enough additional, independent reason to justify one of these theories and perhaps one particular reference assumption that accords with that theory. Indeed it may be that in some cases the resulting reason is sufficient by itself to justify a particular resolution of a metaphysical problem, and perhaps, in addition, a certain theory of reference.

The relevant question for our present purpose is whether applying certain of these tests directly to the various metaphysical hypotheses about perception and the external world will produce enough reason to favor one theory over the others, independently of any assumptions about reference. My contention is that the thesis I have called compatible common-sense realism will prove to be the most reasonable when three of these tests are incorporated as premises in the argument we shall consider. Furthermore, as I shall try to indicate after the examination of the argument is completed, this theory has no counterintuitive implications about reference. This will increase the theory's plausibility, because its reference implications will be among those specified by initially credible reference assumptions.

I shall begin with three tests expressed as principles of reason, in the sense that they provide sufficient conditions for one statement or theory being more reasonable than certain others. The first one is a version of Occam's razor which is spelled out in more detail than usual and is adapted to be clearly relevant to metaphysical theories. The second test is used to argue from the implausibility of assuming certain entities to the rejection of theories that require those entities. The last, which is somewhat similar to a test found among Carnap's conditions for successful explication, assumes the initial plausibility of common-sense beliefs.[2] The first test is used to facilitate the inference from there being no reason to accept sensa to the conclusion that there is reason to reject sensa. The second is used to argue from this rejection of sensa to the rejection of sensum theories. The third is crucial in supporting the compatibilist form of common-sense realism as superior to any theory that rejects either the basic beliefs of common sense or the minimum require-ments of scientific realism. The general approach will be that, independent of one of these tests, each of these hypotheses will be shown to be at least as reasonable as its competitors; but once the appropriate test is applied, each one will prove more reasonable than its alternatives. Of course, how much an "edge" these tests will provide is debatable. It may be quite minimal, but in this realm, where inclining reasons are so difficult to find, every modi-cum of evidence is important.

A PRINCIPLE OF REASON AND GROUNDS FOR REJECTING SENSA

Let us turn to the first principle of reason and its use in the first stage of the argument we shall consider. As often stated, Occam's razor is the principle that entities are not to be multiplied beyond necessity. But this version is elliptical because it does not state for which purpose or purposes the entities to be avoided are unneces-sary. It is clear that science should postulate no more entities and

---

[2] See R. Carnap, *The Logical Foundations of Probability* (Chicago: University of Chicago Press, 1955), p. 7. I have discussed explication in *Metaphysics, Reference, and Language* (New Haven: Yale University Press, 1966), pp. 218–22.

no more kinds of entities than are needed for its explanations. For our purpose we need a version of the razor that will apply to metaphysical theories about what there is, in a way that will distinguish among them according to the entities they assume. For example, the principle that no kind of entities should be assumed if it is not necessary to include any entities of that kind in a catalogue of what there is, clearly applies to all ontological theories, but it is of no help in deciding among them. I think, however, that we can specify a set of conditions which are jointly sufficient—although some are not necessary—for rejecting entities of certain kinds, and which can be applied specifically to sensa.

In brief, there seem to be four different sorts of reasons for or against believing that there are entities of a certain kind. They are empirical non-theoretical evidence, as for the existence of water; empirical, scientific theoretical reasons, as for the existence of positrons; philosophical reasons, as for the existence of universals; and linguistic reasons, as for the existence of meanings and pro-positions. The version of Occam's razor we shall use states that if there are no reasons of these four kinds for the existence of any entities of a certain kind, and furthermore, if philosophical problems are avoided or more easily resolvable without such entities, then the existence of such entities should be denied. We can state this principle as follows:

> P1. *If* there are no empirical reasons or evidence for the existence of any entities of kind K, no scientific theoretical reasons and no metaphysical reasons to assume any entities of kind K, no linguistic reasons for entities of kind K, and fewer recalcitrant philosophical problems without any entities of kind K, *then* it is more reasonable to deny than to assert that there are any entities of kind K.[3]

When P1 is applied to sensa, there are obviously five different tasks to be completed, the first four of which will be attempted in Chapter 2. One is to discover whether there is any empirical

[3] It should be noted that in stating P1, I have equated philosophical reasons for entities of kind K with metaphysical reasons. Thus, for present purposes, I am assuming that there are no other sorts of philosophical reasons for entities of certain kinds. This assumption is questioned, however, in the concluding chapter where I discuss whether there might be reasons for sensa taken from epistemology, aesthetics, and ethics.

evidence for the claim that there are sensa. Because I have already examined this evidence in Chapter 6 of my *Materialism and Sensations*, I shall here primarily summarize the results reached there. I showed the failure of the four main arguments of this sort, namely, the argument from perceptual relativity, the argument from hallucination, the argument from the causal facts of perception, and the time-gap argument. The second task is to examine whether there are any reasons derivable from the explanatory requirements of science for the postulation of sensa. This is considerably more difficult to ascertain because of the unsettled and unclear situation in the relevant sciences. Nevertheless I shall examine some specific instances of scientists who seem to postulate sensa in order to see whether the postulations are necessary for their explanatory purposes. If sensa seem to be avoidable in these cases, I shall inductively infer that it is likely none are needed for theoretical purposes of science. Of course, for all such arguments future developments may override the present evidence. However, while this should be remembered, it does not affect the present justification of a claim, and that is all we can achieve now.

It might be that although neither scientific facts nor theories give reason to accept sensa, there are certain uses of language, which are independent of scientific uses, for which sensum terms are best suited. If there are such uses, then some of them might provide some reason for sensa. But which uses of language would provide such a reason? Clearly, what is necessary for ease or convenience in communication is not relevant. However, if there is a descriptive need for sensum terms, whether or not it is a scientific descriptive need, then there is some reason for the existence of sensa. If, however, as previously suggested, there is no scientific reason for sensa, then any attempt to justify a descriptive need for sensum terms must be made on some other grounds. The important problem, then, is whether all alternative terminologies are descriptively inadequate in some way, perhaps because they are inaccurate, or incomplete, or they embody syntactic or semantic flaws. We shall approach this problem by considering two different claims, each of which proposes a certain terminology as a descriptively adequate replacement for the sensum terminology. The first proposal is that no sensation terminology of any sort is necessary because whatever is described using such a terminology is at least equally well described using a purely physicalistic vocabulary. The second proposal is that a sensation vocabulary which uses sensing terms rather than sensum terms is at least as adequate for descriptive purposes as the sensum terminology. I shall try to show that although the first proposal fails, the second succeeds.

The last task relevant to P1 to be attempted in chapter 2 is to consider all philosophical problems that arise if there are sensa, and all that arise if, to the contrary, there are adverbial sensings. An examination of the discussion of sensa-data, for example in the writings of G. E. Moore, H. H. Price, and A. J. Ayer, reveals a large budget of unresolved, and seemingly unresolvable, problems that do not arise for adverbial sensings. For example, there are the problems of whether sensa are two or three dimensional, whether they have only the properties they seem to have, and whether two people can sense the same sensum. I shall argue that the corresponding problems for sensings are resolvable, and on the grounds that there are no unresolvable problems unique to sensings, I shall conclude that the relevant condition of P1 is met for sensa.

The last task relevant to P1, which constitutes by far the largest part of the book, is to argue that there is no metaphysical reason to assume sensa, because there are phenomenalistic and realistic theories without sensa that are at least as reasonable as any versions of those theories that require sensa. As previously mentioned, I shall begin by constructing the most reasonable form of reductive phenomenalism from the raw material of Berkeley's writings, and then I shall contrast it with the several versions of eliminative phenomenalism. This will constitute Part I. In Part II, I will critically evaluate alternative realistic theories and attempt to justify a conclusion about which versions are most reasonable. After rejecting naive realism because of its excessively naive acquaintance view of the perception of physical objects, I shall examine Lockean and Sellarsian versions of indirect realism and Kantian nondirect realism. I shall reject the Kantian theory because, in part, of its restrictive theory of the applicability of concepts. I shall also argue that a Sellarsian type scientific realism that substitutes adverbial sensings for sensa is at least as reasonable as either Lockean or Sellarsian forms of indirect realism. I shall claim, however, that this form of direct realism is not one of the most reasonable versions of realism, because of objections to all forms of scientific realism. While these objections are not fatal, they are damaging, especially to those versions of scientific realism, such as the Sellarsian version, that reject the common-sense view of the external world. Because of this, and because I find no objections to compatible common-sense realism, I conclude at the end of Part II that this last theory is at least as reasonable as any form of realism, whether direct or nondirect, and whether scientific or not.

At this point we shall not be quite ready to use P1 to conclude that we can plausibly reject sensa. We must first show that some theory which avoids sensa is at least as reasonable as the sensum versions of phenomenalism. I shall do this by showing that compatible common-sense realism is at least as reasonable as any sensum phenomenalism, because this will be crucial for the second stage of the argument. Once this has been done in the concluding chapter, we can reject sensa. This will take us a long way, but not all the way, towards achieving the goal of this book, namely, to justify compatible common-sense realism. To see this in detail, let me lay out the argument adumbrated above:

> I. There is no empirical, nontheoretical evidence or reason sufficient to justify the existence of sensa.
> II. There is no scientific, theoretical reason to justify the existence of sensa.
> III. No sensum terms are needed for describing what there is.
> IV. If I and II and III, then there are neither empirical nor linguistic reasons to justify the existence of sensa.

Therefore

> V. There is neither empirical nor linguistic reason to justify the existence of sensa.
> VI. There are fewer recalcitrant philosophical problems without sensa.
> VII. Compatible common-sense realism is at least as reasonable as any metaphysical theory of perception and the external world that requires sensa.
> VIII. If VII, then there is no metaphysical reason for sensa.
> IX. Principle P1.

Therefore

> X. It is more reasonable to deny than to assert that there
> are sensa.

A Second Principle of Reason and Grounds for Rejecting Theories with Sensa

It is at this point that the second principle of reason becomes
relevant. Its purport is that if one theory is at least as reasonable
as a second theory, and the second theory requires entities that it is
more reasonable to reject than accept, then the first theory is more
reasonable than the second. We can formulate this version of the
principle as follows:

> P2. *If* a theory, *T*, which does not require entities of kind *K*,
> is at least as reasonable as any theory that requires entities
> of kind *K*, and it is more reasonable to deny than to assert
> that there are entities of kind *K*, *then T* is more reasonable
> than any theory that requires entities of kind *K*.

There is an objection to this formulation, however. For our particular use of this principle, some of the reasons that show compatible
common-sense realism to be as reasonable as any sensum theory,
do so by justifying VII, which is then used to show, in addition,
that the theory is more reasonable than any sensum theory. The
objection is that the same bit of evidence should not be continually
invoked to keep increasing the reasonableness of a theory. The
reasons or evidence used to show that *T* is more reasonable than
another theory, *T'*, should in some sense be in addition to, or
independent of, what has been used to show that *T* is as reasonable
as *T'*.

There is a false assumption in this objection, namely, that the
same evidence is used first to establish one level of reasonableness
of *T*, and then again to increase the reasonableness of *T*. This
would be true if the evidence is first used to establish that *T* is
exactly as reasonable as *T'*, and thus at most as reasonable as *T'*,
and then later used to show that *T* is more reasonable than *T'*.
But the evidence is used merely to show that *T* is *at least* as reasonable as *T'*, and this is consistent with this same evidence also being
used to show *T* to be more reasonable that *T'*, without thereby

being used to increase the reasonableness of T. Whether the evidence does show T to be more reasonable than T' is left an open question by P2. Nevertheless, to make sure this objection is avoided, let us amend P2 as follows:

P2a. *If* (1) a theory, T, which does not require entities of kind K, is at least as reasonable as any theory that requires entities of kind K, (2) it is more reasonable to deny than to assert that there are entities of kind K, and (3) the conjunction of the reasons used to justify (1) with the denial of (2) still justifies that T is at least as reasonable as such theories, *then* T is more reasonable than any theory that requires entities of kind K.

We can now use VII, X, and a premise to instantiate Condition (3) in the antecedent of P2a to derive another important conclusion in the attempt to justify compatible common-sense realism. This second stage of the argument is as follows:

VII. (As above)
X. (As above)
XI. The conjunction of the reasons used to justify VII with the claim that it is as reasonable to assert as to deny there are sensa, still justifies VII.
XII. Principle P2a.

Therefore

XIII. Compatible common-sense realism is more reasonable than any metaphysical theory of perception and the external world that requires sensa.

A THIRD PRINCIPLE OF REASON: FAVORING COMMON SENSE

Certain obstacles still remain to block the justification of compatible common-sense realism, because the preceding two stages of the argument do not eliminate any nondirect realism or phenomenalism which does not assume sensa. This can be remedied, however, by invoking the third principle of reason previously mentioned. This principle is derived from the assumption that there is some reason to reject a scientific or philosophical theory if it is incompatible with a pretheoretical, commonly accepted belief of mankind. Of course, this claim is compatible with there being overriding reason to accept the theory and thereby to reject the *prima facie* reasonable belief. However, for our purposes we need not worry about when a point is reached on the scale of evidence at which the weight shifts from the belief to the theory. We need only use a principle which provides a way of choosing among theories already found to be equally reasonable based on all other evidence. It is in such a situation that compatibility with commonly accepted beliefs will tip the scale. We can express this principle in the following way:

> P3. *If* a theory, *T*, is at least as reasonable as another theory, *T'*, and *T* is consistent with more pretheoretical, commonly accepted beliefs of mankind than *T'*, *then T* is more reasonable than *T'*.

It might be objected that this principle is too heavily weighted in favor of common-sense, even naive, realism, and against scientific realism and phenomenalism. I agree that it provides, and indeed should provide, some initial weight on the side of common sense. However, with its first, *ceteris paribus* clause, P2 allows this factor to be considered only when all the rest of the evidence available leaves the one theory at least evenly balanced with the other. This is clearly a much weaker principle than one that permits no theory to override common sense, or one that requires significant agreement with common sense.[4] It is indeed one of the weakest forms of a principle which grants some initial plausibility to what men commonly believe. This is not to imply that a stronger principle might not also be acceptable, but needing only the weaker one, I invoke it with the confidence that it is surely acceptable. Furthermore, its initial weight in favor of common sense is so minimal that it is easy to see how it could be used ultimately in favor of something quite different from common-sense realism. Indeed, Berkeley seemed to use some such principle to help justify his claim that phenomenalism is more reasonable than any nonnaive realistic theory. It might even turn out that a theory is wildly counterintuitive, yet of those theories that are equally most reasonable, it is the one selected by P3. This is because it may be that all theories that are even remotely similar to what is commonly

---

[4] See, for example, the discussion in Chapter 8 of Stebbing's attempt to establish the supremacy of common-sense realism over scientific realism.

accepted are eliminated on independent grounds.

Principle P3 is relevant to my purposes in the following way.
I shall argue that any theory that rejects the minimal tenets of
scientific realism (such as all forms of phenomenalism and Kantian
realism, and some forms of common-sense realism), and any theory
that rejects even the most basic claims of common sense (such as
many forms of scientific realism), contradict more commonly
accepted beliefs than a theory which accomodates both sorts of
minimal claims. Consequently, once the theory I have called
compatible common-sense realism is shown to be more reasonable
than naive realism and at least as reasonable as the most reasonable
versions of these other opponents, then we can use P3 to help
conclude that compatible common-sense realism is the most
reasonable theory of perception and the external world. The third
stage of the main argument I shall use to show this can be exhibited
as follows:

XIV.   Compatible common-sense realism is more reasonable
       than naive realism and is at least as reasonable as any
       form of direct or Kantian realism, or sensing phenome-
       nalism.

XV.   Compatible common-sense realism is consistent with
       more pretheoretical, commonly accepted beliefs than
       sensing phenomenalism, or Kantian realism, or any
       other form of direct realism, except for naive realism.

XVI.   Principle P3.

Therefore

XVII. Compatible common-sense realism is more reasonable
       than any form of direct realism, or Kantian nondirect
       realism, or sensing phenomenalism.

XVIII. If XIII and XVII, then compatible common-sense
       realism is the most reasonable metaphysical theory
       of perception and the external world.

XIII. (As above)

Therefore

XIX.   Compatible common-sense realism is the most reason-
       able metaphysical theory of perception and the
       external world.

EXAMINATION OF THE AUXILIARY PREMISES

The last task to be completed in the present chapter is to evaluate three subsidiary premises before the detailed examination of those concerning sensa in the next chapter, and those concerning metaphysical theories of perception and the external world throughout the rest of the book. Premises I, II, III, and VI concern sensa; premises VII, XIV, and XV are about metaphysical theories; XI must await the statement of reasons for VII; and we have already discussed IX, XII, and XVI, which state the three principles of reason. Consequently, we have only premises IV, VIII, and XVIII to consider now. Of these, XVIII is the easiest to justify. By conclusion XIII, compatible common-sense realism is preferable to any realism with sensa and any phenomenalism with sensa. This leaves only two sorts of theories to consider as rivals to compatible common-sense realism—sensing phenomenalism and opposed versions of realism without sensa. But both sorts of theories are eliminated by XVII, and so XIII and XVII are sufficient for the final conclusion, XIX, as stated by XVIII.

Premise IV is acceptable for the following reason. It is clear that premises I and II entail that there is no empirical evidence and no reason, either theoretical or nontheoretical, for sensa. And, although it is perhaps not immediately clear, if III is true then there are no linguistic reasons for sensa. Linguistic evidence justifies that there are sensa only if it justifies that there is some descriptive need for sensum terms. That is, I would claim that the following is a crucial—and surely debatable—premise for any linguistic reason for sensa:

(i) If there is a descriptive need for sensum terms then there is linguistic reason for sensa.

For example, there being a need for sensum terms for convenience in communicating or for a merely expressive use of language would not provide linguistic reason for sensa. This is because neither need implies a descriptive need, and thus neither one provides reason to think there are entities corresponding in some way to sensum terms.

On the other hand, there are three other linguistic considerations which, if they applied to sensum terms, would provide at least plausible arguments for sensa. In each case it would be the relation of the linguistic consideration to a descriptive need that would provide the justification. Thus each argument would consist of (i) plus one of the following premises:

> (ii) If there is a reporting need for sensum terms, then there is a descriptive need for sensum terms,

or

> (iii) If there is an explanatory need for sensum terms, then there is a descriptive need for sensum terms,

or

> (iv) If all terminologies which are alternative ways of describing sensory experience have linguistic inadequacies, then there is a descriptive need for sensum terms.

Thus given the above premises and (i), if it is established that sensum terms are crucial for certain explanations, or for making identifying reference to sensory experience, that is, reporting it, or if all alternative terminologies, such as the sensing terminology, are inadequate to express certain facts about sensory experience, then there would be linguistic reasons for sensa. It will be part of the task of Chapter 2 to examine these three linguistic reasons for sensa, but their present relevance is that these, the most plausible linguistic reasons I can find, succeed only if they establish a descriptive need for sensum terms. For this reason we can accept premise IV.

Premise VIII is like IV in enabling us to infer from certain information that there is no reason for a certain hypothesis. We can justify VIII as follows. If there is a metaphysical reason for sensa, then there is a metaphysical reason for sensa as constituents of perceptual experiences ("perceptual" sensa), or for sensa in internal experiences, such as feelings, emotions, and bodily sensations ("internal" sensa). But, I would argue, there is no reason for internal sensa if there is none for perceptual sensa. Any reason I can find for internal sensa is also one for perceptual sensa. Furthermore, although the argument from perceptual relativity and the causal argument could be adapted to apply to internal sensa, the two strongest arguments—the argument from hallucination and the time-gap argument—are much less plausible when adapted to internal sensa. Now it is also true that there is a metaphysical reason for sensa in perceptual experiences only if, contrary to VII, some metaphysical theory about perception and the external world that requires sensa is more reasonable than any such theory without sensa. Consequently, if VII is true, then there is no metaphysical reason for sensa.

CONCLUSION AND SUMMARY OF WORK TO BE DONE

With the justification of the three principles of reason and premises IV, VIII, and XVIII, we have fixed the tasks remaining before us throughout the rest of the book. We can summarize the order in which the work is to be done as follows: consideration of reasons for or against sensa; evaluation of various forms of phenomenalism; critical comparison of direct realism with indirect realism; critical evaluation of the attempt to conjoin common-sensa realism with scientific realism; and organization of the preceding results to show how they affect the justification of those premises still to be considered. Let us begin with reasons for or against sensa.

2   On Sensa and Sensings

The primary task of this chapter is to examine whether there is any reason or evidence for the existence of sensa, but we are also interested in whether sensa raise recalcitrant problems we can resolve if we deny there are sensa. I shall consider this second question after the primary task is completed. As implied in the preceding discussion, I take it that there are four different sorts of reasons which might be used to justify the existence of sensa. I find it helpful to divide these reasons roughly into two exclusive and exhaustive kinds: linguistic and nonlinguistic reasons, that is, reasons that are minimally sufficient for sensa only if they include a statement about some linguistic entities, and reasons that do not require any statement about language. Among the latter there are two exclusive and exhaustive kinds, namely those which are philosophical reasons and those which are not. For our present purposes I shall distinguish these two kinds as those that are and those that are not minimally sufficient reasons for sensa only if they include some metaphysical claims about what there is. For example, if we find that a Sellarsian indirect realism is justified, then there will be a metaphysical reason to accept some sort of sensum, that is, some sort of phenomenal individual.

Among the nonphilosophical reasons for sensa, I shall delineate two exclusive kinds without claiming they are exhaustive, namely, empirical theoretical reasons and empirical nontheoretical reasons. Both sorts include premises that are empirically confirmable statements, but the former, unlike the latter, are minimally sufficient reasons for sensa only if they include some scientific theoretical statements that explain some observable data. These theoretical reasons, then, include statements that are not verifiable independently of the confirmation of some scientific theory. The nontheoretical reasons, however, await the confirmation of no scientific theory. That these two classifications are not exhaustive is seen by noting that I have omitted mentioning logical and mathematical reasons for sensa. However, since I can think of no *a priori* reasons of either sort for sensa, I shall not bother with delineating such a class of reasons. The preceding divisions will, I believe, be sufficient to classify all the plausible reasons we should consider.

While I find the preceding distinctions helpful in searching for, discovering, and clarifying what reasons there might be for sensa, we shall find that often, as with reasons for entities of other sorts, the reasons that have actually been given are not easy to classify using the distinctions. This is especially true among empirical scientific reasons where there is no clearly enunciated scientific theory. For example, consider the sorts of reasons offered for and against the existence of flying saucers. One sort of reason, which consists of perceptual reports of people who claim to have witnessed relevantly unusual flying objects, seems clearly to be nontheoretical. However, it might be claimed that some of the counterreasons are theoretical, because they are based on explanation of the observed phenomena by other objects for which there is independent evidence. We should indeed count this second sort of reason as theoretical if justification by explanatory power were sufficient for something being theoretical, but since this explanation requires no scientific theory at all, we can classify such explanatory reasons as nontheoretical. There are, however, examples of two different sorts of theoretical reasons. As the atomic theory of matter became developed, it posited many entities to explain different sorts of observed phenomena. For example, granting scientific realism, the postulation of positrons was justified because certain observed tracks in cloud chambers could be explained by assuming such an elementary particle but could not be explained by the theory of atomic physics with only those elementary particles previously posited. However, the postulation was also justified independently of the discovery of those tracks by requirements of the elaborated mathematical atomic theory. In both cases, the reasons for the existence of positrons are minimally sufficient only if they include essential statements in a version of the atomic theory that explains certain observable data in a mathematically satisfactory way. With these somewhat rough, but I hope helpful, distinctions made, we are ready to begin a search for and examination of empirical, nontheoretical reasons for sensa.[1]

---

[1] Because I have already examined in detail these arguments in *Materialism and Sensations* (New Haven: Yale University Press, 1971), Chap. 6, the present discussion is less detailed and intended to highlight the crucial premises of the strongest versions of the arguments.

EMPIRICAL, NONTHEORETICAL REASONS FOR SENSA

There are two arguments often used to justify the existence of sensa whose empirical premises are not only nontheoretical, but are also thought to be verified by reflecting on our own and others' experience, independent of any scientific discoveries. These are the facts of perceptual relativity and hallucinatory experiences.

Argument from Perceptual Relativity

The crux of the argument from perceptual relativity is expressed in a statement Berkeley puts in the mouth of Philonous:

> But, as we approach to or recede from an object, the visible extension varies, being at one distance ten or a hundred times greater than at another. Does it not therefore follow from hence likewise that it is not really inherent in the object?[2]

The same point is crucial in Ayer's statement of the argument:

> It is held to be characteristic of material things that their existence and their essential properties are independent of any particular observer ... But this, it is argued, has been shown not to be true of the objects we immediately experience. And so the conclusion is reached that what we immediately experience is in no case a material thing.[3]

Since Philonous is not merely interested in "visible extension" but rather in all sensible, or directly preceivable, properties, he would agree with Ayer that the following is a crucial premise in the argument from perceptual relativity:

(1) All directly perceived qualities depend on (vary with certain changes in) perceivers.

As I have argued previously in *Materialism and Sensations*, (1) is not the minimal claim that can be made to describe the phenomenological facts of perceptual relativity. Another contrary interpretation of the facts is:

---

[2] G. Berkeley, *Principles, Dialogues, and Philosophical Correspondence,* C. M. Turbayne, ed. (New York: Bobbs-Merrill, 1965), p. 128.

[3] A. J. Ayer, *The Foundations of Empirical Knowledge* (New York: St. Martin's Press, 1955), pp. 9–11.

(2) No directly perceived qualities depend on perceivers, but which qualities are directly perceived by a perceiver depends on the perceiver.

From this we can derive what might seem to be the minimal claim:

(3) Which qualities are directly perceived by a perceiver depends on the perceiver.

But even (3) implies more than a minimal description if we assume, as seems reasonable, that (3) implies that there are directly perceived qualities. There is at least some plausibility to the view that no qualities are directly perceived. For example, on a sensing version of a Kantian theory, the only qualities to be directly perceived are the properties of things-in-themselves, but since they are not perceivable, they are not directly perceived.

Our problem in stating the minimal claim is to discover some way to describe the shifting and variable nature of our perceptual experiences in a way that will beg no question against any theory of perception and the external world. There are two ways we can do this, and I shall use them interchangeably. One is to use an intensional sense of 'to appear' as in 'A dagger appeared to Macbeth,' and the other is to use an intensional sense of 'to have an experience of' as in 'Macbeth had an experience of a dagger.' In these uses, neither 'An x appears to y' nor 'y has an experience of an x' implies that there is an x. Furthermore, both 'to appear' and 'to have an experience of' can be modified to specify different sense modalities, such as 'visually appear,' 'auditorially appear,' and 'tactually appear.' Then, allowing 'x' to range over properties and relations as well as individuals, we can make claims such as "The redness of blood on her hands appeared to Lady Macbeth," and "Lady Macbeth had an experience of the redness of blood on her hands." Now we can state the minimal description of the phenomenological facts:

(4) Which qualities appear to a perceiver depends on (varies with changes in) the perceiver.

Unlike (3), which as I shall interpret it, implies that there are directly perceived qualities, (4) is consistent with any theory that denies that there are directly perceived qualities, or even one that states that no qualities that appear to perceivers are properties of any sort of entity.

Our problem at this point is to decide whether the phenomenological facts described in (4) provide reason to accept the interpretation of those facts expressed in (1), or whether they show that a different interpretation, such as the first conjunct of (2):

(2a) No directly perceived qualities depend on perceivers,

is at least as reasonable as (1). In order to discover this, let us assume here:

(5) There are directly perceived qualities,

because if there are no such qualities, then both (1) and (2a) are true, and there is no reason to choose one interpretation rather than the other. But once we assume (5), the following objection to (2a) arises. If a quality is directly perceived, then some entity has the quality, and, because some qualities directly perceived under unusual conditions are clearly not properties of external physical objects, they are, therefore, qualities of sensa. While this argument does not establish (1), if it is sound, it certainly provides reason to interpret the facts expressed in (4) and (5) as (1) requires, because of its conclusion about qualities of sensa.

There are two ways to rebut this argument. One is to defend the denial of the first premise, that is, that some properties are directly perceived yet nothing has those properties. While we have agreed that a property which nothing has can appear to someone, it is certainly reasonable to claim that a property is perceived, either directly or indirectly, only if something has it. We can make this explicit by characterizing the direct perception of properties, or more precisely, I would claim, their instances, as we did the direct perception of objects, in the Introduction:[4]

S directly perceives (an instance of) the property ϕ at $t =_{df}$.

(1) For some p at t, S perceives p's (instance of) property ϕ, *and*

(2) $(x)\{[Sx \lor Gx] \cdot x \neq p \cdot Cxp \cdot Cpx] \supset \sim Psp\phi tx\}$

[4] For a short discussion of instances, see my "In Search of Criteria for Property Identity and Difference" (unpublished). Nothing in the present work depends on whether properties or their instances appear or are perceived, so I shall not distinguish carefully between them in subsequent discussions.

Here $Psp\phi tx = S$'s perceptual experience of p's (instance of) property ϕ at t consists in S experiencing x at t. This leaves only the second premise to attack. Can a defender of (2a) justify its denial, namely, that all directly perceived qualities are properties of physical objects? Actually, he need only show that there is no more reason to accept this premise than its denial, without assuming that there are sensa.

To see how he could proceed, let us consider the two most difficult sorts of cases for him. The first consists of standard cases of perceptual relativity. For example, there are cases where a red sign appears white, a sweet drink tastes bitter, cold water feels warm, and a round table appears elliptical. The second sort of case involves illusion, as when a gnarled tree in a graveyard appears to a frightened trespasser to be moving towards him and grabbing at him. Another is where a wall of one solid color appears to have a continually shifting kaliedescope of various colors to someone under the influence of drugs.[5]

In both sorts of cases, the question is whether there is reason to think, without assuming sensa, that qualities that are not properties of any external objects, not only appear to someone, which we can grant, but also are directly perceived. There are two ways someone who wishes to deny there is such a reason can proceed with many cases of the first sort. He can claim that in each case a property of an external object is directly perceived, but it appears differently to the perceiver from the way it is. Although this may sound odd, we do often talk this way in specific situations. Not only do we sometimes say that a round table appears elliptical, a red sign appears white, and cool water appears warm, we also sometimes say that the round shape of the table appears elliptical from here, the red color of the sign appears white as the sunlight glances off the sign, and the cool temperature of the water appears warm to my freezing hands. The second way to handle these cases, and the most reasonable way to handle many cases of the second sort, is to claim that while qualities appear in all these cases, no qualities are directly perceived in any of them. It is true that this would require some explanation, but no more than the claim that in all cases of perception we directly experience qualities which no

---

[5] See W. R. Brain, *The Nature of Experience* (London: Oxford University Press, 1959), p. 10, for a vivid description of such an experience.

external objects have. While qualities of sensa would explain the latter, objectless sensing events would explain the former. For some sensing theories, in these cases when a quality appears to someone, this event consists in the person merely sensing in some way rather than directly perceiving some quality. And, whether or not the theory allows some properties of external objects to be sometimes directly perceived in conditions where they would appear markedly different from the way they are, some sensing theories clearly allow for direct perception of qualities when conditions are optimal and perceivers are normal for that particular sort of property.[6]

I have pointed out that how one explains the facts expressed in (4) and (5) depends on how one interprets those facts. Sensa are used to explain the facts on one interpretation and objectless sensings are used on another. But since the argument we have examined to provide reason for the interpretation expressed in (1) has a premise which seems not to be justifiable independently of assuming sensa, we have found no reason, independent of theoretical considerations, for sensa. Furthermore, because I can find no other way the facts of perceptual relativity can be used to provide such a reason, we can conclude these facts do not justify the existence of sensa. However, although we did consider some examples of illusions in reaching this conclusion, we should not yet conclude that illusory experiences, especially those involving hallucinations, do not provide reasons for sensa. Hallucinations, it is thought, provide quite different grounds for accepting sensa than does perceptual relativity.

Arguments from Hallucination

In all the versions of arguments from hallucination that I have seen, the crucial premise concerns indistinguishability. In particular, the central claim is that for some perceptual experience there is no way to distinguish, first, whether they are veridical or hallucinatory, and, second, whether in these experiences physical objects or sensa are experienced. According to the usual argument, if only sensa are experienced in some of these experiences, then because of this indistinguishability as to kind, sensa are also experienced in the others. However, although some of these experiences are

---

[6] See Chapter 6 for a discussion of optimal conditions.

probably veridical, others are probably completely hallucinatory and so do not include physical objects but only sensa. Thus it is probable that sensa are directly experienced in at least some veridical experiences, and, if in some, then also in all other veridical experiences.

There are several problems for such an argument. One concerns the claim about indistinguishability regarding kinds. If this indistinguishability is to justify identity of kinds, it must be indiscernibility in principle, not merely indiscernibility because of the information which is in fact available. But, whether or not discernible in practice, it is reasonable to think that the causal ancestors of veridical experiences are always different in kind from those of completely hallucinatory experiences. Thus it is always in principle possible to discern what sort of experience any particular one is. However, it may be replied, this does not show it is always possible to discern whether the objects experienced are the same or different in kind. Indeed, it might be argued that if it is granted that sensa are experienced in purely hallucinatory experiences because physical objects are not experienced, then we are justified in saying that sensa are experienced in veridical experiences as well. This is because neither causal ancestors nor any features discernible in the experience itself provide a means for discerning a difference regarding the kind of object directly experienced. That is, different sorts of causal ancestors help us to determine whether an experience is veridical or not. But neither such facts nor any discoverable features of these experiences themselves enable us to discern any difference between any kinds of objects being directly experienced in the two sorts of cases. Thus we should assume they are the same kind, namely, sensa.

It might be replied to this that these facts and features fail to provide a way to discern such a difference because they do not provide a way to discern whether or not physical objects are directly, rather than indirectly, perceived in veridical experiences. In other words, these facts and features can be conjoined with direct experience of sensa when hallucinating, but also direct perception of physical objects in veridical perception. For example, we might sense adverbially in veridical perception, but experience sensa when hallucinating.

I think, however, that there is reason to reject this combined

sensing-sensum theory and to construct another argument from
hallucination which avoids the preceding problems. It is based
upon a quite different kind of indistinguishability which can be
uncovered by concentrating on the proximate, rather than remote,
causally sufficient ancestors of perceptual experiences. It is clear,
I believe, that qualitatively identical physiological states that are
these (total) proximate causes of different perceptual experiences,
can result from quite different remote causes. But given two
qualitatively identical states as (total) proximate causes of two
experiences, the experiences would be qualitatively identical. Thus,
if one cause results in sensa being sensed, then the other does also.
In this way, based on a different sort of indistinguishability, it
could be concluded that sensa are constituents of all cases of
verdical perception. We can lay out this argument as follows:

(1) If the proximate causal ancestor of x is qualitatively
identical with the proximate causal ancestor of y, then
x is qualitatively identical with y.

(2) For any veridical perceptual experience, x, whose proximate causal ancestor is c_1, there is some set of causal
factors that results in c_2, which is qualitatively identical
with c_1, but which also results in a (completely) hallucinatory experience.

Therefore

(3) For any veridical perceptual experience, x, there is a
qualitatively identical hallucinatory experience, y.

(4) If two experiences, x and y are qualitatively identical,
then an entity of kind K is a constituent of x if and only
if an entity of kind K is a constituent of y.

Therefore

(5) For any veridical perceptual experience, x, there is an
hallucinatory experience, y, such that an entity of kind
K is a constituent of x if and only if an entity of kind K
is a constituent of y.

(6) No external object is perceived by someone who has a
(completely) hallucinatory perceptual experience.

(7) If no external object is perceived by someone who has

a perceptual experience, then a sensum he senses is a constituent of that experience.

Therefore

(8) Sensa are constituents of all (completely) hallucinatory perceptual experiences.

Therefore

(9) Sensa are constituents of all veridical experiences.

In premise (1), this argument invokes the principle of same cause then same effect to refute the combined sensing-sensum theory and support the sensum theory. While remote causal facts and experiential features will not help us decide, this principle supposedly provides reason to prefer the sensum theory. However, it may be objected that there is no reason to accept premise (2), because there is no reason to think that for each set of causal ancestors of c_1 there actually is a quite different set that results in c_2, which is qualitatively identical with c_1. But there is contrary evidence accumulating as knowledge of brains increases that certain direct electrical stimulations of parts of the brain, which do not involve any sense receptors, will produce experiences which are qualitatively indistinct from those produced from stimulation of sense organs by external objects. Consequently, although at present we do not know how to produce such complex brain processes, this does not override the reasons to think that qualitatively identical brain effects result from different causal ancestors. We can, therefore, accept premises (1) and (2). It is clear that (4) is also acceptable.

Once premises (1), (2), and (4) are justified, the combined theory is refuted, because it denies conclusion (5) which follows from those three premises. But this is not enough to justify the sensum theory. A rejection of the combined theory leaves both the sensum theory and the sensing theory unscathed. It is Premise (7), unsupported by any facts of hallucinations, that eliminates the sensing theory. The following premise is equally reasonable, given only those facts:

(7a) If no external object is perceived by someone who has a perceptual experience, then an adverbial sensing by him occurs in that experience.

It might be objected here that it is quite counterintuitive to interpret all hallucinatory experiences adverbially so that there are no phenomenal individuals such as apparitions. It surely seems to many people that apparitions are experienced in at least some cases. But while I agree that this is counterintuitive, it will not help the sensum theorist, because conclusion (9) of the preceding argument is at least as counterintuitive as (7a). It surely seems to many people that we do not sense a sensum whenever we perceive an external object. Indeed, the conclusion we get using (7a), namely:

> (9a) Adverbial sensings are constituents of all veridical perceptual experiences,

is closer to our intuitions about veridical perception than is (9). Unlike (9), statement (9a) is consistent with direct perception of external objects. Interestingly, though, the combined theory best accords with our intuitions. However, with it already eliminated, our intuitions provide no way to decide between the two remaining theories.

Once again we have not found perceptual facts that provide reason for accepting sensa. Hallucinatory experiences and certain facts about their causal ancestors fare no better than the facts of perceptual relativity. However, we have not considered all the causal facts that have been thought to be relevant. In particular, it has been claimed that some of the specific features of a causal chain, which begins with an external object transmitting stimulus and ends with a perceptual experience, justify the existence of sensa. Let us see whether this is so.

The Time-Gap Argument

The most forceful argument for sensa derived from causal facts of perception is based on the fact that the finite speed of light results in a time-gap between transmission of the light from an external object and the perceptual experience of the object. However, there may be other causal reasons for sensa, as well. Physiologists, such as Brain and Eccles, have described these complex causal processes as culminating in experiences of sense-data or percepts, but they seem to provide no reason for preferring this description to one that mentions adverbial sensings.[7] Indeed, it would seem that, given their description of the preceding causal chain as consisting of certain neural events resulting from other events, it would be reasonable to construe the culminating effects as being events rather than individuals. This is in accordance with the plausible principle that only events are causes and effects. However, on the sensum theory, not only do these neural events cause events of persons experiencing sensa, but also they either generate the sensa themselves, or they cause certain brain parts to have phenomenal properties. I should think it is at least as reasonable to hold that adverbial sensing events are effects of neural events as to hold that these effects are phenomenal objects or properties. Reasonable, that is, unless the time-gap data prove otherwise.

We can begin a discussion of time-gap arguments by quoting Brain, who first states what he claims are

> physiological and psychological reasons why what we perceive cannot be identical with a state of the physical object which it represents. There are physical reasons as well, for example the time taken for light waves emanating from distant objects to reach the eye of the observer. In the case of the sun this is about nine minutes, but owing to the relative motion of the earth and the sun, even that short interval is enough to ensure that, when we see the sun, what we see is not where the sun is at that moment. The distance of the more remote celestial objects is so great that their light may take millions of years to reach us. Consequently, the star which we 'see' now may have become extinct hundreds of thousands of years ago without our being aware of the fact.[8]

As Brain seems to do, others have used the time-gap to argue that we do not see the sun and stars, but only sensa. However, an indirect realist can point out that the present nonexistence of a star is compatible with my indirectly perceiving it now, if my present perception of it consists in my presently experiencing a star-like

[7] See J. Eccles, *The Brain and the Unity of Conscious Experience* (Cambridge: Cambridge University Press, 1965), pp. 17–18.

[8] Brain, *Science and Man* (London: Faber and Faber LTD., 1966) pp. 46–47.

sensum as a result of my eyes being suitably affected by stimulus previously transmitted from the star. This is how an indirect realist would describe all our perceptions of physical objects. It is one of the advantages of the sensum theory.

It is obvious, however, that the preceding way to rebut the preceding argument from the time-gap by relying on sensa is of no help to someone who wishes to claim that there are no empirical reasons for sensa. Furthermore, someone can use this rebuttal to argue that since some extinct stars are perceived but none are directly perceived, sensa are directly experienced in at least some cases of veridical perception. And, just as the previously discussed sensing-sensum theory is ruled out, so also, for like reasons, is a theory that proposes sensa for perception of nonexisting and, perhaps, distant stars, but sensings for perception of existing and nearby things. Consequently, according to this argument, sensa are directly experienced in all veridical perceptions, and then surely in all hallucinatory experiences. The crucial premise here is:

> Stars are perceived when they do not exist, but no stars are directly perceived when they do not exist.

We have seen how the sensum theory can accommodate the first conjunct of this premise, and so I think that if denying it is required to rebut this argument, the rebuttal fails. But this leaves the second conjunct available, and the way to attack the argument is by considering a more general form of that conjunct:

> All objects exist at the time they are directly perceived.

Often, when someone claims that we directly see a physical object, such as a hand, he takes this to imply that we are perceptually acquainted with the hand, that is, that the hand is not only presented to us when we see it, but it is present with us when we see it. This is clearly the view of the perception of physical objects that a naive realist and, initially at least, a Berkeleyan would have, and it is the view of the experience of sensa that an indirect realist and a Berkeleyan have.[9] However, we have already seen that it is not required for direct perception of physical objects. If my

---

[9] See Chapter 6 for a more detailed discussion of this view that perception is perceptual acquaintance. See the concluding chapter for a problem for a Berkeleyan who holds the view that we are perceptually acquainted with physical objects.

present perceptual experience of a distant star consists in my being in a state of star-sensing now as a result of my eyes being suitably affected by stimulus previously transmitted from the star, then I directly perceive the star now, even if it does not exist now and I am not perceptually acquainted with it. And, as previously shown, the causation of such a sensing event is at least as reasonable an affect of physical and neurophysiological events as is a sensum. Thus the causal facts involved in the time-gap, like the other causal facts of perception we considered, provide no reason to accept the existence of sensa.

Conclusion about Nontheoretical Reasons for Sensa

We have found that three kinds of perceptual facts—relativity, hallucinations, and causal facts—provide no empirical evidence for the existence of sensa. Furthermore, these are the only facts I can find that are plausible candidates for empirical reasons for sensa. On the basis of this I conclude that there are no empirical, nontheoretical reasons for sensa. That is, there are no empirical reasons for sensa that contain no empirical statements whose verification depends on the confirmation of some scientific theory. This justifies, consequently, our acceptance of premise I of the central argument of this book. It does not show, however, that there are no empirical reasons for sensa. It might be that some physiological or psychological theory that explains certain facts of perception, or some other facts, will require there to be sensa. Consequently, although it is difficult at this early stage in the development of theories of perception to foresee whether sensa are or will be required, we should nevertheless try to get some idea of the likelihood of there being such reasons, and, thereby, to see whether or not it is reasonable to accept premise II.

EMPIRICAL, THEORETICAL REASONS FOR SENSA

Previously when drawing the distinction between empirical reasons which are theoretical and those which are not, I claimed that the distinction is somewhat rough and that it would be difficult to classify some reasons for sensa precisely. For example, it might be thought that the reason based on the time-gap could equally well be classified as theoretical, because although the reasons for a time-gap do not depend on any physiological or psychological theory, they do depend on physics. However, the speed of light is measurable by experiment, and so its having a certain finite velocity need not be postulated as part of a theory in order to be confirmed. For this reason I called it nontheoretical. Or again, it might be claimed that my discussion of the other two sorts of empirical reasons vascillated between construing them as theoretical and as nontheoretical because I often considered how well the sensum theory and sensing theory explained the various perceptual facts. However, my aim in bringing in the two theories was only to help show that a sensing interpretation of certain of these facts is at least as reasonable as a sensum interpretation. This involves showing that these facts are as easily explainable under the one interpretation as under the other. By so doing, I tried to justify the rejection of certain premises in the arguments. But this does not imply that the arguments themselves include or depend on theoretical claims. Thus the reasons we have examined so far are nontheoretical. Of course, although we have shown that these uses of the perceptual facts fail, it may be that those facts, and perhaps others, are best explained by a theory that postulates sensa. Let us consider that possibility now, remembering, as we proceed, that much of what we do will be somewhat speculative because of the states of the relevant sciences.

A Theoretical Reason for Sensa: Greater Explanatory Power than Sensings

It is clearly quite easy and natural to use sensa to explain the phenomenal facts that there is widespread perceptual variation, and that people are often deluded in illusory and hallucinatory experiences. They also fittingly explain the common belief that we sometimes experience apparitions when hallucinating, and that we see small, bright specks when seeing distant, and sometimes nonexistent, stars. It seems especially appealing to use sensa to explain experiences in which physical objects and apparitions seem to intermingle, as, for example, when "an apparition hides from view an object in front of which it is standing, or opens and passes through a door known to be locked."[10] Indeed, I think that it is because of the ease and naturalness of these explanations that this

[10] Brain, *The Nature of Experience*, p. 20.

first sort of theoretical reason for sensa is intuitively most convincing.

Of these facts that seem so easily explainable using sensa, I find only one fact more difficult to explain using a theory with sensings, namely, the phenomenological fact that when hallucinating it is often difficult to resist the belief that some sort of individual, that is, an apparition, is experienced. Such convictions about objects are especially strong in the cases where, given sensa, what turn out to be apparitions seem to intermingle with physical objects. As briefly indicated in the preceding discussion of nontheoretical reasons, there is no reason to think that sensing events would not equally well explain why there are phenomenal variations, illusions, hallucinations, and even delusions which result from these phenomena. Sensing events can also be used to explain easily the phenomenon of apparitions intermingling with physical objects. A theory with sensa would explain some of these experiences as ones in which a complex sensum, or complex of sensa, is experienced as the result of the joint effect of different causal chains, some of which include stimuli from physical objects. A theory with sensings would explain the same sort of experience as consisting of sensing events, where the complex way in which the person senses is a joint product of different causal chains. More generally, as causal factors change for various reasons, the way in which a person senses varies. And, depending on what affects these causal factors, the result is perceptual variation and relativity, and sometimes illusion or hallucination which often involves delusion. Such explanations, however, do not explain why people who are hallucinating so often believe they are experiencing objects, even if they doubt the objects are physical. It seems that a theory with sensa can provide the additional explanation merely by pointing out that these people are indeed experiencing objects, but a theory with sensings has no corresponding, simple explanation. This, it might be claimed, is a clear explanatory advantage for sensum theories.

I find it dubious, however, that the simple task of merely positing sensa provides adequate explanations. More is needed, and once that is added, sensum theories lose their advantage. People tend to reify not only when hallucinating, but also in cases of veridical perception and when they have nonperceptual (internal) experiences, feelings, emotions, and moods. Merely assuming phenomenal objects in all these different sorts of cases is not enough. Such sensa would usually be, as Berkeley said, "perpetually fleeting and variable," and, even when hallucinating, perceivers usually believe they are experiencing objects relatively invariant and permanent. Thus explanations of why people believe they are perceiving such objects require more than merely the claim that they actually are experiencing phenomenal objects. What is also needed would seem to be an explanation of people's ability or tendency to pick out or concentrate on invariant (or at least relatively invariant) features of the perceptual flux that affects them. And, as an example will illustrate, there is no reason to think that sensa are any better suited for this task than sensings.

Gibson, in his important book, *The Senses Considered as Perceptual Systems*, not only realizes the significance of invariant features in perception, but he builds his information-based theory of perception on the recognition of such features. Essential to his rejection of a "sensation-based" theory—that is, a theory implying that we both have sensations and also respond or attend to them when perceiving—is this thesis: It is not merely the amount of stimuli affecting sense receptors that is essential to perceiving the external word, it is also the structure of that array of stimuli. He claims that it is by means of attending to invariant elements in stimulus structure, rather than to sensations, that a perceiver obtains information about physical objects. A child, through his various perceptual systems "must learn to separate the invariants from the variants more and more precisely as he grows up, and to focus his attention on them if he is to learn more and more about the world."[11] He gets information about the relatively permanent objects in the world in this way, because "these invariants correspond to the permanent properties of the environment."[12] If Gibson's theory is correct, it is reasonable to explain our strong propensity to reify our experiences as being a result of our natural tendency to concentrate on the invariant elements in arrays of stimuli which is then strengthened by our apparent success in obtaining information about the external world in that way. And, clearly, this explanation is independent of whether sensations are construed adverbially or as involving sensa. This is bolstered by

[11] J. Gibson, "New Reasons for Realism," *Synthese*, 17 (1967): 165–66.
[12] Ibid., p. 162.

realizing that for Gibson, since information about the external world comes from stimuli rather than from sense impressions, the latter "are occasional and incidental symptoms of perceptions."[13] Thus it would seem that how they are interpreted makes no difference for explanations of our perception of the external world.

Of course, Gibson's theory may prove to be unsuccessful and another requiring sensa may become justified. However, we can do no better now than to work with what is available now, and based upon that, I find no reason to think that our tendency to respond in perceptual situations in terms of enduring objects is best explained by a theory assuming sensa. Indeed, even if Gibson's theory that there are perceptual systems that respond to invariant elements in stimulus flux is rejected, it would seem, nevertheless, that what is needed is a theory that involves some sort of response to and concentration on invariant elements of something. Without some such postulation, I find it hard to understand how a theory would explain our tendency to believe we experience relatively invariant and permanent objects given the constantly changing flux of stimuli. But, again, at the present time, I find no more reason to claim these invariants are features of sensa rather than stimuli, or even retinal images, brain processes, sensings or perhaps something else.

Based on present evidence, we can reject the claim that theories with sensa have the preceding explanatory advantage over theories with sensings. But even if they proved to have this advantage, theories with sensa have one disadvantage compared with sensing theories, which might well counterbalance this advantage. A theory with sensa has to assume that whenever someone has a perceptual experience, one of three events is taking place: either a phenomenal object is generated, as I have been interpreting these theories; or some object such as a part of a brain comes to have phenomenal properties; or the perceiver comes to be aware of an object that had previously existed with sensible properties even when he did not experience it. But surely a theory that avoids unsensed sensa, the creation of fleeting individuals, and causing things to have phenomenal properties is to be preferred. Of course, this disadvantage for sensa might be overbalanced if rejecting sensa for sensings creates

---

[13] Ibid.

some explanatory disadvantage. But, again, it is premature to judge that issue and, given present evidence, there is no reason to think that explanations with sensings will result in a more serious problem. Thus far, then, we have found no theoretical, explanatory reasons for sensa.

A Second Theoretical Reason for Sensa: To Explain Seeing in Perspective

It is difficult to predict all the theoretical reasons that might arise for assuming sensa rather than sensings, but I shall try to consider what I think is a fair sample of such reasons. In particular, I shall consider three more purported reasons: two derived from Gibson's discussion of his own theory, and one based on certain claims about measurement made in the field of psychophysics. The first reason comes from Gibson's attempt to explain certain cases of what he calls "deficiencies in perception." Although, as I have tried to indicate, Gibson's way of explaining perception of the external world does not require any sort of sensum, he uses what seems to be one sort of sensum to explain what he calls cases of "incomplete perceptual constancy," such as when parallel railroad tracks appear to converge. Gibson admits that sensation-based theories have less difficulty explaining such facts than his own theory. These other theories state that "the conversion of the pictorial sensation into the tridimensional perception is incomplete, and that a compromise results." But Gibson cannot give this explanation because his theory states that "perception can be independent of sensation, depending only on the pickup of invariants that specify shape and size."[14] He suggests the following explanation:

> In certain conditions for the perception of the layout of things, visual sensations obtrude themselves on the perception of true layout and cause the illusions of seeing partially in perspective. Putting it another way, sometimes we attend to the pictorial projections in the visual field instead of exclusively to the ratios and other invariants in the optic array. The pictorial mode of perception then asserts itself, since pictorial attention interferes with attention to information. The compromise is

[14] Gibson, *The Senses Considered As Perceptual Systems* (Boston: Houghton-Mifflin Co., 1966), p. 306.

not between the raw data and the complete processing of this
data, but between two alternative kinds of attention.[15]

I would guess that Gibson's point here is that in certain situations
we cannot avoid attending and responding to visual sensations or
"pictorial projections" (that is, pictorial sensations or images), and
this interferes with our attending and responding to the invariant
features of the arrays of stimuli that affect our sense organs. It
would seem that he would also explain disease and drug induced
hallucinations similarly, except that in those cases there would be
only mental images for us to respond to. But, although Gibson
agrees that we do have mental images when hallucinating,[16] it is
not clear whether *responses* to such sensa play any role in his
explanation of hallcinations. As he says, hallucinations result
from "purely internal excitation of the nervous system" by the
disease or drug.[17]

As stated, it seems that Gibson's theory requires some sort of
individuals as objects of attention in certain experiences which are
not what we attend to in our usual perception of the external world.
These seem to be some sort of mental images, and thus some sort of
phenomenal individuals or sensa. It would seem, then, that these
explanations of Gibson's theory require that perceivers both shift
and divide attention, sometimes voluntarily, sometimes involun-
tarily between arrays of stimuli and sensa. I find this to be a very
unsatisfactory consequence of his theory. It would seem that these
changes in attention are not done by means of perceptual systems,
because their function is to attend to structured stimuli. It seems,
then, we must postulate some additional attending mechanism
if we accept such explanations. This is especially bothersome,
because, except for this point, Gibson would seem to want to
identify each event of a person attending to and obtaining stimulus
information with some event of one of his perceptual systems
responding to stimuli and obtaining this information in a self-
correcting and self-adjusting way.[18]

It is tempting, while at the same time quite speculative, to wonder

[15] Ibid., pp. 306–07.
[16] See J. Gibson, "On the Relation Between Hallucination and Perception," *Leonardo*
(1970): 425–27.
[17] Gibson, *The Senses Considered as Perceptual Systems,* p. 318.
[18] Ibid., p. 271.

whether a sensum-based explanation of hallucinations might be as plausible as Gibson's explanation. Certainly, assuming that there are sensa that we experience and to which we respond, we would seem to be able to attend to relatively invariant features of the shifting sensa (that is, apparitions or images) when hallucinating, and it is not clear to me why this could not also be the explanation of what occurs in veridical perception. Gibson wants to avoid such indirect perception for epistemological reasons, but there seems to be no better reason for assuming that arrays of stimuli give us reliable information about the external world than that the structural relationships in or among experienced sensa so inform us. Furthermore, for reasons similar to those to be discussed in the concluding chapter, there is no reason to think that the epistemological problem of justifying claims about the external world is more easily solved for one of these theories than for the other. And if such a sensum theory should be at least as plausible as Gibson's, then I think it would be reasonable to replace a perceiver's attending and responding to sensa with his merely sensing sensa, and then to replace that with his sensing adverbially. In this way we would arrive at a sensing theory that would be at least as reasonable as these other two theories.

Such speculation proves very little, however, and it does nothing towards showing whether Gibson's own theory can be adapted to accomodate sensings. To see how this might be done, let me consider Gibson's explanation of incomplete perceptual constancy, and also the related phenomenon of complete pictorial perception, or, as he says, "perception in perspective," which occurs voluntarily for a representational artist. Furthermore, let us utilize Gibson's thesis that each event of a perceiver obtaining perceptual information is identical with one of his perceptual systems responding in some way. We might, then, construe his explanation as follows. Usually, when a person sees an object, his whole visual system responds in a self-correcting way to invariant structural features in the array of stimuli transmitted from the object. Sometimes, however, the system, or some part of it, responds to some other effect of the stimulus flux on the system; that is, it responds to a sensum. This additional response affects the behavior of the system and thus changes the way the object appears. When this occurs, incomplete perceptual constancy results.

There are two points to note about this speculative reconstruction. The first is that it accords with Gibson's claim that sensations are only occasional symptoms of perception, because they occur in seeing only when perceiving in perspective. The second is that the reconstruction does not seem to accord with Gibson's view that sensations are incidental symptoms of perception rather than essential explanatory factors in it, because they are required in some explanations as objects to which systems sometimes respond. Perhaps, then, we should look for a different reconstruction. Indeed, I think we should look for one that makes sensations incidental to perception but which, contrary to what Gibson seems to hold, assumes that these symptoms, or by-products, occur in all cases of perceiving rather than only occasionally. The latter is surely counterintuitive, because phenomenological evidence supports the view that if sensations—whether sensa or sensings—occur in some cases of perception, then they occur in all cases.

I believe we can easily amend Gibson's theory so that it can accommodate sensa as incidental effects that always occur in perceiving. What is needed is to find a substitute for the explanation that incomplete perceptual constancy is an effect of sensa (visual sensations) obtruding on the perception of structural relationships. Let me suggest two plausible alternatives. One is to explain this phenomenon as an effect of some brain processes on the internal workings of the perceptual system. As a result, the system responds differently to stimulus flux, and what is seen appears differently. It might be, for example, that these brain processes are just those that, on Gibson's original view, cause the sensations that obtrude on perception. This would make these explanations to be like those Gibson gives for drug-induced hallucinations: they occur when a drug internally affects the behavior of a perceptual system so that it causes the person to have a mental image. For both of these explanations there is no explanatory need for responses to sensa, yet just as sensa are assumed as effects in hallucinations, so they can be assumed as effects in all perceptions. And, because they would be merely effects, there seems to be no more reason to view such effects as sensa rather than sensings.

Another amendment, which seems more plausible to me, is to postulate that incomplete perceptual constancy results from the obtrusion of certain *variant* structural features of arrays of stimuli rather than the obtrusion of sensations. Although Gibson is not clear about which structural features of the array remain invariant when, for example, someone moves around a table, it seems clear that they are certain quite general features, rather than any specific features. At any one moment, the specific features of a certain structured visual array of stimuli at the eye of a perceiver which corresponds to the straight edge of the table is a sharp discontinuity in intensity of the stimulus energy. But as the perceiver moves around the table, the precise location and length of the discontinuity in the array constantly varies. What is invariant is the continually transforming discontinuity in intensity. It may be, then, that learning to attend to such general invariant features consists in part in coming to ignore habitually the specific variant features. However, under some conditions, as when perceiving railroad tracks, it may be psychologically or physiologically impossible to ignore certain of the specific, variant discontinuities in intensity of stimulus energy, because they are so obtrusive. That is, visual perceptual systems would be incapable of avoiding responses to these specific variant features, such as the precise nonparallel spatial relationships between two discontinuities in intensity that correspond to two railroad tracks.

If either of these amendments proves acceptable, then sensations would not be needed to affect responses of perceptual systems in order to explain incomplete perceptual constancy. They could then be construed as incidental, epiphenomenal effects of all perceptual responses of perceptual systems, and it would be as reasonable to view them as sensings as it would be to posit sensa. Of course, once reduced to incidental by-products with no explanatory function, it might be argued that we should employ Occam's razor and eliminate them. However, this is to treat them as pure theoretical entities, which, as I have argued elsewhere, is dubious.[19] It might be better, however, to identify them with, but not reduce them to, the relevant neural processes. This view, which may be Gibson's, is briefly discussed in the Appendix.[20] Nevertheless, without going into that issue, we can conclude that we have found an example of a stimulus-based theory that can

[19] See my *Materialism and Sensations,* Chap. 2.
[20] See Gibson, *The Senses Considered As Perceptual Systems,* p. 56.

accommodate sensings as easily as sensa. Furthermore, we have found no reason to prefer a sensum-based theory, with its assumption that we respond to sensa, to a theory that replaces such responses to sensa with adverbial sensings. Indeed, our speculations have so far provided no reason to prefer any sort of theory with sensa to any with sensings.

A Third Theoretical Reason for Sensa: Visual Fields

Another purported theoretical reason for sensa I wish to consider can be generated from the part of Gibson's discussion of his theory which deals with visual field. He say that "the temporary array of perspective appearances of the world is called the field of visual sensations, or the visual field."[21] He also says that this field is "unstable and bounded," unlike what he calls the visual world, which is the stable and unbounded world we perceive.[22] Clearly, if there are entities fitting these descriptions, they are "fleeting and variable" visual appearances, that is, individual visual sensa or groups of visual sensa. Of course, a sensing theorist could immediately ask why we should assume there are such phenomenal individuals rather than sensings. The answer would be that there are good scientific reasons to have individuals whose dimensions are measurable and to specify their boundaries, but sensings allow for no such objects, whereas sensa will. Yet this prompts the further question of whether there is any reason or need to claim that the dimensions that are measured are boundaries of such phenomenal individuals.

In order to answer the last question, let us consider another phrase used by Gibson, 'the field of view of a head,' which he says "can be defined as the light intercepted by the ocular system of any animal without a complete panoramic field. For a man it is roughly a hemisphere. ... It spans about 180° horizontally and 150° vertically."[23] I suggest that it is these fields, these "temporary samples" of structured visual stimulus flux, that Gibson should construe as unstable, yet bounded with measurable dimensions. Visual fields should be reconstrued roughly as oval areas of structured visual stimuli, the dimensions of which set out the outer

---

[21] Gibson, "Are There Sensory Qualities of Objects?" *Synthese* 19 (1968–69): 409.
[22] See Gibson, *The Senses Considered As Perceptual Systems,* pp. 253–56.
[23] Ibid., p. 257.

limits of any area of visual stimuli to which a visual perceptual system can respond at any one time. This construal of what is measured is reenforced by realizing that the measurement of these areas is done in terms of response to physical objects at the periphery. Measurement in these cases would be of physical dimensions rather than phenomenal dimensions of appearances or visual sensa.

Given the preceding plausible construal of the entities whose dimensions are scientifically measured, it is clear that sensa are not required. The scientific investigation of such entities could be accommodated as well by a sensing theory, as by a sensum theory or a stimulus-based theory, because measuring the dimensions of such entities implies nothing about sensations, not even that there are any sensations. However, there are other measurements that are scientifically useful, which, it has been claimed, require the existence of sensa. Indeed, one central task of the science of psychophysics has been thought to be to find a way to measure certain features of sensations, such as seen brightness, heard loudness, and felt weight, so that quantitative psychophysical laws about these qualities can be established. This is the fourth and last theoretical reason for sensa we shall examine.

A Fourth Theoretical Reason for Sensa: The Science of Psychophysics

Consider a recent statement describing the task of psychophysics:

As the light-energy increases, the light appears brighter; as the sound-pressure waves carry more energy to the ear, the sound gets louder. Here, then, is one way in which sensations change as the stimulating physical energy changes. The magnitude of the sensation increases when the stimulus energy increases. How are the two kinds of increase related? Does doubling the weight in grams result in double the sensation of heaviness? In order to answer that question, we would need a measuring scale of units of heaviness with which we could tell whether doubling the number of grams of weight, as a physical measure, is observed as doubling the number of those units of heaviness, as a sensation. But how can we construct scales with which to measure sensations?[24]

[24] J. Hochberg, *Perception* (Englewood Cliffs, N. J.: Prentice-Hall, Inc., 1964), pp. 9–10.

The task here is to establish quantitative psychophysical laws on the basis of measurements of the relevant psychological and physical entities. The classical attempt to do this was made by Fechner who thought of psychophysics as the science that would bridge the scientifically bothersome and metaphysically puzzling gulf between the intersubjective world, which is measurable and explainable by the physical sciences, and the seemingly private and immeasurable realm of the mental. Briefly, Fechner attempted to derive a psychophysical law that correlates measurable properties of sensations with measurable properties of the corresponding stimuli, from a law stated by Weber. Weber based his law on certain experiments to determine just noticeable differences among certain sorts of stimuli. The resulting law states that a just noticeable difference for any sort of stimulus is a function of the magnitude of the stimulus, namely:

$$\Delta I = k I.$$

Here I = stimulus intensity, ΔI = a just noticeable difference in stimulus intensity, and k is a constant for the particular sort of stimulus being considered. What Fechner did was to extend this to:

$$\Delta I/I = k\Delta S$$

and integrate to get:

$$S = k \log I.$$

Here S = sensation magnitude. Where the stimulus is light, for example, then, according to Hurvich and Jameson, the corresponding statement of Fechner's law is:

$$B = k \log L$$

where B = apparent brightness, and L = luminance, that is, stimulus intensity for light.[25]

Initially, at least, Fechner's law seems to require that there are sensa with properties, and, *a fortiori*, sensa. Thus, it seems that psychophysics requires sensa. But before drawing a final conclusion we should ask, as we did in the preceding discussion, whether, given the procedures actually used to measure brightness, there is

[25] My source for the preceding discussion is L. Hurvich and D. Jameson, *The Perception of Brightness and Darkness* (Boston: Allyn and Bacon, Inc., 1966), pp. 57–59.

need or even any reason to claim that the brightness being measured is a property of sensations. Consider the following brief description by Hurvich and Jameson of one of the usual methods for measuring "perceived apparent brightness."

> One of the classical psychophysical methods for perceptual scaling is based on discriminability between two stimuli. Suppose we start our experiment in a dark room with a central, foveally fixated test field in which we can expose lights of continuously variable luminance. Assume that the test field is at first dark, and our test light is then turned up until it appears to be just-perceptibly brighter than the totally dark test area with which we started. We measure the luminance of this light with our photometer, and we record this luminance value as the first step on our brightness scale. Starting from this minimally bright test field, we may now increase the luminance again until the observer reports that the test area has become just-perceptibly brighter than it was. This second luminance value, which appears just-perceptibly brighter than the first one, now represents the point on the stimulus scale that is equivalent to the second step on our perceptual scale. The experiment may be continued progressively with each consecutive step representing a just-perceptible increase in apparent brightness over the previous one until we have reached the maximal brightness level that can be obtained.[26]

What seems to be measured here is not a property of a sensum, but rather a "just perceptible increase in apparent brightness" *of a test area*. That is, it seems that changes in luminance are being correlated with certain ways certain physical areas appear to observers under certain test conditions. Indeed, the observer reports that an area is just noticeably brighter than it was previously. Thus, he clearly seems to report a relationship among certain features that one physical entity has at different times, rather than a relationship among his own sensa. This seems to be implicit not only in the preceding description of the method by Hurvich and Jameson, but also in their statement of the law just after this passage where they claim that B is brightness. It is when they later claim that the

[26] Ibid., p. 7.

law is an instance of Fechner's law that they mention brightness sensitivity and increments in sensation. There is certainly no need to subsume the law under Fechner's law. Brightness need not be construed as a property only of sensations, and so it is not necessary to claim that an observer, in spite of his sincere belief that he is talking about a test area, is really reporting, misleadingly and unknowingly, about his own sensa. Furthermore, I see no sufficient reason to construe brightness this way. To show this, let me consider the only two reasons I can find for such a construal.

Both reasons depend on the claim that the brightness measured is *apparent* brightness. The first involves what Chisholm calls "the sense-datum fallacy."[27] Presumably the observer says that one area appears brighter than the other. It might be inferred from this that one area has a brighter appearance than the other, and, consequently, there are two appearances, one of which is brighter than the other. Thus sensa are inferred. However, both inferences are unwarranted. The second is invalid unless something having a bright appearance entails there exists a bright appearance. Not only is this not an entailment, it certainly is no more reasonable than its denial, unless there is independent reason to reject sensings for sensa. Thus this argument does not justify sensa. The first inference is also dubious, because it is reasonable to take the observer to be using an epistemic sense of 'appear,' and so his "*P* appears just noticeably brighter than *Q* to me" would be equivalent to "It seems to me that *P* is just noticeably brighter than *Q*." From this nothing about appearance follows. This is not to deny that the observer could use a nonepistemic sense of 'appear,' but rather to claim that in the test situation he is trying to report what he thinks are actual relationships concerning test areas.[28]

The second reason for believing the observer to be talking unknowingly about his own sensations is based on an implicit assumption, quite common among scientists, that all properties of a physical phenomenon are those quantitative properties that scientists ascribe to it in order to explain its behavior scientifically. Given this rather strong version of scientific realism and the proposition that perceived brightness is not needed for such scientific explanations, perceived brightness is merely an apparent,

[27] See R. Chisholm, *Perceiving* (Ithaca: Cornell University Press, 1957), pp. 151–53.
[28] Ibid., Chap. 4, for epistemic and nonepistemic uses of 'appear.'

and therefore not an actual, property of physical entities. Consequently, perceived brightness is a property of entities of another sort, namely, sensa. There are two objections to this argument. The first will be merely mentioned now and discussed in more detail in Chapter 8. It is aimed at any form of scientific realism that denies that physical entities have observable properties such as brightness and color. My reasons for this objection will become clearer in the later discussion when I argue for what I called "compatible common-sense realism" in the Introduction. This theory implies that physical entities have both sensuous properties, such as color and brightness, and theoretical properties attributed to them in science.

It might be noted before leaving the first objection that this compatible theory is consistent with each directly perceived sensuous property being identical with some theoretical property. As was noted when discussing the argument from perceptual relativity, it is possible that although a property (or an instance of a property) is directly perceived, it always appears differently from the way it is. Thus it might be that the property someone directly perceives when brightness appears to him is not brightness, but rather some theoretical property, such as intensity. Thus intensity might be both sensuous and theoretical.

The second objection is this. Even on the assumption that brightness is not a property of any physical entity, at most it follows that some physical entities sometimes appear to have the property of brightness, and that brightness sometimes appears to some observers. However, as previously pointed out when discussing the argument from perceptual relativity, it does not follow from this that there is an entity which is bright, as would follow if brightness appearing to someone implies that he directly perceives brightness. Thus, as previously concluded, merely apparent or seeming brightness of physical entities does not require actual brightness of sensa.

The conclusion at this point may be put thus: based on the methods used and the reports made by observers, there seems to be no reason to claim that it is really properties of sensa that are measured, and, therefore, no reason to construe the laws established by these methods as psychophysical laws. It might be argued in reply, however, that someone such as Fechner who wishes to measure sensation brightness, could do it indirectly by postulating a correlation between that property and the perceived or apparent brightness of physical entities. This requires that sensa be assumed. Furthermore, whether Fechner's particular law is correct or not, which is clearly questionable, the attempt to find genuine psychophysical laws is surely justified and such laws, according to this reply, require sensa with quantitative properties rather than sensings. For example, it is irrelevant whether the correct relationship between sensation-brightness and stimulus-intensity is Fechner's logarithmic relation, or a relation proposed by Stevens in terms of powers, or some other.[29] If one of them is correct, as is not unreasonable, then, according to this argument, sensa are justified.

There are two objections to this reply. First, the desire to measure properties of sensa is hardly a good reason for postulating that there are sensa with quantitative properties. This would be postulating data to be explained rather than entities that were to be used to provide explanations. But the preceding use is not one in which data are postulated, but rather one where the agreed upon data are interpreted in a certain way. And, it is surely justified to interpret data in a certain way if that interpretation is required for the only, or the clearly most effective, way to formulate the sort of generalizations needed for scientific explanation of the data. Thus, if it can be shown that a sensum intepretation of sensations is needed for the best or only way to produce the kind of scientific generalizations needed for scientific explanations of sensations and their relationships to external objects and stimuli, then sensa would be justified on theoretical, empirical grounds. Consequently this first objection fails.

QUANTITATIVE PROPERTIES OF SENSA VERSUS QUANTITATIVE
SPECIFICATIONS OF SENSINGS

The crucial question, then, is whether sensa with measurable phenomenal properties, such as loudness, brightness, and weight, are better suited to interpreting the relationships expressed in psychophysical laws than are events of loud-sensing, bright-sensing, and weight-sensing. The second objection to the preceding

[29] See Hurvich and Jameson, pp. 14–15, for a discussion of Stevens' law.

reply denies that they are better suited for this purpose. To show this, we can begin by realizing that the present case differs, initially at least, from the one concerning visual fields. If someone measures the phenomenal dimensions of a visual field, then there is a phenomenal object with those dimensions, contrary to the sensing theory. Thus a sensing theorist must argue that the dimensions measured are not phenomenal, but are rather, for example, the physical dimensions of what Gibson calls the "field of view" of a person. In the present case, however, there is no obvious reason to think that the measurements cannot be applied to sensing events. For one reason, there clearly are measurements that apply to events, such as an event of something moving from one place to another, or changing in size, weight, physical brightness, physical loudness, or temperature from one time to another. For example, measurements are used to verify that events of the following sorts occur: a person growing two inches or gaining 10 pounds, the sound of a siren increasing 10 decibels, and the air temperature increasing 10 degrees. Consequently, there is no general problem about applying measurements to events. This does not show, of course, that there are no unique problems confronting the sorts of measurements the sensing theory requires, but I have been able to find none.

The kind of measurement stated in the preceding examples is not the only kind applicable to events, but it is the one most helpful for understanding how to transform quantitative properties of sensa into measurable internal specifications of events. Each of the measurements is used to verify that a certain quantitatively specified event has occurred; none are used to verify that an event has a certain quantitative property. Examples of this second sort of measurement are those used to verify that the event of the person growing two inches has the property of taking a year, or those used to verify that the temperature increase of 10 degrees took only five minutes. Such quantitative measurable properties of events are not the kind a sensing theorist can use, because quantitative properties of sensa do not correspond to properties of sensing events. For example, John's present sensum having the property of phenomenally weighing (P-weighing) 10 phenomenal pounds (P-pounds) does not correspond to 10 P-pounds being a property of the event of John weight-sensing. Properties of sensa correspond to internal specifications of an event rather than to its properties. The difference is illustrated by the difference between specifying the event of John growing as John growing two inches, and modifying it with the property of occurring rapidly. Indeed, the analogy of specifying the event of John sensing with specifying the event of John growing is quite close and, I find, helpful for understanding the sensing theory. Consider the following two lists, each consisting of different ways of quantitatively describing the same event:

John growing a growth of 2 inches	John sensing a sensum of 10 P-pounds
John growing a 2 inch growth	John sensing a 10 P-pound sensum
John growing 2 inches	John sensing 10 P-pounds
John 2-inches-growing	John 10-pounds-sensing

These lists show how the same event can be equally well specified as consisting in John in relationship to some individual with a measurable property and as consisting in John in some state that is nonrelational, but quantitatively specifiable. And because there seems to be no relevant difference between P-weight and, for example, P-loudness and P-brightness, the kind of transformations on the second list from descriptions of quantitative properties of sensa to quantitative specifications of sensings can also be accomplished without problems. Given this, there is no reason to claim that sensing descriptions are not suited to interpreting quantitative relationships expressed in psychophysical laws. Consider the following two ways to derive a quantitative psychophysical law relating physical weight to quantitative features of sense experience. In each case, the first premise would be a law that expresses the apparent weight of an object as a function of its physical weight. Such a law is verified by examining normal perceivers in certain standard test situations. It might be stated as follows:

(1) If an object weighs m pounds, then its apparent weight is n units, where n is a function of m, that is, $n = f(m)$.

The second premise would be a theoretical postulation stating quantitative features of sense experience to be a function of apparent weight under certain conditions. It can be formulated equally well by reference to sensings as by reference to sensa. Thus we might use either:

(2a) If the apparent weight of an object is *n* units, and a normal perceiver in standard test conditions holds the object, then he senses an *r* P-pound sensum, where *r* is a function of *n*, that is, $r = f'(n)$.

or

(2b) If the apparent weight of an object is *n* units, and a normal perceiver in standard test conditions holds the object, then he *r*-pound-senses, where $r = f'(n)$.

For both versions of (2) a psychophysical law is entailed, and there is no reason to prefer the sensum version, (2a), to the sensing version, (2b).

CONCLUSION ABOUT EMPIRICAL REASONS FOR SENSA

I have tried to take a representative sample of reasons for sensa derived from theoretical considerations of those scientific theories that explain perceptual data. I have given examples of two sorts, one where sensa are postulated to explain certain facts as in Gibson's explanation of partial and complete seeing in perspective, and one where it seemed initially that some of the data to be explained must be interpreted as involving sensa in order to make them amenable to the quantitative formulations of science. We found, however, that none of the examples we examined provided reasons for assuming sensa rather than sensings. On this basis I conclude that it is reasonable to deny that there are theoretical empirical reasons for sensa. Since this is what Premise II of the central argument of the book states, we can also conclude that it, like Premise I, is acceptable. It should be noted, however, that not only have I not relied on all the presently available evidence, but also new contrary evidence may become available later. Thus, while I believe the conclusion is justified, it should be considered provisional and constantly open to review. Nevertheless, with this provisional conclusion and with the previous rejection of non-theoretical reasons for sensa, we are justified in concluding that there are no empirical reasons for sensa. Let us turn to the different, yet related, task of considering linguistic reasons for sensa.

LINGUISTIC REASONS FOR SENSA

It might seem that having rejected empirical reasons for sensa, there would be no need to consider whether there are any linguistic reasons for them. If none of the facts of perceptual experience require that sensory experience be interpreted as involving sensa, it might seem that there is no descriptive need for sensum terms and, therefore, no linguistic reasons for sensa. In Chapter 1, however, I stated three different linguistic reasons used to justify asserting that there is a descriptive need for sensum terms, and I delayed discussion of them until now. If we can justify rejecting all three reasons, then, because they are the most plausible I can find, I shall conclude we are justified in accepting Premise III of the central argument: There are no linguistic reasons for sensa. The first argument is that there is a reporting need for sensum terms, thus there is a descriptive need for sensum terms, and thus there is a linguistic reason for sensa. The second is, similarly, that an explanatory need for sensum terms shows there to be a linguistic reason for sensa. And the third is that there is a linguistic reason for sensa because of linguistic inadequacies of all alternative terminologies.

We can use the preceding discussion of sensa to help justify rejecting, for similar reasons, the first two arguments. It is true that if there is a reporting need for a general term, such as 'sensum,' then there is *some* sort of descriptive need for it. There being a reporting need for a general term, T, implies that T is needed to make an identifying reference to something, o. This in turn implies that o is not identifiable without using T. But since identifying requires describing—although not always truly describing—a reporting need for a general term implies some sort of descriptive need for that term. But, as the preceding discussion emphasizes, there is no need to think some sensory experience can be identified using sensum terms, but cannot be identified by use of sensing terms. Furthermore, given the reasonable assumption that a unique correlation between sensory experience and certain brain processes can be established, then instantiations of the following purely physicalistic schema could be used to make identifying references to sensory experience:[30]

---

[30] For more detail, see *Materialism and Sensations,* pp. 170–73.

An entity of the kind for which it is contingently true that things of that kind happen to someone, s, when and only when brain processes of kind K occur in s.

Thus, for two reasons, there seems to be no reporting need for sensum terms.

We can also reject the second linguistic reason for sensa which is based on an explanatory need for sensum terms. In this case, not only is there reason to reject an explanatory need for sensum terms, but the premise that an explanatory need implies a descriptive need is far from obvious, as the discussion in Chapters 4 and 8 of arguments for scientific instrumentalism will show. For our purposes here, however, we need only show that there is no explanatory need for sensum terms. But this, in effect, has already been done because, if there are no empirical reasons for sensa, especially no theoretical reasons, then there is no reason to think there is an explanatory need for sensum terms. The examples taken from Gibson's theory and psychophysics were used to try to find whether there is any reason to think that explanations of perceptual phenomena require sensa. With our rejection of such a need, we can also reject an explanatory need for sensum terms.

The third linguistic reason might seem to be as quickly disposable as the first two, because I have used the sensing terminology throughout the preceding discussion as a replacement for the sensum terminology with no ill effects. Thus, it would seem, at least one alternative terminology escapes linguistic inadequacies. It might further be argued that another linguistically adequate alternative is a purely neurophysiological terminology. I find, however, that we have not yet considered all objections to the sensing terminology, and that a purely physicalistic terminology is unable to provide all the descriptions of sensory experience which we are justified making with the sensing or sensum terminology. Thus, it is descriptively inadequate for that purpose.

I know of two arguments to show that no sensation terminologies, and so neither the sensum nor sensing terminologies, are needed to make any descriptions that it is reasonable to claim are both true and accurate. In both arguments the reason for this claim is that all such descriptions can be made at least as well by a purely

physicalistic vocabulary.[31] Since I have written against both arguments elsewhere, I shall consider them quite briefly here.[32] The
first involves the claim that purely physicalistic terms can accommodate the true descriptive roles now played by sensation terms.
Thus, not only must they be able to describe the same entities that
these sensation terms describe, but they must also provide or entail
the same descriptions of those entities. This requires that for any
sentence that is entailed by a true descriptive sensation sentence,
there is some physicalistic sentence that also entails it. This is
because any sentence that takes over the descriptive role of another
must have at least all the entailments of the second. The problem
for this attempt is that, given all available evidence, it is unreasonable to hold that a physicalistic sentence has all the entailments of
a sensation sentence, such as 'John senses a red-hen-like sensum'
(or 'John red-hen-senses') which it is surely reasonable to think is
sometimes true. Of course, if no sensation sentences of this sort are
true, their descriptive roles need not be considered, but this seems
quite unreasonable and I can find no way to make it reasonable.

The second argument involves the premise that the descriptive
roles of sensation sentences that we now consider true will not be
taken over by, but rather will be replaced by the different and more
nearly accurate roles of certain physicalistic sentences. On this view,
sensation sentences are related to the relevant physicalistic sentences much as the sentence, 'It is somewhat likely that it will rain
tomorrow,' is related to more precise sentences of the form, 'The
probability that it will rain tomorrow on evidence e, is n.' In
neither case must the second have all the entailments of the first and,
supposedly, in neither case is the first needed for either true or
accurate descriptions. However, this premise is reasonable only if
it is plausible to accept the claim that all descriptive sensation
sentences which surely seem to be true and relatively accurate, are
really very inaccurate means of providing the same descriptions
much more accurately provided by certain physicalistic replacements. This is because what is ascribed to someone by, for example,
'John red-hen-senses' is very different from what is ascribed to him

---

[31] See R. Rorty, "Mind-Body Identity, Privacy, and Categories," *Review of Metaphysics* 19
(1965–66): 24–54.

[32] See *Materialism and Sensations*, Chap. 5; and my "Materialism and Some Myths about
Some Givens," *The Monist* 56 (1972): 228–29.

by any suitable physicalistic replacement describing neural processes, cells, synapses, and the like. Consequently if we accept the
claim, we would have to conclude that a person's own sensory
experience is not even remotely like the way it seems to him when
he believes he red-hen-senses. Not only would he have no special
epistemological status about his own sensory experiences, he would
not even have any true beliefs whenever he expresses his beliefs
using sensation terms. But these consequences of this claim are implausible. Thus the claim, the premise that is plausible only if the
claim is, and the argument that uses the premise should be rejected.

We can, I believe, conclude that there is some descriptive need
for some sort of sensation terminology, because, based on scientific
claims (such as in psychophysics) and personal observations, there
is reason to think that no purely physicalistic terminology fulfills
the true and accurate descriptive roles of every sensation term. Thus
the remaining question is whether only the sensum terminology
fulfills all these roles without generating linguistic problems. Based
upon the preceding discussions, there seem to be no linguistic
problems confronting the sensing terminology, but before drawing
a final conclusion I wish to examine the only two troublesome
linguistic problems for the sensing terminology that I have been
able to find.

Two Problems for the Sensing Terminology

The first problem is stated and then rejected by Chisholm, who
champions the sensing terminology. The problem, according to
him, is that it seems difficult to use the sensing terminology to
express what would correspond to a statement that the appearance
of a part of an object is included in the appearance of the whole
object.[33] Consider again a person who sees a hen. According to
Chisholm, when using the terminology of appearances,

> we can say of the hen that it is a whole in which these various
> parts (among others) are contained; we can also say of the
> appearance of the hen, that it, too, is a whole in which the
> appearances of the various parts are contained. Indeed we
> might say of the appearance of each part, that it is a part of the
> appearance of the whole. The appearance of the outer part of

[33] I wish to thank Edwin McCann for his helpful suggestions about this problem.

the tip of one of the feathers is a part of the appearance of the feather; the appearance of the feather is a part of the appearance of the wing; the appearance of the wing is a part of the appearance of the side of the hen; and the appearance of the side of the hen is a part of the appearance of the hen. And these facts, it must be conceded, are difficult to formulate, either in the terminology of "appearing" or in the terminology of "sensing".[34]

Chisholm suggests that we can restate these facts using the language of sensing in the following way:

The way in which a man senses with respect to a thing includes ways in which he senses with respect to some, but not all, of the parts of the thing, and the way in which he senses with respect to any part of the thing is included in the way in which he senses with respect to the thing.[35]

To see if this suggestion is adequate we should first unpack the phrase 'an appearance of a P,' because it is ambiguous. The ambiguity can be shown by two rough definitions:

D1. x is an appearance of a $P =_{df.} x$ is an appearance that (normally) results from the effect on a perceiver of stimulus from a P.

D2. x is an appearance of a $P =_{df.} x$ is a P-like appearance.

While D2 requires that an appearance of a P has something like a pictorial likeness to a P, D1 requires instead that it results from a P. Chisholm seems to use D1, because he reformulates 'an appearance of a hen' as 'a sensing with respect to a hen' rather than as 'a hen-sensing,' and he unpacks 'with respect to' in causal terms.[36] However, the problem arises for both interpretations, and so we must see whether the sensing terminology can be used to reformulate the part-whole statements about appearances of entities, no matter which definition is used.

We have two different sentences to reformulate, depending on which definition is used:

[34] Chisholm, *Theory of Knowledge* (Englewood Cliffs, N. J.: Prentice-Hall, Inc., 1966), p. 98.
[35] Ibid.
[36] See Chisholm, *Perceiving*, pp. 143–49.

A1. In some cases, the appearance resulting from the effect on a perceiver of stimulus from a wing of a hen is part of the appearance that results from the effect on the perceiver of stimulus from the hen.

A2. In some cases, the wing-of-a-hen-like appearance is part of a hen-like appearance.

Following Chisholm's suggestion, the corresponding statements in the sensing-terminology would be:

S1. In some cases, the way of sensing that results from the effect on a perceiver of stimulus from a wing of a hen is included in the way of sensing that results from the effect on the perceiver of stimulus from the hen.

S2. In some cases, the wing-of-a-hen way of sensing is included in a hen way of sensing.

I find two objections to these two sensing formulations. The first is that the notion of one way of sensing being included in another is at best unclear and perhaps meaningless. Does it make any more sense to talk of some way of sensing as including another, than it does to talk of some way of running as including another? If someone walks in a limping manner, and more specifically, in a dragging-the-left-foot manner, does the former way of walking include the latter? The only sense I can make of this inclusion is that it is partial class inclusion. That is, that the class of walkings done in a limping manner includes some members of the class of walkings done in a dragging-the-left-foot manner. Similarly, for sensings we can say that some sensings in certain ways are also sensings in certain other ways. Let us, then, reject S1 and S2 in favor of:

S1a. In some cases, the sensing which results from the effect on a perceiver of stimulus from a wing of a hen is also the sensing which results from the effect on the perceiver of stimulus from the hen.

S2a. In some cases, the sensing in a wing-of-a-hen way is also a sensing in a hen way.

With these replacements for Chisholm's formulations we can avoid the first objection because we need no longer talk of one way or manner of sensing including another, but rather of one sensing in a certain way also being a sensing in another way.

The second objection can grant the preceding revision, however, because it states that the sensing terminology requires sensum terms to be replaced by terms expressing manners or ways of sensing, and this is mistaken. The point is that the sensing terminology is an adverbial terminology according to which the phenomenological content of someone's sensory experience is to be described by a sentence of the form, 'S senses x-ly.' That is, for example, S's sensory experience of redness is to be described by 'S senses red-ly' rather than by 'S senses a red sensum.' And according to this objection, 'S senses x-ly' is logically equivalent to 'S senses in an x manner,' but the content of sensory experience is not to be described by an adverb that expresses a manner of sensing. Thus the adverbial sensing terminology should be rejected. This argument, which states the second linguistic problem, is:

(1) If it is correct to use the adverbial sensing terminology to describe the phenomenological content of sensory experience, then if S senses x-ly, he has a sensory experience of x-ness.

(2) If it is correct to use the adverbial sensing terminology, then S senses x-ly just in case S senses in an x manner.

(3) It is false that if S senses in an x manner (for example in a dazed manner), then S has a sensory experience of x-ness (for example, dazedness).

Therefore

(4) It is not correct to use the adverbial sensing terminology to describe the phenomenological content of sensory experience.

The argument seems sound, given the way Chisholm seems to construe the sensing terminology. For example, he compares sensing in some way with moving in some way, for example, slowly, and he explicitly talks of sensing in some manner.[37] He might, however, object to (2) on the grounds that the equivalence holds for only certain values of 'x,' namely, for what he calls

[37] See Chisholm, *Theory of Knowledge*, p. 96; and *Perceiving,* p. 137.

"sensible characteristics."[38] I believe, however, that there are stronger grounds for rejecting (2), because not even a term such as 'red,' which expresses a sensible characteristic, forms an adverb of manner when substituted for '*x*' in 'sense *x*-ly'. Unlike 'slowly' in 'moves slowly,' 'red-ly' serves to describe a species or kind of sensing. In this it resembles 'to waltz-dance,' that is, 'to waltz,' which describes a kind of dancing rather than merely a manner in which dancing is done. Because of this, it might be useful to use 'to *x*-sense' rather than 'to sense *x*-ly' to help mark this difference.[39] Then we would have 'to red-sense' as quite similar to 'to waltz-dance,' or, that is, 'to waltz.' And just as someone could "waltz-dance" slowly, so also someone could "red-sense" dazedly. I do not think, however, that it matters which locution is used. The important point is to realize that they are equivalent and so, contrary to (2), '*x*-ly' in 'to sense *x*-ly' is not equivalent to 'in an *x* manner.' Thus the second linguistic reason for sensa is avoidable, and an adverbial version of the sensing terminology can be adopted without ill effect. We can, then, continue to use the phrases 'sensing theory' and 'adverbial theory' interchangeably without the fear of saddling the ontological sensing theory with the undesirable consequences of one linguistic adverbial theory.

Conclusion about Reasons for Sensa

We have examined and rejected three different attempts to show that there is some descriptive need for the sensum terminology, and thereby that there are linguistic reasons for sensa. Based on the rejection of these reasons and on my claim that there are no other troublesome linguistic problems for the sensing terminology, we can conclude that there is no descriptive need for the sensum terminology and therefore no linguistic reasons for sensa. Thus we have justified premise III of the central argument of the book, and having previously justified premises I, II, and IV, we can conclude:

> V. There are neither empirical nor linguistic reasons to justify the existence of sensa.

This takes us to premise VI: There are fewer recalcitrant philo-

---

[38] See Chisholm, *Perceiving*, pp. 83–84.

[39] This same point is made by W. Sellars in *Science, Perception and Reality* (London: Routledge and Kegan Paul, 1963), pp. 94–95.

sophical problems without sensa. If found acceptable, it is to be used to help tip the scales of evidence in favor of the final rejection of sensa.

PHILOSOPHICAL PROBLEMS WITH SENSA

Our present concern is to discover whether recalcitrant philosophical problems arise if we assume sensa, and to see whether we can solve or dissolve these problems by assuming objectless sensings instead. As characterized in the Introduction, sensa are phenomenal individuals, that is, individuals which exist when and only when experienced and which have at least one phenomenal property. While I think this expresses logically necessary and sufficient conditions for something being a sensum, it leaves many unanswered questions about other properties and relations of sensa. Some of these questions give rise to problems that are recalcitrant in the sense that no plausible solutions have been found and it seems unlikely that any will be found.

It might be objected at this point, however, that it is premature to consider such problems, because the preceding characterization of sensa faces an objection that should be rebutted first. In particular, the objection is that this characterization begs the question against two theories about sensa, and, therefore, it should be rejected. As I have characterized sensa, there are no unsensed sensa, and consequently, there are no unsensed sense-data. This falsifies by definition any theory implying that sense-data are surfaces of physical objects, and any selective theory of sensory experience that requires unsensed sense-data as some sort of constituents of physical objects, some of which are "selected" to be directly perceived in a particular sensory experience.[40] The answer to this objection is that, although physical surfaces and elements of physical objects may be data for our senses and, in *that* way, may be "sense-data," they are not phenomenal individuals and so are not sense-data in the way relevant to our concern throughout the book. We can keep this distinction clear by using 'sense-data' to refer only to phenomenal individuals, and 'data of the senses' as a more general term to apply to whatever is directly perceived, whether it be physical objects, their surfaces, sensa, or

---

[40] For a discussion of the view that sense-data are parts of surfaces of physical objects, see
    G. E. Moore, *Philosophical Papers* (New York: Humanities Press, 1970), pp. 53–59.

something else.

When we turn to the more troublesome problems that sensa generate, the most puzzling and disturbing is expressed by the question:

(1) Does anyone fail to experience a property that one of his own sensa has?

The case of the striped tiger pinpoints this problem well. If someone gets merely a quick glimpse of a striped tiger as it runs past him, he might experience numerous stripes but not have an experience of any particular number of stripes. In this example, the difficult question for a sensum theorist that corresponds to (1) is:

(1.1) Does anyone who experiences numerous stripes, as an 80-striped tiger runs past him, but does not have an experience of any particular number of stripes, sense a sensum with some definite number of stripes, such as 80 stripes?

If a sensum theorist answers question (1.1) negatively, then he must either say that the person senses a many-striped sensum that has no specific number of stripes, or claim the answer is vacuously true because whenever someone has an experience of stripes he has an experience of some definite number of stripes, whether he realizes it or not. But it is surely implausible that the brief amount of stimulus from the tiger that affects the perceiver would result in such an experience, especially given a strong contrary belief by the perceiver. On the other hand, a sensum with no specific number of stripes is a most puzzling individual. A. J. Ayer, however, is not bothered by this, because although he admits it would be self-contradictory to say that a tiger has merely an indefinite number of stripes, he also claims,

But it does not follow that it is self-contradictory to say of the visual sense-field, which corresponds to the physical expanse of the tiger, that it contains a number of stripes without containing any definite number. For the characteristics which are supposed to be ascribed to this sense-field are not necessarily those that the tiger really has, but only those that it appears to have, so that the model on which we have to base our usage of the expression 'being numerous,' in this context, is not the physical characteristic of being numerous but the physical characteristic of looking numerous; and... to say that the stripes on the tiger look numerous does not entail saying that they look to be of any definite number. Thus, in saying that the sense-field in question contains a number of stripes, we need to be saying no more than that it has the *Gestalt* quality of being striated; and, while the presence of this quality is compatible with there being some definite number of stripes, it does not logically necessitate it.[41]

Ayer's reply seems to be that the sense-datum (sense-field) terminology is to be modeled on the appearing terminology, and thus the former has only the entailments that correspond to those of the latter. Consequently, because there appearing to be numerous stripes does not entail that there appears to be some definite number of stripes, so also, according to Ayer, there being a sensum with numerous stripes does not entail that there is a sensum with some definite number of stripes. But this does not solve the problem for a sensum theorist who gives a negative answer to (1.1), because his theory conjoined with that answer and the statement that some perceivers have experiences of numerous stripes but no definite number of stripes, does entail that there are sensa with an indefinite number of stripes. If this is not self-contradictory, it is at least exceedingly odd. Ayer, who claims to be interested in the sense-datum terminology rather than sense-data, claims that when " 'numerous' is applied to sense-data, it need not have the same meaning as it has when it is applied to physical objects."[42] I suppose he would say that its difference in meaning results from its being understood on the model of 'appear numerous' in the appearing sentence. I would guess he would say the same thing about 'definite number.' But this suggestion is vague at best, and does nothing to dispel the oddity of the original sentence. Furthermore, it does not outweigh the fact that there seems to be no equivocation in the two uses of 'numerous' and 'definite number.' Aside from being forced to assume an ambiguity by his version of the sensum terminology, I see no reason to assume there is one.

[41] A. J. Ayer, *Philosophical Essays* (New York: St. Martin's Press, 1965), p. 93.
[42] Ibid.

Thus Ayer fails, and I know of no one who succeeds, in attempting to justify the initially puzzling and implausible solution that a sensum theorist is forced to accept if he answers questions (1) and (1.1) negatively.

The natural move at this point is to agree that sensa can have properties that they are not experienced to have. Indeed, I think that this is a plausible answer to (1), because, as I have argued elsewhere, there are no sound objections to each sensum being identical with some part of the brain, and thereby having certain neurophysiological (and thus nonphenomenal and nonexperienced) properties.[43] As I have characterized sensa, the only restriction on their properties is that they have at least one phenomenal property. However, even granting that a sensum has theoretical, neurophysiological properties which it is not experienced to have, can we also grant that it has sensible properties, such as having 80 stripes, of which its perceiver is not aware? If not, then this second, and last, way out of the problem is also unsatisfactory. One problem for this affirmative answer to (1.1) is that the claim that a sensum in such a case has a definite number of stripes eliminates one basic use of sensa for a sensum theory. Generally on such theories, something is an event of having a perceptual experience of some definite number of stripes if and only if it is an event of sensing sensa with that number of stripes. But given this identity claim, the answer to question (1.1) cannot be affirmative, because that answer and the identity claim entail that the perceiver in question both does and does not experience a sensum with a definite number of stripes.

Another problem is that it is quite unreasonable to say that the sensum someone briefly experiences because of a quick glimpse of a tiger, has a definite number of stripes, although he does not experience it to have some definite number of stripes. Furthermore, it seems most unlikely that the brief amount of stimulus from the tiger that affects the perceiver would result in a precisely striated sensum, just as it seems unlikely it would result in an experience of a precise number of stripes. Surely Ayer would be right to claim that the effect would be correctly described, using the appearing terminology, as the stripes of the tiger appearing numerous but not appearing to be of any specific number. And Ayer would also

---

[43] See *Materialism and Sensations,* esp. Part I, and also the Appendix of this book.

be right to claim that no equally justified description should import more definiteness into sensory experience than the appearing statement. Thus in this case it is implausible to claim that the person senses a sensum with some definite number of stripes. Contrary to Ayer, however, this would not show that the sensum description would be justified on the grounds that it is modeled on the appearing description. It would show instead that the sensum description is not justified, because the appearing statement expresses the maximum amount of definiteness justified by the facts, and the sensum terminology is unable to express exactly that amount of indefiniteness in any plausible way. Of course, if sensa were independently shown to be required, and the affirmative answer to question (1) were more reasonable than the negative answer, then there would be some reason to accept these undesirable consequences. But with no reason to think sensa are required, these undesirable consequences show the second answer to be, like the first, an unsatisfactory solution of the problem.

As Chisholm points out, if we assume sensings rather than sensa, the sensory experience can be characterized in a way that captures the indefiniteness and also avoids the preceding objections.[44] It is even difficult to state a corresponding question for the sensing theory, because all properties of sensa transform into internal specifications of objectless sensings. Such specifications, unlike sensible properties such as redness, are not entities that we experience or are aware of. We can, however, be aware of a sensing event whose particularity is given by its specifications. And we can ask whether someone is aware of the specific way in which he is sensing, if this is taken either to be asking whether what he is aware of is, for example, the event of his 80-stripes-sensing, or to be asking whether he is aware that this sensing event is the event of his 80-stripes-sensing. In the first case, the question is about whether a particular event of sensing is something that he is aware of, and, in the second, it is about whether he has propositional sensible knowledge about an event. Neither question corresponds to (1) but to a different question about the event of sensing a sensum with 80 stripes. And in neither case is "a way an event is specified" an object of awareness.

[44] See Chisholm, *Perceiving*, pp. 117–24.

It is a mistake, then, to ask whether or not the entity that someone is experiencing is the way his numerous-stripes-sensing is specified. Because of this, there is no question for sensings that corresponds to (1) for sensa, and so there is no problem for sensings comparable to the one raised for sensa by question (1). For example, neither of the following two questions corresponds to (1):

(1a) Does anyone fail to experience one of his own specified sensings?

and

(1b) Does anyone's sensing fail to seem to him to be sensibly specified in the way it is sensibly specified?

The first question concerns either whether someone is aware of some sensing event or whether he is aware that he is sensing in a certain way. As the preceding discussion shows, neither question corresponds to (1). Furthermore, both answers are clearly affirmative. Question (1b) does not correspond to (1) but rather to:

(1) Does anyone's sensum fail to seem to him to have sensible properties that it has?

Both (1b) and (1′) concern whether or not anyone's sensory experience has any sensory features that he does not believe it to have. Although (1′) is like (1) in being difficult to answer, it differs from (1) because neither answer to (1′) has the implausible consequences that both answers to (1) have. Incidentally, (1b) has no advantage over (1′), and so it is of no use in arguing for sensings instead of sensa.

The question about sensings that seems to come closest to (1) is:

(1c) Does anyone fail to sense in a way that one of his sensings is specified?

However, the answer to this is clearly and unproblematically negative. There is, nevertheless, a question about sensings that corresponds to (1.1) namely:

(1a.1) Does anyone who experiences numerous stripes, as an 80-striped tiger runs past him, but does not have an experience of any particular number of stripes, sense in a way that is specified in some definite numerical way, for example, does he 80-stripes-sense?

This also clearly requires a negative answer. Furthermore, this answer raises no problem for a sensing theorist who identifies the event of 80-stripes-sensing with the event of having an experience of 80 stripes. Thus the sensing theory avoids the most difficult and recalcitrant problem that sensa generate.

Four More Puzzling Questions about Sensa

There are at least four other questions about sensa that have continually plagued philosophers. While they are not as puzzling as question (1), they nevertheless remain unanswered while the corresponding questions about sensings either can be quickly answered, or the conditions required for a satisfactory answer can be quickly discovered. They are:

(2) Does anyone have an experience of one of his own sensa having a property, but the sensum does not have it?

(3) Where, if anywhere, are sensa located?

(4) Are sensa two or three dimensional (phenomenally)?

(5) Can more than one person experience the same sensum?

There is no easy way to justify an answer to any of these questions. Of course, we could stipulate answers to them, but with at least sixteen different sets of answers, it is not clear how to justify one stipulated set rather than another. Indeed, it is in part because no one has found a way to justify one of these sets of answers that the questions remain open to debate and unresolved. It has been pointed out, however, that there may be one way to resolve them.[45] If scientific explanations of sensory experience should require there to be sensa with certain properties, and, moreover, their having these properties implies answers to these questions, then one set of answers would be justified. If the preceding discussion of scientific explanations and sensa is correct, however, then there is no reason to think science will require sensa. But, even if it should require sensa, it is far from clear that it would require them to have properties that would provide ways of answering the preceding questions.

---

[45] Philip Ostien's comments were very helpful for clarifying some of the issues involved here.

That is, it is not clear the properties needed for explanation would help answer these questions. Thus, not only have the problems posed by these questions remained unresolved, there is no reason to think that they will some day be resolved. In this sense, at least, they are recalcitrant.

Let us consider the corresponding questions about sensings. Corresponding to (2), there is the following:

(2a) Are anyone's sensings specified in ways in which the sensings are not specified?

Here (2a) and its trivial answer are essentially the same as (1a). This again shows how difficult it is to transform (1) and (2), which are clearly different, into two corresponding, yet distinct, questions about sensings. And, while (2) is by no means as troublesome as (1), there is no easy answer to it as there is to (2a).

The question of where, if anywhere, to locate sensa is puzzling. Is a toothache to be located in a tooth and does this eliminate the theory that sensations are identical with brain phenomena? Where does one locate an afterimage? It often seems to someone who experiences one that it is physically distant from him. Yet other mental images, such as eidetic images and dream images seem to lack such locations. If we reject sensa for sensings, however, we have a much easier and less puzzling question to answer, namely:

(3a) Where are sensings located?

A precise answer to (3a) depends on finding a way to locate events precisely, but we can at least say that each event of a person sensing, such as afterimaging or hallucinating, is located where the person is when sensing. This is true of any event, such as locating the event of a horse running a race. However, more precision is possible than this if it can be shown that the particular event is identical with one that is more precisely located. Thus if the event of a person tooth-aching—that is, tooth-ache-sensing—is identical with the C-fibers of his brain firing in a particular way, then the tooth-aching event is located more precisely where his brain's C-fibers are located. Consequently, not only is there a straightforward way to locate sensings, but it is a way that does not make the mind-body identity theory implausible.

The most puzzling problem that question (4) generates is not one about how to decide the correct number of dimensions, but rather how to make sense of nonphysical spatial dimensions. If sensa have dimensions, whether two or three or more, they are not physical dimensions. The seeming dimensions of an apparition or dream images are surely not physical. But then what sort of dimensions are they and what is the difference between two and three of them? It might be tempting to try to avoid these last questions and dissolve the corresponding puzzles by considering question (4) to be in the material mode of speech, and by claiming it transforms, in the formal mode of speech, into:

> (4) Should a two or a three dimensional sensum terminology be used to describe the sensa involved in sensory experience, as in 'flat-disk sensum' vs. 'spherical sensum'?

The answer to this Carnapian sort of external question depends upon choosing one terminology and justifying that it is at least as suitable for best explaining sensory experience as the other one.[46] But if one terminology were chosen to describe sensa, it would then seem to be correct to claim that sensa have a certain number of dimensions and the puzzles would rearise.

When question (4) is rephrased for sensings, the puzzles dissipate, because sensings, being events, are nondimensional. The corresponding question is:

> (4a) Are sensings specified two or three dimensionally?

Now, while the question remains debatable, the puzzle about nonphysical dimensions has disappeared. No solution to the problem about whether a sensing is a flat-disk-sensing or a sphere-sensing implies there is an individual with dimensions that seem to be nonphysical. This is further emphasized by the fact that the "formal mode" rendition of (4a) seems to express the crux of the problem in such a way that not only is it solvable, but also no solution to it resurrects the original puzzle. The question becomes:

> (4a′) Should a two or three dimensional sensing terminology be used to describe the sensings involved in sensory experience?

---

[46] For Carnap's characterization of an external question, see *Meaning and Necessity* (Chicago: University of Chicago Press, 1956), pp. 205–21. For my distinction between two kinds of external questions, see *Metaphysics, Reference, and Language* (New Haven: Yale University Press, 1966), pp. 161–75.

Again, the answer depends on a justified decision about which terminology to use for explanatory purposes, but neither choice of a terminology has puzzling consequences about nonphysical space. Indeed, it would seem that both should be used, although not used to describe the same specification. Once again, then, a puzzling, unsolved problem is avoidable by assuming sensings.

The last question is about one sort of privacy of sensa and is very troublesome for someone who assumes sensa. Consider the question of whether Siamese twins experience the same sensum when each experiences a sensum to be in the same common part of their bodies, for example, a pain in the side they share. Part of the problem here derives from the previous problem about the location of sensa. If all sensa are located in the brains of those who experience them, then, because no two persons actually have the same brain, no two people experience the same sensum. But if sensa are located where they are experienced, it might be that Siamese twins sometimes feel the same pain and experience the same tactile and kinaesthetic sensum. By assuming sensings, however, we can transform question (5) so that it is as easily answerable as was (3a), which concerned the spatial location of sensings:

    (5a) Can one person's sensing event be identical with another
           person's sensing event?

If this 'can' in (5a) expresses merely logical possibility, then the answer to (5a) can be settled by deciding whether it is logically possible that there is some bodily process common to two persons that is identical with a sensing by one and also with a sensing by the other. If, as seems true, it is logically possible that two persons have the same brain and each sensing by each person is identical with some brain process of that brain, then it also seems logically possible that a sensing by one person and a sensing by the other are identical with the same brain process. We should then answer (5a) affirmatively. However, if the 'can' expresses physical possibility, then a negative answer is reasonable, because the only bodily processes that are plausible candidates for such "joint" identities are brain processes and it seems physically impossible that two persons have the same brain. Once again, by assuming sensings we find a way to answer a question that remains perplexingly unanswered with sensa.

CONCLUSION ABOUT SENSA

We have finished our extended discussion of sensa. By seeing that five perplexing and unanswered questions about sensa can be transformed into questions about sensings which can be satisfactorily answered, we have completed the discussion of sensa relevant to justifying premise VI of the central argument. That is, we have found what is needed to justify that there are fewer recalcitrant philosophical problems without sensa. Sensings allow us to answer the transformed questions in ways that avoid the disquieting puzzlement generated by answers to the corresponding questions that arise for sensa. And, because throughout the long discussion of sensa and sensings we have found no intractible problems unique to sensings, we can conclude that premise VI is justified.

We have previously justified premises I, II, III, and IV, and from them concluded V: There are neither empirical nor linguistic reasons to justify the existence of sensa. It might seem, then, that we have reached the point where we can conclude that we are justified in rejecting sensa, but this would be premature. As was discussed in setting up the central argument, there may be metaphysical reasons for sensa that would counterbalance the reason for jetisoning sensa we have just found, namely, that recalcitrant problems are avoided in that way. In particular, I claimed that if some form of sensum realism or sensum phenomenalism is more reasonable than any form of direct realism or sensing phenomenalism, then we are not justified in rejecting sensa. Thus we have one enormous task left to complete before we draw a final conclusion about sensa, that is, to examine premise VII: Compatible common-sense realism is at least as reasonable as any metaphysical theory of perception and the external world that requires sensa. This will occupy most of the rest of the book, because it involves a detailed examination of the most plausible versions of sensum realism and sensum phenomenalism. Of course, this lengthy examination is important for more than the rejection of sensa; it is also crucial for helping us find and explicate the most reasonable metaphysical theories of perception and the external world.

The next task, which comprises the next section of the book,

is to develop and examine the most plausible versions of phenomenalism. My strategy will be to start with the historical Berkeley
and to amend and strengthen his theory until we have developed
a Berkeleyan theory that is truly a worthy opponent for any version
of realism. However, while investigating this theory we should
also examine the various sensum and sensing versions of eliminative
phenomenalism that eliminate physical objects rather than identify
them with groups of sensa. It may be that difficult problems will
arise for the Berkeleyan theory that can be avoided by one of the
eliminative versions, and our aim is not only to discover the most
plausible sensum theories, but also to uncover the strongest
phenomenalistic opponents of compatible common-sense realism.

Part I
PHENOMENALISM

3 Berkeleyan Phenomenalism

In the Introduction, I claimed that the basic distinction between realists and ontological phenomenalists is that the former accepts and the latter denies:

> (8) There are external objects, that is, objects (perhaps unknowable) which are not perceivers and which exist independently of and unaffected by any (finite) perceivers.

For many realists these objects are physical objects, but a Kantian realist claims that no physical objects are external. In this he agrees with all phenomenalists. I further distinguished two sorts of phenomenalists: Berkeleyan phenomenalists, who are reductive phenomenalists because they reduce physical objects to groups of sensa, and eliminative phenomenalists, who deny there are any physical objects. In addition, I distinguished three kinds of eliminative phenomenalists who differ in their construals of physical-object terms. The central task of this part of the book is to explicate and develop the most reasonable versions of phenomenalism as preliminary to a critical comparison with the strongest realistic theories.

In order to accomplish this task I shall begin with that version of phenomenalism most fully developed by an historical figure, and then, using contemporary tools developed in linguistic philosophy and the philosophy of science, I shall reconstruct it to make it as plausible as possible. Once this is finished we can compare it with the opposing versions of phenomenalism to discover which, if any, is the most reasonable. Historically, the principle phenomenalist has been Berkeley. Thus we shall begin with his version and then examine the three versions of eliminative phenomenalism.

Using the approach of *Three Dialogues between Hylas and Philonous* as a model, we can construe Berkeley as proceeding in a quite standard and acceptable way to develop, explain, and justify his version of phenomenalism. He first attacks the extant versions of realism by trying to show that some of their consequences are falsified by certain facts of perception and that the way to avoid these consequences is to adopt his theory. Then, in the third dialogue, he tries to defend his position by showing that it has no unacceptable consequences. Based upon these two sets of results, he can go on to conclude that his phenomenalistic thesis is the most reasonable theory of perception and the external world. However, as has happened so often to others, Berkeley's ingenious efforts in both endeavors fail to justify his conclusions, as a short review of his central arguments will show.

BERKELEY'S OBJECTIONS TO REALISM

In the first two dialogues Berkeley attacks three versions of realism: naive realism, a modified naive theory, which is adumbrated in writings of Galileo, and indirect realism. His primary attack on both naive theories is based on the argument from perceptual relativity, but he first argues that sensible (sensuous) secondary qualities are dependent on perceivers and, therefore, are not properties of external physical objects. The argument is that since intense degrees of sensible heat and cold, and certain sensible tastes and odors are identical with pains, and since all pains are perceiver-dependent sensa, at least some sensible secondary qualities are nothing but sensa (see *Dialogues* I 3).[1] This argument, however, assumes there are pains with which to identify felt heat and cold, and we have found no reason to prefer a sensum theory of pain to a sensing theory of hurting. Without pains, there would be no perceiver-dependent entities in these situations with which the felt heat and cold would plausibly be identified.

It might be objected at this point that although on a sensing theory, sensible intense heat is not to be identified with someone's pain or with someone's hurting, his feeling intense heat would be identical with his hurting. Consequently, because the latter is perceiver-dependent, so also would be the former. There are, however, two replies to this. First, such an argument at most establishes that certain events of someone feeling intense heat, rather than the intense heat which he feels, are perceiver-dependent, and this will not support Berkeley's thesis about secondary

[1] In this chapter all references to and quotations from Berkeley's *Principles* or *Dialogues* or *Correspondence* refer to *Principles, Dialogues, and Philosophical Correspondence*, C. M. Turbayne, ed. (Indianapolis and New York: Bobbs-Merrill, 1965). All others refer to *The Works of George Berkeley*, A. A. Luce and T. E. Jessop, eds. (Edinburgh: Thomas Nelson and Sons, 1948–1957). Vols. I and IV.

qualities. Second, whether we grant that there are pain-sensa or accept only objectless events of hurting, the crucial identity claim is no more reasonable than a contrary thesis. That is, as the sensible heat of a stove, for example, becomes more and more intense, someone whose hand is on the stove feels increasingly intense pain (hurts more intensely), until finally he becomes incapable of perceiving the heat of the stove with his hand and is aware only of the pain in his hand (his hand hurting).

This counterthesis is bolstered by a different example in which it is clear that a pain (a hurting) is not to be identified with a sensible quality that is perceived while the pain is felt. Consider someone whose finger aches intensely because it was badly mangled in an accident. This person rubs his finger lightly across a glassy smooth table top, but he is not aware of the smoothness of the table as distinct from the pain in the finger. In this case it would be implausible to claim that he perceives the sensible smoothness and it is identical with his felt pain. Rather we should conclude that he does not perceive the smoothness of the table, but only feels the pain. A similar conclusion is reasonable about a person whose finger is slowly becoming numb, because of a shot of novocaine, as he holds it on a hot surface. It would certainly be mistaken to conclude that when the finger is numb he can still feel the heat, but it is identical with a feeling of numbness. The reasonable conclusion is that he feels only the numbness, just as in the previous case he felt only the pain. Similarly, on a sensing interpretation, it would be unreasonable to conclude that the event of his finger hurting is identical with his perceiving the smoothness, or that the event of his finger feeling numb is identical with his feeling heat. The only significant difference between these two cases and Berkeley's example is that in the former cases the sensible smoothness and heat are not causally related to the hurting or the numbness. But this gives no reason to claim identity in Berkeley's case and not in these others. Consequently, I find we are justified in rejecting the identity claim that is crucial for the first Berkeleyan argument concerning sensible secondary qualities.

While the preceding argument, if sound, would refute the naive theory, it would leave the modified theory unaffected, because that theory agrees with Locke that sensible secondary qualities are really sensations. It differs from Locke in stating that sensible primary qualities are properties of external physical objects. As Hylas says when he abandons naive realism:

> Sensible qualities are by philosophers divided into 'primary' and 'secondary'. The former are extension, figure, solidity, gravity, motion, and rest. And these they hold exist really in bodies. The latter are ... briefly, all sensible qualitites besides the primary, which they assert are only so many sensations or ideas existing nowhere but in the mind (*Dialogues* I 6).

Berkeley, however, has two arguments to refute this position. One is to apply the argument from perceptual relativity to primary qualities, and the other, from *The Principles*, assumes that the sensible secondary qualities have already been shown to be perceiver-dependent:

> For my own part, I see evidently that it is not in my power to frame an idea of a body extended and moved, but I must withal give it some color or other sensible quality which is acknowledged to exist only in the mind. In short, extension, figure, and motion, abstracted from all other qualities are inconceivable. Where therefore the other sensible qualities are, there must these be also, in the mind and nowhere else (*Principles* 10).

Essentially, the point here is that there is no way to avoid the conclusion that sensible primary qualities are perceiver-dependent once this has been shown of sensible secondary qualities.

The basic problem with this argument is that while we cannot doubt that many physical objects appear to be both colored and extended, and while it is inconceivable that something is sensibly colored yet not extended, many people have found it to be not only conceivable but true that external physical objects have only primary qualities. Galileo, who may have held the modified naive view, says,

> I say that upon conceiving of a material or corporeal substance, I immediately feel the need to conceive simultaneously that it is bounded and has this or that shape; that it is in this place or that at any given time; that it moves or stays still; that it does or does not touch another body; and that it is one, few, or many. I cannot separate it from these conditions by any

stretch of my imagination. But that it must be white or red, bitter or sweet, noisy or silent, of sweet or foul odor, my mind feels no compulsion to understand as necessary accompaniments. Indeed, without the senses to guide us, reason or imagination alone would perhaps never arrive at such qualities. For that reason I think that tastes, odors, colors, and so forth are no more than mere names so far as pertains to the subject wherein they reside, and that they have their habitation only in the sensorium. Thus, if the living creature were removed, all these qualities would be removed and annihilated.[2]

Eddington in his famous discussion of two tables, describes the scientific table, similarly, as not colored because it consists of a system of swarming, colorless particles.[3] Whether or not Galileo is right (a topic to be discussed in Chapter 8), it is surely false that sensible extensions must be perceiver-dependent if some sensible secondary quality that appears to accompany the extensions is perceiver-dependent.

The failure of the two preceding arguments is of little consequence for Berkeley if the argument from perceptual relativity succeeds, because it applies to both primary and secondary qualities, and, if sound, it destroys any form of direct realism, whether naive or not. We have already found reason to reject that argument in Chapter 2, however, because it depends essentially on interpreting the facts of perceptual relativity so that all sensible qualities vary with certain changes in perceivers and conditions of perception. We saw not only that this is merely one way to construe these facts, but also that it is no more reasonable than a construal that destroys the argument, namely, that it is only how properties appear to someone and which properties he perceives that depend on perceivers and conditions of perception. On this interpretation, no sensible qualities are perceiver-dependent and thus none are reducible to sensations as Berkeley's own phenomenalism and his attack on both naive theories require. Furthermore, since we have found no other cogent empirical or linguistic arguments for sensa, and thus none against all forms of direct realism, we can conclude

[2] Galileo, *The Assayer* in *The Controversy on the Comets of 1618*, S. Drake, trans. (Phila.: University of Pennsylvania Press, 1960), p. 309.
[3] See A. Eddington, *Nature of the Physical World* (New York: The Macmillan Co., 1929), Introduction.

that no Berkeleyan attacks on direct realism succeed. This, however, does not affect his arguments against indirect realism.

One main defect with Berkeley's refutation of indirect realism is that it is generally aimed at nonessential features found in Locke's particular version.[4] Berkeley attacks a Lockean conception of material substance and Locke's claims that properties of external objects cause sensations and that those sensations caused by primary properties resemble their causes. But an indirect realist can easily avoid Berkeley's attack. An indirect realist does not need to consider physical objects to be material substrata underlying, in some figurative way, various properties. Nor need he take a stand on what causes sensations. As defined in the Introduction, the claim that someone indirectly perceives physical objects has no causal implications, and so he can avoid any stand about causal conditions of perception. However, if he wishes to assert that there are causal relations—indeed necessary causal connections—among stimuli transmitted from an object and a perceptual experience of the object, he is not thereby committed to any view of what the causes of sensations are. He could even embrace Berkeley's view that only entities with active powers are causes, assume only God is active, and proclaim Malebranche's occasionalism. On this somewhat implausible view, the necessary causal connections between stimuli and experiences would result from God necessitating that the latter follow the former when conditions are appropriate. Of course, he could take instead a Humean view of these causal relations, and leave open the question of whether some active power necessitates them.

Another of Berkeley's main objections can be construed to be that indirect realism assumes unnecessary entities to explain the production of perceptual sensa, and thus it should be rejected on the basis of Occam's razor. In this regard, Berkeley considers various attempts to justify the postulation of external physical objects. He rejects postulating them, first, as causes of sensa, then as "instruments" that the author of nature uses to help produce sensa, and finally, as Malebranchean "occasions," that is, entities such that when certain things happen to them, God causes certain perceivers to sense certain sensa (*Dialogues* II 6–8). In each case Berkeley

[4] See Chapter 7 for a discussion and definition of Lockean representative realism.

(through Philonous) can be taken as offering a simpler, more plausible explanatory hypothesis, namely, that there is one author of nature who is the proximate cause of the sensa of physical objects that we experience. Consequently, if Berkeley is correct, then not only is the postulation of external physical objects not justified, but the rejection of those postulated entities is justified.

The issues involved in justifying one explanatory schema with its postulated entities as superior to another schema with its postulations are too complex to resolve here. This is in part because a resolution awaits a decision about whether scientific realism or instrumentalism is acceptable. This will be discussed in detail in Chapters 4 and 8. It also awaits a discussion about what conditions are required for a completely adequate explanatory schema. Here I shall say only that although a Berkeleyan schema is simpler than any realistic schema—whether scientific or common sensical— with respect to the number of entities it assumes, such simplicity is just one of several factors relevant to the acceptability of explanatory schemas. Because Berkeley has not considered these other factors, he has not succeeded in showing his schema to be superior to realistic ones. We can, then, reject this argument as we did his previous ones. However, we cannot also conclude here that no Berkeleyan would succeed; such a conclusion must await the more detailed discussion in Chapter 8.

A Berkeleyan Defense of Phenomenalism

When we turn to Berkeley's defense of his own view in the third dialogue, we find greater success than in his attacks on realism in the first two dialogues, because he refutes many of the objections to his theory. Yet there are crucial objections he fails to meet adequately. In particular, there are four important, well-known objections, which must be countered if a Berkeleyan phenomenalism is to be a plausible theory of perception and the external world. As I hope to show, these objections are interrelated in such a way that by construing Berkeley as one sort of theoretical phenomenalist, we shall be able to produce plausible replies to all four objections. The first objection is that Berkeley verges on contradiction because he seems to say that we have knowledge of something only if we have an idea of it, we have no ideas of minds, and we have knowledge of minds. He saves himself from this contradiction by the introduction of "notions" as the concepts we use to think about minds. The problem is that saving his theory in this way seems at best to be merely an unjustified *ad hoc* adjustment. I shall argue, however, that construing notions as theoretical concepts which function differently in thinking from the observational concepts that represent physical objects and sensa, will open the way to justifying the introduction of notions.

The second objection is that Berkeley's claim that physical objects are groups or bundles of sensa is badly in need of clarification and justification. But the only interpretation that succeeds in clarifying the claim is clearly mistaken, namely, that physical objects are logical constructions out of sensa. I shall argue, however, that Berkeley can also be interpreted as a theoretical phenomenalist, and this will enable us to construe the relationship more plausibly in terms of physical objects being one sort of theoretical construction out of sensa.

The third objection is related to the second, because it concerns the problem of how it is possible that two perceivers perceive the same physical object when it is nothing but a group of sensa and only one person can experience any one sensum.[5] Berkeley's answer, through Philonous, is clearly unsatisfactory:

> If the term 'same' be taken in the vulgar acceptation, it is certain (and not at all repugnant to the principles I maintain) that different persons may perceive the same thing, or the same thing or idea exist in different minds... But if the term 'same' be used in acceptation of philosophers who pretend to an abstracted notion of identity, then according to their sundry definitions of this notion (for it is not yet agreed wherein that philosophic identity consists), it may or may not be possible for diverse persons to perceive the same thing (*Dialogues* III 18).

However, the beginning of a more plausible reply is that each bundle that is a physical object consists in different sensa experienced by different perceivers, yet no one of these sensa is experienced by more than one perceiver.

The last objection we shall consider is that Berkeley apparently

---

[5] For a discussion of this problem and one proposed solution to it, see R. Van Iten, "Berkeley's Alleged Solipsism" *Revue Internationale de Philosophie*, XVI (1962); 447–52.

introduces God into his theory in a way that is not only *ad hoc*, but unjustifiably demeans the explanatory capacity of science. According to R. J. Hirst, the main objection to Berkeley's theory is that it is unscientific:

> Just as the Greek dramatists sometimes introduced one of the Olympian Gods into their plays to unravel a hopelessly tangled plot by supernatural means, so Berkeley seems to try to solve his problem of a continuing cause of our impressions by bringing in his God. This seems perilously near cheating and is certainly to abandon science and philosophy; if one can "solve" theoretical problems by postulating God's intervention, and attribute to ·him just the powers and intentions necessary to fill the bill, then scientific investigation and reasoning are nullified, for any theory you like can be patched up in this way.[6]

The crucial tasks for rebutting this objection are to see whether a Berkeleyan theoretical phenomenalist needs to postulate God, and if he does, whether the postulation is plausible at least, and does not imply the abandonment or demeaning of scientific reasoning and investigation. A central issue here is whether a Berkeleyan can plausibly adopt a realistic view of apples, an instrumentalist view of electrons, and also allow for the importance of scientific explanations in conjunction with explanations in terms of what Berkeley calls "the author of nature." I believe he can.

The First Objection: Knowledge, Ideas, Notions, and Minds

To see the first objection clearly, consider the following quotations from the beginning of Berkeley's *Principles*. First:

> It is evident to anyone who takes a survey of the *objects* of human knowledge that they are either ideas actually imprinted on the senses, or else such as are perceived by attending to the passions and operations of the mind, or lastly, ideas formed by help of memory and imagination—either compounding, dividing, or barely representing those originally perceived in the aforesaid ways (*Principles* 1).

[6] G. Wyburn, R. Pickford, R. Hirst, *Human Senses and Perception* (Edinburgh and London: Oliver and Boyd, 1964), p. 260.

And also:

> This perceiving, active being is what I call "mind," "spirit,"
> "soul," or "myself." By which words I do not denote any one
> of my ideas, but a thing entirely distinct from them, wherein
> they exist, or, which is the same thing, whereby they are
> perceived—for the existence of an idea consists in being
> perceived (*Principles* 2).

From these two quotations it seems we can derive two statements:

(1) All objects of human knowledge are ideas;
(2) No idea is denoted by the word 'mind';

which taken together allow us to deduce:

(3) No objects of human knowledge are denoted by 'mind.'

AN APPARENT CONTRADICTION IN BERKELEY'S PHILOSOPHY

The preceding conclusion would seem to be unpalatable to
Berkeley because his whole philosophy is so intimately dependent
upon the existence of minds. Nevertheless, in his earlier writings
there is evidence that he had previously accepted the conclusion.
In the *Philosophical Commentaries*, written before the *Principles*
and the *Dialogues*, he says in Entry 581:

> Say you the Mind is not the Perceptions, but that thing w^{ch}
> perceives. I answer you are abus'd by the words that and thing
> these are vague empty words w th out a meaning.

In this entry it certainly seems that Berkeley is claiming that the
word 'mind' does not denote some thing. Indeed, even to talk of
'mind' denoting some thing is to misuse the word 'thing.' And,
clearly, if it is without meaning to talk of some thing denoted by
'mind,' then there can be no human knowledge of what thing 'mind'
denotes. Later in the *Commentaries* Berkeley again agrees with (3):

> The substance of Body we know, the substance of Spirit we do
> not know it not being knowable. It being purus actus (*Com-
> mentaries* 701).

It would make a consistent interpretation of Berkeley's position
easier if he had continued to hold the theory of mind expressed in

the *Commentaries*.[7] His later position, however, and what seems to be his final position, is the position stated in both the *Principles* and *Dialogues*. It is quite different:

> We may be said to have some knowledge or notion of our own minds, of spirits and active beings, whereof in a strict sense we have not ideas (*Principles* 89).[8]

This by itself seems inconsistent with (3), yet it may not be. Statement (3) asserts there is no knowledge of things denoted by 'mind,' but the quotation implies nothing about whether or not 'mind' is a denoting term. Indeed, Berkeley's claim in that quotation would be compatible with (3) if, as some commentators have claimed, Berkeley considered the word 'mind' to be more like the word 'number' than like the word 'apple.'[9] According to Berkeley, 'number' is not a denoting term. He says:

> There are no ideas of number in abstract denoted by numerical names and figures. The theories therefore in arithmetic, if they are abstracted from the names and figures, as likewise from all use and practice, as well as from the particular things numbered, can be supposed to have nothing at all for their objects (*Principles* 120).

Nevertheless, Berkeley would not deny we can have arithmetical knowledge, knowledge we might call knowledge of numbers, and surely knowledge which in the strict sense does not involve ideas.

Thus Berkeley could avoid contradicting (3) by taking an instrumental or nondenoting view of mental terms, but it seems quite clear that this is not his position in the *Dialogues* and *Principles* where, in addition to the above, he says:

> For by the word "spirit" we mean only that which thinks, wills, and perceives; this, and this alone, constitutes the

---

[7] For a view that the concept of mind found in the *Commentaries* is closer to Berkeley's final position than the one I am defending here, cf. C. M. Turbayne, "Berkeley's Two Concepts of Mind", *Philosophy and Phenomenological Research*, 20 (1959): 85–92, and 22 (1962): 577–80. Turbayne claims that Berkeley continued to maintain the nondenoting view of 'mind' found in the *Commentaries*, but that he gave up his view in the *Commentaries* that talk of 'mind' denoting things is meaningless. Rather, according to Turbayne, Berkeley says it is metaphorical.

[8] See also *Dialogues* III 4.

[9] Cf. Turbayne, and for an article pursuing the line Turbayne takes, J. Murphy, "Berkeley and the Metaphor of Mental Substance," *Ratio* 7 (1965): 170–79.

significance of that term... What I am myself, that which I denote by the term "I," is the same with what is meant by "soul," or "spiritual substance" (*Principles* 138, 139).

From this and the quotation from *Principles* 89 we can conclude from what Berkeley asserted in these two major works:

(4) Some objects of human knowledge are denoted by 'mind.' This statement flatly contradicts (3).

BERKELEY'S WAY TO AVOID THE CONTRADICTION: TWO KINDS OF OBJECTS OF KNOWLEDGE

Can Berkeley be saved from this contradiction? It is clear, I think, how he would claim to avoid it: by modifying premise (1). In the *Principles* he says:

Human knowledge may naturally be reduced to two heads— that of *ideas* and that of *spirits* (*Principles* 86).

This adjustment may seem to contradict the quotation from which we extracted premise (1), but, although in that passage it may seem Berkeley calls all objects of knowledge "ideas," the section relevant to minds does not mention ideas:

or else such as are perceived by attending to the passions and operations of the mind

Here 'such' may seem to refer to ideas, but if we take it to refer to objects of knowledge and take seriously Berkeley's repeated claims that we have no idea of, that is, no idea represents, either minds or operations of the mind, then even in this initial quotation there is a hint of two quite disparate objects of knowledge.[10]

ANOTHER CONTRADICTION AVOIDED BY BERKELEY: NOTIONS AND MINDS

We have not yet dissipated all traces of contradiction, however, because a second problem arises from one of Hylas' challenges to Philonous:

You even affirm that spirits are a sort of beings altogether different from ideas. Consequently, that no idea can be like a

---

[10] This position has been stated by A. A. Luce, *Berkeley's Immaterialism* (Edinburgh: Thomas Nelson and Sons, 1945), pp. 39–40.

spirit. We have, therefore, no idea of any spirit. You admit nevertheless that there is spiritual substance, although you have no idea of it, while you deny there can be such a thing as material substance because you have no notion or idea of it. Is this fair dealing? (*Dialogues* III 4)

We might lay out an argument to express this problem as follows:

(5) If humans have knowledge about some object, then they have an idea of it; that is, they think about the object by means of an idea that (pictorially) represents the object.

(6) A mind "being an agent, cannot be like unto, or represented by, any idea whatsoever" (*Principles* 27).

Therefore

(7) There is no human knowledge of minds.

Clearly Berkeley cannot accept (7), which is even a stronger claim than (3), and is inconsistent with even an instrumental theory of mind. Consequently, because he accepts (6), Berkeley must reject (5). This is what he does:

We may not, I think, strictly be said to have an *idea* of an active being, or of an action, strictly we may be said to have a *notion* of them. I have some knowledge or notion of my mind, and its acts about ideas, in as much as I know or understand what is meant by those words. What I know, that I have some notion of (*Principles* 142).

Given the addition of notions to ideas, it is easy to absolve Berkeley of being committed to the inconsistent conjunction of (4) and (7). Instead of holding (5) as it first seems, Berkeley would agree to:

(5a) If humans have knowledge about some object, then they have either an idea or a notion of the object.

This does not entail (7) when taken with (6). Berkeley, then, by the introduction of notions can avoid holding (3) and (7), and his philosophy avoids contradiction. But to many people it surely seems he avoid contradiction only by the sudden, unjustified introduction of something like an idea in all respects, except that it does what ideas cannot do: represents active rather than inert entities. That is, their view is that for Berkeley (5a) is to be construed as:

> (5b) If humans have knowledge about some object, then they have either an idea or a notion that (pictorially) represents the object.

If this is the most plausible interpretation, then it surely seems Berkeley avoids contradiction only at the price of making his theory rest upon an *ad hoc* assumption so tenuous and so little developed that it makes his whole position implausible.

A DEFENSE OF NOTIONS: THEORETICAL TERMS AND NOTIONS

My present aim is to show that although Berkeley has hardly given us enough to conclude that notions are any more than a weak *ad hoc* addition to his thesis, and although, as he presented it, his position has an important weakness, it is possible, nevertheless,to use the little Berkeley said as the basis for constructing a viable theory of notions that complements and makes plausible his whole theory of mind. Whether Berkeley held anything remotely like the theory I shall propose is something I am afraid we shall never know because it seems his more detailed writings on mind are irreparably lost.[11] My aim, then, is not to speculate about what Berkeley thought, but rather to flesh out the little Berkeley gave us in a plausible way. In short, I shall argue that a Berkeleyan can justifiably reject (5b) because he can quite plausibly assign notions a role in thinking that is quite different from the representational role of ideas.

Berkeley, like many contemporary philosophers, was keenly interested in language and its importance for philosophical problems, particularly the problems of what kind of words are denoting words and what kind of objects are denoted. For example, as previously quoted, he claims that arithmetical terms do not denote objects. They, as many other terms, have a different function. Berkeley realized that "the communication of ideas marked by words is not the chief and only end of language, as is commonly supposed" (*Principles*, Introduction 20). And, although many general terms do denote objects, none denote abstract ideas,

---

[11] This seems to be the most plausible interpretation of the subject matter of a manuscript lost by Berkeley. Cf. *Correspondence* II 6.

but rather they "signify indifferently a great number of particular ideas" (*Principles*, Introduction 18).

Berkeley claims that words such as 'apple' denote collections of ideas, but, as we have seen above, that mental substance words such as 'mind,' 'soul,' or 'spirit,' which I shall call "mind-terms" to distinguish them from the broader class of mental terms, denote things that are not ideas and not constituted of ideas. My claim is that if we understand terms such as 'apple' to be one kind of observation term and mind-terms to be one kind of nonobservational, theoretical term, and couple this with an empiricist view of the meaning of theoretical terms, we shall arrive at a distinction between ideas and notions that is neither vague nor baseless. One result will be the view that our ideas of apples, that is, the ideas we use to think about particular apples, are expressed by the observation term 'apple.' In this regard, an idea I use to think about apples can be said to picture representationally particular apples, themselves bundles of particular ideas, and, derivatively, the term 'apple,' which refers to particular apples, can also be said to represent or picture apples.[12] Furthermore, our *notions* or concepts of mind will be construed as being expressed by the theoretical term 'mind' and are what we use to think about minds, which are not like ideas and therefore cannot be pictorially represented by ideas. Whereas apples, stones, trees, and other sensible things are observable entities, minds and the like are unobservable theoretical entities.

ELABORATION OF THE DEFENSE: EMPIRICISM AND THE MEANING OF THEORETICAL TERMS   But there is still the question of what reason there can be for distinguishing notions from ideas in this way. It will not do to answer that the reason is that, because ideas can represent only ideas, something else is needed to represent minds. A much more plausible answer will come from considering one

---

[12] I have here interpreted Berkeley as claiming that each particular object consists of sensible ideas that are themselves particulars. R. J. Van Iten disagrees in "Berkeley's Alleged Solipsism." He claims that Berkeley can consistently escape solipsism only if he construes the constituent ideas as universals, because if the constituents of each object are particular ideas, then, because no two minds can perceive the same particular idea, it follows that no two minds can perceive the same object. But there is a missing premise here, namely, if no two minds can perceive the same constituents of an object, then no two minds can perceive the same object. This premise is debatable and surely not a necessary truth. For a discussion of when two perceivers perceive the same physical object, see the examination in Chapter 5 of the third major objection to Berkeley's phenomenalism.

widely accepted empiricist theory of the meaning of theoretical terms and observation terms. Like all empiricist theories about how terms and concepts come to have meaning, it requires that any nonlogical term derives whatever meaning it has from certain of its relationships to observable situations. It differs from other empiricist theories of meaning and concept formation, however, in having less restrictive requirements about what this relationship must be. This theory, as expounded by Carnap, distinguishes between the vocabulary, V_o, of an observation language, L_o, and the vocabulary, V_t, of a theoretical language, L_t. He first considers the observation vocabulary:

> The terms of V_o are predicates designating observable properties of events or things (e.g., 'blue,' 'hot,' 'large,' etc.) or observable relations between them (e.g., 'x is warmer than y,' 'x is contiguous to y,' etc.).[13]

Because all these terms designate properties we are aware of by observation, there is no problem of their applicability to what they designate. In this respect, their role in language is completely determined by what can be observed. That is, their meaning can be completely and clearly determined by specifying the observable conditions of their application. Thus, as Carnap says, "L_o is intended for the description of observable events and therefore is meant to be completely interpreted."[14] Observation terms, then, are completely meaningful according to this or, indeed, any empiricist theory of meaning. Using Berkeley's terminology, we can say that such terms are used to express the ideas we have of observable properties. And, we could also say, the observation terms picture in some derivative way these same observable properties.

Theoretical terms, on the other hand, have always raised problems for empiricist theories of meaning and concept formation.

---

[13] R. Carnap, "The Methodological Character of Theoretical Concepts" in *Minnesota Studies in the Philosophy of Science*, H. Feigl and M. Scriven, eds. (Minneapolis: University of Minn. Press, 1956), Vol I, p. 41. It should be noted that Berkeley would not agree that there are observable relations. Cf. *Principles* 142. Furthermore, while Berkeley would seem to claim that sensation words such as 'pleasure' and 'pain' are part of the observation vocabulary because they, like 'blue' and 'hot,' refer to sensory ideas (perceptual sensa), Carnap, at least in his later works, would disagree. For Berkeley the observation language would include part of a phenomenal language, but for Carnap it would be only the thing-language.

[14] Ibid.

For many of these theories, if a term is not an observation term, it is cognitively meaningful only if and only insofar as it is definable by observation terms.[15] Because of this, empiricists have tried to construe theoretical entities as logical constructions out of observables by using observation terms to provide explicit definitions of theoretical terms. When this procedure failed, however, they turned to partial definitions in reduction sentences to give the terms a clear, yet incomplete meaning. This procedure also failed and it is now generally agreed that many theoretical terms are not observation terms, and not definable—either explicitly or partially—by observation terms.[16] The relationship of theoretical terms to what is observable is much more tenuous, and, consequently, on empiricist theories of meaning, they have at best both unclear and incomplete meaning. The problem for the empiricist, however, is to show that they have any meaning at all.

Carnap's solution of this problem is to construe the theoretical vocabulary, V_t—the vocabulary containing only theoretical terms, and, therefore, no observation terms—as connected by correspondence rules, C-rules, to the observation vocabulary, V_o. For example, let us assume that we have a very simple theoretical system, T, with two purely theoretical statements:

$$(x)[T_1 x \supset T_2 x], \quad \text{and} \quad (x)[T_2 x \supset T_3 x],$$

and two C-rules:

$$(x)[O_1 x \supset T_1 x], \quad \text{and} \quad (x)[T_3 x \supset O_2 x].$$

According to Carnap, whatever significance the theoretical terms T_1, T_2, and T_3 have is provided by the contingent connection they have to the fully and clearly meaningful observation terms O_1 and O_2. That is:

> There is no independent interpretation for L_t. The system T is in itself an uninterpreted postulate system. The terms of V_t obtain only an indirect and incomplete interpretation by the fact that some of them are connected by the rules C with observational terms, and the remaining terms of V_t are connected with the first ones by the postulates of T. Thus it is

---

[15] See Chapter 7 for a discussion of empiricist theories of concept formation and learning.
[16] Carnap, pp. 66–69.

clear that the rules C are essential; without them the terms of V_t would not have any observation significance. These rules must be such that they connect sentences of L_o with certain sentences of L_t, for instance, by making derivation in the one or the other direction possible.[17]

On this empiricist view of theoretical terms, they are meaningful, but, because they are neither completely nor partially definable by observation terms, they have only an incomplete and unclear meaning. We cannot, therefore, be said to have a complete and clear understanding of whatever a theoretical term might refer to. Instead of a full and clear understanding, or idea, we have at best something like a Berkeleyan notion of what it signifies. Strictly speaking, then, for theoretical terms, unlike observation terms, we do not have an idea of—an idea that represents or pictures— anything at all. While we can "visualize" those things that 'apple' or 'stone' denote, we cannot "imagine" in the same way what 'electron' or 'mind' might denote. Nevertheless we do have a conception of, an understanding of, what an electron or mind is. It is true that a grasp of theoretical entities is often aided by a picture, such as a tinker toy "picture" of an atomic structure. But this is picturing only in the sense of using something observable, something we can have an idea of, as a model to help us better understand what we cannot visualize or completely understand.

I have suggested that Berkeleyan notions be construed as what we can call "theoretical concepts," concepts that we use in thinking about theoretical explanations of what we observe and that we express using theoretical terms. I have suggested that, as required by one empiricist theory of meaning, such concepts are neither completely nor clearly understood and do not represent whatever they might denote. On this view of notions, therefore, premise (5b) is false, because notions do not function to represent pictorially what ideas cannot picture. Indeed, their function in thinking is not a representational one at all. Notions are rather conceptual devices we use to explain what we observe and represent by ideas. To add to ideas, which function in thought descriptively, something quite different that functions to explain, is not to make a mere *ad hoc* adjustment. It is to take into account something essential for any

[17] Ibid., p. 47.

adequate theory of mind, because any such theory must be able to account for explanatory thinking, as exemplified in science, as well as descriptive thinking.

AN OBJECTION: THE TERM 'MIND' IS NOT A THEORETICAL TERM   We have not reached the end of the matter, however, because construing 'mind' and other mind – terms as theoretical terms immediately gives rise to two new objections. The first is this. 'Mind' is surely not an observation term, because minds are not observable, that is, no ideas can pictorially represent them. But also, it is surely not a theoretical term, because it is always used to refer to what someone is aware of, unlike theoretical terms such as 'electron.' It is true, I believe, and also recognized by Berkeley that 'mind' refers to what someone experiences. In *Principles* 89, he says, "We comprehend our own existence by inward feeling or reflection,..." and in *De Motu* 21, "the sentient, percipient, thinking thing we know by a certain internal consciousness." We should, consequently, construe 'mind' for Berkeley as what I call a "reporting term," that is, a term used to make an identifying reference to something that someone is conscious or aware of, something he experiences.[18]

In this way it is like 'apple,' but it differs from 'apple' because we do not observe its referent through the senses. Rather, we are aware of it through "internal consciousness." Yet, having granted this much, must we conclude that Berkeley could not consistently hold that 'mind' is a theoretical term? And, because of this, must we agree after all that Berkeley's notions can have no function in thinking except the one forced on him by his own theory, namely, that of representing what ideas cannot represent?

We can avoid these conclusions, but in so doing we must draw a distinction between mind-terms that are theoretical terms and certain other theoretical terms such as 'electron.' This distinction will not only allow us to avoid this objection, but will prepare the way for the answer to the second and more serious objection.

REPLY: TWO KINDS OF THEORETICAL TERMS   There are two reasons why mind-terms should be contrued as theoretical terms, albeit a unique kind, and why it is plausible to fill out Berkeley's view in this way. The first reason is that whether or not mind-terms have a

---

[18] See my *Materialism and Sensations*, pp. 81–82 for a discussion of reporting terms.

reporting use, surely one of their primary roles is to explain various sorts of observable human behavior. And since they are clearly not observation terms, they meet what is generally accepted as a sufficient condition for being a theoretical term. That is, they are nonlogical constants in an explanatory vocabulary that are neither observation terms, nor definable by observation terms.[19] Because terms that meet this sufficient condition can also be reporting terms, we can distinguish between theoretical terms that are also reporting terms such as 'mind' (what I call "theoretico-reporting" terms), and nonreporting or "pure" theoretical terms such as 'electron.'

There is a second reason for construing mind-terms as theoretical terms. When someone uses them self-ascriptively—in their first person use—they are, like observation terms, used to refer to what the person experiences, but this is not true when someone uses them other-ascriptively. They function very similarly to 'electron' when so used, because in both these cases when I make an assertion using either term, I do not experience whatever the term refers to, but rather must justify my assertion by inference from what I observe. It might be concluded from this that when they are used other-ascriptively, mind-terms are pure theoretical terms, but that when used self-ascriptively, they are nontheoretical or "pure" reporting terms. But I find the claim that mind-terms, contrary to appearances, are ambiguous in their first and other-person uses to be reasonable only if there are grounds for concluding that no theoretical terms are reporting terms. I can think of no reason for this, however.[20] Let us conclude, consequently, that Berkeley can agree with what seems reasonable: Mind-terms are, in both their first and other-person uses, theoretico-reporting terms. They differ, therefore, from both the pure theoretical term 'electron' and the observation term, 'red.'

It is interesting to note at this point how Berkeley's concept of mind on the above extrapolation both differs from and is, I think, more plausible than either Locke's or Hume's view. For Locke, a mind is a mental substance which is something like a material substance:

The one being supposed to be (without knowing what it is) the

[19] Ibid., pp. 72–78, for a definition of 'theoretical term.'
[20] Ibid., pp. 84–100 for a discussion and defense of theoretico-reporting terms.

substratum to those simple ideas we have from without; and
the other supposed (with a like ignorance of what it is) to be
the *substratum* to those operations which we experiment in
ourselves within.[21]

That is, minds are pure theoretical entities postulated to "support"
mental activities. If, however, Locke is right about mental substance
and Berkeley is right about the inadmissibility of material substance, then it seems we should conclude with Hume, and with
those words Berkeley put into the mouth of Hylas against his
defender Philonous:

> it should follow that you are only a system of floating ideas
> without any substance to support them. Words are not to be
> used without meaning. And, as there is no more meaning in
> *spiritual* substance than in material substance, the one is to be
> exploded as well as the other (*Dialogues* III 4).

But Philonous' answer stresses the important differences between
the two kinds of substance:

> I know or am conscious of my own being, as that I *myself* am
> not my ideas, but somewhat else, a thinking, active principle
> that perceives, knows, wills, and operates about ideas... But
> I am not in like manner conscious either of the existence or
> essence of matter (*Dialogues* III 4).

As Berkeley realizes, someone experiences himself when he is
active, as in willing, just as surely as he senses any idea. Someone's
mind, an active entity, is not, therefore, merely a postulated
theoretical entity, but rather a theoretical entity he is aware of when
he is active. Thus, on this plausible view, Locke is wrong, but not
completely wrong, because someone's mind, unlike his ideas, is
more than what he is aware of. To paraphrase Locke, a mind is a
something I do not know *completely* what. For one thing, as
Berkeley says in a letter to the American Samuel Johnson, "That
the mind is passive as well as active I make no doubt" (*Correspondence* IV 3). Thus, reinforcing what was previously claimed,
we have at best an incomplete and unclear understanding of our
minds.

[21] J. Locke, *An Essay Concerning Human Understanding*, Book II, Chap. 23, sec. 5.

Hume would also be wrong, and on two counts. First I am not, as Hume says, merely:

> a bundle or collection of different perceptions, which succeed each other with an inconceivable rapidity, and are in a perpetual flux and movement.[22]

I am an active being, and no collection of ideas is active. Furthermore, when I am active I am aware of myself, so Hume is also wrong in claiming:

> when I enter most intimately into what I call *myself*, I always stumble on some particular perception or other...[23]

Sometimes I "stumble on" myself which is not a perception. Hume, like Locke, however, may not be completely wrong, for when I introspect it may well be I come across only ideas. What Hume overlooked, however, is that self-awareness comes primarily, if not exclusively, when I am active; it is not some object I find by introspection.

ANOTHER OBJECTION: BERKELEY'S INSTRUMENTAL VIEW OF THEORETICAL TERMS　The second objection is more serious, for it is aimed at the claim that the view of mind stated above is consistent with the rest of Berkeley's philosophy. By construing mind-terms as theoretical terms and by claiming that for Berkeley they are denoting terms, what results is a realistic interpretation of theoretical terms, whereas Berkeley actually maintained an instrumental view of theoretical terms. Consequently, according to this objection, the elaborated construal of Berkeley's position I have offered here may help save him from one inconsistency only by involving him in another.

It must be admitted that there is good reason to claim Berkeley adopts instrumentalism. This is the view that the sentences that formulate the purely theoretical part of science are merely complex linguistic devices used to warrant inferences from certain factual claims expressed in the observation vocabulary, to certain other factual claims also expressed in the observation vocabulary. And, according to instrumentalism, because theoretical terms function

---

[22] D. Hume, *A Treatise of Human Nature*, Book I, Part IV, sec. 6.
[23] Ibid.

merely as integral parts of these nonformal rules of inference, they are, like the terms used to express formal rules of inference, non-denoting "auxiliary marks, which serve as convenient symbolic devices in the transition from one set of experiential statements to another".[24] We have already seen that Berkeley is an instrumental-ist regarding mathematical terms. One reason to think he has the same view about theoretical terms is his comparison of the two:

> And just as geometers for the sake of their art make use of many devices which they themselves cannot describe nor find in the nature of things, even so the mechanician makes use of certain abstract and general terms, imagining in bodies force, action, attraction, solicitation, *etc.* which are of first utility for theories and formulations, as also for computations about motion, even if in the truth of things, and in bodies actually existing, they would be looked for in vain, just like the geo-meters' fictions made by mathematical abstraction (*De Motu* 39).

REPLY: CAUSAL EXPLANATIONS, THEORETICAL TERMS, AND REALISM
There is good reason to think Berkeley an instrumentalist, then, at least for some theoretical terms.[25] But Berkeley would not be an instrumentalist regarding those terms previously called "theore-tico-reporting terms." Berkeley would interpret all pure theoretical terms instrumentally, and so he would agree that they are not denoting terms. This is true of the pure theoretical terms of physics, which are surely not reporting terms. But a reporting term is a denoting term, and so, by definition, some theoretical terms, such as mind-terms, are also denoting terms. There is, therefore, nothing in the view of mind-terms presented here that is inconsist-ent with the rest of Berkeley's philosophy, for he can be an instru-mentalist regarding the pure theoretical terms of science because they do not denote anything we experience, and be a realist regard-ing theoretico-reporting terms because they do denote things we experience.

---

[24] C. Hempel, "The Theoretician's Dilemma" in *Minnesota Studies in the Philosophy of Science*, H. Feigl, M. Scriven, and G. Maxwell, eds., (Minneapolis: University of Minn. Press, 1958), Vol. 2, p. 86.

[25] For more textual evidence of Berkeley's instrumentalism, cf. K. R. Popper, "A Note on Berkeley as Precursor of Mach and Einstein," *Conjecture and Refutations*, 2nd ed. (London: Routledge & Kegan Paul, 1965), pp. 166–74.

We have not done enough yet, however. Although the above account works for such terms as 'myself,' 'mind,' and, 'spirit,' which are clearly reporting terms and therefore can be distinguished from pure theoretical terms, it might be objected that this is not true of 'God,' 'Creator,' and 'author of nature.' These terms are not reporting terms. Thus, if we are to construe them as theoretical terms, it seems we must admit they are pure theoretical terms and not denoting terms, contrary to Berkeley. It is true that no finite perceivers experience what such terms might denote, so it seems we should claim they are pure theoretical terms. Someone might try to resolve this problem by claiming these particular pure theoretical terms are denoting terms on Berkeley's view because the notions that each of us has corresponding to these terms are "obtained by reflecting on [his own] soul, heightening its powers, and removing its imperfection" (*Dialogues* III 4). But, although this may explain how each of us can have a notion of God derived from his notion of his own mind, I do not think it sufficient to show that 'God' is a denoting term because 'mind' is a denoting term.

Fortunately, there is another way to justify the claim that 'God' and all other mind-terms are denoting terms, whether or not they are reporting terms. We can divide theoretical terms in another way, according to the kind of explanatory role they play. As Berkeley puts it when discussing the physical sciences:

It is not, however, in fact the business of physics or mechanics to establish efficient causes, but only the rules of impulsions or attractions, and, in a word, the laws of motions, and from the established laws to assign the solution, not the efficient cause of particular phenomena. . . . The true, efficient and conserving cause of all things by supreme right is called their fount and principle. But the principles of experimental philosophy are properly to be called foundations and springs, not of their existence but of our knowledge of corporeal things, both knowledge by sense and knowledge by experience, foundations on which that knowledge rests and springs from which it flows. . . . These laws of motion are conveniently called principles, since from them are derived both general mechanical theorems and particular explanations of the phenomena. A thing can be said to be explained mechanically then indeed

when it is reduced to those most simple and universal principles, and shown by accurate reasoning to be in agreement
and connection with them (*De Motu* 35–37).

One explanatory role, the role of the pure theoretical terms of the
physical sciences, is to warrant the derivation of inferential
relationships, both deductive and inductive, among observable
facts.[26] This is an important kind of explanation because it allows
us to make inferences beyond our present observations and thereby
attain the knowledge needed to guide the course of our lives. For
this explanatory role, Berkeley's instrumentalist or "inference
ticket" construal of theoretical terms is plausible. But it is not
plausible for the other role, the role Berkeley assigns to mind-terms.
    The second explanatory role described by Berkeley is that of
explaining the causation, or production, of the various observable
phenomena. It is clear why Berkeley thinks that the physical
sciences cannot deal with these causes. The subject matter of
science is observable phenomena. These are nothing but ideas, and
no ideas, being inert, can cause anything. Only active entities, such
as minds, can be causes and, consequently, the second kind of
explanation requires mind-terms, and, clearly, denoting terms,
because the terms used to explain the production of ideas must
denote active entities. They cannot, therefore, be merely nondenoting parts of inference tickets. Consequently, any theoretical
term, whether pure or not, is a denoting term, if its explanatory role
is the explanation of the production of ideas, rather than the
establishment of inferential relations among ideas.

Preliminary Conclusion about the First Objection

We can conclude that it is plausible for a Berkeleyan to distinguish among theoretical terms in two different ways. First, there is
the distinction between those that are also reporting terms, and
those that are not. Second, there are those whose explanatory
function is to explain in terms of causes, and those whose function
is, primarily at least, to warrant inferences. We can also conclude
that it is plausible for a Berkeleyan to claim that all theoretical
terms that are reporting terms and all those that explain by means
of causes, are denoting terms that succeed in denoting or standing

[26] Cf. Hempel, p. 87, and the discussion of scientific instrumentalism in Chapters 4 and 8.

for things, whenever they succeed in explaining. Similarly, it is also plausible that theoretical concepts or notions that have causal explanatory roles in thinking stand (in thought) for things they do not picture, whenever they succeed in explaining. With this established, there remains only one question for this Berkeleyan reply to the first major objection, namely, whether it is also plausible that no nonreporting theoretical terms whose primary explanatory function is to warrant inferences, are denoting terms. In other words, the crucial remaining issue is whether it is reasonable to construe all the pure theoretical terms of science instrumentally, that is, whether it is reasonable to reject scientific realism for scientific instrumentalism.

To decide about this last issue requires a detailed examination of what I have found to be perhaps the strongest argument for scientific instrumentalism, namely, the argument from the theoretician's dilemma. Because this involves an extensive investigation of many complex issues, I shall set it aside for separate treatment in Chapter 4. Here we can say only this: If the argument shows scientific instrumentalism to be plausible, then the first objection will be refuted, because we will have found a plausible Berkeleyan theory of mind-terms, notions, and minds that fits with and supplements what little Berkeley gave us.

Second Objection: Cherries and Groups of Sensa

Let us turn to the second of the four major objections to Berkeley's theory which were stated previously. It concerns the relationship between physical objects and ideas. It may be that I have given a plausible Berkeleyan theory of mind, but one current view is that his theory of physical objects is implausible, and so, taken as a whole, Berkeley's philosophy is implausible. I shall reply to this objection by showing that a Berkeleyan can avoid it by adopting a certain view of physical objects, and that, contrary to how it may seem at first, this theory and the theory of mind I have stated above can be plausibly conjoined.

The objection to Berkeley's theory of physical objects is from G. Warnock. According to Berkeley, physical objects are collections or bundles of ideas. Warnock says that we should construe this bundle theory as follows:

Any statement about any material thing is really (can be analyzed into) an indefinitely large set of statements about what it seems, or in suitable conditions would seem as if the speaker and other people *and God* were hearing, seeing, feeling, tasting, smelling—that is into an indefinitely large set of statements describing the ideas of which any material object is a collection.[27]

Thus Warnock interprets Berkeley to be an analytic phenomenalist much like the early A. J. Ayer. But Warnock claims that physical-object statements cannot be analyzed in this way, and "this is fatal to Berkeley's case".[28] We can agree that if Berkeley is most plausibly construed as an analytic phenomenalist, then his theory of physical objects is indeed implausible. This is because, as the later Ayer and Chisholm have shown, there is good reason to reject phenomenalistic analyses of physical-object statements.[29] Let us see why this is so.

ANALYTICAL PHENOMENALISM AND LOGICAL CONSTRUCTS

Ayer states a thesis which he calls "phenomenalism," but I have called it analytical phenomenalism. Unlike other species of phenomenalism, including theoretical phenomenalism, his thesis requires the analysis of physical-object statements by sensum statements. As Ayer puts it, the thesis is:

Every empirical statement about a physical object, whether it seems to refer to a scientific entity or to an object of the more familiar kind that we normally claim to perceive, is reducible to a statement, or set of statements, which refer exclusively to sense-data. And what is meant by saying that a statement S is 'reducible' to a class of statements K is first that the members of K are on a lower epistemological level than S, that is, that they refer to 'harder' data, and secondly that S and K are logically equivalent.[30]

[27] G. J. Warnock, *Berkeley* (Baltimore: Penguin Books, 1953), p. 180.
[28] Ibid.
[29] See A. J. Ayer, *The Problem of Knowledge*, pp. 118–129; and R. M. Chisholm, *Perceiving*, pp. 189–97.
[30] Ayer, pp. 118–19.

In short, the thesis as stated by Ayer is that physical objects are logical constructions out of sensa, because all statements about physical objects are reductively analyzable into statements that refer only to sensa. This is an acceptable statement of the thesis, but one thing should be noted. Ayer's statement of the thesis implies that sentences about physical objects are logically equivalent to sentences that refer exclusively to sensa. This way of stating analytical phenomenalism implies that it is not purely linguistic, for it is not enough to show that each statement using physical-object terms is found to be logically equivalent to some statement using only the sensum terminology. It must also be shown that each of these particular sensum sentences refers exclusively to sensa. But the most that can be justified by the linguistic claim that two sentences, A and B, are logically equivalent is that A and B refer to the same entities of some sort or other. It is true that a Berkeleyan who wishes to use an analysis of physical-object statements by sensum sentences to explicate his ontological thesis about the relationship between physical objects and sensa, would wish to make the additional claim that the common referents are exclusively sensa or groups of sensa. Nevertheless, it should be noted that this is neither trivially true, nor entailed by the purely linguistic claim.[31]

We need not worry about this problem, however, because the objections which refute analytical phenomenalism do not depend on any claims about reference. They depend only on showing that there are sentences containing physical-object terms that are not logically equivalent to any sensum sentences. Although neither Ayer nor Chisholm state their objections independently of claims about reference, such claims play no part in the arguments to establish the objections. It is clear that one can attack an equivalence claim by attacking either or both of the logical entailments of which it consists. Ayer attacks both entailments, but Chisholm attacks only one, namely, that each physical-object statement entails some sensum statement.[32] It is interesting to note that this is not the entailment essential to one who wishes to refute the epistemological skeptic by showing that sensum statements are

---

[31] This is discussed in more detail in my *Metaphysics, Reference, and Language* (New Haven: Yale University Press, 1966), pp. 200–10. See also *Materialism and Sensations*, pp. 132–43, for a similar discussion about analytical behaviorism.
[32] See Ayer, pp. 124–29; and Chisholm, pp. 193–94.

certain and physical-object statements are justified because derivable from them.

Both Ayer and Chisholm seem to make stronger claims than they need. Chisholm implies that no ordinary physical object statements entail "statements referring solely to appearances," and Ayer doubts that "the occurrence of a given series of sense-data can ever be a sufficient condition for the existence of a physical object."[33] But to refute analytical phenomenalism we need only justify that *some* physical object statement either does not entail or is not entailed by any purely sensum statement. We can, however, easily show that there are cases in which both sorts of entailments fail.

REJECTION OF A SUBJUNCTIVE ANALYSIS   Although Chisholm considers only one of the entailments, we can use his general strategy, but not his specific tactics, to find counterexamples to both entailment claims. Since the most likely and most suggested candidates for the analysis of physical object statements are subjunctive conditionals, I shall use such a conditional as the crucial example. Let us take a relatively simple sentence as the analysandum:

(1) This table is red.

In selecting an analysans, let us be as generous as possible and not limit the sensum terminology merely to words expressing "simple ideas." Thus we can allow ourselves to talk not merely of red, loud, sweet, smooth sensa, but also of table-like sensa. Furthermore, let us allow ourselves to use the seeming or appearing terminology in any case where it is clear it does not entail the existence or nonexistence of a physical object. Thus we can use expressions such as 'There appears to me to be a red table here,' and also, following our stipulation in Chapter 2, 'The table here appears red to me.' We can make one more concession already suggested in allowing the preceding use of 'me.' Since Berkeley and Descartes can use 'perceiver' so that, in spite of Strawson's claims about persons, it entails nothing about objects with physical properties, we can replace 'me' with terms such as 'a perceiver' and use them

[33] Chisholm, p. 190; and Ayer, p. 127.

in the analysans.[34]

There is one point left to make before proposing an analysans. As the objections by both Ayer and Chisholm show, the crucial objection to any phenomenalistic analysis centers on perceptual relativity, that is, on how perceptual experiences of unchanging objects vary with changes in conditions and perceivers. Thus it is important to try to include in the analysans a specification in sensum terms of the conditions in which the perception occurs. Keeping all this in mind, I shall propose the following sentence as a close approximation of the most plausible phenomenalistic subjunctive analysis of sentence (1). If it fails, then I shall claim there is reason to reject a subjunctive analysis of (1). It is:

(2) If a perceiver, who would appear to most perceivers to be normal and to be in normal conditions, were to have a table-like sensum here and now, then this sensum would be a red-table-like sensum.

Chisholm's particular tactics are to show that the analysis of some physical-object statement, P, in terms of a conditional appearance statement, R, fails, because there is a statement, S, consistent with P, which with P entails not-R. It follows from this that P does not entail R. However, the particular sentence Chisholm picks as S only allows us to infer the weaker claim that P and S do not entail R.[35] Nevertheless this is enough for Chisholm's purposes, because it follows from this also that P does not entail R. Let us, then, interpret the general Chisholmian strategy for showing that one sentence does not entail another to be to find a third sentence which, when conjoined with the first, *clearly* does not entail the second. Of course, we can use this strategy to attempt to show (2) does not entail (1), as well as to show (1) does not entail (2).

To show (1) does not entail (2), we can use an example of a person who is daydreaming:

(3) Jones and the conditions here and now appear to be normal to most perceivers, but Jones, who is mentally picturing

[34] See P. F. Strawson, *Individuals* (London: Methuen, 1959), Chap. 3. I have argued against Strawson's objection to Cartesian egos as subjects of experiences in "Strawson's 'Person'," *Theoria* 30 (1964): 149–55.

[35] Chisholm, p. 193.

a brown table here and now, does not notice this red table
before him.

Here (1) and (3) do not entail (2), unless they are inconsistent, but
they are clearly consistent. It might be thought that (1) and (3)
entail the denial of (2), but they do not, because (3) is compatible
with Jones also having a red-table-like sensum here and now. We
could achieve an entailment, however, by amending (3) to state
that Jones has *only* a brown-table-like sensum. Then Jones'
situation would be an instantiation of the antecedent of (2), but
a denial of its consequent. We can similarly show that (2) does not
entail (1) by using:

(4) There is a painting of a red table here and now which is
so realistic that everyone who merely looks at it believes
he is seeing a red table.

Here (2) and (4) clearly do not entail (1), and so (2) does not entail
(1). The analysis of (1) by (2) fails. Furthermore, I can find no way
to amend either the antecedent or consequent of (2) to avoid
counterexamples of the preceding form. There is, then, reason to
reject the analysis of (1) in terms of conditional sensum sentences.

REJECTION OF A PROBABILISTIC ANALYSIS   Although neither (1) nor
(2) entails the other, it does seem that when there is a red table
somewhere, perceivers who are there *generally* sense a red-table-like
sensum if they sense a table-like sensum. It might be tempting,
then, to consider that some probability statement about sensa is
the analysans of a physical object statement. This, indeed, seems
to be the claim of C. I. Lewis, the only one I know who has considered this possibility. He says:

What the statement of a perceptually learned objective fact,
such as "This (seen object) is red" or "This is square" means—
in one specific and specified sense of the word 'meaning'—
is explicable by some set of statements representing predictions
of possible experience and having the form, "If *S* be given
and act *A* initiated, then in all probability *E* will follow," where
'*S*,' '*A*,' and '*E*' each refers to some recognizable item of
direct experience, and the colloquial phrase "in all probability"

is intended to suggest a probability approximating to certainty.[36]

Although there is some problem about how to interpret Lewis' probability statement I shall construe it as:

(5) The probability of E, given S and A, that is $P(E, S \cdot A)$, is almost 1.[37]

Here 'E,' 'S,' and 'A' are sentences about particular experiences and actions. Then, according to Lewis, any physical object sentence, 'P,' means the same as some sentence of the form of (5).

We can examine Lewis' particular example by letting L = A sheet of real paper lies before me; S = A visual sheet-of-paper presentation is given; A = I act to pick up and tear; and E = A torn paper presentation follows. Although Lewis does not state the following mutual entailment, it follows from his other claims:[38]

$$\Box[L \equiv P(E, S\cdot A) \text{ is almost } 1].$$

However, we still have a problem with each entailment. It is easy to see that:

$$\Box[P(E, S\cdot A) \text{ is almost } 1 \supset L]$$

is false. Its probability statement does not entail that anything exists, and so does not entail L. Furthermore the claim that the antecedent probability of L is almost 1 does not entail L. And, on some interpretations of probability not even $P(L) = 1$ entails L.

The converse entailment is more difficult to refute, but it can be done using the same strategy we just used to refute the subjunctive analysis.[39] If we assume, as is reasonable, the *possibility* of a Cartesian-like malicious demon, we can also assume:

(1) $\Diamond[L \cdot P(\overline{E}, S\cdot A) > .5]$

That is, it is possible that there is a sheet of paper before me, and

[36] C. I. Lewis, "Professor Chisholm and Empiricism", *Journal of Philosophy* XLV (1948): 517.

[37] See Lewis, "The Philosopher Replies," in *The Philosophy of C. I. Lewis*, P. A. Schilpp, ed., (La Salle, Ill.: Open Court, 1968), p. 657.

[38] See Lewis, *An Analysis of Knowledge and Valuation* (La Salle, Ill.: Open Court, 1946), p. 248. His Statement (1) expresses one entailment, and the other follows from his (6) and $\Box$ [P(B, A) is high $\supset$ ~P($\overline{\text{B}}$, A) is high].

[39] Cf. Chisholm, "Lewis' Ethics of Belief," in *The Philosophy of C. I. Lewis*, pp. 236–38.

it is probable no torn paper presentation will occur, given a sheet-of-paper presentation and I act to pick up and tear. But because, by the probability calculus, $\Box[P(B, A) + P(\overline{B}, A) = 1]$ we also have:

(2) $\Box[P(\overline{E}, S \cdot A) > .5 \supset \sim P(E, S \cdot A)$ is almost 1]

Therefore

(3) $\Box[L \cdot P(\overline{E}, S \cdot A) > .5 \supset \sim P(E, S \cdot A)$ is almost 1]

Therefore

(4) $\sim \Box[L \supset P(E, S \cdot A)$ is almost 1]

Although we have seen that the particular analysis taken from Lewis fails, this obviously does not show that no analysis using probability sentences succeeds. However, I find no way to avoid the two kinds of objections we found fatal to Lewis' analysis. Certainly both a conjunction and a disjunction of probability statements face the same problems, and I see no more hopeful way to proceed. I conclude, then, that we have examined a fair sample of the two most plausible kinds of phenomenalistic analysis of physical object sentences, namely, a subjunctive analysis and a probabilistic analysis, and both fail. Therefore it is reasonable to conclude on inductive grounds that analytic phenomenalism which requires some such analyses is false. But, of course, this does not affect a theoretical phenomenalist who agrees that the relationships among physical-object sentences and sensum sentences are logically contingent. Perhaps he will fare better than the analytic phenomenalist in replying to the second major objection to Berkeleyan phenomenalism.

INTRODUCTION TO THEORETICAL PHENOMENALISM

Although we have seen that Warnock's objection to Berkeley's bundle theory is sound if the theory is construed as implying the analysis of physical-object statements, there is another and, I shall try to show, more plausible way to construe the claim that physical objects are collections of sensory ideas, that is, sensa that are constituents of perceptual experiences (perceptual sensa). It is hinted by Ayer just after his rejection of analytic phenomenalism, when he says that "in referring as we do to physical objects we are

elaborating a theory with respect to the evidence of our senses."[40]
That is, physical objects are theoretical constructions rather than
logical constructions out of our sensa. On this view, the relationship
between any physical-object statement and any sensum statement
is logically contingent, and is analogous to the contingent relationship between theoretical statements and observation statements,
mediated by correspondence rules. Furthermore, when the term
'cherry' denotes a cherry, it also always denotes a particular
collection of individual sensa that is identical with the denoted
cherry. For example, such a collection might contain sensa "of
softness, moisture, redness, tartness" (*Dialogues* III 19). Thus,
'What I see is a cherry' might sometimes refer to the same things as
certain sensum statements, perhaps 'What I sense are sensa of
redness and tartness,' but no sensum statement would have the
same meaning as the physical-object sentence. In short, on this
reconstruction of Berkeley as a theoretical phenomenalist, 'cherry'
is a theoretical term that refers to sensa whenever it refers to
anything, and cherries are theoretical entities identical with groups
of sensa.

THREE NEW OBJECTIONS TO PHYSICAL OBJECTS AS THEORETICAL   Three
objections immediately arise to construing 'cherry' as a theoretical
term for Berkeley and combining this view with the preceding
Berkeleyan theory of mind. First, in the previous discussion,
physical-object terms such as 'apple' and 'cherry' were said to be
observation terms, but here they are said to be theoretical terms.
How can these two claims be reconciled? Second, construing
'cherry' as both a theoretical and a referring term is inconsistent
with the preceding Berkeleyan theory of mind, because 'cherry'
would have an inferential rather than a causal explanatory role
and consequently would be merely a nonreferring inferring device.
Third, even if 'cherry' should be a referring term, if it also is a
theoretical term, then, like 'electron' and 'neutrino,' it would refer
to unobservable entities rather than ideas. Berkeley cannot accept
this.

In answer to the first objection, it must be admitted that I have
previously called 'cherry' an observation term and that I said that
mind-terms are theoretical terms because they are explanatory

[40] Ayer, p. 132.

terms that are neither observation terms nor definable by observation terms. But I only claimed this reason was a sufficient condition for being a theoretical term. It is not a necessary condition, and thus it is at least possible that some observation terms are also theoretical. Indeed, it is even plausible. If we agree that for Berkeley all terms that refer to observable entities, whether to individual perceptual sensa or to collections of them, are observation terms, then physical-object terms, such as 'cherry,' are observation terms.[41] They are not, however, what we can call "pure" observation terms. Because of this, as we shall see, they can also be theoretical terms. On some empiricist theories of meaning, pure observation terms would be those whose meaning can be completely determined by observation. A Berkeleyan could interpret this to require that such terms are truly applicable to what, as Berkeley says, can be "perfectly known" by an individual (finite) perceiver. On the basis of this, we can construct the following Berkeleyan definition:

'O' is a pure observation term $=_{df}$. 'O' is an observation term that is truly applicable to what can be perfectly known by a (finite) perceiver.[42]

According to Berkeley, individual sensa "are perfectly known, there being nothing in them which is not perceived" (*Principles* 87). Consequently they have only phenomenal properties. Furthermore, for a Berkeleyan, only individual sensa and other ideas are perfectly known. We have already seen that no mind would be perfectly known, not even by the perceiver whose mind it is. And, although there is no more to a physical object than the sensa that compose it and each of these sensa is perfectly knowable by someone, a physical object is usually more than any set of sensa experienced by any one (finite) perceiver. Physical objects, then, are not perfectly known by any one (finite) perceiver. Consequently, given the preceding definition, only terms that are truly applicable to

---

[41] A Berkeleyan could devise a more precise definition of 'observation term' by using the one in *Materialism and Sensations*, p. 69, and omitting the requirement that what is observable be physical.

[42] This definition differs considerably from the one given in *Materialism and Sensations*, p. 102. A *theoretical* phenomenalist could, however, use that definition instead of the present one.

individual sensa are pure observation terms. But no physical-object terms are truly applicable to individual sensa. Therefore, 'cherry' is an observation term but not a pure observation term.

The preceding conclusion helps to show how a Berkeleyan can also construe 'cherry' as a theoretical term, because it is plausible for him to construe a term to be theoretical if it is not a pure observation term and it functions to warrant inferences among pure observation sentences. Hume makes a relevant point here in saying,

> There is scarce a moment of my life, wherein ... I have not occasion to suppose the continu'd existence of objects, in order to connect their past and present appearances, and give them such an union with each other, as I have found by experience to be suitable to their particular natures and circumstances.[43]

We can say, then, that the term 'cherry' is used as a part of inferring devices to warrant inferences from sentences about past sensations to others about future ones. It functions like a theoretical term related to pure observation terms by correspondence rules. Physical-object terms are, on this Berkeleyan reconstruction, both observation terms and theoretical terms.

But the second objection arises immediately at this point, for I have construed 'cherry' as an inference-warranting term. I did not, however, claim that it is *merely* an inferring device. And indeed it is not. It is an observation term and thus one species of a reporting term because it is used to refer to what is experienced, that is, sensa. In this way 'cherry' would, for Berkeley, differ from 'electron,' which is also an inferring device, but not a referring term, because it is not used to refer to anything experienced. The term 'cherry' also differs from mind-terms. Although both 'cherry' and 'mind' are theoretico-reporting terms, only 'cherry' "pictorially" represents what it refers to, because only 'cherry' refers to sensa, and only sensa can be pictured by ideas. Thus although 'cherry' is a theoretical term, it does not correspond to a notion, but rather to ideas we have that we use to represent cherries.

This answer to the second objection is sound, however, only if

---

[43] Hume, Book I, Part IV, sec. II.

'cherry' does indeed refer to sensa. But, according to the third objection, if physical-object terms are inferential theoretical terms and they refer to something, then, as with 'electron', what they refer to is unobservable. As I tried to show elsewhere, there are many terms whose referents are not easy to uncover.[44] If, however, an analogy with scientific theoretical terms is used to provide reason for this claim about the referents of physical-object observation terms, then a counter analogy with reporting phenomenal terms can be used to vitiate the strength of that reason. Furthermore, there are scientific theoretical terms that have an inferential explanatory role, but which surely seem to refer to what is observable. There are not only terms such as 'conglomeration of molecules composed of two hydrogen ions and one oxygen ion,' but also others of a quite different sort such as '100 degrees centigrade.'[45] Thus I find nothing implausible in supposing that terms such as 'cherry' are theoretical terms with an inferential explanatory role, that they are referring terms, and that they refer to what is observable, which for Berkeley is perceptual sensa.

Preliminary Conclusion about the First and Second Objections

The preceding discussion provides, I believe, considerable plausibility to the replies a Berkeleyan can give to the first and second of the four major objections to his theory. In each case, the reply depends in part on interpreting mind-terms and physical-object terms as referring theoretical terms, but interpreting other, scientific theoretical terms as nonreferring, inferring instruments. This initial plausibility, however, is somewhat tenuous, and surely provisional, because there are important problems for the reply to each objection that we have not yet considered. The first is that, as previously indicated, throughout the preceding discussion of Berkeleyan theories of minds and physical objects as theoretical entities, I have relied on the thesis of scientific instrumentalism to help avoid objections and to argue for the plausibility of a Berkeleyan position. Thus, if instrumentalism is implausible, then my efforts have been of little value. It is, then, incumbent upon a Berkeleyan phenomenalist, indeed, all phenomenalists, to argue

---

[44] See especially my *Metaphysics, Reference, and Language.*
[45] For a discussion of 'temperature' as both a theoretical term and an observation term, see *Materialism and Sensations*, pp. 103–05.

for the plausibility of scientific instrumentalism. If no such attempt succeeds, then there would be a serious objection to all versions of phenomenalism. Consequently, the next task before us will be to examine the strongest available argument for instrumentalism. We shall do this in the next chapter, where we will consider an argument based on the theoretician's dilemma which uses the consequences of Craig's theorem and the techniques of Ramsey-sentences to show that there is no need for theoretical entities. If this argument succeeds, the phenomenalistic position will be considerably strengthened. Not only would this justify a final Berkeleyan theory of mind, it would also bolster considerably the grounds for rejecting the second objection, and provide the crux of the reply to the fourth objection that Berkeley's theory is unscientific.

A second problem we have not yet considered is that the viability of the reply to the second objection depends crucially on theoretical phenomenalism, which, according to Sellars, is deficient. Theoretical phenomenalism entails that relationships among sensum statements and physical-object statements are analogous to those between the theoretical sentences of science and observation sentences. Thus, as in our preceding simple model of a theory, it would seem that we should be able to segregate four sets of sentences: physical-object sentences, correspondence rules relating physical-object terms and sensum terms, sensum generalizations, and singular sensum sentences. It seems that a theoretical phenomenalist should at least give some examples of how this segregation is to be achieved in order to justify using the analogy. Sellars' objection is that this analogy breaks down for significant reasons, and thus theoretical phenomenalism fails as did analytical phenomenalism. We must examine this crucial objection, then, to see whether it can be rebutted in such a way that plausible examples of a theoretical-like relationship between physical-object sentences and sensum sentences can be constructed.

Such a reply to Sellars' objection is obviously important for justifying the rejection of the second objection, but more is needed. As I briefly argued above, a Berkeleyan must also justify the claim that whenever physical-object terms refer, they refer to sensa. And even more is needed. He must at least indicate those conditions in which a term such as 'cherry' refers to sensa, and give some way of determining which sensa it refers to when it refers. The latter problem is essential to unpacking what it is for a physical object to be identical with a bundle of sensa. Without some understanding of the relationship between a particular cherry and the individual sensa which constitute it, the bundle theory remains too imprecise to be acceptable. Consequently, examples are needed of the sorts of correspondence rules that relate "theory" to "observation" in ways that clarify the theoretical interpretation of the bundle theory. It will be the task of Chapter 5 to see whether this can be done in a way that avoids Sellars' objection. If this is done successfully, then we shall also be able to reply to the third objection by showing, with the use of other correspondence rules, how it is that different people perceive the same cherry by sensing different sensa that are constituents of the group of sensa that is identical with the cherry. If all this is achieved and scientific instrumentalism is shown to be plausible, then the four important objections to Berkeleyan theoretical phenomenalism will be rebutted, and it will be shown to be a strong contender for the most plausible theory of perception and the external world.

4   The Theoretician's Dilemma and Scientific Instrumentalism

Science has had amazing success in explaining a wide variety of observable phenomena. In the course of forming these explanations it has also predicted occurrences it is very unlikely that men would ever have looked for if it had not been for the scientific theories that provide the explanations. And many people think it is no less amazing that these explanations and predictions of what is observable are achieved by the assumption of a whole realm of minute and often ephemeral entities forever hidden from view. Others, such as a Berkeleyan, not so much amazed as puzzled, find the idea of explaining what is known through observation by an unknown array of entities to be almost unintelligible. This division of opinion about the theoretical entities of science exists not only among philosophers but also among scientists. In general the division is equivalent to that between scientific realists who affirm the existence of entities supposedly denoted by the terms scientists use in their explanations and predictions, and scientific instrumentalists who claim that because no entities need be assumed for the kind of explanation science requires, the purely theoretical terms of science are nonreferring symbolic devices that function solely as integral parts of inference rules to warrant inferences among observation statements.

This debate between scientific realists and instrumentalists is about the reality of theoretical entities and is not, therefore, to be decided on purely linguistic or logical grounds. And, because empirical evidence, whether scientific or not, will also not decide it, it appears to be a metaphysical issue. Yet it has often been mistaken for a linguistic issue. One reason for this is that it is often stated, as I have stated it above, as a debate about whether theoretical terms are referring terms. This is enough to show that linguistic considerations are relevant to the issue, but, as we shall see, they alone are not sufficient to settle it. Another reason is that many of the primary attempts to establish instrumentalism have essentially involved purely linguistic and logical claims about theoretical terms. The purpose of this chapter is to examine in detail and defend against a wide variety of attacks what I find to be the strongest argument for instrumentalism. This is the argument taken from what is called the "theoretician's dilemma." Later, in Chapter 8, I shall examine other attempts to justify instrumentalism. Most of these will be taken from current situations in specific sciences, such as quantum theory. Because of their dependence on the present state of particular sciences, these arguments are less forceful than the one we shall examine here, even assuming they are equally successful. Unlike these others, the argument from the theoretician's dilemma is independent of future changes in sciences. I shall argue in Chapter 8, however, that except for the problems raised by quantum physics, none of these other objections cause trouble for a scientific realist. On the other hand, quantum physics and the theoretician's dilemma raise serious doubts about a realistic interpretation of science. They provide, therefore, at least some reason to accept instrumentalism, the doctrine that is so crucial to Berkeley and, indeed, any phenomenalist.

THE THEORETICIAN'S DILEMMA AND INSTRUMENTALISM

The argument I shall examine is based on what has been called "the theoretician's dilemma," which by itself is an argument to establish that theoretical terms are unnecessary for the purposes of science. The main argument goes on to state that this fact about the language of science can be used to justify a denial of the existence of the theoretical entities of science. For our first approximation of the dilemma we can do no better than turn to Hempel's statement in his classical discussion of the dilemma. He first states the crucial first horn of the dilemma:

> . . . if the terms and the general principles of a scientific theory serve their purpose, i.e., if they establish definite connections among observable phenomena, then they can be dispensed with since any chain of laws and interpretative statements establishing such a connection should then be replaceable by a law which directly links observational antecedents to observational consequents.[1]

[1] C. Hempel, "The Theoretician's Dilemma," in H. Feigl, *et al.*, eds., *Minnesota Studies in the Philosophy of Science*, 4 vols. (Minneapolis: University of Minnesota Press, 1956–1970), vol. 2 (1958), p. 49.

He then finishes the dilemma as follows:

> ...if they don't serve their purpose they are surely unneces-
> sary. But given any theory, its terms and principles either serve
> their purpose or they don't. Hence, the terms and principles of
> any theory are unnecessary.[2]

In order to see clearly which premises need to be defended or
amended I shall begin by laying out the argument in the following
form:

(1) Theoretical terms either serve their purpose or they do
    not serve it.
(2) If they do not serve it, then they are unnecessary.
(3) If they serve their purpose, then they establish relation-
    ships among observable phenomena.
(4) If they establish such relationships, then the same
    relationships are established without theoretical terms.
(5) If these same relationships are so established, then
    theoretical terms are unnecessary.

Therefore

(6) Theoretical terms are unnecessary.

Thus far the argument has remained on the linguistic level. To move
from language to ontology we can use a version of Occam's Razor
that applies specifically to the purported referents of unnecessary
theoretical terms. In this regard, it differs from the general version,
P2a, we used in the central argument of the book. According to the
present version, we should not multiply the postulated theoretical
entities of science beyond necessity in the sense expressed by the
conjunction of the following two premises:

(7) If theoretical terms of science are unnecessary, then
    there is no reason to postulate the existence of any
    referents of theoretical terms, that is, any theoretical
    entities.
(8) If there is no reason to postulate the existence of any
    theoretical entities, then it is unreasonable to believe that

---

[2] Ibid., pp. 49–50.

there are any theoretical entities, that is, it is reasonable
to accept scientific instrumentalism.

And the conjunction of (6), (7), and (8) yields the desired conclusion:

(9) It is reasonable to accept scientific instrumentalism.

We can certainly grant premises (1) and (2) in this argument.
Premise (3) is also acceptable, because one necessary condition for a
theoretical term serving its basic explanatory purpose is that it
establishes some relationships among observable phenomena.
Indeed, as we proceed we shall make a more precise characterization of these relationships. This will be required by our examination
of other premises in the argument, but it will not affect the reasonableness of accepting (3). I shall also assume that (8) is acceptable.
Incidentally, unlike principle P2, there may be reasons to doubt
generalizing (8) to apply to all entities, as there would be, for
example, if William James' pragmatic justification of belief in God
were acceptable, However, (8) is limited to postulated scientific
theoretical entities, such as the ether, effluvium, or phlogiston,
where its application seems fully justified. As it stands, premise (7)
also seems fully justified because it provides the rest of the relevant
formulation of Occam's razor. Although this is true, we shall find
that, like (3), (7) must be amended as a result of our examination of
the argument. For (7), however, we shall find that the amended
version will be susceptible to certain important objections. We
must, then, withhold judgment about (7).

Premise 4 and the Transcription of Theories

It is clear that premises (4) and (5) are crucial and, at least as
first formulated, are far from clearly acceptable. One way people
have tried to establish (4) is by attempting to provide definitions in
use of theoretical terms. If successful, then it would be established
that theoretical terms are unnecessary because they could be
replaced by observation terms in all their occurrences. This attempt
has failed and now it is generally agreed that theoretical terms are
related to observation terms only contingently by means of cor-

respondence rules.[3] There are two other attempts to establish (4) which have more chance of success. Both are attempts to show how any theory can be restated or transcribed so that it no longer contains theoretical terms. But, it is claimed, all and only the relationships among observation statements that are established by the original theory are also established by the transcribed theory. The first method of transcription, called "Craigian transcriptionism," applies Craig's theorem to theories as axiomatized systems, and shows how all and only those axioms and theorems of the original theory that contain only observation terms or terms either explicitly or partially definable by observation terms (I shall call these "empirical" terms) can be retained. The second method, called "Ramseyan transcriptionism," relies on the use of Ramsey-sentences to replace all theoretical predicates with variables.[4]

To see how these methods of transcription apply to our argument, let us make our initial amendment by replacing (4) with:

> (4a) If theoretical terms in a theory, T, establish relationships among empirical statements, then either the Craigian transcription of T or the Ramseyan transcription of T establishes the same relationships.

This requires a corresponding change in (5) to:

> (5a) If such transcriptions will establish these same relationships, then theoretical terms are unnecessary.

The fourth premise will be established if either a Craigian or a Ramseyan transcription succeeds. The major task of this chapter is to examine each method separately in order to evaluate this fourth premise.

Craigian Transcriptionism and Deductive Systematization

Given one standard view of the relationship between theoretical terms and observation terms, we can see how easy it is to transcribe

---

[3] For an opposing view, see D. Lewis "How to Define Theoretical Terms," *Journal of Philosophy*, 67 (1970): 427–46. However, because his method of defining a theoretical term, T, of the theory, S, implies that T names a component of the unique realization of S, it is not a sort of definition an instrumentalist can use.

[4] The term 'transcriptionism' is used by C. Hooker, "Craigian Transcriptionism," *American Philosophical Quarterly*, 5 (1968): 152–63.

theories. The system, *S1*, is a simplified view of this standard relationship:

$$S1 \quad P1 \quad (x)(T_1x \supset T_2x)$$
$$C1 \quad (x)(O_1x \supset T_1x)$$
$$C2 \quad (x)(T_2x \supset O_2x)$$

Here we have one theoretical postulate, P1, and two correspondence rules from which we can deduce the empirical generalization:

$$G1 \quad (x)(O_1x \supset O_2x)$$

Furthermore, exactly those relationships among empirical statements which can be deduced using *S1* can also be deduced using *T–S1*, the transcribed version of *S1*, with *G1* as its one postulate. That is, let us say, *T–S1* achieves the same deductive systematization as *S1*, where a system, *S*, achieves some *deductive systematization* just in case *S* and some empirical premise, E_1, yield an empirical statement, E_2, not entailed by E_1 alone. In other words, $E_1 \supset E_2$ is a theorem of *S*, and E_1 does not entail E_2. Thus, the theoretical terms of *S1* are unnecessary to achieve the same deductive systematization that *S1* achieves. But, although we can easily transcribe systems of the form of *S1*, other theories that have different relationships to observation statements may not be so easily transcribable. What would be helpful would be a general procedure to transcribe theories no matter how related to observation statements. This is what Craig's theorem shows can be done.

Craig's theorem shows that, given certain preconditions, for any axiomatic system with two sets of terms that are clearly demarcated, there is a way to retain exactly the assertions of the system that contain only the terms of one of the sets, and to retain proofs for exactly those assertions that are theorems of the system and contain only the terms of that same set. Thus Craig's theorem has much wider application than the elimination of theoretical terms, but I shall discuss it only in that narrower context. We are, then, interested in whether Craig has shown a way to produce exactly those axioms and theorems of any scientific theory that are empirical statements, that is, contain only what I have called empirical terms, and a way to reproduce each empirical axiom as an axiom and each empirical theorem as a theorem. The following is a brief summary of the method that Craig's theorem justifies.[5] First, there are the preconditions that a system, S, must meet if the Craigian procedure is to be applied successfully to it. There are those that apply to any axiom system. The two most important for our purposes are:

> C1 The nonlogical axioms of S are specified and are distinct from the logical axioms of the underlying logic, L, of S;
> C2 The logical axioms of L are specified and are distinct from the nonlogical axioms of S.

Of course these two preconditions imply another; that the Craigian procedure is to be applied to a set of sentences only if the set is axiomatized. In addition there are preconditions required for the Craigian procedure in particular. The two most important for our purposes are:

> C3 The theorems of S constitute the sentences which formulate the scientific theory which is to be transcribed, and at least some of them express its subject matter;
> C4 There is an effective criterion for deciding which terms of the theory and its subject matter are theoretical and which are not.

Second, for a system, S, that meets the preconditions, four steps are required to achieve a Craigian transcribed system, C–S:

> (1) Assign to each sequence of symbols in S its unique Gödel number, n;
> (2) Ascertain which empirical statements are theorems of S and which are axioms of S, and include the latter among the axioms of C–S;
> (3) Ascertain which sequence of symbols of S constitute a proof of each empirical theorem of S,
> (4) For each empirical theorem, E, of S form an axiom of C–S by conjoining E with itself the number of times equal to the Gödel number, n, assigned to the sequence of symbols of S which is the proof of E.

---

[5] For more detail, see W. Craig, "On Axiomatizability Within a System," *Journal of Symbolic Logic*, 18 (1953): 30–32; and "Replacement of Auxiliary Expressions," *Philosophical Review*, 55 (1956): 38–55.

Having gone through this procedure, exactly the empirical statements that are axioms of S remain among the axioms of $C-S$, and exactly the empirical statements that are theorems of S, because derivable from the axioms of S, remain to be the theorems of $C-S$. Consequently, S and $C-S$ have the same deductive systematization. This is because S achieves some deductive systematization in just those cases where some sentence of the form $E_i \supset E_j$ is a theorem of S, and E_i does not entail E_j. But for any sentence of that form, just those that are theorems of S are also theorems of $C-S$.

OBJECTIONS TO CRAIG'S METHOD AS APPLIED TO SCIENTIFIC THEORIES

I. SCIENTIFIC THEORIES ARE NOT FORMAL SYSTEMS Have we now justified Premise (4a)? Two sorts of objections remain. There are objections, to be considered later, that the preservation of deductive systematization is not sufficient to show that a Craigian theory established all the relationships established by the untranscribed theory. There are also objections that the Craigian procedure cannot be applied to scientific theories because they do not meet all the preconditions for application of the procedure, and thus there is no transcribed theory to establish any relationships. In particular, three objections have been raised. One is directed at Precondition $C3$, a second concerns $C4$, and a third arises because of the requirement that the theories to be transcribed must be in the form of an axiom system. Beginning with the third, it has been argued that most scientific theories are not axiom systems and, therefore, Craig's method is not applicable to them. The answer to this, of course, is that to make premise (4a) reasonable, a theory need not be actually axiomatized, it is only required that there is good reason to think this can be done. But, it might be replied, this is reasonable only if it is reasonable to think that a fixed theory with fixed subject matter is available, and the latter is not reasonable. This reply is essentially an objection to $C3$, which implies that there is a fixed scientific theory and subject matter.

II. SCIENTIFIC THEORIES DO NOT MEET PRECONDITION $C3$ This objection to $C3$ has been stated by Ernest Nagel, who says: "In order to specify the axioms of L* [the transcribed language] we would have to know, *in advance* of any deductions made from them, *all* the true statements of L*—in other words, Craig's method shows us how to construct the language L* only *after* every possible inquiry into the subject matter of L* has been completed."[6] And, because science is far from that completed state now and, furthermore, that state is an ideal it is unlikely man will ever reach, we can conclude that it is unreasonable to claim there is or will be a fixed set of sentences available for axiomatization.

Hilary Putnam has given the crux of an answer to this objection, although Nagel later rejects it. Putnam points out that we do not have to know all the true statements of scientific theory and subject matter, "we need only be given the theory."[7] Nagel thinks Putnam's reply is mistaken because, it seems, he thinks that to be given a theory is to be given an axiomatized theory, and thus Putnam's comment is irrelevant to Nagel's point.[8] But clearly Putnam's point is that we need only be given a set of sentences that at some time are thought to express the theory and its subject matter, and, given that set, it can be axiomatized. If it is objected that in the present state of many sciences there is a large body of statements that are neither accepted nor rejected, the reply is that it is enough to have three distinct sets of statements: those accepted, those rejected, and those neither accepted nor rejected. Any accepted statement is to become an axiom or a theorem, the denial of any statement rejected will become either an axiom or a theorem, and no statement neither accepted nor rejected and no denial of such a statement will be either a theorem or an axiom if it is not entailed by some set of accepted statements. Of course, no axiom system constructed in this way is complete, but this is as it should be, given that the science in question is not finished. Furthermore, it is quite reasonable that once the three sets of sentences are demarcated, the science in question can be axiomatized and Craig's method applied to it.

At this point the objection might arise that very often there is no agreement about which sentences expressing the subject matter of a science are to be placed in each of the three classes. Thus the

---

[6] E. Nagel, *The Structure of Science* (New York: Harcourt, Brace, and World, 1961), p. 23.

[7] H. Putnam, "Craig's Theorem," *Journal of Philosophy*, 62 (1965): 256.

[8] See E. Nagel, "A Rejoinder to Putnam," *Journal of Philosophy*, 62 (1965): 431.

preceding reply fails, because it is premised on three clearly distinguished sets of sentences. Where there is no such tripartite division there is no way to set up axioms. The reply to this objection is that where scientists disagree, alternative axiomatizations can be devised for each different tripartite division that is plausible to accept. Furthermore, even if it is unreasonable to think that some day there will be no undecided sentences in science, it is nevertheless reasonable to claim that someday one tripartite division will be more reasonable than any other. This is certainly sufficient for the purpose of justifying premise (4a) by means of Craig's procedure.

III.   SCIENTIFIC THEORIES DO NOT MEET PRECONDITION $C4$ Let us turn to the objection to precondition $C4$, which I find to result from a more serious problem. As stated in $C4$, the Craigian method can be applied to a theory only if there is a clear distinction between those terms that are to be permitted in the transcribed theory and those that are not. Usually, this distinction is thought to be that between theoretical terms and observation terms, but I shall make the distinction in a somewhat different way. I have argued elsewhere that some theoretical terms, such as 'temperature,' are also observation terms, and others, such as 'pain,' are also phenomenal terms. Consequently we should limit the rejected terms to any theoretical term, 'T,' for which 'There is a T' entails 'There is a P,' where P is what I have called a "pure" theoretical term. That is, very roughly, where 'P' is a theoretical term such that 'No P is experienced' is true. Consequently, not only are pure theoretical terms, such as 'electron' and 'proton,' to be eliminated, but also certain terms that can be used to report what is experienced. For example, if we let 'T' be 'conglomeration of molecules each consisting of one oxygen ion and two ions whose nuclei contain only one proton,' then, although 'T' can be used to report about water, it should be eliminated. This is because 'There is a T' entails 'There is a proton.' Furthermore, as I have also argued elsewhere, there may be terms which are what I have called "empirical" because they are defined by observation terms, but which are not themselves observation terms.[9] Yet because all such terms are to be permitted

---

[9] For more precise characterizations of empirical terms and pure theoretical terms, see my *Materialism and Sensations*, pp. 64–78 and pp. 102–03.

in transcribed theories, we should make the relevant distinction to be one between empirical terms and the two sorts of theoretical terms. (These, for convenience, I shall call merely "theoretical" terms throughout the rest of this chapter.)

The crucial objection to precondition *C4* is that no results of a Craigian procedure based on any such distinction are sufficient to justify premise (4a). This objection has been supported in two ways. First, it is claimed that there is no general way to make such a distinction, because what is observable, and thus empirical, and what is theoretical differ for different contexts, purposes, and background knowledge. What is observable in one context is not in another, and what is theoretical relative to one theory is not theoretical for another. Second, it is claimed that even if some general means can be devised for separating the terms of a theory into the two classes, so that precondition *C4* is met, any such procedure is purely arbitrary and thus the resulting distinction cannot be used in an attempt to justify (4a).

A.   THERE IS NO GENERAL DISTINCTION BETWEEN OBSERVABLE AND THEORETICAL.   Let us consider the first claim that there is no general distinction. Those who argue for this, use basically three different arguments, often conflating them. The first two of these are very similar but they are also importantly different, as the differences in the objections to each will show. The first is:

(1) There are many different distinctions between what is observable (theoretical) and what is unobservable (non-theoretical), and therefore there is no general or universal way to make such a distinction.[10]

The problem with this argument is that it confuses the claim that there is no *single* way to make this distinction, with the claim that there is no method for making the distinction that applies to all terms. The first follows from the premise but the second does not. Clearly, if there should be several different ways to make this distinction, there would be at least one. The only question remain-

---

[10] See M. Spector, "Theory and Observation," *British Journal for the Philosophy of Science,* 17 (1966): 3 and 20; and P. Achinstein, "The Problem of Theoretical Terms," *American Philosophical Quarterly,* 2 (1965): 193.

ing for us would be whether any one would be suitable for justifying (4a).

People who seem to use the first argument often, I think, confuse it with the second:

> (2) Any criterion for making a distinction between what is observable (theoretical) and what is unobservable (non-theoretical), produces a distinction which is "tied to a particular context and to some intended contrast." Therefore, no such distinction applies to all contexts, and, therefore, there is no general or universal way to make such a distinction.[11]

We can interpret this as a valid argument if we construe the premise that there is a tie between criteria and particular contexts to be equivalent to the conjunction of the following two statements. First, all criteria for making the distinctions are of a form such as: 'If term T has property P in context C, then T is an observation (theoretical) term in context C.' Second, for some terms shown to be observational (theoretical) in some context by some such criterion, there is at least one context in which it is shown not to be observational (theoretical). Although valid, there is reason to question the soundness of this argument. Both conjuncts of the premise are open to doubt. First, many counterexamples clearly show it to be dubious that a completely context-free criterion, such as one of the form: 'If T has property P, then T is an observation (theoretical) term,' will be devised. But it does not follow that it has been shown that one of the form: 'If T has property P in context C, then T is an observation (theoretical) term' is dubious. Of course, the latter may be independently shown to be dubious, but if it is, that would not show that being an observation (theoretical) term is context relative. At most, such a fact would show that it is either context relative or no term is an observation (theoretical) term. Thus the first conjunct of the premise is not established in this way. However, such a fact alone would be sufficient to substantiate the objection, but what results would be an entirely different argument for the objection. Indeed, it would be the third one we shall consider.

---

[11] Achinstein, p. 196. See also Achinstein, pp. 194–95, and p. 202.

The same can be said about the evidence relevant to the second conjunct of the premise, for it would be established by showing it to be likely that for any criterion, whether or not it is relativistic, there is some term that meets the criterion but is not an observation (theoretical) term in some context. In this case, however, such evidence would not only establish the second conjunct, but the third argument as well. And, because the third argument, if sound, is sufficient, and because what shows it to be sound is needed for the second argument but is not sufficient for it, the third argument is the crucial one. It is an inductive argument based on past attempts to state a nonrelativistic criterion, namely:

> (3) All attempts to provide a criterion to mark a general distinction between observation (theoretical) terms and nonobservation (nontheoretical) terms have been shown to fail, and, therefore probably, all attempts will fail.

The evidence that has been adduced for the premise of this argument is that every attempt that is known to have been examined has been shown to fail. This is the same evidence used to support the premises of the first two arguments. The difference is that while the first argument is invalid and one conjunct of the second is not supported by this evidence, it is initially plausible that the third argument is shown to be inductively sound by the evidence. Nevertheless there are still ways to attack this argument. One is to argue that, even if those attempts that have been examined are the only ones available, there is an important sense in which they do not constitute a fair sample. Another is to find some plausible attempt which has not yet been shown to fail. I shall argue both points.

I would claim that it is not sound to generalize from those attempts thus far examined, because, with one exception, they are not meant to be more than quick and rough sketches of the sort of characterizations the authors in question wished to indicate. This is true of the statements of Carnap, Hempel, Nagel, Braithwaite, Ryle, and Hanson, the men whose attempts are usually discussed.[12] It is easily seen that any criterion will have to be more precise and more complicated than the simple sketches of these men. On the other hand, Maxwell, who has attempted a more

---

[12] See Achinstein and Spector for detailed references to and discussions of these men.

detailed analysis of 'observation term' has been shown to fail because of his reliance upon the unhelpful notion of a quickly decidable sentence.[13] But one failure of one detailed attempt and several failures of oversimplifed sketches do not constitute the kind of evidence sufficient to support this generalization. More attempts must be made in the light of the sound criticisms of the preceding attempts before an inductively sound conclusion is drawn.

Regarding the second point, I shall say only that I have proposed definitions of 'observation term,' 'empirical term,' and 'theoretical term' which I believe are plausible, and if not ultimately acceptable, give reason to reject the conclusion that no attempts will succeed.[14] At least these definitions avoid many of the objections raised against other proposals. This is partly because many of the objections depend on a dichotomy between everything theoretical and what is observable. But I claim the dichotomy applies only to one sort of theoretical term. It is also because the concept of being observable and the context in which being observable is relevant to the definition of 'observation term' are both characterized in considerable detail. Furthermore, I believe that these terms, as so defined, can be used to provide a criterion to mark the distinction that the instrumentalist who used Craig's method wants. Of course, all criteria may fail for this purpose, but if they do, I think it likely that they would be shown to fail on the basis of a distinction drawn according to the intuitions of the instrumentalist. This may be all he needs. While a criterion is preferable, an intuitive sorting can also succeed. The objection to this is that such a division is arbitrary. Indeed some claim that any general division between observation (and thus what is empirical) and theory is arbitrary, and thus Craig's method cannot be used to justify premise (4a) of the original instrumentalist argument. Let us turn to this objection.

B. ANY DISTINCTION BETWEEN OBSERVABLE AND THEORETICAL IS ARBITRARY The arguments usually used to deny there is any nonarbitrary, general distinction between empirical terms and (pure) theoretical terms are based on one of two claims about a continuous series. One is based on a continuum in the decreasing

---

[13] See G. Maxwell, "The Ontological Status of Theoretical Entities," in *Minnesota Studies* 3 (1962), p. 13; and, for a discussion of Maxwell's views, Spector, pp. 5–12.

[14] See my *Materialism and Sensations*, pp. 64–77.

size of objects. As Hempel says, "There is a gradual transition from the macroscopic objects of our everyday experience to bacteria, viruses, molecules, atoms, and subatomic particles; and any line drawn to divide them into actual physical objects and fictitious entities would be quite arbitrary".[15] The second claim is about a continuum in the series of observations, from observing through a vacuum, to observing with binoculars, then with an optical microscope, and finally with an electron microscope. Maxwell concludes, "The important consequence is that, so far, we are left without criteria which would enable us to draw a nonarbitrary line between 'observation' and 'theory.' Certainly we often find it convenient to draw such a to-some-extent-arbitrary line; but its position will vary widely from context to context . . . . But what ontological ice does a mere methodologically convenient observation-theoretical dichotomy cut?"[16]

Although the two preceding series are different, they are obviously related, and although the two objections differ, they both make the same point. One is directed against an attempt to place a nonarbitrary limit on which objects are observable and, as a consequence, to determine nonarbitrarily which terms are not observation terms. The other one tries to counter the placing of a nonarbitrary limit on which conditions for observing are to count as determining what is observable and, consequently, which terms are observation terms. The joint point of these objections is that because there is a continuous series, making a cut at one place is as good as, and no better than, making it at some other place. Therefore, any cut is arbitrary and of no ontological significance.

These two objections are unsound as stated. The mere fact that there is a continuous series is not enough to justify that any cut made in the series is arbitrary, no matter what the purpose for the cut. Obviously many cuts are made in the series of real numbers, as in measuring, which are fully justified and are, therefore not arbitrary. What would be arbitrary would be merely to pick a certain cut in one of these series and proclaim that there exist no objects falling on one side of the cut. This, of course, is not what is stated in premise (4a), nor is it stated or implied by any other premise in the argument.

[15] C. Hempel, *Philosophy of Natural Science* (Englewood Cliffs, N.J.: Prentice-Hall, 1966), p. 82. See also Spector, p. 19.
[16] Maxwell, p. 7.

Nevertheless, although unsound, both versions of this objection do emphasize that an instrumentalist using Craig's method must give some reason for using a criterion to distinguish between empirical terms and pure theoretical terms, such that the reason does not depend on, and the criterion does not imply, any particular arbitrary cuts in these series.

An instrumentalist who uses Craig's method would claim to have a good, independent reason for his criterion. He would be trying to explicate those relationships among empirical statements that are mentioned in premise (4a) and that express the observable subject matter that scientific theories attempt to explain and predict. He would, consequently, be trying to isolate precisely the terms that can be characterized very roughly as those that describe the unaided observations made in standard observation conditions by standard observers through any of their sense modalities.[17] This would be the first step in defining 'observation term,' then 'empirical term,' and finally 'pure theoretical term' for the purpose of applying Craig's procedure. If he is successful in making these three definitions in a way that will allow him to distinguish two sets of terms as required by condition $C4$, he would have justified his procedure without assuming or implying any cuts in the series of observation conditions or in the series of objects. His procedure concerns only certain terms of language, and has no ontological implications.

Furthermore, his distinction (either alone or when conjoined with the conclusion of his argument that there are no objects referred to by pure theoretical terms) entails no particular cut in the two series. Certain scientific statements are also needed. But all such entailed cuts would be arbitrary in a sense that makes them unjustified for ontological purposes, only if some premise in the instrumentalist argument is unjustified. This would be true of premise (4a) if the charge of arbitrariness could be lodged against it. But we have seen it neither implies an arbitrary cut nor needs to be justified by assuming such a cut. Thus it is not to be rejected for this reason. Of course, whether there are other reasons to reject (4a) or some other premise, and thus the justification of the conclusion, remains to be seen. We can, nevertheless, dismiss the charge of

---

[17] For more detail, see Cornman, pp. 64–71.

arbitrariness against (4a) and, with it, also dismiss the last objection I have found that attempts to show premise (4a) is not to be justified in a Craigian way because scientific theories fail to meet one of the preconditions for the use of Craig's method. There are, however, other objections to (4a) that we must consider now.

Craigian Transcription and Inductive Systematization

We have found reason to think that scientific theories meet the preconditions for the application of Craig's method and that, given this applicability, a Craigian transcribed theory has the same deductive systematization as the original theory. But, even so, we have not done enough to establish premise (4a) because the relations among empirical statements established by scientific theories are not only deductive, but also inductive. And the crucial objection to (4a) is that theories of certain forms establish certain inductive relationships that are not established by either the Craigian or the Ramseyan transcribed versions of the theories. Thus premise (4a) is false. To make this objection and the instrumentalist's argument more precise, let us amend (4a) so that it specifically refers to both deductive and inductive systematization. We can characterize inductive systematization in terms of inductive derivability, which, in turn, will be characterized later. Let us say that a system, S, achieves some *inductive systematization* just in case some empirical statement, E_2, is inductively derivable from S and an empirical statement, E_1, but E_2 is not inductively derivable from E_1 alone. And, as a first approximation, let us say that S achieves some *epistemic systematization* just in case it achieves either some deductive or some inductive systematization. We can now replace (4a) with:

> (4b) If theoretical terms in a theory, T, establish epistemic systematization, then either the Craigian transcription of T or the Ramseyan transcription of T preserves its epistemic systematization.

This requires we change (5a) to:

> (5b) If either of such transcriptions preserve epistemic systematization, then theoretical terms are unnecessary.

The present objection to (4b) was first raised by Hempel and constituted his primary way out of the theoretician's dilemma. It was later echoed by Scheffler, and its central thrust was accepted by Hooker. However, as we shall see, none of these men established a crucial premise in his argument, as was noted by Bohnert and by Lehrer. Indeed only Lehrer has worked out the objection in any detail. We shall first examine a rather simple version of the objection as stated by Hempel and the others, and conclude with a close examination of Lehrer's version.

HEMPEL ON INDUCTIVE SYSTEMATIZATION

To see how the objection arises we need to consider theories with a form different from that of $S1$, because $C-S1$ with the postulate $G1$ has the same inductive systematization as $S1$. The theory used by Hempel in his objection can be given the following simplified form:[18]

$S2$ $P1$ $(x)(T_1x \supset T_2x)$
 $C1$ $(x)(T_1x \supset O_1x)$
 $C2$ $(x)(T_2x \supset O_2x)$

There are two parts to Hempel's argument. First, if we conjoin $S2$ with the empirical statement, O_1a, we will get inductive results we cannot achieve with O_1a alone. Second, because $S2$ has no contingent empirical axioms or theorems, $C-S2$ will consist only of the underlying logic of $S2$, and this will not yield inductive results with O_1a. We can agree with the second part of Hempel's argument about the Craigian transcription of $S2$, but objections have been raised about his argument concerning $S2$. To see the objections, let us first assume that given only the empirical statement, O_1a, we cannot derive that the probability of the empirical statement, O_2a, relative to O_1a is greater than one half, that is, $P(O_2a, O_1a) > \frac{1}{2}$. Then we can lay out the core of Hempel's argument as follows:

(1) $(x)(T_1x \supset O_1x)$ $\hspace{2cm}$ ($S2$)
(2) O_1a $\hspace{4.2cm}$ (assume)
(3) $P(T_1a, O_1a) > \frac{1}{2}$ $\hspace{2.3cm}$ (1, 2)
(4) $(x)(T_1x \supset O_2x)$ $\hspace{2cm}$ ($S2$)

---

[18] See Hempel, "The Theoretician's Dilemma."

(5) $P(O_2 a, O_1 a) > \frac{1}{2}$ (3, 4, prob. axioms)

(6) S2 achieves some epistemic   (5, definition)
systematization

Note that step 5 is justified by reference to axioms of the probability calculus. Previously we referred only to the nonlogical axioms of a system, S, and the axioms of the underlying (deductive) logic, L, of S. This was sufficient for deductive systematization, but for inductive systematization we need also axioms of an "underlying" probability calculus, P.[19] This addition distinguishes in part between deduction and what I have called "inductive derivation."

The problem with the argument is step (3). It cannot be derived from (1) and (2) using S2 and L. Nor will the addition of P help. The following counterexample illustrates the problem. Let $T_1 x = x$ is a conglomeration of H_2O molecules, and $O_1 x = x$ is a solid at $-100°$ centigrade. Here (1) is true and we can assume $O_1 a$, but that assumption with (1) surely does not make $T_1 a$ probable relative to $O_1 a$, because $O_1 x$ has so many true values other than groups of H_2O molecules. While it is true that Hempel's interpretations of $T_1 x$ and $O_1 x$ make the inference seem somewhat plausible, the present example has the same form, which is enough to cast doubt on the inference.

POSITIVE RELEVANCE AND INDUCTIVE SYSTEMATIZATION

While we cannot derive (3) from (1) and (2), we can derive that $P(T_1 a, O_1 a)$ is greater than $P(T_1 a)$ (the antecedent probability of $T_1 a$) from S2 and an empirical statement, E_1, using L and P. That is, following Lehrer, we can derive that $O_1 a$ is *positively relevant* to $T_1 a$.[20] Furthermore, we can say that a system, S, achieves some inductive systematization if it can be inductively derived from S, or from S and some empirical statement, E_1, but not from E_1 alone, that some empirical statement, E_2, is positively relevant to another empirical statement, E_3, that is, $P(E_3, E_2) > P(E_3)$. We can now construct the Hempelian argument that from S_2 with an empirical statement, it can be derived that $O_1 a$ is positively relevant to $O_2 a$, but from C–$S2$ this cannot be derived. Therefore, the

[19] Step (5) can be derived using a set of axioms that includes $0 \leqslant P(B, A) \leqslant 1$; $P(B \cdot C, A) = [P(B, A) \times P(C, A \cdot B)]$; and $(x)(Fx \supset Gx) \supset P(Gx, Fx) = 1$.

[20] See K. Lehrer, "Theoretical Terms and Inductive Inference," *American Philosophical Quarterly Monograph Series 3* (1969), pp. 32–33.

Craigian transcription of $S2$ does not achieve the same epistemic systematization as $S2$, and premise (4b) is mistaken about Craigian transcriptions. Again we can agree with the claim about $C-S2$, but, again, there is an objection to the argument about $S2$. The argument in question is:

(1) $(x)(T_1 x \supset O_1 x)$ ($S2$)
(2) If $P(O_1 a) < 1$ then $P(T_1 a, O_1 a) > P(T_1 a)$ (1, prob. axioms)

(3) $P(O_1 a) < 1$ (assume)
(4) $P(T_1 a, O_1 a) > P(T_1 a)$ (2, 3, L)
(5) $(x)(T_1 x \supset O_2 x)$ ($S2$)
(6) $P(O_2 a, O_1 a) > P(O_2 a)$ (4, 5)
(7) $S2$ is positively relevant to $O_2 a$ (6, def.)

Here it is assumed that statements about the probabilities of observation statements are empirical statements.[21] Thus $P(O_1 a) < 1$, which is to be conjoined with $S2$, is assumed to be empirical. In the present argument the step corresponding to the incorrectly derived (3) of the previous argument is (4), but (4) is correctly derived. The problem for the present argument is that (6) cannot be derived using L and P. The reason in this case is that from step 5 we can only derive $P(O_2 a) \geq P(T_1 a)$, and not $P(O_2 a) = P(T_1 a)$. If we could derive the latter, then the argument would go through, but with the former it will not. One way to see this is to interpret $T_1 x$ and $O_1 x$ as previously, and to let $O_2 x = x$ is a clear, tasteless liquid at $50°$ centigrade. Here we can assume $P(O_1 a)$ is extremely high but less than 1, and the statements in steps (1) and (5) are true. Furthermore, given all this, there is no reason to think that the probability that a is a clear, tasteless liquid is at all increased. Another, quicker way to show the problem is to let $O_2 x = x$ is either O_3 or not O_3. Thus $P(O_2 a) = 1$ and cannot be increased.

We have found no way to show that $C-S2$ does not achieve the same inductive systematization as $S2$. But, of course, theories might have forms quite different from those of $S2$. However, of the three forms of theories that differ from the form of $S1$ and $S2$ and

----

[21] Some people claim that probability statements are analytic and therefore not empirical. However, on my definition of 'empirical sentence,' in Cornman, p. 78, a probability statement with only empirical terms is an empirical sentence if the probability function is a logical constant, whether or not the sentence is analytic.

which have been examined, two face problems similar to those confronting *S2*. The third, proposed by Lehrer, is importantly different from the others, and we will examine it in detail later. One of the first two has basically the converse relationships of *S2*:

> *S3*   *C1* $(x)(O_1x \supset Tx)$
> *C2* $(x)(O_2x \supset Tx)$

Because Lehrer has highlighted the problem for showing that *C–S3* does not achieve the same inductive systematization as *S3*, we need not discuss it here.[22] It is enough to note here that the mistake is inferring $P(O_2a, O_1a) > P(O_2a)$ from $O_1a \supset Ta$ and $P(O_2a, Ta) > P(O_2a)$.

SCHEFFLER ON INDUCTIVE SYSTEMATIZATION

The second system is that discussed by Scheffler. It can be simplified as one of the following form:[23]

> *S4*   *C1* $(x)(y)[(Tx \cdot O_1xy) \supset Ty]$
> *C2* $(x)(Tx \supset (y) O_2xy)$

Scheffler's claim about *S4* is the same as Hempel's about *S2*, namely, that *S4* achieves some inductive systematization, but *C–S4* achieves none because it consists only of the underlying deductive and inductive logic of *S4*. But again the problem is to show that *S4* achieves some inductive systematization. We can reconstruct Scheffler's attempt to show that it does as follows:

(1)	$O_2ab_1, O_2ab_2, \ldots O_2ab_n$	(assume)
(2)	$P[(y)O_2ay] > \frac{1}{2}$	(1, Confirmation Rule)
(3)	$P(Ta) > \frac{1}{2}$	(2, *C2* of *S4*)
(4)	O_1ac	(assume)
(5)	$Ta \supset O_2cd$	(4, *S4*, L)
(6)	$P(Ta, O_2cd) = P(Ta)$	(5, *P*)
(7)	$P(O_2cd) \geqslant P(Ta)$	(6, *P*)
(8)	$P(O_2cd) > \frac{1}{2}$	(3, 7)
(9)	*S4* achieves some epistemic systematization	(8, def.)

---

[22] See Lehrer, pp. 32–34, for Lehrer's discussion of his *S2*.

[23] For this system and Scheffler's discussion of it, see I. Scheffler, *The Anatomy of Inquiry* (New York: Alfred A Knopf, 1969), pp. 197–203.

There are two steps in this argument that cannot be established with just L and P. The first is step (2), which a rule of confirmation is used to warrant. In this case let us grant here that if n is high enough, there is some inductive rule that warrants the inference from (1) to (2). This addition of an inductive rule that is not a theorem of the calculus of probability will have important consequences which we shall consider later. The second questionable step is the move to (3). It is the same problem facing Hempel's argument concerning $S2$, and thus Scheffler's argument fails for the same reason. Furthermore, if we construe the argument to be concerned with positive relevance, then the objection to step (6) of the second argument concerning $S2$ arises. Scheffler seems to be somewhat aware of the problem for deriving step (3) of the above argument. In discussing his step (7), which corresponds to $C2$ of $S4$, with x instantiated to a, he says;

> The consequent of (7) in turn may be taken as providing inductive grounds for its antecedent, under suitable conditions — for example, when likely alternatives have been eliminated, or when no likely alternatives are available.[24]

Here, in a very rough way, Scheffler seems to be suggesting another inductive rule which may warrant inferences to step (3) from $C2$ of $S4$ and step (2) when certain conditions, not specified by either L or P, are met. It seems likely that we shall need some inductive rules in addition to the axioms of L and P if we are to begin the task of showing premise (4b) false by showing some Craigian transcribed theories do not preserve inductive systematization. The only attempt of which I am aware that uses inductive rules and, in addition, presents a detailed argument against the Craigian preservation of inductive systematization, is that of Lehrer. Let us turn to his work now.

LEHRER ON INDUCTIVE SYSTEMATIZATION

In his detailed approach to the problem, Lehrer does three things not done by either Hempel or Scheffler. First, he specifies two inductive rules, $RD1$ and RI, which are neither theorems of L nor

[24] Ibid., p. 199.

theorems of P.[25] The first rule concerns direct inducibility. It states a sufficient condition for one statement, k, being directly inducible from another statement, e, that is, D(k, e). It can be stated as follows:

> RD1. D(k, e), if P(k, e) > P(h, e), for any h not entailed by ($k \cdot e$).

Lehrer's second rule gives a sufficient condition for k being inducibile (either directly or indirectly) from e, that is, I(k, e). The version I shall use is a modification, indeed oversimplification, of Lehrer's *RI*. This change is to make it easier to see the point of his argument against Craigian transcriptionism. Lehrer, rightly, would not accept the modification, but that does not affect his argument or my objection to it. Both concern only the kind of rule, not the particular version, he proposes. The modified rule is:

> *RIa* I(k, e) just in case there is an hypothesis, h, such that D(h, e) and D(k, $h \cdot e$) are derivable by *RDI*.

This rule allows for indirectly inducing k from the initial evidence and some hypothesis that has been directly induced.

The second thing Lehrer does is to propose a system (his "*S3*") in which two of the three postulates are probability statements rather than universally quantified statement.[26] He does this, I assume, because he finds no way to show that a transcribed theory with universally quantified postulates does not preserve inductive systematization. Third, he states a set of assumptions which, with his *S3* and his two inductive rules, yields an empirical statement of the form I(p,q). He goes on to conclude that *S3* achieves inductive systematization, but:

> No system of probability statements relating [only] observation terms can achieve the same inductive systematization as *S3*. Therefore, the theoretical terms in *S3* are logically

[25] See Lehrer, pp. 36–38. The kind of inductive rules Lehrer proposes are also called acceptance rules and rules of detachment. Some people are opposed to such rules, but my claim that the Craigian method preserves inductive systematization would not be affected if they are right.

[26] Ibid., pp. 34–35.

indispensible to the inductive systematization achieved by that
system.[27]

If this is correct we can further conclude that premise (4b) is
false, because its consequent is false for a Craigian transcription
of Lehrer's *S3* and also for a Ramsey-sentence transcription in
which theoretical constants are replaced with variables.

It is important to note that Lehrer's inducibility is not what I
previously called "inductive derivability," which we can now
characterize as follows:

> q is inductively derivable from p = $_{df.}$ q is derivable from p,
> using L, P, and the inductive rules, R, but q is not derivable
> from p using L alone.

However, q being inducible from p, that is, $I(q, p)$, is similar to
q being probable relative to p, that is, $P(q, p)$. Each is here
construed as a relationship between pairs of sentences and is
governed by a set of rules, the latter by the axioms or probability
and the former by the set R (for Lehrer, *RDI* and *RI*).[28] The
relevance of $I(q,p)$ to inductive derivability is that certain inductive
rules, such as Lehrer's, sometime allow us to derive inductively a
sentence of the form of $I(q,p)$ from some system, S, conjoined with
a statement, r. And if r and $I(q,p)$ are empirical, and r alone does
not yield $I(q,p)$ using L, P, and R, then S achieves some inductive
systematization. This is shown by the characterization of inductive
systematization which we can now unpack completely:

> S achieves some inductive systematization = $_{df.}$
>
> (1) some empirical statement, E_2, is derivable from S and

---

[27] Ibid., p. 39.

[28] This differs from my misleading original characterization of Lehrer's inducibility as a
species of inductive derivability in "Craig's Theorem, Ramsey-Sentences, and Scientific
Instrumentalism," *Synthese*, 25 (1972): 101. This seems to have misled I. Niiniluoto,
"Inductive Systematization: Definition and a Critical Survey," *Synthese*, 25 (1972):
25–81, into confusing 'p being inductively derivable from q' with '$I(p, q)$'. See especially
his discussion on pp. 40–43 and pp. 67–75. This confusion leads him to argue incorrectly
that because on some interpretations, '$I(p,q)$' does not satisfy the inductive analogue of
the converse of the deduction theorem, it follows that inductive derivability fails to
satisfy that analogue. But inductive derivability satisfies both the theorem and the
converse themselves, as Steven Kaufman has very helpfully shown in "The Preservation
of Epistemic Systematization within the Extended Craigian Program," *Synthese*, 27 (1974):
215–22.

an empirical statement, E_1, using L, P and R, but not using L alone, *and*

(2) E_2 is not derivable from E_1 alone, using L, P, and R.

With these definitions completed we can also substitute our final characterization of epistemic systematization for the previous first approximation:

S achieves some epistemic systematization $=$ $_{df.}$
(1) some empirical statement, E_2, is derivable from S and an empirical statement, E_1, using L, P, and R, *and*
(2) E_2 is not derivable from E_1 alone using L, P, and R.

This differs from the first attempt, which mistakenly allowed S to achieve epistemic systematization where E_2 is derivable from E_1 alone when not only L, but also P and R, are used.[29] Surely, if S is unnecessary to derive E_2 using L, P, and R, then it does not achieve epistemic systematization even if it is required in order to derive E_2 using L alone. Perhaps the characterization of deductive systematization should be amended so E_2 is in no way derivable from E_1 alone. If it were, the original definition would be equivalent to the present one. We need not worry about this, however, because our present and future interest concerns only inductive and epistemic systematization.

Lehrer's system, which I shall call $S5$, consists of three correspondence rules:

$S5$ $C1$ $P(Tx, O_1 x) = r$
       $C2$ $P(O_2 x, Tx \cdot O_1 x) = s$
       $C3$ $(x) [(O_1 x \cdot O_2 x) \supset Tx]$

There are three steps in Lehrer's procedure, but only two are crucial for our purposes. First, he argues that, given $S5$, a pair of his assumptions, and his two inductive rules, it follows that $O_2 a$ is inducible from $O_1 a$, that is, $I(O_2 a, O_1 a)$, and thus $S5$ achieves some inductive systematization. Lehrer's second move is to show that, given a second pair of assumptions and the two inductive rules, $I(O_2 a, O_1 a)$ cannot be derived solely from probability statements relating observation terms. From this he concludes that $S5$ achieves some inductive systematization not achieved by

---

[29] What I have here called the first approximation is the version used in my "Craig's Theorem, Ramsey-Sentences and Scientific Instrumentalism."

a system which does not use theoretical terms.

We can lay out the argument to establish his first point as follows:

(1) For any h not entailed by $(O_1b \cdot Tb)$,
   $P(Tb, O_1b) > P(h, O_1b)$ $(A1)$

(2) $D(Tb, O_1b)$ $(1, RD1)$

(3) For any h not entailed by $(O_2b \cdot Tb \cdot O_1b)$,
   $P(O_2b, Tb \cdot O_1b) > P(h, Tb \cdot O_1b)$, $(A2)$

(4) $D(O_2b, Tb \cdot O_1b)$ $(3, RD1)$

(5) $I(O_2b, O_1b)$ $(2, 4, RIa)$

(6) $I(O_2b, O_1b)$ is derivable from $S5$ by
   L, P, and R. $(1-5)$

(7) $S5$ achieves some inductive systematization. $(6, \text{def.})$

I have used the two inductive rules $RD1$ and RIa in this proof. Lehrer's assumptions $A1$ and $A2$ are each an instantiation of the antecedent of $RD1$. Furthermore, Tb instantiates h in RIa, and so given $D(Tb, O_1b)$ and $D(O_2b, Tb \cdot O_1b)$, we can derive $I(O_2b, O_1b)$ by RIa.

We can reconstruct Lehrer's argument to establish his second point as follows. We shall use one bit of additional symbolism: $Ef = f$ is an empirical statement.[30]

(8) For some h not entailed by $(O_2b \cdot O_1b)$, $P(h, O_1b)$
   $\geqslant P(O_2b, O_1b)$. $(A3)$

(9) For any f, if Ef and $I(f, O_1b)$, then for some h not entailed
   by $(O_2b \cdot f \cdot O_1b)$, $P(h, f \cdot O_1b) \geqslant P(O_2b, f \cdot O_1b)$. $(A4)$

(10) If $A3$ and $A4$, then $I(O_2b, O_1b)$ is not derivable solely
   from probability statements relating only observation
   constants using L, P, $RD1$, and RIa.

(11) If $I(O_2b, O_1b)$ is not derivable from such probability
   observation statements using L, P, $RD1$, and RIa, then
   it is not derivable in such a way from any system consisting solely of observation statements.

---

[30] Lehrer does not explicitly include Ef in his statement of what I have called $A4$ (see Lehrer, p. 38). Nevertheless I have added it because it seems implicit in his discussion of the assumption, and, more importantly, without such amendment, (9) would contradict the conjunction of (2) and (3). This addition will also play a central role in a later discussion of an objection to the Craigian transcription of system $S6$.

(12) If I(O_2b, O_1b) is not derivable in such a way from such a system and I(O_2b, O_1b) is derivable from $S5$ to produce some inductive systematization, then no system without theoretical constants preserves the inductive systematization of $S5$.

(13) Neither $C-S5$ nor $R-S5$ (the Ramsey-sentence transcription of $S5$) uses theoretical constants.

(14) Neither $C-S5$ nor $R-S5$ preserves the inductive systematization of $S5$ (and premise (4b) is false).

(7 through 13)

In this argument, assumption $A3$ functions to guarantee that O_2b is not directly inducible from O_1b, because $A3$ is essentially an instantiation of the denial of the antecedent of $RD1$. Assumption $A4$ similarly functions to guarantee that O_2b is not indirectly inducible from O_1b using R and some empirical hypothesis directly inducible from O_1b. Relative to the conjunction of any empirical statement with O_1b, there is always some nonentailed hypothesis with a probability at least as high as O_2b. Thus premise (10) is acceptable.

OBJECTION TO LEHRER'S PROOFS There are objections to each of the preceding arguments. The first is sound through step (5), but there is a problem about step (6) unless it is interpreted properly, and step (7) is mistaken. What Lehrer has shown is that there are two assumptions that are compatible with $S5$ from which I(O_2b, O_1b) can be derived using $RD1$ and $R1a$. No postulate of $S5$ is used in any step in the derivation of I(O_2b, O_1b). Nevertheless (6) is acceptable if we construe 'derivability' so that if P is derivable from Q alone then P is derivable from Q and S, even if P is not derivable from S alone. This is a plausible interpretation, even if it is also plausible to require that S be an essential part of the proof of P, if P is to be derivable from S.

While we can save step (6) this way, it points up two reasons to deny step (7). The derivation of this step fails because the steps (1) through (6) do not yield that theory $S5$ meets the two conditions individually necessary and jointly sufficient for inductive systematization. We have seen that $S5$ achieves some inductive systematization if some empirical statement, in this case I(O_2b, O_1b), is inductively derivable from $S5$ and an empirical statement,

E, but $I(O_2b, O_1b)$ is not inductively derivable from E alone. First, if we assume that E is the conjunction of $A1$ and $A2$, then while $I(O_2b, O_1b)$ is derivable from $S5$ and E, it is also derivable from E alone. Second, it is wrong to assume that $A1$ and $A2$ are empirical statements, because they contain theoretical terms. Thus even if $S5$ were essential for the derivation of $I(O_2b, O_1b)$ from $A1$ and $A2$, this would not establish that $S5$ achieves some inductive systematization. Thus Lehrer's argument does not show that $S5$ achieves some inductive systematization. There is, however, a way to avoid this objection. This is to replace $S5$ with $S6$, which has as postulates or theorems the three postulates of $S5$ and either Lehrer's four assumptions or the universally quantified statements of which they are instantiations. Then, because $I(O_2b, O_1b)$ is derivable from $S6$ alone, it is also derivable from $S6$ and some empirical statement, E, from which it is not derivable alone. Thus step (7) is sound for $S6$. Let us, then, replace '$S5$' with '$S6$' throughout both stages of Lehrer's argument.

However, even with the first stage of Lehrer's argument made sound, the second stage faces a separate set of objections. We can now grant (7), we have already found premise (10) to be acceptable, and we can also agree to the assumptions stated in (8) and (9). Surely premise (13) can also be granted, because $C-S6$ contains only empirical terms and $R-S6$ replaces all theoretical terms with variables. This leaves premise (11) and (12), both of which face objections. One objection is that even if (12) is correct about the Craigian procedure, it is false if the Ramsey-transcription of $S6$ preserves epistemic systematization and if we construe an observation sentence to have only observation constants as predicate terms and no predicate variables. Ramsey-sentences, with their predicate variables, would not be observation statements. If, however, we construe an observation sentence to be one with an observation constant but no theoretical constants, then Ramsey-sentences would be observation statements and this objection would be lodged against (11). Because, as we shall see later, the Ramsey method is successful, either (11) or (12) is false. Nevertheless, if we restrict Lehrer's argument to the Craigian approach, then we can avoid this objection and grant (12) as so restricted. While this would not refute premise (4b) of the original argument, it would certainly show a defect in the Craigian approach. Let us, then, assume the restriction.

Premise (11) is crucial. It faces two initially plausible objections. Both agree that Lehrer has established the antecedent of (11) and concentrate on the consequent. The first one claims that the antecedent does not provide reason to deny that $I(O_2b, O_1b)$ is derivable from universally quantified observation statements. If it should be so derivable, then the consequent of (11) and thus (11) are false. I feel sure that Lehrer's reply to this would be that given his two assumptions $A3$ and $A4$ and the two inductive rules, $I(O_2b, O_1b)$ is not derivable from any system that replaces the postulates of $S6$ with a set of universally quantified observation statements. For example, we could not use $(x)\ (O_1x \supset O_2x)$ so that $P(O_2b, O_1b) = 1$, and then derive $D(O_2b, O_1b)$ by $RD1$, because by $A3$ there is some hypothesis, h, not entailed by O_1b, such that $P(h, O_1b) = 1$. Similarly, $A4$ would block deriving $I(O_2b, O_1b)$ recursively using both $RD1$ and $R1a$. Thus if we used $(x)\ [(O_1x \cdot E) \supset O_2x]$, where E is an empirical statement (and thus different from Tb), so that $P(O_2b, O_1b \cdot E) = 1$, then by $A4$ the probability of some nonentailed h also equals one and that stops the use of $RD1$ and $R1a$. We can consequently agree with Lehrer and reject this objection.

The second objection to (11) claims that there are observation statements that are neither probability statements nor universal statements, and that certain of these would have the same inductive systematization as $S6$. Indeed, $I(O_2b, O_1b)$ is just such a statement. Why can we not substitute that statement for $S6$ and as a result preserve the inductive systematization of $S6$? This would falsify (11) by falsifying its consequent, while its antecedent would remain true. Two replies might be made here. The first is that $S6$ achieves some additional inductive systematization while $I(O_1b, O_2b)$ does not. The second is that $I(O_1b, O_2b)$ is not a theorem of $S6$ and so it is not a theorem of C–$S6$. Thus even if $I(O_1b, O_2b)$ were to preserve the inductive systematization of $S6$, we could not preserve it using the Craigian procedure.

Both these points can be answered in the same way. The Craigian procedure guarantees that for any system, S, the Craigian transcribed system, C–S, preserves the deductive systematization of S because S achieves deductive systematization in just those cases where some contingent empirical sentence of the form $E_i \supset E_j$ is derivable from S alone using L, the underlying logic of S. But for any empirical sentence of that form, just those derivable from S are also derivable from $C-S$. In order to handle epistemic systematization in a parallel way, let us extend the Craigian procedure in the following way. First, we add to the deductive axioms and rules of L, a set of axioms for the probability calculus, P, and a set of inductive rules, R (for Lehrer, $RD1$ and RI). Second, we claim that S achieves some epistemic systematization in just those cases where some $E_i \supset E_j$, which is not a theorem of L, P, or R, is derivable solely from S by L, P, and R. Third, for any statement of the form $E_i \supset E_j$, which is not a theorem of L, P, or R, just those that are derivable from S by L, P, and R, that is, those I shall call the "*epistemic*" theorems of S, are to be taken as (deductive) theorems of $C-S$. Consequently, any statement, for example $E_i \supset \mathrm{I}(O_2 b, O_1 b)$, is an *epistemic* theorem of S just in case it is a theorem of $C-S$ that is deducible from an axiom of $C-S$ consisting of the statement itself, in this case, $E_i \supset \mathrm{I}(O_2 b, O_1 b)$, conjoined the appropriate Gödel number of times. Of course, each set of axioms, comprising either S, L, P, or R, should be effectively defined and be distinct from each of the other three sets, and the corresponding proof procedures should also be effectively defined. But given that this can be done for L, I see no additional problems for doing it for P and R, especially for a set of inductive rules like Lehrer's rules. It is true that there may be much more debate about which set of inductive rules to use than about which logical system and which axioms for the probability calculus are to be used. But for our purpose, we need only claim that for any proposed set of inductive rules, whether or not it is correct, the epistemic systematization derived using those rules is preserved by $C-S$.

It seems that we have found a way to guarantee the Craigian preservation of epistemic systematization of any system, but one last objection remains. System $S6$ contains not only $\mathrm{I}(O_2 b, O_1 b)$ as an epistemic theorem, but also $A3$ and $A4$ as theorems. The problem is that by using rules $RD1$ and RIa it seems that from some empirical theorems of $S6$ alone, and thus from $C-S6$, we can derive that there is some theoretical sentence, T, for which $\mathrm{D}(O_2 b, T \cdot O_1 b)$. Thus, it can be objected, no Craigian transcription of $S6$ succeeds. The problem arises as follows. Given RIa and $\mathrm{I}(O_2 b, O_1 b)$, it follows that either $\mathrm{D}(O_2 b, O_1 b)$ or, for some h, $\mathrm{D}(h, O_1 b)$

and $D(O_2b, h \cdot O_1b)$ are derivable by *RD1*. But, given *A3* as a theorem of *S6*, we know that $D(O_2b, O_1b)$ is not derivable by *RD1*. Consequently, there is some hypothesis, h, for which $D(h, O_1b)$ and $D(O_2b, h \cdot O_1b)$ are derivable by *RD1*. But it follows from *A4*, which as stated is restricted to empirical statements, that for no empirical statement, E, such that $D(E, O_1b)$, is $D(O_2b, E \cdot O_1b)$ derivable by *RD1*. The objection concludes from this that h is some nonempirical statement, and, therefore, some theoretical statement is a theorem of any system that has the empirical theorems of *S6*. Consequently, we cannot use Craig's theorem to rid certain theories such as *S6* of all theoretical terms and also preserve epistemic systematization.

There are several ways to reply to this objection. One is to claim that a necessary condition for a scientific theory to be acceptable is that it be grounded in what is empirical in the sense that for any observation statement, O_1, and any theoretical statement, T, there is another observation statement, O_2, for which $P(O_2, O_1) \geqslant P(T, O_1)$. Thus given our two inductive rules, we could not derive $I(Tb, O_1b)$ from *S6* if it is amended to be made acceptable, and the problem would not arise. This reply is too weak to rely on, because it takes us into an area that is still so unclear that we cannot adequately evaluate it. A second reply is stronger. It points out that the most we can derive from *S6* is that there is some nonempirical statement inducible from O_1b. But this statement does not entail that there is some theoretical statement so inducible. It might be a phenomenal statement, such as an appearance statement, or a Ramsey-type statement with predicate variables. Neither of these is the kind of pure theoretical statement that the instrumentalists wish to contrast with empirical statements. Thus, this objection fails to show that some theoretical sentence is a theorem of *S6* and *C–S6*.

We can, however, amend *A4* so that the sentence, 'There is a pure theoretical statement that is inducible from O_1b,' is a theorem of *S6*. We need only to replace *Ef* in the antecedent of *A4* with $\sim Tf$, where $Tf = f$ is a pure theoretical statement. However, it is by no means clear that this theorem is a pure theoretical statement as it must be for the objection to be sound. It is theoretical only if 'pure theoretical statement' is a theoretical term, but we need not worry about this to refute the objection. Either the term is theoretical, or it is not. If it is, then no sentence containing it is an epistemic theorem of *S6* and no such sentence is a theorem of *C–S6*. If the term is not theoretical, then the sentence in question is not theoretical. Therefore if the term is theoretical, then the sentence is not an epistemic theorem of *S6* and, therefore, not a theorem of *C–S6*. The same conclusion holds for the term, 'empirical statement.' Thus there really is no problem here. Incidentally, I think that these two terms are neither pure theoretical terms, nor empirical terms. They are clearly not theoretical terms of any science other than linguistics, and it is not clear they would occur even in that science. They would seem to be technical philosophical terms, rather than explanatory terms of some science which would be enough to show they are not pure theoretical terms. One point is clear, however. They are not empirical terms as they must be if either is to be contained in an epistemic theorem, because they are not observation terms nor definable by observation terms.

Conclusion: Craigian Transcriptionism Preserves Epistemic Systematization

I have found no other objections to extending the Craigian procedure to include all inductive as well as deductive derivations from any theoretical system. This includes those with universally quantified postulates and also those with probability statements as postulates. Thus what Craig has done for the preservation of deductive systematization by systems with no theoretical terms, the extended Craigian procedure seems to do to preserve epistemic systematization. Although Lehrer's attempt shows that an unextended procedure is not sufficient, it does not show that there is no satisfactory Craigian transcription of some theories. Indeed, we can conclude at this point in our examination that we seem to be justified in accepting premise (4b) because it seems reasonable to claim that for any theory, *S*, an extended Craigian transcription of *S* preserves the epistemic systematization of *S*. Although we have done this without considering Ramseyan transcriptions, my claim is that we could also have done it relying on Ramsey sentences. Thus even if the Craigian method had failed, premise (4b) would still be justified because Lehrer's argument would fail for a different reason. Let me briefly explain why I claim this.

Ramseyan Transcription and Epistemic Systematization

The Ramseyan method of elimination differs from the Craigian procedure in what it does with the pure theoretical terms of a theory once they have been identified. While the Craigian procedure is to retain only the empirical statements of the theory, the Ramseyan approach is to replace each pure theoretical term with a unique variable and existentially quantify over each variable.[31] Two points should be noted here. Because of the restrictions on existential instantiation, all sentential functions that result from this replacement are first conjoined and then each required existential quantifier is made to range over the whole conjunction. Thus for any theory, *S*, which consists of several statements, the resulting Ramseyized theory, *R–S*, consists of one existentially quantified sentence. The second point is that the resulting variables are predicate variables and thus at least second order quantification is required for a Ramseyized theory.

As an example, let us consider the Ramsey-sentence corresponding to Hempel's example, *S2*:

$$R\text{--}S2 \quad (\exists\phi)(\exists\psi)(x)[(\phi x \supset \psi x)\cdot(\phi x \supset O_1 x)\cdot(\psi x \supset O_2 x)].$$

As *R–S2* illustrates, the Ramseyan approach has certain advantages over the Craigian method. First, it does not require that a theory be axiomatized, but only that all the sentences thought to express the theory and its subject matter be available and that there is a way to distinguish the relevant theoretical terms. Second, if a theory is axiomatized, the Ramseyan method not only preserves the structure of the theory, as *R–S2* does for *S2*, but it also has only one postulate of finite length rather than the infinite number of postulates resulting from a Craigian transcription.

There are, however, accompanying disadvantages.[32] One is that, *ceteris paribus*, a theory that only requires first order quantification is preferable to one that requires higher level quantification. Generally, two reasons are given for this: one logical and one ontological. There are problems and complexities in logical systems that include higher quantification which are not present in

[31] This approach derives from F. Ramsey, *The Foundations of Mathematics*, ed. R. Braithwaite (New York: Humanities Press, 1931), Chap. 9.

[32] See H. Bohnert, "In Defense of Ramsey's Elimination Method," *Journal of Philosophy*, 65 (1968): 277–79, for a discussion of these disadvantages.

first-order systems. We can agree that it is better to restrict theories to first-order quantification where possible, but it is not clear that higher quantification occurs in scientific theories only if they are Ramseyized. If quantification over predicate variables is required independently of Ramseyizing, then the Ramseyan approach is at no disadvantage for this reason. Even if all scientific theories that are not Ramseyized can avoid higher quantification, it is still not clear it can be avoided altogether. For example, properties of relations are discussed in logic, and for analogical arguments predicate variables are used to state their form and the criteria for evaluating them. Nevertheless it is at least possible that predicate variables can be avoided completely except for Ramseyizing. If this should be the case, which I find unlikely, then the Craigian method would have one advantage over Ramseyan elimination, unless, of course, a linguistic nominalist should succeed in his nominalistic reductions or eliminations. But even if no such success is forthcoming, this logical disadvantage would not by itself be enough to justify rejecting the Ramsey method, nor do I find that this would overbalance its advantages over the Craigian approach.

The second reason for claiming that higher order quantification puts a Ramseyan approach at a disadvantage, is based on ontological nominalism. Scheffler claims that the Ramsey method has "expansive effects on ontological commitment, since it replaces noncommital theoretical-predicate constants with existentially quantified predicate variables ranging over nonindividuals."[33] There are two ways the Ramsey method might result in ontological expansion. One way is to require a commitment to more entities of some kind already exemplified, but not to require commitment to entities of an entirely new kind, for example, require commitment to additional properties when there already is commitment to some properties. The second is to require commitment to entities of a new kind, for example, require commitment to properties when nothing else does. The first sort of expansion of properties has no undesirable consequences, because even granting that the ontological nominalist is right in his aversion to properties, the mere addition of some properties to those he already is trying to eradicate, raises no new problems for him.

---

[33] I. Scheffler, "Reflections on the Ramsey Method," *Journal of Philosophy*, 65 (1968): 270.

The second kind of expansion is undesirable, given nominalistic proclivities, but just as it seems unlikely that predicate variables are avoidable unless we Ramseyize, it also seems unlikely that we are committed to properties only if we Ramseyize. Furthermore, even if we are so committed only if we Ramseyize, there is reason to doubt that the mere use of second-order quantification is sufficient to commit us ontologically to properties. In discussing this problem for the Ramsey method, Bohnert points out that "the effect of quantification in a formalized system depends on its detailed semantics and syntax, and plausible ways have been outlined for making sure that the costs of higher quantification are purely linguistic."[34] I would only add to this, by way of emphasis, that some nontrivial theory or criterion of referring is needed to move from the linguistic use of higher quantification to ontological commitment to properties.[35] Thus, for several reasons, we can reject the second attempt to show that higher quantification creates disadvantages for the Ramseyan method.

The second advantage of Craigian elimination is said to be that it guarantees there is no reference to purely theoretical entities, but a Ramseyized theory does not. None of the empirical terms of the theorems of a Craigian theory would refer to the same entities as any of the pure theoretical terms of the original theory, and so they would not refer to postulated theoretical entities. However, given certain theories of reference, the predicate variables over which there is existential quantification in a Ramseyized theory would have properties as values. And, if no empirical predicates are found to be true substituends, then it is certainly plausible to conclude that the true values are theoretical entities. This is clearly a disadvantage, although it need not be damaging, because some different theory of reference might be correct, or some empirical terms might turn out to be true substituends of the Ramsey variables. A Berkeleyan might even argue that the values are certain ideas of the author of nature.[36] Nevertheless, because of the Craigian guarantee, I think that the instrumentalist case is made stronger by relying ultimately on the Craigian procedure, even with its disadvantages. If both methods of elimination work, as I claim, his case is even stronger.

[34] Bohnert, p. 279.

[35] See my *Metaphysics, Reference, and Language* (New Haven: Yale University Press, 1966), for an extended discussion of the relevance of linguistic claims to ontology.

[36] Cf. G. Maxwell, "Structural Realism and the Meaning of Theoretical Terms," *Minnesota*

One reason for this, as we shall see, is that a joint use of the two methods will enable the instrumentalist to present more convincing refutations of certain objections to other premises in this argument.

RAMSEYAN TRANSCRIPTION AND INDUCTIVE SYSTEMATIZATION

As with Craigian transcription, it can be shown that Ramseyan transcription preserves deductive systematization. That whatever is an empirical theorem of a Ramseyized theory, R–S, is also an empirical theorem of the theory, S, is shown by the fact that R–S is an existential generalization of S in second-order quantification. That the converse is true is more difficult to show, but it has been done by Bohnert as sketched by Scheffler.[37] We can roughly indicate it by pointing out that whatever is an empirical theorem of S can be derived in the same steps as whatever is an empirical theorem of R–S, once the predicate variables of R–S have been existentially instantiated. This is because once instantiation to dummy constants has occurred for R–S, every step that does not involve generalization from these constants and is valid for S is also valid for R–S. But because no generalization from these constants is necessary to derive empirical theorems—those that contain only empirical constants—all empirical theorems of S are also empirical theorems of R–S.

The primary attack on Ramseyan transcription has been that it does not preserve inductive systematization. This claim has less initial plausibility than it does regarding Craigian transcriptions, because Ramseyized theories have the same structure as the original theory, but Craigian theories do not. Nevertheless Scheffler, and as far as I know only Scheffler, has attempted to show that one Ramseyized theory does not preserve inductive systematization.[38] However, this attempt fails for the same reason as

Studies 4 (1970), pp. 181–92, where Maxwell argues that "theoretical" variables in a Ramsey sentence take as values entities whose intrinsic properties are unknown. We know only their structural properties by means of the location of the corresponding variables in the Ramsey sentence. For all we know, then, the values may be such ideas. For a similar point, see the discussion of a "Malebranchean" explanation schema in chapter 8.
[37] See Scheffler, *The Anatomy of Inquiry*, pp. 207–08.
[38] Ibid., pp. 214–20.

Scheffler's and Hempel's attempts to show some Craigian theories do not preserve inductive systematization. Nevertheless, Scheffler's argument is interesting and worth reconstructing. To do so we shall consider not only $S2$ and $R-S2$, but also $S2a$ and its Ramseyized form:

$$R-S2a \quad (\exists \phi)\,(\exists \psi)\,(x)\,[(\phi x \supset \psi x) \cdot (\phi x \supset O_1 x) \cdot (\psi x \supset \sim O_2 x)].$$

We can now reconstruct the argument as follows:

(1) $R-S2$ is analytic and $R-S2a$ is analytic (in second-order logic).

(2) If h_1 is analytic and h_2 is analytic, then h_1 and h_2 are logically equivalent.

(3) If $O_1 a$ inductively supports $O_2 a$, given h_1, and h_1 and h_2 are logically equivalent, then it is false that $O_1 a$ inductively supports $\sim O_2 a$ given h_2.

(4) If $O_1 a$ inductively supports $O_2 a$, given $R-S2$, then $O_1 a$ inductively supports $\sim O_2 a$, given $R-S2a$.

Therefore

(5) It is false that $O_1 a$ inductively supports $O_2 a$, given $R-S2$.

(6) $O_1 a$ inductively supports $O_2 a$, given $S2$.

Therefore

(7) $R-S2$ does not preserve the inductive systematization of $S2$.

I have made two important changes in this argument. First, I have used 'inductively supports' throughout to allow for either of two interpretations of the argument. That is, by 'A inductively supports B, given C,' I mean that either $P(B, A) > \frac{1}{2}$ or $P(B, A) > P(B)$ is inductively derivable from C alone or from C and some empirical statement, E, but not from E alone. Thus both versions of the earlier arguments against the preservation of inductive systematization by Craig's method would be captured by using 'inductively supports.' Second, I have supplied premise (3) to the argument, because, as stated by Scheffler and by Bohnert in his attack on it, it is not clear whether (3) which is acceptable, or some other premise which is not acceptable is assumed.[39] For example, consider:

> (3a) If h_1 is analytic, then it is false that O_1a inductively supports O_2a, given h_1.

and

> (3b) If O_1a inductively supports O_2a, given h_1, and h_1 and h_2 are logically equivalent, then O_1a inductively supports O_2a, given h_2.

We can show both of these to be false by letting $O_1x = x$ is red, $O_2x = x$ is smooth and red, $O_3x = x$ is rough and red, $h_1 = (x)(O_2x \supset O_1x)$, and $h_2 = (x)(O_3x \supset O_1x)$. Here both h_1 and h_2 are analytic, but, first, $P(O_2a, O_1a) > P(O_2a)$ is inductively derivable from h_1 and $P(O_1a) < 1$, and, second, it is not inductively derivable from $P(O_1a) < 1$ alone or from h_2 and $P(O_1a) < 1$ alone.

The argument, with premise (3), is sound through step (5), but, as with both versions of the Hempelian attack on Craigian transcription, and as suggested by Bohnert, premise (6) is false.[40] Neither R–$S2$, R–$S2a$, nor $S2$ achieves any inductive systematization, and so R–$S2$ trivially preserves the epistemic systematization of $S2$. As with the Craigian method, it seems that Ramseyan elimination cannot be shown to change inductive systematization where the postulates of a theory are universally quantified statements. Once again, however, the question can be raised whether there is a change when some of the postulates are probability statements. Let us see.

LEHRER'S SYSTEM RAMSEYIZED AND INDUCTIVE SYSTEMATIZATION   It has already been indicated that the empirical theorems of Ramseyized theory are just those of the original theory. As with the Craigian procedure, we can see that by using not only L, but also P and R, a Ramseyized theory would have exactly the same *epistemic* theorems as the original theory and thus would preserve the epistemic systematization of the original theory. One special problem arises, however, namely, quantifying into probability contexts. The Ramseyized version of Lehrer's system, $S5$, is:

---

[39] Ibid., pp. 218–19; and Scheffler, "Reflections on the Ramsey Method," p. 273; and Bohnert, p. 280.

[40] See Bohnert, p. 280.

$$R\text{–}S5 \quad (\exists\psi)\ \{P(\psi x, O_1 x) = r \cdot P(O_2 x, \psi x \cdot O_1 x) = s \cdot$$
$$(x)\ [(O_1 x \cdot O_2 x) \supset \psi x]\}$$

Such probability statements are intensional or opaque, because substitution *salva veritate* fails, both for individual constants and for predicates.[41] Some probability statements about fictional characters are true, and while it seems probable that blood is red, given that it appears red to most people, it is not probable that blood is the color of fire engines, given that blood appears red to most people. Furthermore, existential generalization over individuals within probability contexts is invalid because of the case of fictional individuals.

The question before us, however, is whether existential quantification over properties fails in probability contexts. It would fail if there is a case where $P(Fa, Ga) = r$ is true but $(\exists\psi)\ [P(\psi a, Ga)] = r$ is false in second order logic. That is, it would fail if the property in question is "fictional" in the sense that *it* does not exist. It will not do to say that if a property is not instantiated, then it does not exist, because if nothing has the property of being a bachelor and married, then given second-order logic, there is some property that nothing has. Furthermore, given that there are such contradictory properties, then it seems justified to assume that existential generalization is valid over any property ascribed to an individual, whether in probability contexts or not, and whether instantiated or not. Consequently, I think that the intensionality of probability contexts does not invalidate the existential quantification over properties as required by Ramseyizing.

Conclusion about Premise (4b): Both Craigian and Ramseyan Transcriptions Preserve Epistemic Systematization

We previously concluded that the extended Craigian procedure can be used to preserve epistemic systematization. We can now draw the same conclusion about the Ramseyan method once it is similarly extended. Both methods preserve deductive systematization and, when the underlying logic of a system is supplemented with a set of axioms for the probability calculus and a set of

---

[41] See W. Quine, *Word and Object* (Cambridge, Mass: Massachusetts Institute of Technology Press, 1960), pp. 166 ff. for a general discussion of quantification over individuals in intensional or opaque contexts.

inductive rules, both methods preserve epistemic systematization, whether the system includes probability statements or only universally quantified systems. Thus premise (4b) of the original instrumentalist argument is doubly justified. We can leave it at last, and turn to premise (5b): If either Craigian transcriptions or Ramseyan transcriptions preserve epistemic systematization, then theoretical terms are unnecessary.

OBJECTIONS TO PREMISE (5b): OTHER WAYS THEORETICAL TERMS ARE NECESSARY

The basis for attacks on premise (5b) is that it is elliptical as it stands. No group of predicates is unnecessary, *simpliciter*. It is either unnecessary for some particular purposes, or, possibly, for all purposes. According to the objections to (5b) the most that has been established so far in this discussion is that theoretical terms are unnecessary for the purpose of achieving epistemic systematization, but that is not enough to show they are unnecessary for all purposes as (5b) seems to imply. Indeed, according to the various objections to (5b), there are various scientifically relevant purposes for which theoretical terms are necessary, and thus (5b) is false when it is unpacked to express what is intended:

> (5c) If either Craigian transcriptions or Ramseyan trans-
> criptions preserve epistemic systematization, then no
> theoretical terms are necessary for any purposes
> relevant to science.

There are two sorts of objections to (5c). One sort states there are certain requirements for scientific explanation other than the achievement of epistemic systematization that, for certain kinds of theories, cannot be met without theoretical terms. The other is that there are conditions for an acceptable science, other than the specific requirements of scientific explanation, for which theoretical terms are necessary. Let us consider the second sort first.

Three Objections: Acceptable Theories and Purposes of Scientists Require Theoretical Terms

I have found three objections of the second sort. The first claims that theoretical terms are needed to achieve two necessary features of an acceptable scientific theory, that is, that it produce a reasonable amount of integration of the relevant subject matter, and that, *ceteris paribus*, it be at least as simple in structure as any other competing theory.[42] It is clear that the kind of simplicity and integration imposed on a subject matter by an axiomatized theory with a small number of postulates is lost when an infinite number of postulates is required. The second and third objections state that theoretical terms are necessary for scientifically relevant purposes of scientists.

According to Maxwell,

> Both Craig's method and the Ramsey device must operate upon theories (containing, of course, theoretical terms) which are "already there." They eliminate theoretical terms only after these terms have already been used in intermediary steps. Neither provides a method for axiomatization *ab initio* or a recipe or guide for invention of new theories. Consequently neither provides a method for the elimination of theoretical terms in the all-important "context of discovery."[43]

This passage points up two species of the second objection. The first is that it is not possible to begin the development of a new science with a transcribed theory, because transcription can occur only after a nontranscribed theory is available. The second is that even if it were possible to begin with a transcribed theory, it is psychologically necessary to use the much simpler and better integrated nontranscribed version in the invention and development of the theory. The third objection, from Putnam, is that theoretical terms are necessary for scientists, because "without such terms we could not speak of radio stars, viruses, and elementary particles, for example—and we *wish* to speak of them, to learn more about them, to explain their behavior and properties better."[44]

The first objection would be quite plausible if it were amended to state that the two features are necessary for the development of acceptable scientific theories, and if only Craigian transcriptions preserved epistemic systematization. The amendment is needed,

---

[42] See N. Goodman, "Review of William Craig" *Journal of Philosophy*, 22 (1957): 317–18.
[43] Maxwell, "The Ontological Status of Theoretical Entities," p. 17.
[44] Putnam, p. 257.

because, although it is reasonable to claim that integration and relative simplicity are psychologically necessary for scientists to develop complex theories successfully, they are by no means necessary in any sense for the function of a fully developed theory to explain and predict empirical data scientifically. This requires at most that its epistemic theorems be correct and readily derivable from the axioms of the theory. But this is equivalent to the theorems of the Craigian version of the theory being correct and readily derivable from the Craigian axioms, as they surely are. Once the objection is amended, (5c) would be implausible, if only the Craigian procedure preserved epistemic systematization. A Craigian transcription does not preserve such integration and simplicity, and so theoretical terms would be needed for some purpose relevant to science. Nevertheless, the objection fails even when amended, because whatever integration or postulate simplicity is achieved by a theory is also achieved by its Ramseyized version. Thus a Ramsey transcription preserves not only epistemic systematization, but also simplicity and integration. Premise (5c) does not fail for this reason. Here is a case where the acceptability of Ramsey elimination, in addition to Craigian elimination, is of special aid to the instrumentalist.

As Bohnert indicates, Ramsey elimination can also be used to reply to both species of the second objection. In this case, however, its use allows the Craigian method to avoid the objection also. Bohnert says that from the beginning of theory construction we can assume a theory is devoid of theoretical terms if we do two things.[45] First, we should treat purported theoretical terms such as 'pi-meson' and 'mu decay,' as predicate variables from the start. Thus instead of using 'phi' and 'psi' we have different spellings of some predicate variables. Second, in order to avoid having to work and communicate with one existentially quantified postulate at any stage of development, we drop the existential quantifiers and communicate with the resulting clauses instead of sentences. Another way to interpret the latter move is to treat the terms as special constants reached by existential instantiation, instead of variables. Thus again we would have sentences from the beginning,

---

[45] See Bohnert, pp. 275–77; and "Communication by Ramsey-Sentence Clause," *Philosophy of Science*, 34 (1967): 341–47.

but no theoretical terms, because the predicate constants just function as proxies for the predicate variables once instantiated. Of course, these constants would be encumbered by the restrictions resulting from their introduction by existential instantiation, but this would cause no problem for a transcriptionist.

Furthermore, although it may be helpful for many scientists to act as if these variables or restricted constants are theoretical terms that refer to theoretical entities, it does not seem psychologically necessary to think of them in this way. There are instrumentally minded scientists who would seem to be more at ease when thinking of them as uninterpreted constants or variables.[46] This, I find, answers the second objection, and does it in a way that allows the Craigian transcriptionist to avoid the objection as well. He can derive his Craigian theories from theories construed from the beginning as containing predicate variables or restricted constants. Thus, the acceptability of both the Craigian and the Ramseyan methods again makes the instrumentalist case stronger. Consider theories as in Ramseyan form while developing to provide an integrated and relatively simple structure to aid scientists. Then, once developed, apply the Craigian procedure, which because it allows only empirical constants and variables, fully justifies no reference to theoretical entities.

There are two ways to interpret the third objection, depending upon how 'speak of elementary particles' is interpreted. It may be a purely linguistic claim equivalent to 'speak using elementary particle terminology,' or it may have ontological significance when it means to speak using terms that denote and describe elementary particles. Because theoretical terms are obviously necessary for both purposes and because some scientists have such purposes, they are purposes relevant in some way to science. And because these purposes cannot be achieved using the Craigian or Ramseyan transcription of a theory, premise (5c) is shown to be false by this objection. Clearly, the problem is that (5c) is too general. The instrumentalist wishes to consider only the purposes relevant to science that are necessary either for the development of acceptable scientific theories, or for their use to explain and predict scientif-

---

[46] Consider, for example, some who hold the Copenhagen interpretation of quantum theory, as discussed in Chapter 8.

ically the empirical data with which they deal. This is because he would claim in premise (7), suitably revised, that if theoretical terms are not necessary for the first purpose, and not even "theoretical" variables are needed for the second purpose, then there is no reason to postulate referents of theoretical terms. Let us amend the fifth premise again so that it specifies just these purposes, and, as a result, avoids the third objection:

> (5d) If either Craigian transcriptions or Ramseyan transcriptions preserve epistemic systematization, then no theoretical terms are needed for scientists to develop acceptable scientific theories, and neither theoretical terms nor variables are needed to provide acceptable scientific explanations and predictions of empirical data.

Of course, the third objection can be raised now against premise (7) as amended, but, as indicated above, and as we shall see later when we examine (7), we can reject the objection once again.

Objection: Scientific Generalizations Require Theoretical Terms

The fifth premise, as finally amended, avoids all three objections of the second sort. This leaves us with one objection of the first sort, namely, that theoretical terms are necessary for scientific explanations in certain situations. Scientific theories explain empirical generalizations directly, both universal and statistical, and singular empirical statements indirectly by explaining generalizations from which the singular statements can be derived. But as Wilfrid Sellars points out in countering instrumentalism and arguing for realism,

> Microtheories not only explain why observational constructs obey inductive generalizations, they explain what, as far as the observational framework is concerned, is a random component in their behaviour, and in the last analysis it is by doing the latter that microtheories establish their character as indispensable elements of scientific explanation and as knowledge about what really exists.[47]

[47] W. Sellars, *Science, Perception and Reality* (New York: The Humanities Press, 1963), p. 122.

The point here is that if all empirical generalizations were either universal or statistical of the form: n/m O_1's are O_2's, where $n/m >$ $\frac{1}{2}$, then it is plausible to argue that some of these generalizations could be accepted without being derived from theoretical statements, and used to provide the explanations of other empirical generalizations and of singular empirical statements. Theoretical terms would be unnecessary on this "standard account" of theories. But as Sellars points out, because of observational randomness, for some empirical statistical generalizations, $n/m < \frac{1}{2}$. Such randomness needs to be explained, and any scientific explanation of a generalization requires not only other generalizations, but ones where $n/m > \frac{1}{2}$. But in some cases of this kind, some generalization essential to the explanation has $n/m > \frac{1}{2}$ only if it contains a theoretical term. Furthermore, a statistical generalization explains a singular empirical statement only if it has $n/m > \frac{1}{2}$. Consequently, the explanations of some singular statements also require theoretical terms, because, again, some generalization essential to the explanation has $n/m > \frac{1}{2}$, only if it contains a theoretical term. Thus, on what I shall call the "Sellarsian account" of theories, there are two kinds of explanation required of some scientific theories for which theoretical terms are necessary: explanation of empirical generalizations where $n/m < \frac{1}{2}$, and explanation of singular empirical statements. The result is there are two different reasons why (5d) is false.

We can illustrate the sort of situation envisaged by this objection by considering, first, three empirical generalizations:

> G1 n/m O_1's are O_2's (where $n/m < \frac{1}{2}$)
> G2 $(1-n/m)O_1$'s are O_3's
> G3 $(x) (O_2 x \supset \sim O_3 x)$.

And, second, a theory designed to explain generalizations G_1 and G_2:

> S7 C1 n/m O_1's are T_1's
>   C2 $(1-n/m)O_1$'s are T_2's
>   C3 $(x) [(O_1 x \cdot T_1 x) \supset O_2 x]$
>   C4 $(x) [(O_1 x \cdot T_2 x) \supset O_3 x]$

This captures the form of what Sellars calls an "artificially simple" example, if we let $O_1 x = x$ is a piece of gold, $O_2 x = x$ is something that dissolves in *aqua regia* at rate p, $O_3 x = x$ is something that dissolves in *aqua regia* at rate q, $T_1 x = x$ is something with microstructure r, and $T_2 x = x$ is something with microstructure s.[48] Since p does not equal q, a scientific explanation of $G3$ is not required. If we assume with Sellars that $G1$ needs to be explained and that there is no empirical term, E, such that u/v E's are T_1's, where $u/v > \frac{1}{2}$, then we can distinguish a species of each of the two objections to (5d). The first is that theoretical terms of $S7$ are needed to explain generalization $G1$, and the second is that they are needed to explain the singular statement that something a which is O_1 is also O_2. Both are explained by $S7$. $G1$ is deducible from $S7$ alone, with dependence on its theoretical terms. That a which is O_1 is also O_2. Both are explained by $S7$. $G1$ is deducible rather than the more usual T_2. Clearly, $T_1 a$ is essential to this explanation.

Consider the first objection. We can explain observational randomness, such as expressed in $G1$, by means of theoretical statements, such as $S7$, but according to the objection we cannot do so without theoretical terms. However, if we assume, as we have, that a system explains a generalization only if it is an epistemic theorem of the system, then, the randomness can be explained by generalizations that contain no theoretical terms, and the first objection fails. This can be illustrated with $S7$ and $G1$. One reason this objection fails is that the Ramseyan transcription of $S7$ yields $G1$, and R–$S7$ has no theoretical terms. Another reason it fails is that the Craigian transcription of $S7$ would have $G1$ conjoined a certain number of times as an axiom because $G1$ is an empirical theorem of $S7$. But $G1$ conjoined is a conjunction of empirical generalizations, and thus no theoretical terms are necessary. This is true, of course, of any system that explains observational randomness. If a system explains randomness by having the generalization that expresses the randomness as an epistemic theorem, then the system transcribed in either way also explains it.

Let us turn to the second objection and apply it to the Craigian method. Given just $S7$, $T_1 a$ is essential to the explanation of why a, which is O_1, is also O_2, and thus it seems to be that the Craigian transcription of $S7$ would not explain this, because no empirical

[48] Ibid., pp. 121–22.

statement that does not entail O_2a yields O_2a when conjoined with $C–S7$. Thus it seems that while $C–S7$ preserves the epistemic systematization of $S7$, it does not preserve the explanatory power of $S7$, where $S7$, or any theory, requires a singular theoretical statement to explain something. It seems, then, that scientific explanation and epistemic systematization differ. Consequently, initially at least, this objection seems sound when directed against Craigian transcriptions, but this does not refute premise (5d) if the objection can be refuted when lodged against Ramseyan transcriptions. And, this can be done if one precaution is taken. Furthermore, the way it is done will show us how the Craigian method can avoid the objection also.

As Scheffler points out, when it is necessary to assert a singular theoretical statement, such as T_1a, to achieve a certain explanation, we must include the clause that results from Ramseyizing it within the scope of the Ramseyan quantifiers.[49] Then $R–S7a$ ($R–S7$ with the additional conjoined clause) and O_1a yield O_2a. An important consequence of this is that this derivation of O_2a counts as part of the epistemic systematization of $R–S7a$. It might be objected here that such a derivation goes beyond the epistemic systematization of $S7$, and so $R–S7a$ does not preserve epistemic systematization because it increases it. But the reply is that if $S7$ is an attempt to systematize a theory that explains why a is O_2, then $S7$ should be replaced by $S7a$ which includes T_1a as a postulate or theorem, because any theoretical statement of a scientific system that is necessary for explanation must be derivable from the postulates of the system. If this cannot be done, then the system does not preserve the explanatory power of the preaxiomatized theory and it is importantly incomplete as a result. But once all such theoretical statements are included, the empirical statements explained by a system are just those through which it achieves its epistemic systematization, and both the Ramseyan and Craigian transcriptions of the system preserve the explanatory power of the system. Thus the second reason given for requiring theoretical terms is also mistaken.

It can be objected at this point that although the Ramseyan reply to the second objection is sound, the Craigian retort is not.

---

[49] See Scheffler, *The Anatomy of Inquiry*, pp. 211–12.

For example, the relevant empirical theorem of $S7a$ is $(O_1a \supset O_2a)$, which in $C\text{--}S7a$ is derivable from an axiom consisting of that theorem conjoined a certain number of times. But this conjunction is not a generalization, and thus O_2a is not explained by being derived from a generalization as required of scientific explanation. A way to meet the letter if not the spirit of this objection is by pointing out that, if $O_1a \supset O_2a$ is a theorem of a system, then so also is the generalization $(x)\,[(x = a) \supset (O_1x \supset O_2x)]$ and the explanation of why a is O_2 can be given using that generalization. Two other replies are more substantial. The first claims that if, as for $S7a$, there is no empirical test for T_2x and thus none for T_1a, then there is no way to give a justified explanation of O_2a using $S7a$, because there is no way to justify T_1a. Surely $C\text{--}S7a$ provides at least as satisfactory an explanation as that. If, however, there is a test for T_1x, then because $S7a$ does not include a statement of it, it fails as a systematization of the theory in question. Thus, either way, $C\text{--}S7a$ is not found to be less adequate an explanation of why a is O_2 than $S7a$ is.

The third reply grants that explaining particular facts by generalizations may well be important in developing and constructing acceptable scientific theories, but denies that generalizations are required where the purposes are only explanation and prediction. If two theories have the same epistemic systematization, then what one explains is exactly what the other explains and there seems to be no reason to deny that the explanations are equally acceptable in both cases. We can say, then, as previously, that in the context of discovery and development, it seems best for an instrumentalist to give a Ramseyan construal of theories, but thereafter a Craigian version can be adopted because it preserves the explanatory power of the original and fully justifies no reference to postulated theoretical entities.

CONCLUSION ABOUT PREMISE (5d): NO THEORETICAL TERMS
NEEDED FOR DEVELOPMENT OF THEORY OR SCIENTIFIC
EXPLANATION

We have found several reasons to amend the fifth premise of the original argument, but when it is finally stated as (5d), we have uncovered no sound objections to it. We can, consequently, accept (5d), but must now examine the seventh premise. In its original form it seemed acceptable because it stated that if theoretical terms are unnecessary, then there is no reason to postulate referents for the terms. But in amending the fifth premise we have substantially restricted the ways in which theoretical terms are claimed to be unnecessary, and thus it is not immediately clear that no term being necessary in these specific ways is sufficient for there being no reason for the postulations. We must examine the seventh premise when amended as required by (5d):

> (7b) If no theoretical terms are needed for scientists to develop acceptable scientific theories and neither theoretical terms nor variables are needed to provide acceptable scientific explanations and predictions of empirical data, then there is no reason to postulate the existence of any referents of theoretical terms.

OBJECTIONS TO PREMISE (7b): OTHER WAYS TO JUSTIFY THE EXISTENCE OF THEORETICAL ENTITIES

The seventh premise is unique in the argument, because in it the inference is made from a claim about certain linguistic terms to a metaphysical claim about theoretical entities. All the premises preceding the seventh concern theoretical terms and their roles in theories, while the eighth premise concerns only theoretical entities. After some revision we found the premises about theoretical terms to be acceptable, and we accepted premise (8) from the start. If (7b) is found acceptable then the needed link between language and ontology will be justified and the instrumentalist will have reason to accept his position.

I believe that (7b) is initially plausible. This rests on the fact that when theoretical terms, such as 'ether' and 'phlogiston,' are found to be unnecessary for theory development and explanation, we are fully justified in claiming they have no referents. In (7b) this claim is extended to all theoretical terms because of the success in transcribing theories. Of course, this extension can be questioned by pointing out a difference in the way in which 'ether' is unnecessary. It is unnecessary even if no method of transcription works, because as its use developed it came to have no testable consequences and thus it failed to provide a *scientific* explanation. Clearly the case with 'electron' is different. Nevertheless the basis of the case for (7b) is that whatever the reasons may be, both 'ether' and 'electron' are unnecessary for theory development and explanation, and whenever this is true of such pure theoretical terms, then whether or not the terms are used for convenience, no referents should be postulated for them.

There are, however, objections to (7b). Thus far, I have found just two which are based either on facts about science or facts concerning scientists. Whether there are objections to (7b) that are not based on science must await Chapter 8, where I shall try to develop just such an objection. Both of the science-based objections grant that theoretical terms are not needed for the purposes of theory-development and explanation, but state that there is a reason independent of these purposes of science that justifies the postulation of referents for the terms. One is Putnam's objection that forced a revision of the fifth premise. Does the desire of scientists and philosophers "to speak of elementary particles" (either in the sense of merely using elementary particle terminology, or in the sense of using terms that denote and describe elementary particles) justify postulating referents for certain theoretical terms, given that no theoretical terms are needed for theory development or explanation? We can see that postulation is not justified in this way for either interpretation of 'speak of'. It is clear that the use of theoretical terminology is fully justified, but not only is this justified use consistent with an instrumentalist's interpretation of the terminology as a helpful but unnecessary inferring device, it surely does not justify postulating referents of the terms when they are unnecessary for theory development and explanation. Scientists can use the terminology for explanation, and can test sentences of the terminology for acceptability without being committed to holding either that those that are acceptable are merely satisfactory inferring devices or that they are, in addition, factually true assertions. These sentences are found acceptable in terms of their ability to warrant inferences, to explain, and to predict. Whether they also denote and describe entities is not settled merely by their being found scientifically acceptable in this way.[50] Because of this, Putnam's objection fails for both interpretations of 'speak of

---

[50] For two opposing views on this, see Nagel, *The Structure of Science*, pp. 129–52; and Sellars, *Philosophical Perspectives* (Springfield, Ill.: Charles C. Thomas, 1967), Chap. 14.

elementary particles.' For the first interpretation, speaking "of" such entities is fully justified by procedures of science and desires of scientists, but this alone does not justify postulating the entities. But the second interpretation with its ontological commitment to entities denoted and described by theoretical terms is not justified in the same way. More is needed to justify a move from scientifically acceptable terminology to a realistic ontology, and, given the success of transcribing theories, it is not clear what would qualify for the task.

The second objection to (7b) is an attempt to argue from the success of scientific theories to the justification of postulating theoretical entities. Maxwell, in his discussion of the role of theories in the context of discovery, points out that present theories have been devised for the purpose of discovering new empirical facts and that one fact is that many of them serve this purpose extremely well. According to Maxwell, "this fact, itself, cries out for explanation." He concludes, "The only reasonable explanation for the success of theories of which I am aware is that well-confirmed theories are conjunctions of well-confirmed, genuine statements and that the entities to which they refer, in all probability, exist."[51] Maxwell's proposed explanation is interesting because it seems to be a nonscientific explanation of the success of scientific explanations and discoveries. It is not scientific because it is *ad hoc*. It explains only the one fact it is designed to explain, and that fact is its only empirically testable consequence. I would also claim that it is a metaphysical explanation because its central claim about theoretical terms referring to unobservable entities not only is not itself empirically testable, but it is a claim about a relationship between language and ontology that is similar to the Wittgensteinian claim that atomic sentences picture atomic facts.

There are four general ways to reply to an objection such as Maxwell's: first, to deny that the success of science requires any kind of explanation; second, to claim that such nonscientific or metaphysical explanations are illegitimate; third, to claim that if they are legitimate, there are alternative explanations of the same kind at least as plausible; and, fourth, to claim that whether or not such explanations are legitimate, there is an explanation of the

---

[51] Maxwell, "The Ontological Status of Theoretical Entities," p. 18.

success which is scientific, or at least empirical and not meta-physical. I shall here sidestep the issues involved in the first two sorts of replies and shall assume that some sort of explanation is required and that metaphysical explanations are generally legiti-mate. Then I shall briefly sketch again the Berkeleyan alternative metaphysical explanation and also offer an explanation which, even if it does not qualify as scientific, is empirical and not meta-physical.

Although it is sometimes overlooked, we have seen that Berkeley's phenomenalism combines scientific explanations of observable facts with metaphysical explanations of the same facts by embracing scientific instrumentalism. And his metaphysical explanation of these facts also provides a metaphysical explan-ation of the success of science. If we assume with Berkeley that it is not "the business of physics or mechanics to establish efficient causes, but only the rules of impulsions or attractions, and, in a word, the laws of motions, and from the established laws to assign the solution, not the efficient cause of particular phenomena,"[52] then the causation or production of observable phenomena requires a different kind of explanation. For Berkeley, such production requires active entities, that is, minds. And, the fact that humans can discover these laws, construct theories that explain the laws and theories, requires that the kind of mind postulated to explain the production of observable phenomena be of a certain sort. This mind—the author of nature—must be a powerful, orderly, rational being. It must not only be capable of presenting lesser minds with a multitude of sensory ideas in ways that allow for explanation and prediction by laws and theories, but it must also be capable of endowing human minds with the ability to uncover the laws and devise the theories. Whether Berkeley is justified in claiming that the author of nature is also benevolent, we need not discuss here. We can, however, end by noting that Berkeley need postulate just one pure theoretical entity instead of the many required by Maxwell's rival metaphysical explanation. Occam's Razor would seem to require that we find Berkeley's theory preferable, at least in this respect.

We need not however, turn to metaphysical explanations of the

---

[52] *Berkeley, George, The Works of*, 9 vols., eds. A. Luce and T. Jessup, (Edinburgh: Thomas Nelson and Sons, 1948–57), *De Motu*, 35.

success of scientific theories in the context of discovery. The following is a rough outline of an empirical explanation. As Quine says, scientific theories are "empirically underdetermined," and they have more empirical consequences than just those that they are designed to explain and predict. Thus they explain, predict, and lead to discoveries of new empirical phenomena no one had ever imagined before the theories were developed. Of course, this is not true of all proposed theories, but only of some that are well developed and tested. Many theories have been abandoned, and many of those now accepted have been constantly revised. Those we now accept seem so admirably suited to discovery, explanation, and prediction because they have been devised for that purpose, are empirically underdetermined, and have been able to accomodate unexpected observations by acceptable revisions instead of being rejected. Of course, based on the evidence of the past, it is likely that some of those that now may seem so admirably suited, will be drastically altered or even abandoned. It is the self-corrective nature of the scientific enterprise that forms the core of this empirical explanation of the success of scientific theories, rather than some metaphysical fitting of either theory or observation to something purely theoretical. It may be that both kinds of explanations of the success are acceptable, but whether either kind is acceptable, regardless of which kind it is, we have found plausible alternatives to Maxwell's explanation, and thus have reason to reject the second, and last, objection to (7b) from science.

CONCLUSION ABOUT SCIENTIFIC INSTRUMENTALISM AND BERKELEYAN PHENOMENALISM

We have not yet found a reason to reject (7b), and, based on the preceding discussion, we have found the other premises facing objections to be acceptable. Thus this argument to justify scientific instrumentalism stands unrefuted, and scientific realism remains unjustified. This is an important conclusion for our evaluation of all forms of phenomenalism, whether Berkeleyan or eliminative. We found in Chapter 3 that no form of phenomenalism is a plausible theory of mind, perception, and the external world, unless scientific instrumentalism is plausible, because, while Berkeley's version allows observational theoretical terms and mind-terms to be referring terms, no version of phenomenalism allows the pure, nonreporting theoretical terms of science to refer to anything. Thus, having found no reason to reject instrumentalism, we have overcome the last obstacle for our reconstruction of the Berkeleyan theory of mind. This allows us to refute the first of the four major objections to Berkeleyan phenomenalism that remained unanswered at the end of Chapter 3. However, although we still have not done enough to refute the last three objections, significant progress has been made.

Consider the fourth objection, which claims that the theory is unscientific. We have found that there is no need to postulate theoretical entities in order to develop acceptable scientific theories and to provide acceptable scientific explanations and predictions of empirical data. Thus by adopting scientific instrumentalism, a phenomenalist has done nothing to nullify, limit, retard, or in any way demean scientific investigation and progress. So, in one important sense Berkeleyan phenomenalism is not unscientific, that is, it is not anti-science. Of course, this does not refute that it is unscientific in the different sense of postulating an entity for explanatory purposes in an *ad hoc*, untestable, and implausible way. Whether a Berkeleyan author of nature is unscientific in this sense is not decided by the preceding conclusions. Consideration of this problem must await, however, until Chapter 8 where the Berkeleyan explanatory schema will be contrasted with the schema available to a scientific realist in order to discover which schema more closely approaches the ideal of explanation as clear and precise understanding of what is explained in terms of its antecedent or constituent causes. It is, incidentally, in this discussion that a new objection to premise (7b), which is independent of the requirements of science and scientists, will be developed.

Much remains to be done before the second and third major objections to Berkeleyan phenomenalism are refuted, but we are now closer to replies. The second objection is that there is no way to make plausible the crucial Berkeleyan claim that physical objects are bundles of sensa. I replied in Chapter 3 that this claim could be explicated and shown to be plausible by construing physical objects as theoretical constructs out of sensa. Thus the relationships between observational theoretical terms and sensum terms is to be taken as analogous to that between scientific theoretical terms and observation terms. The remaining task, then, regarding the second objection, is to state this version of theoretical phenomenalism as clearly as possible while refuting the major objection to it, which I have said stems from Sellars. A crucial part of this task will be to give some helpful examples of correspondence rules in the form of identity statements that identify a physical object with a group of sensa. Once such examples are given, we shall also be able to answer the third objection that for Berkeley no two perceivers perceive the same thing. This can be handled by means of correspondence rules that relate two sorts of events: events of different perceivers sensing different sensa in the group that is identical with a certain physical object, and events of those same perceivers perceiving that physical object. Once this is done, we will have found, I believe, a quite reasonable version of Berkeleyan phenomenalism.

5   Theoretical Phenomenalism

We have seen that one of the major objections that faces a phenomenalist who claims that there is nothing over and above ideas, or
sense-data and, perhaps, perceiving minds, is how to account for
the seemingly evident truth that there are physical objects. Berkeley's answer to this objection is to say that "a certain color, taste,
smell, figure and consistence having been observed to go together,
are accounted one distinct thing signified by the name 'apple'; other
collections of ideas constitute a stone, a tree, a book and the like
sensible things."[1] Our primary task is to give a plausible explication
of this Berkeleyan thesis that will enable us to refute not only the
principle objections to the thesis, but also the objection that
Berkeley can make no sense of two perceivers seeing the same
physical object.

Our problem is to find a defensible explication of the thesis that
a physical object, such as an apple or, using Philonous' example, a
cherry is nothing but a collection of ideas, sense-data, or percepts,
that is, what I have called "sensa." We have seen that it is of no
help to interpret the thesis as would an analytical phenomenalist,
such as the early A. J. Ayer, who claims that physical objects are
logical constructions out of sensa. This is because of well known,
successful objections to such analyses raised by Ayer, later, and also
by R. M. Chisholm. I have, however, offered another interpretation, namely, that physical objects are theoretical constructions
rather than logical constructions out of our sensa or ideas. On this
thesis the relationship between physical-object statements and
sensum statements is logically contingent, and is analogous to the
relationship between theoretical statements and observation statements, as mediated by correspondence rules, which is also contingent. It is this thesis I shall explicate and defend. To do this I
shall consider the principle objection to the thesis as it has been

---

[1] Berkeley, *Principles, Dialogues, and Correspondence* (New York: Bobbs-Merrill, 1965),
p. 22.

raised by W. Sellars.[2]

THEORETICAL PHENOMENALISM AND THEORETICAL CONSTRUCTS

Sellars begins his discussion of theoretical phenomenalism, which he calls the "new" phenomenalism, to contrast it with "old," that is, analytical phenomenalism, by stating the thesis he wishes to refute:

> Although the framework of physical objects is not translatable into the framework of sense contents, this is not because it refers to entities over and above sense contents. It is merely a conceptual device which enables us to find our way around in the domain of what we directly observe in a manner analogous to the role played by scientific objects with respect to the domain of the observable in a less stringent sense of this word.[3]

He goes on to say why he rejects this view:

> It is my purpose to argue that this won't do, *not* however, on the grounds that 'real existence' should not be denied to theoretical entities—though indeed, I agree that it should not —but rather on the ground that the relation of the framework of physical objects to the framework of sense contents cannot be assimilated to that of a micro-theory to its observation base.[4]

His reason for this rejection is that the assimilation requires an analogy with what I called in Chapter 4, following Sellars, "the standard account" of theories. According to this view, the relationship between theory and observation can be expressed by four kinds of statements: theoretical statements, correspondence rules, observation generalizations, and singular observation statements. An overly simple example of this kind of relationship is a theoretical system with theoretical postulates $(x)(T_1 x \supset T_2 x)$ and $(x)(T_2 x \supset T_3 x)$, correspondence rules $(x)(O_1 x \supset T_1 x)$ and $(x)(T_3 x \supset O_2 x)$, observation generalization $(x)(O_1 x \supset O_2 x)$, and various singular

---

[2] See W. Sellars, *Science, Perception and Reality* (London: Routledge and Kegan Paul, 1963), Chap. 3.
[3] Sellars, p. 86.
[4] Ibid.

observation statements such as O_1a and O_2a. In this case the theory explains why a which is O_1 is also O_2, by explaining the observation generalization which is derivable from the theory. However, if a theory is to be satisfactory, at least some of the generalizations that it explains must be inductively confirmed independently of the theory itself. This is important for testing the theory. On the standard account these are observation generalizations. Thus if a close analogy with the standard account is to hold for a theoretical phenomenalist, there must be independently confirmable *sensum* (or sensing) generalizations that are derivable from the "theoretical" physical-object statements and correspondence rules. But, Sellars argues, there are no such sensum generalizations.[5] Thus the analogy on which theoretical phenomenalism relies fails, and the theory is refuted.

We can lay out a first approximation of Sellars' argument as follows:

(1) If theoretical phenomenalism is correct, then the relation between some physical-object statements and some sensum statements is closely analogous to the relation between theoretical statements and observation statements on the standard account of theories.

(2) If the preceding close analogy is correct, then some physical-object statements explain independently inductively confirmable sensum generalizations.

(3) There are no independently inductively confirmable sensum generalizations.

Therefore

(4) Theoretical phenomenalism is not correct.

Of the three premises, only (2) is clearly acceptable, because, as we have just seen, the analogy requires that the role of observation generalizations on the standard account corresponds to the role of sensum generalizations for a theoretical phenomenalist. The other two premises, however, require more extensive examination.

Premise (3) and Essentially Autobiographical Generalizations

As stated, premise (3), which supposedly states a crucial dis-

[5] Sellars, p. 87.

analogy, is dubious, but Sellars would admit to this. His claim is that some "essentially autobiographical" sensum generalizations would be independently confirmable, but that theoretical phenomenalism requires sensum generalizations that are merely "accidentally autobiographical" and none of these are independently confirmable. Consider, for example:

> G1   Whenever I have gustatory sensa immediately preceded by red cherry-like visual sensa, I have a sensum of tartness.

Such a generalization is merely accidentally autobiographical, if it is true and it is reasonable that it remain true when 'anybody' is substituted for 'I' throughout to produce what we can call, following Ryle, an "open" generalization, that is, $(x)(O_1 x \supset O_2 x)$.[6] But if its remaining true with the substitution is clearly unreasonable, then it is essentially autobiographical. Sellars' claim is that all independently confirmable sensum generalizations are essentially autobiographical and thus no open sensum generalizations are inductively confirmable independently of physical-object claims. Thus, while (3) is dubious, Sellars would claim the following is acceptable:

> (3a) There are no independently inductively confirmable *open* sensum generalizations.

We can agree with Sellars that it is unlikely that there are any confirmable, universally quantified, open sensum generalizations, because our sensory experience is too disorderly for any constant conjunction of sensa. It is far from clear, however, that it is so disorderly that there are no confirmable, probabilistic, open sensum generalizations. Consider, for example:

> G2. It is probable that someone has a sensum of tartness at a time, t, given that at t, he has gustatory sensa immediately preceded by red cherry-like visual sensa, that is, $P(O_2 x, O_1 x) > .5$.

Furthermore, we can explain this "observation" generalization by deriving it from a "theoretical" postulate: $(x)(T_1 x \supset T_2 x)$, where $T_1 x = x$ tastes a red cherry, and $T_2 x = x$ tastes a physical object

---

[6] See Sellars, p. 81, and G. Ryle, *The Concept of Mind* (New York: Barnes and Noble, 1949), pp. 120–21.

that is tart; and two probabilistic correspondence rules: $P(T_1x, O_1x) > .7$, and $P(O_2x, O_1x \cdot T_2x) > .8$.[7]

There are two replies to the preceding move suggested by Sellars' discussion. The first is that it is unlikely such open probabilistic generalizations are true because their non-open or autobiographical form that is restricted to me depends on the contingent peculiarities of my environment and myself in such a way that they cannot be made open and true. The second reply is that even if some of these autobiographical generalizations are true when made open, there is no way to confirm them inductively that does not "presuppose our common sense knowledge of ourselves as perceivers, of the specific physical environment in which we do our perceiving and of the general principles which correlate the occurrence of sensations with bodily and environmental conditions."[8] Thus such generalizations are not confirmable independently of the "theory" used to explain them.

Sellars' reason for the first reply would seem to be that an autobiographical sensum generalization is true only if its antecedent expresses a very complex pattern of sensa. Supposedly, this is the only way to eliminate disconfirming instances that would arise because of many interruptions in and interferences with the uniformities in my own sensory experience. And, once these statements are tied to my peculiarities they are clearly essentially autobiographical. It is unclear, however, that any clauses in an acceptable sensum generalization require this complexity if it is probabilistic and it is not offered as an analysis of a physical-object statement. It may be because most of Sellars' discussion of sensum generalizations occurs in the context of his objection to analytical phenomenalism that he rests so much on the claim about complexity. But $G2$, with its quite simple clauses, seems to be not only quite reasonable, but also the sort of generalization that uniformities in sense experience would inductively confirm.

At this point the second Sellarsian reply becomes appropriate. Just how am I to confirm $G2$ inductively and independently of any reliance on evidence expressed in terms of physical objects and

---

[7] This derivation can be made using a set of assumptions that includes:
$0 \leqslant P(B, A) \leqslant 1$; $P(B \cdot C, A) = P(B, A) \times P(C, A \cdot B)$; and $(x)(Fx \supset Gx) \supset P(Gx, Fx) = 1$

[8] Sellars, p. 84.

persons? If we must make reference to such "theoretical" entities in stating our evidence, then the analogy with the standard account of theories is broken. To confirm $G2$, I would have to get the testimony of other persons and observe their bodily behavior in relevant physical environments. I would have to use statements about the verbal and nonverbal behavior of other persons to justify statements about which sorts of sensa are constantly, or usually, conjoined in their sensory experiences. Thus, according to this objection, "theoretical" evidence would be more basic than "observational" evidence.

Is this reply sound? It is clear that I can get some inductive evidence for some sensum generalizations from my own experience. Furthermore, these generalizations need not be autobiographical in form. I can, for example, merely list the times I have found $O_1 x$ true of someone, without relying on theoretical evidence, and compare this with the corresponding number of times I found $O_2 x$ to be true of the same perceiver, namely, myself. The resulting relative frequency is certainly independent inductive evidence for $G2$, but it can surely be objected that it is not strong enough to confirm $G2$. Three points can be made here. First, more evidence that is not expressed in physical-object statements can be found to support $G2$. The testimonial evidence of other perceivers which I see or hear can be construed as sensa produced by other perceivers after I produce certain sensa relevant to $G2$ that they experience. For example, I might express my desire to get evidence about $G2$ by producing certain auditory sensa for other perceivers to experience. And then, when I get certain returning auditory sensa, I interpret them as expressing the thoughts of these other perceivers about those of their sensa which are relevant to $G2$. In doing this, neither I nor these other "finite" perceivers need to postulate physical objects, or use physical-object terms. Of course, the existence of these other perceivers is assumed, but, contrary to Sellars, this raises no problems, because no physical properties of perceivers are assumed and phenomenalists need not view perceivers as purely theoretical. As Berkeley says, "the sentient, percipient, thinking thing we know by a certain internal consciousness."[9] Thus a theoretical phenomenalist can allow reference

---

[9] Berkeley, *De Motu*, Sec. 21.

to perceivers in the sensum generalizations. Indeed, as *G2* shows, reference to perceivers is surely needed in such generalizations, but this allows *G2* to be confirmed in a way that does not depend on any physical-object statements.

It is not clear, however, that a theoretical phenomenalist must argue for this testimonial source of evidence. If only autobiographical evidence is allowed, then, even granting that no autobiographical evidence is strong enough to confirm *G2*, it is likely to be at least strong enough to call for a theory to explain the uniformity stated in *G2* which I perceive at least in my own case. Then, once such a theory is developed, it can be used, as are other theories, not only to explain *G2*, but also to derive other sensum generalizations which I can partially confirm with new autobiographical evidence. This will help confirm the theory and thereby *G2*, which is derivable from it. However, even without this additional, dependent confirmation of *G2*, and thus with only the insufficient autobiographical evidence for *G2*, there is still a third defense available for the theoretical phenomenalist. The autobiographical evidence can certainly confirm or disconfirm an autobiographical version of *G2*. Although this would not be an open sensum generalization as the standard account requires, it is an independently confirmable generalization. Thus except for this one point, the analogy would hold, and I see no reason to deny that this is close enough for the theoretical phenomenalist. If, contrary to my preceding points, he is forced to this defense, he could even forego his refutation of (3a) and still resist defeat. He could justify rejecting either (1) or (2), when (2) is amended to correspond to (3a), depending on how strictly a close analogy with the standard account is construed. If the analogy's being close requires that the sensum generalizations are open, he could reject (1). If it lacks this implication he could reject (2). However, his main point would remain that (3a) is at least dubious enough to forestall its use as a premise to justify a conclusion.

AN AMENDED PREMISE (3): THE STANDARD ACCOUNT AND THE ORDER
OF CONCEPT FORMATION

There is another objection to the analogy we have not yet considered. It can be stated by amending (3) in a different way:

(3b) There are no inductively confirmable generalizations that can be stated with no physical-object terms and no terms which are derivatives of physical-object terms, e.g., 'cherry-like.'

Once (2) is amended accordingly, this objection is that all three premises are true and the conclusion (4) is established. Although we can perhaps be generous in allowing derivatives of physical-object terms in a sensum sentence used to analyze a physical-object sentence, it can be objected that we cannot do so in the present case because it depends upon a close analogy with the standard account. Observation terms, it is argued, are not derivatives of scientific theoretical terms.

The most decisive reply to this objection is to produce a generalization using "pure" sensum terms. We might try:

G3. It is probable that some one has a sensum of tartness at a time, t, given that at t he has gustatory sensa immediately preceded by red, globular, small, shiny, smooth, moist, soft, plump sensa, that is, $P(O_2x, O_3x) > .5$.

If the sensum adjectives used in G3 seem not to be enough to increase the probability to greater than .5, then it is possible to supply more to raise the probability. However, it can still be objected in the spirit of Sellars that 'red,' 'globular,' 'firm,' and the rest are also derivatives of physical-object terms, because they are analogically derived, in the orders of concept formation and concept learning, from physical-object terms. If this reply is allowed, then there is a disanalogy between sensum terms and the observation terms of the standard account.

The crucial question for this objection is whether priority in the orders of the formation and the learning of concepts is a feature of the standard account itself, or whether it is merely a feature of those terms that supposedly fit the standard account of scientific theories, that is, observation terms. It is clear that at least some epistemological independence of the nontheoretical terms from the theoretical terms is essential. However, a term P being derivative from some term Q in the orders of concept formation and learning, is consistent with the confirmation of sentences using P being independent of and even prior to the confirmation of sentences using Q. Epistemological independence is compatible with dependence of concept formation and learning.[10] And, because it is epistemological independence that is essential to the standard account, I conclude that a phenomenalist who utilizes the standard account can grant this disanalogy between sensum terms and observation terms without damaging consequences. Thus he can grant (3b), because when (2) is amended to correspond to (3b) it becomes dubious. An analogy with the standard account does not prohibit this disanalogy. The second attempt to find a crucial disanalogy fails as did the first.

Premise (1) and a Nonstandard Account of Theories

Throughout the preceding discussion I have been assuming that theoretical phenomenalism requires the standard account of the relationship between physical-object statements and sensum statements, but it is now time to question that assumption, that is, premise (1). Sellars thinks that the standard account of the relationship between scientific theories and observation is mistaken and proposes a different model, which I have called the "Sellarsian account." It can be asked, however, why he insists on a different model for scientific theories but claims that theoretical phenomenalism needs the standard account. To answer this, let us first recall the Sellarsian account and then see why Sellars thinks a theoretical phenomenalist cannot accept it. If the standard account of theories is correct, then there are independently confirmable observation generalizations that are either universal or probabilistic, such as $P(O_2 x, O_1 x) = n$, where $n > .5$. Such generalizations could be accepted without being derived from theoretical statements, and used to provide the explanations of other observational generalizations and singular observation statements. Theoretical terms would be unnecessary. But, as Sellars points out, because of observational randomness, for some probabilistic observational generalizations, $n < .5$. Such randomness needs to be explained, and any scientific explanation of a generalization requires not only other generalizations, but at least some where $n > .5$. But, says Sellars, in some cases of this kind, no acceptable generalization essential to the explanation has $n > .5$ if it does not contain a

[10] For a related discussion, see Chapter 7 and also my "Materialism and Some Myths about Some Givens," *The Monist* (1972), esp. pp. 217–18, and pp. 224–27.

theoretical term. Consequently, he concludes, some theoretical terms are needed to formulate certain inductively confirmable generalizations that are needed for certain explanations. This is the Sellarsian account of theories. And, if it is correct, then the standard account, which implies that no theoretical terms are needed to formulate any such explanatory generalizations, is mistaken.

We can illustrate how the sort of situation envisaged by Sellars can be applied to our example of sensum statements if we let $O_4 x = x$ has only a hot, peppery sensum, and assume that $P(O_4 x, O_1 x) < .5$. We can explain why a who has O_1, also has O_2, by using the observational generalization $P(O_2 x, O_1 x) > .5$. But $P(O_4 x, O_1 x) < .5$ does not explain why b who has O_1, also has O_4. However, if we let $T_3 x = x$ tastes a red cherry marinated in Tabasco sauce, and assume $P(O_4 x, O_1 x \cdot T_3 x) > .7$, then we can explain that b has O_4, because $T_3 b$, and thus $P(O_4 b, O_1 b) > .7$. The crucial point here is that we cannot use $P(O_4 x, O_1 x) < .5$ or, let us assume, any other open observational generalization to explain why b has O_4. The result is that the standard account is wrong if, as surely seems likely, there are cases such as b's having O_4. Consequently, according to Sellars, theoretical terms are indispensable for explaining certain singular observational statements, whether they are sensum statements or observational physical-object statements, and the Sellarsian account is correct.

We have seen that Sellars seems to think that theoretical phenomenalism is correct only if the standard account of theories correctly specifies the relation between sensum statements and physical-object statements, and that the standard account is mistaken. He also seems to agree that the standard account of the relationship is sufficient for theoretical phenomenalism, because he says:

> *If* the observation framework permits the formulation of inductive generalizations—statistical or non-statistical— which hold within limits which can be accounted for in terms of such concepts as accuracy of measurement and experimental error ..., then the positivistic interpretation of theoretical entities is inescapable.[11]

---

[11] Sellars, p. 96.

It is clear that if we adapt this to the "sensum framework," an instrumental interpretation of physical-object terms is implied. This in turn implies theoretical phenomenalism, given a realistic interpretation of sensum terms. Although I believe Sellars overstates the reasonableness of the first implication by saying the consequent is "inescapable" given the antecedent, we have seen in Chapter 4 that it is plausible because of the theoretician's dilemma. But why should Sellars hold the converse?

AN ARGUMENT FOR PREMISE (1): THEORETICAL PHENOMENALISM AND INSTRUMENTALISM

The most plausible argument I can devise for showing that the standard account is necessary for theoretical phenomenalism involves the converse of the two preceding implications. This is to argue, as I believe Sellars would, that theoretical phenomenalism requires an instrumental view of all physical-object terms, which in turn requires that no such terms are needed for explanations of singular sensum statements. Thus they can be explained merely by open sensum generalizations as the standard account states. In more detail the premises for this argument are:

(5) If theoretical phenomenalism is correct, then all physical-object terms are nonreferring inferring devices.

(6) If all physical-object terms are such devices, then none of them are needed to explain any singular sensum statements.

(7) If no physical-object terms are needed in this way, then all explainable singular sensum statements are explained by open sensum generalizations.

(8) If all explainable singular sensum statements are so explained, then the standard account of theories is correct for physical-object terms.

Furthermore, we know that if the Sellarsian account is correct, then the standard account is not. Thus, if our preceding assumption about the need for physical-object terms to explain why b has only a hot, peppery sensum is correct, then it follows that the standard account and theoretical phenomenalism are both incorrect.

We can grant premise (8) on the assumption that a sensum statement contains sensum terms and, in addition, at most per-

ceiver terms, individual variables, and logical constants. The other
three premises, however, are open to doubt. The converse of (5)
is acceptable on the grounds that if no physical-object terms are
referring terms, then neither scientific theoretical terms, nor
observation physical object terms, are referring terms and only
sensation terms are left to denote what we perceive. This is sufficient
for theoretical phenomenalism. Nevertheless, it is not necessary,
because it does not allow for the particular species of theoretical
phenomenalism we are presently considering. Berkeleyan reductive
phenomenalism, unlike the eliminative varieties, construes physical
objects as bundles or groups of sensa, and one requirement of
such a view would seem to be that at least some physical-object
terms sometimes denote collections of sensa. Thus the most we
should accept is:

> (5a) If theoretical phenomenalism is correct, then each
> physical-object term is either a nonreferring term or a
> referring term that denotes at most collections of
> sensa.

But this amendment forces a change in (6) which makes it clearly
dubious. It would seem that a physical-object term that denotes
a collection of sensa is as likely as any term to be needed for
explanations of someone's having sensa. Thus, assuming that $T_3 b$
is needed to explain why b has O_4, it is plausible to argue that the
phrase 'a physical object marinated in Tabasco sauce' denotes at
some time certain sensa that b experiences at that time, and is also
needed to explain a singular sensum statement.

However, even if the argument is restricted to instrumentalistic
versions of eliminative phenomenalism, so that (5) and (6) can
remain unamended, (6) is still open to doubt. The converse of (6)
would be acceptable if it were shown that all physical-object terms
are what, in Chapter 4, I called "pure" theoretical terms, that is,
very roughly, nonreporting theoretical terms. Although there is
some reason to doubt this construal, the argument from the
theoretician's dilemma would then be plausible.[12] In short, if no

---

[12] It surely seems that some physical-object terms are observation terms and so are reporting
terms. For the definition of 'pure theoretical term,' see my *Materialism and Sensations*,
p. 102.

pure theoretical terms are needed to establish inferential relationships among observation sentences, then they are not needed for
any explanatory purpose, and, by Occam's razor, no entities should
be postulated as denoted by them. But (6) is not justified in this
way. We can see that it is open to doubt by considering that logical
terms are needed for explanations, and yet it is quite reasonable
to hold that all of them are nonreferring inferring devices. Furthermore, a need for mathematical terms in explanations would not be
sufficient for a realistic interpretation of the terms. It is of course
true that there are differences between physical-object terms, and
logical and mathematical terms, but it is far from clear how to use
these linguistic differences, in a way that does not beg the question,
in order to justify that an explanatory need implies reference in
the former case but not in the latter cases.[13]

PREMISE (7), RAMSEY SENTENCES, AND CRAIG'S THEOREM   The crucial
objection to the preceding argument, however, is that premise (7)
is false, if we assume, as we did when accepting (8), that a sensum
statement contains sensum terms, but, in addition, at most perceiver
terms, individual variables, and logical constants. We shall see
later why this interpretation is crucial for the truth of (8). One
reason (7) is false as so interpreted, is that a Ramsey-sentence
translation of an open generalization explaining singular sensum
statements contains no physical-object terms, because each one is
replaced with a predicate variable. Thus, although the Ramseyized
sentence contains no physical-object terms, it is not a sensum
sentence because it contains predicate variables. For example,
we have assumed that $T_3 b \cdot P(O_4 x, O_1 x \cdot T_3 x) > .7$ explains why b
which has O_1 also has O_4. We also assumed that we cannot drop
$T_3 b$ or replace it with a sensum term in the generalization and still
use the generalization to explain why b has O_4. But we can explain
this by using the corresponding Ramsey sentence, which is an
open generalization but not a sensum statement:

$$(\exists \phi)[\phi b \cdot P(O_4 x, O_1 x \cdot \phi x) > .7].$$

Here no physical-object terms are needed. But this explanation is

[13] I have discussed some of the problems involved in inferring reference claims from logical
and linguistic claims in *Metaphysics, Reference, and Language* (New Haven: Yale University Press, 1966), esp. Chap. 3 and Part III.

not by an open *sensum* generalization, and, it is reasonable to assume, there is no other explanation by an open sensum generalization. Thus (7) is false.

Of course, we can also show that (7) is false by using the Craigian procedure for eliminating theoretical terms. As argued in Chapter 4, this procedure can be extended to cover explanations by probability statements in such a way that neither theoretical terms nor predicate variables are needed. For example, since we derived $P(O_4 b, O_1 b) >$ .7 and used it to explain why b has O_4, the Craigian procedure shows how to achieve a set of observation postulates from which $P(O_4 b, O_1 b) > .7$ is derivable as a theorem. However, while the theorem and relevant postulate are sensum statements, neither one is an open generalization. Thus, unlike the Ramseyized explanation, no open generalization would be included in this explanation. These two objections indicate how to amend (7) to make it acceptable, namely:

> (7a) If no physical-object terms are needed to explain any singular sensum statements, then each explainable singular sensum statement is explained either by an open sensum generalization, or by an open generalization with sensum terms and predicate variables but no physical-object terms, or by a non-open sensum statement.

If we amend (7) this way, we must also amend the antecedent of (8), but such an amendment makes (8) lose its plausibility. As briefly stated above, both the Ramseyan and Craigian procedures show how to provide explanations of singular sensum statements without using either physical-object terms or open sensum generalizations. But if, as is reasonable, there are such explanations, then the standard account is mistaken and (8), as amended to accommodate (7a), would have a true antecedent and false consequent. The truth of (8) depends on restricting its antecedent to explanations made by open sensum generalizations. Furthermore, we were mistaken in assuming that $T_3 b \cdot P(O_4 x, O_1 x \cdot T_3 x) > .7$ is needed to explain why b is O_4. As in this case, theoretical terms are needed only for explanations of certain singular observation (sensum) statements by generalizations that are open and are also observation (sensum) generalizations. There is, however, no reason to require the explaining generalizations to be of that form, because the effects of the Craig and Ramsey eliminations allow the explanatory use of predicate variables and non-open generalizations. Thus there is reason to reject not only the standard account, but also the Sellarsian account because of its claim that theoretical terms are indispensable for certain explanations.[14]

The consequence of this for theoretical phenomenalism is to make clear that it does not require the standard account, contrary to premise (1). This theory can allow many sorts of relationships between physical-object sentences and sensum sentences which differ from the one relationship required by the standard account. Indeed, a Berkeleyan could even accommodate the Sellarsian account and its claim about the indispensability of certain theoretical (physical-object) terms, by making the plausible assumption that all needed physical-object terms are those that denote certain sensa when correctly used in certain of the explanations of why perceivers have the sensa they do. Furthermore, as I shall try to show below, a Berkeleyan can even accomodate the need to use physical-object terms in certain explanations in which it is clearly unreasonable to take them to be denoting any sensa.

PHENOMENALISM AND AN EXPLANATORY NEED FOR PHYSICAL-OBJECT TERMS

A theoretical phenomenalist who accepts the Sellarsian account of theories can easily accommodate those explanations of why someone has certain sensa that involve, but only involve, those physical objects that are perceived. Our previous examples involving tasting are of this kind. If we assume, contrary to fact, that we must use $T_3 b$ to explain why b has O_4, this need not bother a theoretical phenomenalist. He can claim that whenever the event of someone sensing a certain sensum is explained by the postulation

---

[14] If the preceding discussion and that in Chapter 4 is right, then the correct account of theories is as follows: (1) Some confirmable, open observation generalizations are neither universal nor probabilistic with $n > \frac{1}{2}$; (2) all explainable, singular observation statements are explainable without theoretical terms; and (3) some explainable, singular observation statements are not explainable by open generalizations that have no predicate variables and no theoretical constants. The standard account disagrees with the first and third clauses, and the Sellarsian account disagrees with the second.

of that perceiver perceiving some physical object, P, and the explanation is "minimally adequate," then, in the context of that explanatory use, 'P' denotes something, namely the sensum it is used to explain.[15] Thus 'red cherry,' as used in the preceding explanation with T_3b, would denote a sensum, indeed, a hot, peppery sensum, because this minimally adequate explanation of b having that sensum includes the postulation that b tastes a red cherry. Note that it is not claimed that this theoretical postulation is needed for every minimally adequate explanation of someone having a sensum, but only that some minimally adequate explanation includes it. This Berkeleyan claim that relates what a physical object term explains to what it denotes, can be stated more precisely in the following contingent correspondence rule (C-rule):

> $C1$. What 'c' denotes in the sentence 'At time t, someone, P, perceives cherry c,' is sensum s *if and only if* some minimally adequate explanation of the event of p sensing s at t, but not of any other sensation-event, includes the postulation that at t, p perceives c.

This claim about the reference of a physical-object term indicates how a Berkeleyan might begin to explicate what it is for a cherry to be, as Philonous says, "nothing but a congeries of sensible impressions, or ideas perceived by various senses, which ideas are united into one thing (or have one name given them) by the mind because they are observed to attend each other."[16] We need to do more than this, however, because $C1$ is not sufficient to distinguish Philonous' reductionistic claim from the eliminative claims of a 'physical object' elimination theorist. Although both agree that sensa are sometimes denoted by physical-object terms, only a reductionist makes the additional claim that each physical object is nothing but, and thereby identical with, some group of sensa.[17] We can distinguish between the two theories by realizing that only a Berkeleyan would claim that a physical-object term denotes a sensum when and only when the sensum is in the group with which

---

[15] A set of assumptions is *minimally* adequate to explain something just in case the set is adequate to explain it, but no proper subset is adequate to explain it.

[16] Berkeley, *Principles, Dialogues, and Correspondence*, pp. 195–96.

[17] For a discussion of what it is for an entity to be reduced to, that is, be nothing but an entity, see the Appendix.

the corresponding object is identical. We can express this relationship between denotation and identity as follows:

> C2. Sensum s is in the group of sensa that is identical with cherry c *if and only if* for some value of 'x' in 'At time x, someone perceives cherry c,' what 'c' denotes is sensum s.

In these ways, we can begin to understand not only a Berkeleyan conception of the conditions in which physical-object terms denote sensa, but also the conditions for identifying physical objects with particular groups of sensa, and even their reduction to those groups. Furthermore, a Berkeleyan theoretical phenomenalist can use this explication of this part of a Berkeleyan theory of physical objects whether or not he agrees with Sellars that some theoretical terms are indispensible. Even if no theoretical term is needed to achieve adequate explanations, a Berkeleyan can claim that a theoretical term denotes something whenever it is used in certain of the minimally adequate explanations of an event of someone having certain sensa.

There are, however, other explanations of why perceivers have certain sensa which entail that there are unperceived physical objects. Using Hume's example, we would explain why someone, p, has grey-ash-like sensa now when some time ago he had flaming-log-like sensa, by postulating: p had been seeing a burning log in his fireplace at t that continued to burn unperceived until it turned to the ashes he now sees.[18] We can formalize this explanation by letting $O_5 x = x$ has flaming-log-like sensa sometime ago at t, and $O_6 x = x$ has grey-ash-like sensa now; and by expressing the complex postulation using $T_4 py$. Then we can explain why p, who has O_5, also has O_6 by $(\exists y)\, T_4 py$ and $P(O_6 x, O_5 x \cdot T_4 xy) > .5$. If we assume that $(\exists y)\, T_4 py$ is needed to explain why p has O_6, then, it seems initially, there is no way to avoid the conclusion that there exists a log burning unperceived in p's fireplace. This shows the problem the Sellarsian account of theories raises for a phenomenalist who maintains that something exists only if it is either perceived or a perceiver.

There is, however, a clue in Berkeley's work about how to avoid

---

[18] Hume, *A Treatise of Human Nature*, Book I, Part XV, sect. I.

this problem. Consider two passages. First:

> The table I write on I say exists, that is, I see and feel it; and if
> I were out of my study I should say it existed—meaning thereby
> that if I was in my study I might perceive it, or that some other
> spirit actually does perceive it.[19]

Second:

> The question whether the earth moves or no amounts in
> reality to no more than this, to wit, whether we have reason to
> conclude from what has been observed by astronomers, that if
> we were placed in such and such circumstances, and such or
> such a position and distance both from the earth and sun, we
> should perceive the former to move among the choir of the
> planets, and appearing in all respects like one of them.[20]

These two passages indicate that Berkeley would agree to a subjunctive analysis of our ordinary statements that assert the
existence of physical objects, especially those where perception of
the objects is denied. In other words, although Berkeley holds the
metaphysical thesis that, strictly speaking, something exists at a
time t if and only if at t either it is perceived or it is a perceiver
(that is, it is capable of perceiving), he is willing, nevertheless, to use
and analyze another "loose" sense of 'exist.' It is the sense he would
use when "speaking with the vulgar." Notice also that in neither
passage does Berkeley provide a pure sensum sentence for the
analysans as he would do if he were, as Warnock claims, an
analytical phenomenalist. As a theoretical phenomenalist he need
only find a way to analyze certain physical-object statements
which removes their apparent incompatibility with *esse* is *percipi*.
In doing this he can use theoretical (physical-object) terms, because
he can admit the use of, even the need for, theoretical terms.

    We cannot, however, use either of the two passages from Berkeley
to provide the model for a viable Berkeleyan analysis. The first fails
because, even if I might not be able to perceive anything, it would
exist if someone else were to perceive it. It also fails, even if we
replace 'I' with 'we' or 'someone,' because 'might perceive' is too

---

[19] Berkeley, p. 23.
[20] Berkeley, p. 49.

weak. There being no table in the study is compatible with it being possible that someone would perceive it if he were in the room. The second passage fails, because it is too strong to require that we *should* perceive what exists. We fallible beings might not notice the earth move even if we should be in the right spot in the right conditions. We can avoid both these problems in a Berkeleyan way by mentioning an all-perceiving being in the antecedent, and we can do it in a way that does not imply such a Berkeleyan god exists. Consider the following as a model for analysis of this "loose" sense of 'exist' ('exist$_L$'):

> There is (exists$_L$) a table in my study at time $t =$ $_{df}$. If at t someone should perceive everything, then at t he would perceive a table in my study.

Such an analysis allows the use of 'There is a log burning unperceived in x's fireplace' in explanations by someone who subscribes to *esse* is *percipi*:

> There is (exists$_L$) a log burning unperceived in x's fireplace at $t =$ $_{df}$. No one perceives a log burning in x's fireplace at t, but if at t someone should perceive everything, then at t he would perceive a log burning in x's fireplace at t.

Such an analysis shows how a phenomenalist who adopts the Sellarsian account of theories can use unperceived physical objects in his explanations. However, such explanations are incompatible with the existence of an all-perceiving god, and thus they are incompatible with Berkeley's actual position. Consequently, the historical Berkeley cannot use such explanations and also agree that the preceding analysis is correct. However, a Berkeleyan who wishes to use such explanations and to postulate a god—perhaps as the all-perceiving producer of those sensa that constitute the physical world—can reply that these explanations do not require mention of any objects which *no being* perceives. He can easily amend any such explanation by replacing 'unperceived' with 'unperceived by a finite perceiver.' Then the most that his explanations would entail is that no finite perceiver perceives everything.

CONCLUSION ABOUT BERKELEYAN PHENOMENALISM

We have found that Sellars' objection to theoretical phenomenalism refutes neither the theory in general nor the particular Berkeleyan version with which we have been primarily concerned. Not only have we seen that there is reason to reject the Sellarsian account of theories, but we also saw that Berkeleyan phenomenalism can accommodate that account, even for unperceived physical objects. The basic strategy has been to analyze all existence claims about physical objects into claims only about perception of physical objects, and then to argue that whenever the physical-object terms in such claims denote, they denote nothing but sensa and collections of sensa which some perceivers actually sense. In this way a Berkeleyan can relate his primitive theoretical terms to his observational sensum vocabulary by various sorts of correspondence rules. We have already seen that he has at his disposal not only probability statements, such as those relating tasting cherries to having sensa, but also identity claims relating cherries to sensa. In addition, there are others that identify events of perceiving physical objects with events of having sensa. For example, there is:

> C3. Perceiving a table in my study is identical with sensing sensa that are in the collection of sensa which is identical with a table in my study (or, which is denoted by 'a table in my study').

Given such correspondence rules, the various ways to accommodate the explanatory use of theoretical terms, and, if the phenomenalist wishes, the Craigian and Ramseyan resources, it is reasonable to conclude not only that Sellars' objection fails, but also that the second and third major objections to Berkeleyan phenomenalism should be rejected.

Berkeleyan Replies to the Second and Third Objections

The problem the second objection poses for a Berkeleyan is how to give a plausible explication of what it is for physical objects to be bundles or groups of sensa. For a Berkeleyan who is a theoretical phenomenalist, the problem is to make plausible the sense in which physical objects are theoretical constructions out of groups of sensa. That is, he must formulate statements which express certain contingent relationships between each physical object, as a theoretical, explanatory entity, and particular sensa that are pure observation entities whose perception by someone is to be explained. We are now in a position to see how he could do this.

The statements *C1* and *C2* relate the denotation of a physical-object term to its explanatory role, and to a certain group of sensa. We can use these statements to devise necessary and sufficient conditions for each physical object being reductively identical with a group of sensa. For our example of a cherry, we have the contingent correspondence rule:

> *C4*. A cherry, *c*, *is nothing but* the group of sensa, *G*, *if and only if* for each sensum, *s*, in *G*, some minimally adequate explanation of the event of someone, *p*, sensing *s* at some time *t*, but not of any other sensation-event, includes the postulation that *p* perceives *c* at *t*.

Similar statements can be given for other physical objects. Notice that these groups will contain sensa that exist at quite different times, that is, when and only when they are sensed. Thus, often there are times when no members of a certain collection exists, that is, when no one is sensing a sensum to be explained by the perception of an appropriate physical object. Yet, given the preceding Berkeleyan analysis of the existence (existence$_L$) of physical objects, in some of these cases we can claim the group or collection exists$_L$, because if someone were to perceive everything, he would sense a sensum that would be in that collection. Thus, although the members of these groups usually exist for only a very short time and, at times, none of them exists, a Berkeleyan can still maintain that some of these groups themselves, and thus some physical objects, exist$_L$ uninterruptedly for quite a long time.

Statements of the form of *C4*, which give conditions for a physical object being a certain group of sensa, provide a plausible way to explicate the crux of Berkeley's bundle theory when interpreted by means of theoretical phenomenalism. Consequently, because we have also found no objections to theoretical phenomenalism and an unrefuted argument for scientific instrumentalism, we can justifiably reject the second objection to Berkeleyan phenomenalism. Our last major task at present, then, is to discover whether the third objection can also be rejected.

It is clear that if a Berkeleyan is to have a plausible way to understand how two different perceivers see the same physical object, he must allow the group that is identical with the object to include different sensa sensed by different perceivers. This is because only one perceiver senses any one particular sensum and, as stated previously, perceiving a certain object is identical with sensing a sensum in the group which is identical with the object. If we look again at *C4*, we can see that it allows a group to include sensa from different perceivers, because *C4* requires of a particular sensum that is in the group identical with a cherry, only that the event of someone or other sensing it is explained by that perceiver perceiving the cherry. Taking this point with the claim about perceiving a physical object expressed in *C3*, we can devise a reply to the third objection by using the following, plausible Berkeleyan construal of when two perceivers perceive the same cherry:

> *C5*. Perceiver *p* and perceiver *q* perceive the same cherry at time *t* *if and only if* some sensum that *p* senses at *t* and some sensum that *q* senses at *t* are in the group of sensa that is identical with a particular cherry.

Although we have done enough to refute the third objection, it is also worth pointing out that we can similarly handle the problem of how to construe one perceiver seeing the same cherry at one time that he touches at another time. Since, according to Berkeley, no one can visually sense the same sensum he tactilely senses, we must allow each group to contain sensa from all sense modalities. Again, *C4* permits this. What we get resembles *C5*:

> *C6*. A perceiver, *p*, sees at *t* the same cherry that he touches at *t'* *if and only if* some visual sensum that *p* senses at *t* and some tactile sensum that *p* senses at *t'* are in the group of sensa that is identical with a particular cherry.

Throughout the preceding, lengthy discussion and elucidation of the construal of Berkeleyan phenomenalism as a species of reductive theoretical phenomenalism, we have refuted the first three major objections to the theory, as well as many other, subsidiary objections. At the end of Chapter 4, we rejected the most serious part of the fourth objection that Berkeley's theory is unscientific. Based upon this, we are justified in concluding, I believe, that this version of phenomenalism is plausible enough to be one of the leading contenders for the most reasonable theory of perception and the external world. However, much work remains to be done before that final decision can be made. In particular, we have two preliminary tasks remaining. One is to examine various forms of realism to see which, if any, are plausible enough to be serious contenders. This will constitute Part II of the book. The other task is to compare this Berkeleyan variety of theoretical phenomenalism with the three main eliminative versions in order to try to discover which varieties of phenomenalism are the most plausible. Let us attempt this task now.

REDUCTIVE VERSUS ELIMINATIVE PHENOMENALISM

In the Introduction I distinguished between Berkeley's reductive phenomenalism, which reductively identifies physical objects with groups of sensa, and eliminative phenomenalism, which eliminates physical objects instead of reducing them. I said that we would consider one instrumentalistic version of the eliminative theory which construes all physical-object terms as nonreferring, theoretical terms that function solely as parts of inference tickets, and two noninstrumentalistic versions. I further mentioned that there are two subspecies of each eliminative theory, one that assumes sensa and one that assumes objectless sensings. It is clear, I believe, at this stage of our discussion that instrumentalistic phenomenalism has been shown to be at least somewhat plausible by the preceding examinations of scientific instrumentalism and theoretical phenomenalism. Of course, an instrumentalistic phenomenalist must reject all of the preceding C-rules, because they state conditions either for denotation of physical-object terms, or for identity of physical objects with groups of sensa. But this raises no problem; in fact, it simplifies his task of fully fleshing out his theory.

The case is quite different, however, for the two noninstrumental eliminative theories. One, the postulation elimination theory states that physical-object terms are referring terms that fail to denote anything because they are not needed for any explanatory purpose. The other, the 'physical object' elimination theory, states not only that physical-object terms are referring terms, but also that sensa are denoted by some of them. However, because there is no explanatory or descriptive need for these terms, this success in denoting is purely referential, and not attributive or descriptive. Thus it is false to say that there are physical objects. I find both of these theories implausible, considerably more so than their materialistic counterparts.[21] This is because the theories are plausible only if it is plausible that no physicalistic terms (both theoretical and observational) are needed now, or in the future will be needed, for nontranscribed explanations of the empirical subject matter of science, whether it be construed as sensory experience or observable behavior. By 'nontranscribed explanations' I mean explanations that are not transcribed by either the Craigian or Ramseyan procedure. But it is surely implausible that science will develop in such a way, because present evidence points to future scientific explanations becoming more physicalistic rather than less. It is this that makes the corresponding materialistic theories, which depend on the future elimination of *psychological* terms, to be more plausible.

An obvious objection to this argument is that the plausibility of the two theories depends only on it being plausible that no physical-object terms are needed for explanation in transcribed theories, and this is guaranteed by the two transcribing procedures. However, although a mere transcriptional elimination supports an instrumental interpretation, as argued in Chapter 4, it provides reason to reject these two theories with their noninstrumental construal. Often a sentence of the form 'There is a P,' where 'P' is a physical-object term, follows from certain minimally adequate explanations. In one of the previous examples, 'There is a cherry' follows from the use of 'T_3b' to explain someone having a certain sensum. But if 'cherry' is a referring term, and this explanation is correct, then it is reasonable to hold not only that 'cherry' denotes something, contrary to the postulation elimination theory, but also that it truly describes what it denotes, contrary to the physical-object elimination theory. Thus either there are no such explanations, or all of them are incorrect, or 'cherry' is not a referring term, or the two theories are unreasonable. But surely there are such explanations, and it is unreasonable that all of them are incorrect. Furthermore, both theories are mistaken if no physical-object terms, including

---

[21] The two materialistic theories are discussed in *Materialism and Sensations*, Chaps. 4 and 5.

'cherry,' are referring terms. Therefore, it is reasonable to think that these two noninstrumental versions of eliminative phenomenalism are mistaken.

An instrumental phenomenalist avoids the preceding problem. He can allow 'There is a cherry' to follow from a correct, minimally adequate explanation, and also deny that 'cherry' denotes or truly describes anything, because, on his theory, 'cherry' is not a referring term. If, therefore, 'There is a cherry' should be construed as true because it follows from a correct explanation of something, it would be at most "instrumentally true," that is, a nonreferring sentence that is derivable from a correct application of a correct inference ticket. Here a correct inference ticket is, roughly, an inference-warranting device that, given "factually" true premises, warrants inferences to "factual" conclusions such that either all (deductive) or most (inductive) are "factually" true. In such a way, an instrumentalist can grant the "truth" of 'There are cherries,' deny there is anything denoted by 'cherry,' and thus not be ontologically committed to cherries.[22]

CONCLUSION ABOUT THE MOST REASONABLE FORMS OF PHENOMENALISM

We are justified in rejecting the noninstrumental versions of eliminative phenomenalism, but both instrumental species, and, of course, the Berkeleyan reductive theory, avoid the preceding refutation. This raises the final question for our present examination of phenomenalism. Is there any reason to choose any of the three remaining versions of phenomenalism as the most reasonable variety of that theory? To answer this question we must consider the relevant differences among the three theories: Berkeleyan phenomenalism, sensum instrumentalism, and sensing instrumentalism. All three agree that each individual is either a perceiver, or a sensum, or is composed of such entities, and all accept scientific instrumentalism. However, they disagree about five important points:

(1) The existence of physical objects;

[22] Denotation and ontological commitment are discussed in *Metaphysics, Reference, and Language*, esp. Chap. 5.

(2) The construal of physical-object terms as reporting (and thus referring) terms;

(3) The perception of objects of some sort;

(4) The existence of sensa;

(5) The need for correspondence rules (C-rules) that identify physical objects with groups of sensa.

A Berkeleyan accepts all five, a sensum instrumentalist accepts only (3) and (4), and a sensing instrumentalist accepts none of them.

Based upon our common-sense intuitions, our past discovery of problems for sensa, and the recent discussion of correspondence rules, I conclude the following:

(a) Common sense provides some reason to prefer theories that accept (1), (2), or (3) to theories that reject respectively (1), (2), or (3);

(b) The recalcitrant problems facing sensa provide some reason to prefer theories that reject (4) to theories that accept (4);

(c) The fact that devising C-rules expressing identity is a nontrivial task in addition to the task of justifying scientific instrumentalism, is some reason to prefer theories that reject (5) to theories that accept (5).

Of these, I believe only (c) requires additional comment. An instrumentalist regarding all physicalistic terms need only be able to distinguish between psychological terms and physicalistic terms in order to adapt the argument from the theoretician's dilemma to provide at least some reason for his theory. But a reductive phenomenalist must also formulate a wide range of additional C-rules and integrate them with the theories that explain psychological events. And, although I have tried to state a fair sample of such rules, it is far from obvious that such a project will succeed.[23] Thus there is at least some reason to prefer a pure instrumental phenomenalism, which avoids these C-rules, because it avoids one of the ways a reductive variety might be refuted.

There remains the task of evaluating the relative strengths of the

---

[23] For an example of a problem for the C-rules proposed here, see the final chapter for a time-gap argument against Berkeleyan reductive phenomenalism.

preceding reasons to prefer certain theories to others. I believe it is clear that the demonstrated problems for sensa are the most serious, and it seems reasonable to say that the conflicts with common sense are the least serious. Furthermore, in accordance with principle P3, it seems reasonable to believe that common sense should be considered as reason to prefer one theory to another, only once it is independently shown that the theory is at least as reasonable as the other. If both beliefs are correct, then the Berkeleyan theory is the least reasonable of the three phenomenalistic theories, because it is favored only by the factors in (a), but is opposed by both (b) and (c). And sensing instrumentalism seems to be the most reasonable, because it is the only one favored by (b), it is also favored by (c), and it is opposed only by the factors in (a). However, in order to avoid overlooking a plausible theory, I shall not rely on my intuitions of the relative strengths of these reasons, but will assume that they show the three theories to be roughly equally reasonable. Consequently, for the purpose of comparing the most reasonable forms of phenomenalism with the most reasonable versions of realism, I shall assume that these three theories are the most plausible forms of phenomenalism. With that settled, we are ready to turn to the second major task of the book: a critical evaluation of various species of realism.

Part II
REALISM

6   Naive Realism

It has often been claimed that to attack a naive realist is to attack a straw man, because no one—surely no philosopher—is so naive as to be such a realist. The reason, or excuse, usually given for considering so naive a view is that it will help us to see how the theories of past indirect realists and phenomenalists emerged from the rejection of the naive view. Indeed, in an overly historical approach to a perennial problem it is often said that the rejection of naive realism leads to a Lockean representative realism, which, when rejected, in turn leads to phenomenalism. However, not only do I find that I have a strong affinity for the naive view, but I also find strong objections to those arguments that supposedly refuted naive realism in the distant days of the British empiricists and led us through Locke's theory to Hume's sparse ontology and skeptical epistemology. Naive realism has not yet been decisively refuted, and I believe that only a very naive version of it is refutable. It is my present purpose to characterize this version carefully, as must be done to refute it, and then to show how to refute it. Whether some less naive version remains as a strong contender for the most plausible theory of perception and the external world will be considered later. From here on, I shall call *only* this very naive view, "naive realism."

There are two distinct subtheses of naive realism. One concerns the nature of the external world, and the other concerns our relationship to that world when we perceive it. It is my contention that it is the second thesis which, in part, is excessively naive and clearly mistaken. I shall try to show here, and later in Chapter 8, that none of the many attacks launched against the first thesis succeeds, and only one against the second thesis succeeds. Once we see this, we shall also begin to see how a less naive view of perception will, when coupled with the first thesis, result in a plausible version of what can be called "common-sense realism." But first we must clarify naive realism. In doing so I shall attempt to characterize the minimal thesis which is sufficient for someone to be a naive realist. If we find reason to reject this minimal claim, then we will be justified in rejecting the thesis itself.

Being one form of realism, minimal naive realism differs from all versions of phenomenalism in stating that there are objects that exist independently of perceivers and are unaffected by being perceived. Furthermore, many of these objects are physical objects that are directly perceivable. Thus naive realism is one form of direct realism, but this does not sufficiently account for its naiveté. To express this we must be more specific about the properties it ascribes to physical objects and the species of direct perception it maintains. In particular, although minimal naive realism is not committed to the view that all individuals and all properties of individuals are observable, it is committed to the view that there are many perceivable individuals that have certain perceivable, occurrent, that is, nondispositional, properties. More precisely, on this view there are many observable individuals that have *at least* the following observable, occurrent physical properties: size, shape, weight, solidity, texture, motion (rest), location, sensuous color, and hotness (coldness). I shall call these the "minimally required" sensible properties. There is a question, however, whether the minimal position construes other properties of observable objects, such as taste, odor and sound, as occurrent or rather as dispositional, that is, mere powers or capacities.

Consider, for example, the smell of cooking cabbage and the sound of a firing cannon. In these cases a belief that sensuous smells and sounds are not properties of the physical objects is reinforced by the fact that we sometimes smell the odor of cabbage in the living room when the cabbage is cooking in the kitchen, and we often hear the cannon's boom after seeing the smoke. Something seems to be transmitted to us from the objects because of some of their nonsensuous properties. Because of this, the minimal position is compatible with the physical properties of the objects that correspond to sensuous tastes and sounds not being sensuous themselves. Furthermore, I believe that a naive realist is unclear about whether sensuous qualities we experience, or something else, are transmitted from objects to us. This ambivalence is illustrated by the old problem for the naive view of whether there is a (sensuous) sound of a tree falling in a forest when no perceiver is present to hear it. Consequently, I think that a minimal position can leave it to science to explain what, if anything, is transmitted in both sorts of cases.

It is more difficult to decide about the sweetness of sugar. Is a cube of sugar sensuously sweet when no one is tasting it? The fact that the taste of sugar often lingers when the sugar is no longer touching the tongue might incline one to believe that the sweet taste is caused by some different property of the sugar which affects the tongue. However, the fact that contact is made between objects and the tongue reinforces the belief that we actually experience a sensuous property of the sugar. Again, because of this ambivalence, I shall assume that a minimal naive realist does not believe that physical objects have sensuous taste qualities. This will help us to center attention on what is often thought to create the crucial problem for this view, namely, the property of sensuous color. If this problem is resolved, then, I believe, any that involves other sensuous properties, such as tactile and taste qualities, can also be resolved.

MINIMAL NAIVE REALISM: FIRST THESIS

We are now ready to try to define the first thesis of the minimal position. Aside from having the perceivable occurrent properties we have discussed, this thesis also consists in the claim that many physical objects are not affected in any way by being perceived, and, when not perceived, many of them exist with those perceivable properties they have when perceived. Let us, then, adopt the following definition:

> *Minimal Naive Realism (first thesis):* The world consists in large part of perceivable physical objects that are not per-ceivers, that exist unperceived, and that are not affected either by being perceived or, generally, by changes in the usual conditions in which they are perceived; many of these objects have and are perceived to have at least the minimally required sensible properties, that is, the observable, occurrent physical properties of size, shape, weight, solidity, texture, motion (rest), location, sensuous color, and hotness (coldness).

I have not included in this definition anything concerning a naive view about persons or about the powers or capacities of external objects to affect other objects. The former is omitted because I am here interested in the naive view of the purely physical world, and the latter is omitted for brevity because I believe that any minimal naive view about this is noncontroversial. Furthermore, no claims about the speed of light, addition of velocities, or Euclidean space are included. I do not believe the minimal view conflicts with a realistic interpretation of the theory of relativity. For example, the observable property of being at rest can be relativized to become being at rest relative to the earth. Minimal naive realism concerns the observable properties and behavior of observable objects, but not the theories used to explain this behavior. Thus this view can accept any observed behavior no matter how counterintuitive, and, of course, it can accept unobservable, explanatory entities and behavior that are radically unlike anything that is observed. What would clearly raise a problem for this position would be an explanatory theory that requires things not to have any property that closely resembles a property that we clearly perceptually experience them to have. But relativity theory has no such consequences in the realm of things that have the sizes and speeds of observable things. As will be indicated in Chapter 8, I believe that this is also true of the distinctive features of quantum mechanics with its conceptually puzzling consequences. If any theory, it is the atomic theory of matter, as we shall also see in Chapter 8, that seems to have consequences for the observable properties of a physical object that are not compatible with the first thesis of naive realism.

Minimal Naive Realism: Second Thesis

The second thesis concerns the naive view of the perception of objects and properties. It is clear that the view is not fully expressed by the characterization of direct perception given in the Introduction, because that characterization accommodates an adverbial-sensing version of the causal theory which is alien to the naive view. We can begin to explicate the view once we realize that it is the same conception of perception that indirect realists and Berkeleyans have of our experience of sensa. And, because a Berkeleyan claims that physical objects are nothing but groups of sensa, his view of the perception of physical objects also seems to agree with that of the naive realist. In this way, at least, a Berkeleyan can even think with "the vulgar."

If there are sensa that we experience, we do not only experience them directly, but we are also in some way perceptually acquainted with them. I have elsewhere slightly unpacked this by saying that a sensum is presented to and present with the individual who experiences it.[1] But more unpacking than this is needed. To say that a sensum is presented, perhaps given, to someone in an experience, is in part to say that he directly experiences the sensum. It is also to say that in directly experiencing it, his relationship to the sensum is so intimate and immediate that it does not consist in, and is not analyzable in terms of any different relationships of any sort or any nonrelational properties of the person, the sensum, or anything else. That is, let us say, a person immediately experiences a sensum. Consequently, any relation of immediately experiencing that a person has to an object does not consist even partly in a causal relationship, such as being caused to have an experience of the object by stimulus from the object, or in the relationship of experiencing some different object, such as a sensum or brain part.

Except for listing other negative examples of the preceding sort, I believe that little more can be said to characterize immediate experiencing. My only reason for this is that just as I would agree with G. E. Moore that sensuous, occurrent yellow is a simple, unanalyzable property, I would also claim that immediately experiencing something, whether it be an object or a property of something, is a simple, unanalyzable relationship. The best I can do, then, to characterize immediate experiencing is as follows:

> s immediately experiences (object, property) p, at time $t =$ df. At t, s directly experiences p and does so in such a way that this relationship of experiencing between s and p is simple (that is, does not consist in any other relationships or properties) and unanalyzable.

Using this definition, we can see that although immediately experiencing implies directly experiencing, the converse is false. A person would directly experience, but not immediately experience an object, if his experiencing the object consisted in a causal process that begins with stimulus from the object causally affecting him in some appropriate way and ends with his sensing in some way.

Sensa are supposedly immediately experienced, but even this is not sufficient to capture fully the character of the intimate relation-

[1] See my *Materialism and Sensations*, pp. 222–26.

ship we are said to have to them. A person's relationship to a sensum is presumably so intimate that it appears to him "as it is." That is, a sensum has whatever sensible (sensuous) phenomenal properties the person who has the sensum experiences it to have. Similarly, if a physical object should appear as it is, then it would have whatever sensible, physical properties it is experienced as having. We have then:

> A (sensum, physical object) p appears to s at time t as it is at t [that is, at t, s experiences p as it is at t] = $_{df.}$
>
> (1) s immediately experiences p at t, *and*
>
> (2) for any sensible (phenomenal, physical) property, Q, if, at t, s has an experience of p as having Q, then at t he immediately perceives Q, which is a property of p at t.

Notice that the claim that sensa appear as they are does not imply that sensa have phenomenal properties only if we experience them to have the properties. Thus this claim avoids the serious problem, discussed in Chapter 2, that is raised for the sensum theory by experiences of only indeterminate numbers of stripes. Furthermore, it does not prohibit the identity of sensa with brain entities. Notice also that only sensible properties are mentioned, and so it is experiencing something as having *such* a property that is sufficient for it having the property. Finally, it should be noted that 's has an experience of p as having Q (p as Q)' implies neither that p has property Q nor that p exists. It is equivalent to an intensional sense of 'p appears Q to s.' Both sentences are attempts to describe merely the phenomenological content of sensory experience, as in 'Macbeth had an experience of a daggar as bloody red (a bloody red daggar).'

We are almost ready to characterize what it is for something to be perceptually presented to someone. For a sensum, this amounts to it appearing as it is, but this will not do for physical objects. Unlike a sensum, a physical object that is perceptually presented often does not appear to someone as it is when either he or the conditions in which he perceives it are not normal. Thus the general characterization of an entity being presented to someone should at least include reference to normalcy, although, of course, such reference is redundant if the entity is a sensum. We now have the following:

p is perceptually presented to s at time $t = {}_{df.}$
   (1) s immediately perceives p at t, and
   (2) if, at t, s should be a normal perceiver who immediately perceives p in normal conditions of perception, then p would appear to s at t as it is at t.

There remains the less complex task of characterizing what it is for a sensum or a physical object to be perceptually present with its perceiver. This means, essentially, that it exists at the times it is perceived. Notice that this is not a redundant addition. It is clear that the second defining condition of perceptual presentation does not imply that p exists, and, while condition (1) does imply that it exists at some time, it does not imply it exists at t. This was a crucial point in refuting the time-gap argument for sensa, which assumed that direct perception of p at t implies that p exists at t. We want, then, the concept of "being present with" as characterized below:

p is perceptually present with s at time $t = {}_{df.}$ p exists at t when s immediately perceives p.

With this done, we have a preliminary characterization of perceptual acquaintance. Although we can continue to abbreviate its characterization in terms of being perceptually presented to and present with a perceiver, I shall not use the full unpacking of those concepts because of redundancies. In particular, we can express the results of the preceding discussion in terms of the following definition:

s is perceptually acquainted with a (sensum, physical object) p at time $t = {}_{df.}$
   (1) s immediately experiences p at t, *and*
   (2) p exists at t, *and*
   (3) for any sensible (phenomenal, physical) property, Q, *if*, at t, s should be a normal perceiver who immediately perceives p in normal conditions of perception, and in so doing he has an experience of p as having Q, *then*, at t, he would immediately perceive Q, which is a property of p at t.

This gives us a way to unpack the second thesis of minimal naive realism which concerns its acquaintance construal of the perception of physical objects. We must first, however, restrict the sensible physical properties referred to in clause (3) to those that are minimally required, if we are to state the minimal thesis. Let us call perceptual acquaintance when it is restricted in this way "minimal perceptual acquaintance." We can, then, put the second thesis as follows:

> *Minimal Naive Realism (second thesis):* to perceive a physical object is to be minimally perceptually acquainted with it.

Before examining objections to the view consisting of these two theses, it should be noted that this seems to have no epistemic consequences by itself. One quick indication of this is that the elaborated characterization of the view involves no epistemic terms. That is, unlike Russell's notion of acquaintance, no terms such as 'inference,' 'knowledge,' and 'truth,' are used.[2] It is true that condition (3) states that under certain conditions a certain sort of experience of a certain sort of property is sufficient for something, p, having the property, Q. It does not follow from this, however, that someone knows or is even justified in believing that p has Q, even given that he immediately perceives p and that he believes he is experiencing p to have Q. It may well be that some independent reason to think that the person and conditions are normal is required in order to justify his belief that p has Q.

OBJECTIONS TO MINIMAL NAIVE REALISM

In considering the variety of objections raised against naive realism I have found that it is helpful to put them into three rough groups: three objections raised by Berkeley, an objection from hallucinations, illusions, and perceptual relativity, and seven objections based on scientific discoveries and theories. I shall consider them in that order, beginning with a brief review of the three Berkeleyan objections we have already rejected in Chapter 3. All three of Berkeley's objections are directed at the first thesis of naive realism, because they are aimed at showing that some, or all, of the sensible qualities we immediately perceive are not properties

---

[2] See the discussion of direct perception in the Introduction and in the final chapter.

of perceiver-independent objects. The first argument for the identity of extreme degrees of hotness and coldness, bitter tastes, and unpleasant odors with pains or feelings of uneasiness is used to strip some sensible, occurrent secondary qualities from external objects. Of these, the only properties I have claimed a *minimal* naive realist assigns to external objects are hotness and coldness. And, while, interestingly, Berkeley's argument is most plausible when applied to these properties, we have seen that it fails even there. Not only would the argument fail if there should be no pains, as the sensing interpretation implies, but also it is plausible to argue that even if there are pains, what occurs when touching a hot stove is that you are caused to feel pain that is so great in some cases it prohibits you from immediately experiencing the heat of the stove.

The second argument depends on the success of Berkeley's objections to secondary qualities, because it states, basically, that sensible, occurrent primary properties, such as extension, are properties of external objects only if, contrary to fact, this is also true of certain secondary properties. But not only has Berkeley not dispatched sensible, external secondary properties, he does not even show that extension is perceiver-dependent if color is. Although its converse is true, being colored is not necessary for something's being extended, or even having size and shape. The third argument, which is based on perceptual relativity, applies equally to primary and secondary properties. It fails, however, because the uninterpreted facts of perceptual relativity provide no more reason to state that the properties we immediately perceive vary with changes in perceivers than to state that it is how the properties appear to us that varies with such changes. Thus all three of Berkeley's objections to the first thesis fail. But there are others not yet refuted.

An Objection from Hallucination, Illusion, and Relativity

It is often claimed that naive realism cannot accommodate delusory experiences, and, even if it could do that, it could not accommodate the sort of explanations such experiences require. Both of these objections are aimed at the second thesis, which concerns our relationship to external objects when we perceive them. The first objection often concentrates on hallucinatory experiences, such as those involving mirages and phantom limbs, in which someone is deluded into thinking that there is something he is perceiving. In some of these cases, a person has an experience of an oasis, or his own leg, but there is no oasis or leg for him to experience. Consequently, in these cases the persons do not experience things the way they are, and, according to this objection, naive realism is refuted.

It may be that someone has held the extremely naive view that if a person has an experience of something, then he actually perceives it as it is, that is, it appears as it is. However, this view is not the one under discussion and, I believe, it is not one worth discussing. As interpreted here, minimal naive realism states that we perceive many physical objects, and it identifies our perceiving something with our being minimally perceptually acquainted with it. This does not imply that someone's having an experience of something, even when he and conditions are normal, is sufficient for his actually perceiving it, let alone for perceiving it as it is. One must also *immediately* perceive it. How to establish that someone is immediately perceiving something is a difficult epistemological problem, but one need not be extremely naive epistemologically to be a naive ontological realist. Nevertheless I would think a naive realist would at most need to claim that when a person and conditions are normal and something appears to him, then he immediately perceives it, and thus he experiences it as it is. But not even a naive realist who makes this additional claim would be refuted by the above objection, because in the preceding examples either the person or the conditions are not normal.

Because the sufficient condition for something appearing as it is to someone contains the conjunct that he immediately perceives it, the cases of hallucinating do not provide the strongest grounds on which to base this objection. Examples of illusions are better suited for this, especially those where an object that someone perceives lacks a certain property that the perceiver experiences it to have. However, given that sometimes these perceivers and conditions are normal, the object would have the property if naive realism, as previously defined, were correct.

Unless the second thesis of naive realism is amended, the only remotely plausible way I find to avoid this objection is to claim that in all cases of illusion involving normal perceivers, some conditions of perception are abnormal. This is clearly true in many cases of illusion. We can divide these conditions into those that are internal, that is, those that either are spatially within the relevant perceptual systems of a perceiver, or are mental conditions of the perceiver, and those that are external, that is, all other conditions. This will allow us to say that a perceiver's perceptual systems are normal, but perhaps because of excessive fear and nervousness, some of his internal conditions are presently abnormal, so that, for example, a gnarled tree with its branches swaying in a cemetery appears to him to be an approaching figure. It is clear that a naive realist can accommodate many cases of illusion in this way. Certain optical illusions present more difficult problems, however, because it is clear that in many cases the perceiver and all his internal conditions are normal, and it certainly seems that the external conditions are normal. Consider a case where two objects, equal in height, are experienced as being different in height, because they are different distances from the perceiver, but appear to be equidistant because they are placed against a trapezoidal shaped wall that slants away from the perceiver. This illusion and the illusions that sometimes occur when seeing very realistic paintings, do not result from any abnormal conditions of perception but from the objects seen and the relationships among them. Thus the present attempt to avoid this objection fails, and only amending the thesis remains.

Once we see why this objection succeeds, we can also see that the fault lies with the preceding characterization of minimal naive realism rather than with the thesis itself. So an amendment is justified. Quite ordinary examples involving perceptual relativity refute this characterization, but there is no reason to think a naive realist fails to account for them. While Berkeley's argument from perceptual relativity is aimed at the first thesis, the present objection is aimed at the third condition of the characterization of perceptual acquaintance. Often people experience square tables as rhomboidal, parallel railroad tracks as converging, and red polished objects as silver, when bright light glances off their surface. In these cases the perceivers and all conditions are normal. Our naive realist need not be so naive as to overlook these ordinary and plentiful cases. In explicating his view, we should not allow such examples to refute him. He would, I believe, recognize that it is not enough that perceivers and conditions are normal for a physical object to appear as it is. The conditions should also be *optimal* for discerning the particular sort of property in question. For example, the shape of the table and the spatial relationship between the two railroad tracks would be said to appear as they are from directly above the table and tracks, and the color of a surface appears as it is when seen under white light that is neither too strong, nor hits the colored surface at too great an angle. We should, then, change the characterization of perceptual acquaintance to account for this added requirement. We can do this by replacing condition (3) by:

(3a) For any (minimally required) sensible (phenomenal, physical) property, Q, *if*, at t, s should be a normal observer who immediately perceives p in conditions optimal for distinguishing whether or not p has Q, and in so doing he has an experience of p as having Q, *then*, at t, he would immediately perceive Q, which is a property of p at t (*then*, let us say, at t, p would (minimally) appear to s as it is at t).

Of course, the corresponding replacement should also be made for condition (2) of the characterization of perceptual presentation.

The preceding amendment defeats objections from perceptual relativity and optical illusions, given the reasonable assumption that there are optimal conditions for deciding about sensible properties, because none of those examples involves optimal conditions. However, even with the rejection of this first objection from delusion, the second remains unscathed, because its claim is that naive realism cannot accommodate the sorts of explanations these examples of illusion and relativity require. Because this objection takes us into a discussion of certain scientific theories, I have placed it in the third category of objections with six others drawn from science.

Seven Objections to Naive Realism from Scientific Facts and Theories

FIRST OBJECTION: DEPENDENCE OF SEEN COLOR ON THE NERVOUS SYSTEM

The facts of illusion and perceptual relativity require explanations, and these explanations are given in terms of causal processes that involve such causal factors as the positions of stimulus sources, perceivers and objects, the media through which stimuli pass, and the states of perceivers' sense organs and central nervous systems (CNS). Each of these, and other factors, can be crucial in the causation, and thus explanation, of illusory experiences and relativistic variations in perception. But many people believe that if these causal factors, especially those that involve only a perceiver such as the CNS, affect perception, then naive realism is false. As C. W. K. Mundle says:

> The processes in the sense-organs and the CNS on which perception depends must, presumably, function in one or other of two ways—revealing what is there or creating sense-data which represent what is there. If their function is to reveal what is there, we shall have to conclude that each physical surface simultaneously possesses many very different colours. The statement that the same surface cannot simultaneously be wholly and uniformly pervaded by different colours will be, not a truism, but the very opposite of the truth. The paradox disappears if what are visibly coloured are sense-data created by the CNS.[3]

Two quick comments should be made before beginning to evaluate this first objection from science. First, the disjunction of either revealing what is there or creating sense-data is not exhaustive, because, as we have seen, there is also the alternative of causing objectless sensings. Let us add this disjunct before considering the argument, because it will not help the naive realist if the CNS does not function "to reveal what is there." Second, I shall assume that 'to reveal what is there' comes to, roughly, 'to cause someone to experience what is there as it is.'

The crucial premise in this argument is that if the senses and CNS function to reveal what is there, then each physical object has many different colors. Mundle's reason for this, regarding color, is "the fact that, and the extent to which, the phenomenal colours of a thing may vary, when it is viewed from the same place, owing to

[3] C. Mundle, *Perception: Facts and Theories* (Oxford: Oxford University Press, 1971), p. 130.

changes in the CNS."[4] There are two replies to this, one of which we have already considered when rejecting other arguments based on perceptual relativity. It is that Mundle's claim that the phenomenal colors vary is supported only by one particular interpretation of the phenomenological facts of relativity. There is another, equally plausible construal that falsifies this claim. It is that there are no phenomenal colors involved in perception, and so there are none to vary with changes in the CNS. Instead, all sensible colors are observable, occurrent properties of physical objects which do not vary merely with changes in the CNS. What changes is how physical objects appear to us, and this is obviously compatible with our sometimes immediately perceiving the colors that physical objects actually have. This prepares for the second reply. Mundle, and others, seem to assume that if the color of something is ever revealed to us, then it is revealed, that is, appears as it is, under a wide variety of conditions that are surely not optimal and often not even normal. By allowing the naive realist to deny this assumption, as we have done in specifying perceptual acquaintance and as is surely reasonable, he can easily avoid the absurd result that one object is totally colored several different colors at one time because of variations in perceivers and conditions of perception.

SECOND OBJECTION: DEPENDENCE OF SEEING "REAL" COLOR ON WHICH CONDITIONS ARE OPTIMAL

The second objection arises at this point. It is aimed at the assumption in (3a) that under certain conditions, but not others, a perceiver who is in a certain state will perceive the "real" color of an external object. K. Campbell hints at such an objection by saying that to insist that one state of a perceiver enables him

> to see colour aright, while all others turn vision awry, is to be partial beyond reason. It involves determining the real colour of a surface (which is supposed to be an objective, physical property) on grounds totally remote from the physical circumstances of the surface (e.g. that it looks magenta to normal eyes after exposure to room sunlight, although not otherwise).[5]

We can construct one version of the intimated argument as

---

[4] Ibid.

[5] K. Campbell, "Colours," in *Contemporary Philosophy in Australia*, R. Brown and C. Rollins, eds. (New York: Humanities Press, 1969), pp. 145–46.

follows. First, if, as is surely true, which color appears to someone who sees a physical object depends on what internal and external conditions obtain, then it depends on factors that are completely independent of the state of the object seen. But, second, if this is true, then it is unreasonable to claim that some colors that appear are "real" colors, that is, colors of external physical objects. Consequently, naive realism is also unreasonable.

The mistake in this argument is easily seen by comparing a perceiver with a thermometer. Clearly, any temperature reading that is determined by using a thermometer depends, in part, on the state of the thermometer. Nevertheless, one and only one of the readings is the correct one, namely, the one recorded by a correctly functioning thermometer under proper conditions. Of course, if temperature readings were *completely* dependent on the state of thermometers, then we should reject the claim that they can be used to determine "objective" properties of physical objects. But just as the occurring of a thermometer reading depends *in part* on what is being measured, so also when perceiving, the appearing of a color depends in part on what is seen. Thus, contrary to the second premise of the argument, the fact that which color appears depends in part on the state of the perceiver and conditions is not sufficient for it being unreasonable that some color that appears to a perceiver when he sees an object is its "real" color.

It might be replied, however, that the objection can be sustained by a version stressing that the appearing of a color is *partially* dependent on which conditions obtain. According to this second version of the second objection, if naive realism is true, then which one of many colors that appear is the color of an object depends in part on which conditions are optimal and which perceivers are normal. But, second, if there is such a dependence, then certain changes in which conditions are optimal and which perceivers are normal would result in changes in the colors of physical objects. But it is unreasonable that such changes in conditions or perceivers result in changes in properties of external physical objects. Therefore naive realism is implausible.

Once again the mistake involves dependence, although in this case it is not because of a confusion between complete and partial dependence. If 'depends (in part) on' in the first premise of the two arguments is replaced by 'causally results in part from,' then although the first premise of the first argument is true, that of the second argument is false. It is clear that the appearing of a color to someone causally results *in part* from the particular conditions that obtain, but naive realism does not imply that conditions of perception causally affect properties of physical objects. What it does imply is that if the conditions that are optimal or the perceivers that are normal should differ in certain ways, then the "real" colors of physical objects would also be different, because the colors that would optimally appear to normal observers would be different. And this subjunctive conditional implies another: if which conditions are optimal and which perceivers are normal should change in certain ways, then which of various appearing colors are "real" would also change. But it does not imply that mere changes in conditions or perceivers would causally affect or bring about the corresponding changes in "real" colors. Thus, because naive realism does not imply the causal claim required for the first premise of the second argument, we can reject this version of the second objection.

We have not yet finished with the second objection, however, because there is a third version that concentrates on the fact that naive realism implies that there is a relationship between changes in "real" colors and changes in conditions. It is easy to imagine that changes will occur—for example, changes in the sensitivity of the eyes of the great majority of human begins—that would justify claiming that our current views of which conditions are optimal and which perceivers are normal should be replaced by a radically different thesis. And this change in conditions and perceivers could easily be such that we would also have to conclude that if naive realism is correct, then the colors of certain physical objects would also change correspondingly. But it is surely implausible that colors of physical objects would change in such a situation, and so naive realism is implausible.

Although this argument is also mistaken it does highlight one point about naive realism. If the conditions that are optimal or the perceivers that are normal come to change in certain ways, then naive realism should be rejected, because it would require that colors of physical objects change in implausible ways. And this would be true even if we construe 'causal dependence' to express merely causal relationships. Thus a naive realist should argue that it is implausible that such changes in conditions or perceivers will occur. And certainly, given present evidence, there is no reason to claim now that changes will occur in the future that will justify our rejecting present views about these conditions and perceivers. This alone is enough to reject the preceding argument, which requires the mistaken inference from the ease in conceiving a situation requiring us to change our views to its being plausible that such a situation will occur. Although such a situation is possible, it is surely unlikely that it will occur. Furthermore, a naive realist can make his case still stronger. Even if we were now in a situation that required us to change radically our views about optimal conditions and normal perceivers, it does not follow that we should conclude either that certain conditions were once optimal but are no longer, or that certain perceivers used to be normal but are not now normal. It seems to be at least as reasonable to conclude instead that what we had previously thought to be optimal and normal is and was mistaken because it is more reasonable, at least right now, to accept a quite different hypothesis. And since it is reasonable that justifications of claims about conditions, but not the conditions themselves, are relative to available evidence in this way, a naive realist has a second way to refute this last version of the second objection.

THIRD OBJECTION: PERCEPTION BY OTHER CREATURES VERSUS HUMAN
PERCEPTION

Any specific thesis about which conditions are optimal and which observers are normal is an hypothesis that is open to revision or rejection in so far as it does not correctly specify those situations in which we see the colors of physical objects. But this assumes that human eyes in particular are suited to uncover such properties of objects, and gives rise to the third objection. Mundle puts it by saying that, according to the naive realist,

the colors which *we* see presupposes that the visual mechanism with which evolution has endowed (most) human beings *reveals* the inherent colours of things. Can this be defended in view of the varieties of visual mechanisms in other creatures? Many of these respond to slices of the electro-magnetic spectrum different from that which affects our eyes.[6]

This objection can be strengthened by questioning not only the unique suitability of human sensory systems for causing us to perceive the world as it is, but also the special relevance of those conditions of perception I have called "optimal." Is not picking out just human sensory systems and those conditions supposedly optimal for those systems unjustifiably arbitrary?

The reply to this is that such a choice would be unjustifiable if it singled out only human senses and only conditions optimal for those senses. But, according to (3a), naive realism states merely that *if* a normal human perceiver in optimal conditions has an experience of a physical object as having a (minimally required) sensible property, then it has that property. That is, (3a) leaves open the question of whether different conditions are optimal for other creatures to discern these properties, and also the question of whether there are properties that are perceived by other creatures, but not by human beings. Thus examples of other creatures who discern colors, sounds, or smells that we cannot perceive are irrelevant. What is inconsistent with naive realism, as previously defined, is the claim that some creatures perceive the same objects that we perceive and, for example, the colors they optimally experience the objects as having resemble the actual colors of the objects more closely than do the colors we optimally perceive them to have. Two examples illustrate this problem. If physical objects that we experience as having continuous surfaces, should be more precisely discernible by other creatures as not having continuous surfaces, or if other creatures could discern differences among particular instances of certain sensible properties (such as among reds of different shades) that are indiscernible for humans, then naive realism as previously characterized would be refuted. I know of no reason to think there are creatures of the first sort. This, of course, does not avoid the related problem that microscopes raise, but we shall consider that later. It does seem, however, that there are creatures of the second sort, because dogs can distinguish among smells better than humans can. And, more importantly for a minimal naive realist, there may be other animals that can distinguish more precisely among colors.

[6] Mundle, p. 55.

Someone might try to avoid this objection by agreeing with Berkeley that relational properties are not sensible, but that would not succeed.[7] Even if a difference between two colors is not sensible, a humanly indiscernable yet distinct difference between two colors implies that at least one of them is not the color that optimally appears to us, and naive realism as previously characterized is refuted. Assuming that there are such creatures, we have the same choice we had when considering the first objection: either agree that naive realism is refuted, or find a justifiable amendment. Once again I believe the latter course is available. For example, a naive realist need not be put in a quandary when he sees an advertisement with a picture of the extremely sharp edge of a razor blade magnified many times, and he finds it to be jagged rather than a straight line as it normally appears. What would bother him extremely, for example, would be an accurate picture which depicted the edge as curved to such a degree that, in some cases under optimal conditions, unaided, normal human beings discern the difference between such a curved edge and a straight line. The difference between these two cases points out that the naive realist only requires that, for unaided human senses, the sensible properties of objects are indiscernibly approximated by the properties he optimally experiences them as having. This is true of the magnified "jagged" edge, but false of the visibly curved edge, because for the former, but not the latter, there are no instances of such variations from a straight line that an unaided human being is capable of discerning. Thus we can once more make a justified amendment to the third condition that we have used to characterize perceptual acquaintance. Let us replace (3a) by:

(3b) for any (minimally required) sensible (phenomenal, physical) property, Q, *if*, at t, s should be a normal observer who immediately perceives p in conditions optimal for distinguishing whether or not p has Q, and in so doing he has an experience of p as having Q, *then*, at t, he would immediately perceive a property of p that is either Q or some property which is not distinguishable from Q by unaided, normal human

---

[7] See Berkeley, *A Treatise Concerning the Principles of Human Knowledge*, Secs. 89 and 142.

perceivers, even in optimal conditions (*then*, let us say, at *t*, *p* would (minimally) appear to *s* "approximately" as it is at *t*).

We have found a justified way to amend the characterization of perceptual acquaintance so that a naive realist can avoid the objection that it is unreasonably arbitrary to assume that human perceivers are best suited for discerning certain sensible properties of objects. Of course, this reply depends on a two-part assumption: no creatures optimally perceive a physical object *p* to have a property *Q* such that: (1) *Q* is more nearly like a property of *p* than any property *R* that humans optimally experience *p* to have, and (2) there are optimal conditions in which unaided, normal humans are able to distinguish perceptually *Q* from *R*. But I find no reason to doubt this assumption. For example, there is no reason to think that either of the following pairs of claims is true. First, some creatures experience some things to be curved in a humanly discernible way while we optimally experience them to be flat, and the curved shape that appears to these creatures is closer to the shape of these things than the flat shape that optimally appears to us. Second, some creatures find things orange that optimally appear red to us, and the color that appears to these creatures is closer to the actual color of the things than the color that optimally appears to us.

FOURTH OBJECTION: MICROSCOPES AND THE COLOR OF BLOOD

The preceding amendment also permits the naive realist to handle certain of the examples used to generate the fourth objection from science. Consider two examples using magnification by microscopes instead of perception by nonhuman creatures. One concerns the edge of a razor blade magnified enough to appear jagged, and the other concerns a drop of blood that optimally appears red to unaided human perceivers, but which appears quite translucent and almost clear when magnified sufficiently. Surely, if microscopes reveal colors as well as shapes of things more precisely, then razor blade edges are jagged rather than straight and blood is almost clear rather than dark red. The first example can be handled easily by the preceding amendment, because the edge of the razor blade appears "approximately" as it is, but the second is not accommodated so easily. Although the variations from a straight line are so minuscule that they are not humanly discernible without perceptual aid even under optimal conditions, the difference between something red and something virtually colorless is clearly discernible by humans. It is not as if the microscope reveals that blood is a humanly indiscernibly lighter shade of red than the shade it optimally appears to us. This would be handled by the amendment. Unfortunately, the difference stated in the example is a clearly discernible one.

As stated above, this objection about the color of blood does not require any reference to a microscope, because the difference in color between a drop of blood and the same blood when thinly pressed between two glass slides is easily discernible by the naked eye. A thin smear also appears almost colorless, whether or not it is viewed through a microscope. Therefore a microscope adds nothing to this objection, unless we find that what a microscope "reveals" is discernibly different in color from what optimally appears to unaided sight. But once we see how a naive realist can rebut the version of the objection that does not rely on microscopes, we shall be almost ready to see that he can also defeat the claim that certain things "revealed" by microscopes show that no drop of blood has any color that approximates the shade of red it optimally appears to have.

It is a mistake for a naive realist to talk about *the* color of blood, except elliptically. Indeed, to be more precise, he should talk, for example, about the color of an unsmeared drop of blood, the color of a thin smear of blood, and the like. He can then say that a drop of blood is dark red and a thin smear is no more than a very pale red, perhaps even almost clear. He can also point out that one must be careful about the conditions in which one observes a thin smear if he hopes to see any color it has. It is, for example, much better to put it on a white background than to let light shine through it from behind, because in the latter case much of the light of many wavelengths will pass completely through the smear and no color it has will appear. By discussing colors of blood in this plausible way, a naive realist can reasonably argue that differences in color between a drop and a thin smear raise no problems for his thesis.

It might be replied that it is unreasonable that the color of a bit of blood is dark red at one moment, and an instant later, after it is pressed between two slides, it is almost clear. According to this reply, merely flattening something should not change its color. But this is surely questionable. The thickness of the blood is changed and thickness is certainly related to color. For example, as a red balloon expands it becomes thinner and its color becomes a noticeably lighter shade of red. When the rubber stretches, any two points on the surface of the balloon become significantly farther apart. Under such conditions we would surely expect that the color would be "thinned out," perhaps to the point where it would no longer appear even faintly red. But this, a naive realist could plausibly argue, would not refute the claim that the unstretched balloon has the red color it is optimally experienced to have when it is not stretched. And, he could conclude for similar reasons that it is also plausible to expect a thin smear of blood to have a much fainter color than an unsmeared drop.

The explanation of this thinning out of color is that the red pigment is in the red blood cells containing hemoglobin molecules. These molecules produce the red color of blood and are the red masses that, as Locke says, are "swimming in a pellucid liquor." The thinner a volume of blood is, the fewer of these red masses there are behind any unit of surface area. The result is that there is a smaller ratio of reflected red light to white light for a thin smear than for an unsmeared drop. Because of this, a thin smear optimally appears much paler in color than the same amount of blood in drop form. A naive realist can use this explanation to argue plausibly that the color of a thin smear indiscernibly approximates a shade of red that is much paler than the dark red of an unsmeared drop. Thus, thickness is crucial for color, contrary to the preceding defense of the fourth objection *sans* microscope.

Will the introduction of a microscope resurrect the objection? It will, only if two claims are jointly reasonable. First, something such as a thin smear of blood of a certain thickness appears noticeably different in color under a microscope from the way the same smear with no change in thickness optimally appears to the naked eye. Second, any color appearing through the microscope is closer to any color the smear actually has than any indiscernible approximation of the color which optimally appears to the unaided eye. Let us assume that some smears of blood appear faintly red without a microscope, but through a microscope, under certain conditions of illumination, the same smears with the same thickness appear quite clear except for certain dark masses. The question, then, is whether a naive realist can justify rejecting the claim that, under these conditions, microscopes "reveal" an absence of any red color in blood. If he fails in this, then it is unreasonable for him to hold that the color of the smear is quite close to the pale red that optimally appears.

We can see how to answer this question by considering the following facts. Any masses that might appear dark under certain conditions of illumination would be the hemoglobin molecules in the blood. They might appear dark, when, for example, light is transmitted through the smear from beneath it. But they generally appear red, especially when light is properly focused on the top of the smear. This is true even when the blood is viewed through the most powerful optical microscopes. In general, the method of illumination that is used is crucial for optimally discerning surface colors. For example, polarized light is often used to eliminate the effects produced by interference among reflected light waves and to cut out much of the regularly reflected and stray white light that hides the surface color.

A naive realist can use the preceding facts to justify the following conclusions. First, some of the conditions of illumination in which the hemoglobin masses in blood appear red are optimal, at least given present technology, for seeing the colors of the masses. Second, the large number of red hemoglobin masses in a visible amount of blood will appear continuously red to unaided eyes. Finally, on the basis of the first two conclusions, the continuous red color that a smear of blood optimally appears to have when viewed without aids indiscernibly approximates the red colors of the many dots of red hemoglobin spread throughout the smear. In this way, a naive realist can rebut the fourth objection even when it relies on microscopes..I can think of one last reply. If magnification should be great enough, then the atomic structures of surfaces with their spatially discrete and completely colorless particles would be visible, and this is discernibly different from the continuous colored surfaces that optimally appear to unaided human beings. This reply takes us to the fifth objection from science.

FIFTH OBJECTION: ATOMIC CONSTITUENTS AND CONTINUOUS COLOR

Whereas the fourth objection substituted microscopes for other creatures, the fifth substitutes the atomic theory of matter for microscopes. It is often argued that a microscope comes closer to revealing what is there than does unaided sight, because it shows surfaces that appear continuous to unaided sight to be composed of spatially discrete masses, and this accords with the scientific view that physical objects are composed of particles. The basic question, then, is whether the atomic theory of matter provides a picture of physical objects that refutes the claim that they optimally appear approximately as they are. Two features of this picture have been cited as providing the refutation, namely, that the basic constituents of physical objects are spatially discrete, and that they are colorless, that is, they are not sensuously colored. From this it is concluded not only that the second thesis of naive realism is refuted, but the first thesis is also, because, independently of whether we are perceptually acquainted with the physical objects, those objects are neither spatially continuous nor colored. It should be noted, incidentally, that if this objection succeeds, objects do not even appear through microscopes approximately as they are, because some of what appears there is at least sensuously dark in color, and, according to this objection, no objects have even these sensuous "colors".

A naive realist might reply to this objection by adopting scientific instrumentalism, which we have already seen is at least somewhat plausible. Then he could argue that the atomic theory does not provide a better picture of what there is than does a description of the way things optimally appear to us, because the theory provides no picture at all. A more interesting and important question for the purposes of this book is whether a naive realist can refute this objection if he adopts some version of scientific realism instead. I believe that he can, and, although I shall not examine this in detail until Chapter 8 where I shall consider common-sense realism, I shall here briefly indicate how a naive realist can proceed. Like the two examples that illustrate the fourth objection, the two features of atomic structures relevant to the fifth example can be handled differently. The first, like the example of the "jagged" edge of a razor, is quite easy, but the second, again

involving color, is more difficult. While admitting that there are
numerous gaps among the discrete constituents of observable
physical objects, a naive realist can also point out that these gaps
are so minuscule that unaided human beings are unable to discern
a difference between such systems and continuous masses. Thus
such systems appear approximately as they are when optimally
seen by unaided human perceivers. It should be noted here that,
contrary to this objection, the preceding characterization of the
first thesis of minimal naive realism does not state that any observable physical objects are continuous in their sensuous color.
The present discussion shows one reason for this.

One point crucial to the species of the fifth objection that concerns color is the inference that because no scientifically basic
particles are colored, no system of these particles is anywhere
colored. As will be discussed in Chapter 8, there are various ways
to attack this inference. One is to claim that sensuous color is an
emergent property of certain of these systems, and, while granting
that no basic particles are colored in isolation, some are colored
when they are components of these systems. Another way is to
grant that basic particles remain colorless even when in systems,
but to postulate that something like fields are set up among the
particles in certain systems, and that these "fields" are colored.
And, because there are so many of these colored areas in an
observable system, such systems optimally appear continuously
colored. On the basis of these brief remarks and the promise of
more detailed comments later, I shall assume here that a naive
realist who adopts a version of scientific realism that allows
objects to have nonscientific properties can accommodate both
initially troublesome features of atomic structures.

SIXTH OBJECTION: NO ONE PROPERTY OF OBJECTS CORRELATES WITH
ONE COLOR

The answer to the second species of the fifth objection seems to
assume that all red physical objects, such as tomatoes, fire engines,
and stop lights, have one property in common. But according to
the sixth objection this is mistaken. As Mundle says, science has
discovered that "there is no single property corresponding to their
visible colour in the various physical objects which [appear to be]

the same colour."[8] His reason for this is that "there is an infinite number of different mixtures of wavelengths whereby you see each of the colours that you can see," and so "in vision there is no one-one correlation between the colours we see and any physical property of the object emitting or reflecting the light which makes us see them."[9] The point here is that selective reflection and absorption of quite different combinations of light waves by surfaces of quite different molecular structures often result in our having experiences of qualitatively identical color. Thus, Mundle concludes that it is mistaken for a naive realist to assign one common property to all these different objects.[10]

As presented, this argument is invalid, because its premises imply only that there is no physical property in a one-one correlation with each perceived color, but its conclusion states that there is no property of any sort in such a correlation. If, however, we amend the conclusion to mention only physical properties, then an additional premise is needed to the effect that sensuous, occurrent color of external objects is a physical property. The problem then is that any seeming plausibility of the amended version depends on an equivocation on 'physical property.' If it is taken to mean, roughly, a "scientific," theoretical property of physics, then the added premise about sensuous color is false. If, however, it is taken to mean, roughly, an observable or theoretical property that is ascribable to physical objects, then the additional premise is true, but the facts about surface structure and light waves do not establish that there is no physical property common to all physical objects that optimally appear to be the same color.[11] According to a naive realist, of course, there is one common physical property, which may not be "scientific," namely, sensuous color itself. He might well bolster his point by postulating, as I suggested concerning the fifth objection, that various molecular surface structures are correlated with, and are perhaps causally sufficient for, the very same *emergent* property of the whole surface, namely,

---

[8] Mundle, p. 51.

[9] Ibid., pp. 54–55.

[10] For a similar argument, see Campbell, pp. 132–38.

[11] For definitions of 'physical property' of these two sorts, see Sellars, "The Identity Approach to the Mind-Body Problem," *Review of Metaphysics* 18 (1965), Sec. 45; and my *Materialism and Sensations*, pp. 9–13, respectively.

one sensuous color.[12] Nothing discovered or postulated by science refutes this. It is only if someone accepts a rather strong version of scientific realism which limits the properties of physical objects to what I called "scientific" properties, that this sort of problem with sensuous color arises. On such a view, each instance of color of an external object would have to be identical with some instance of a scientific property.[13] But there is no reason for a naive realist to adopt such a version of scientific realism. Indeed, as we shall see in Chapter 8, there is reason for no one to adopt it.

We are left with one further objection based on science. So far, we have rejected six science-based objections by showing that naive realism can accommodate both scientifically discovered facts and scientific explanatory theories, even when they are given a realistic interpretation. Throughout these discussions, we have assumed the scientific description of perception as involving stimulus from an external object which affects someone's sense organs, which then affect his brain. When all this occurs properly, he perceives the object. For the naive realist, to perceive the object is to be perceptually acquainted with it. While we have not yet found a way to use these or other scientific claims to refute naive realism, we shall now see that the claim that these causal chains occur over a period of time provides the basis for the last and defeating objection to the naive realistic view of perception.

SEVENTH OBJECTION: THE TIME-GAP ARGUMENT AGAINST NAIVE REALISM

In Chapter 2 we briefly considered the version of the time-gap argument that argues from the claim that light, and thus visual stimulus, travels at a finite velocity, to the conclusion that whenever an external physical object is perceived, a sensum is directly perceived. Crucial to this argument is the false premise that all objects exist at the time they are directly perceived. We rejected that premise because direct perception, as characterized in the Introduction, does not require the presence of what is directly perceived. Indeed, we saw that direct perception of a distant star at a time, t, after it had exploded would occur if an objectless

---

[12] See *Materialism and Sensations*, pp. 249–51 for a definition of 'emergent property.'

[13] This seems to be what Campbell requires in his version of the argument; see Campbell, p. 133.

event of star-sensing, rather than an event of experiencing a
star-like sensum, occurred at *t* as a result of someone's eyes being
appropriately affected by stimulus from the star. Nevertheless,
although that version of the time-gap argument fails, we shall find
that another version, which considers perceptual acquaintance
instead of merely direct perception, is sound and refutes naive
realism. To see this, let me lay out the argument in some detail:[14]

(1) If something is perceived by *s* at a time *t*, then *t* is one
    time at which *s* has a veridical perceptual experience of
    it.

(2) No veridical perceptual experience of an external
    physical object by *s* occurs before the stimulus energy
    transmitted from the object first affects a sense organ
    of *s*.

Therefore

(3) If an external physical object is perceived by *s* at *t*, then
    t is not a time before the stimulus energy from the object
    first affects a sense organ of *s*.

(4) Some external physical objects that are perceived by a
    person, *s*, have ceased existing before stimulus from
    them first affects a sense organ of *s*.

Therefore

(5) Some external physical objects are perceived by a
    person, *s*, at a time when the objects do not exist.

(6) If naive realism is correct, then if a person, *s*, perceives
    an external physical object at *t*, then he is perceptually
    acquainted with it at *t*.

(7) If a person, *s*, is perceptually acquainted with an object
    at *t*, then it exists at *t* and, if *s* should be normal and
    conditions optimal, *s* would experience it approximately
    as it is at *t*.

Therefore

(8) Naive realism is incorrect.

[14] This argument is adapted from the argument for sensa discussed in *Materialism and
Sensations*, p. 219.

This argument is valid and it certainly seems sound. Surely a naive realist will not refute it by attacking premises (1), (6), or (7). They are not only clearly true, but are true by definition. His only hope, then, is to attack one of the two empirical premises, (2) and (4). But (2) is an obvious truth and, moreover, is surely accepted by a naive realist. While he *might* deny that a veridical perceptual experience of an object first occurs after light reflected from the object first affects his eyes, because he might believe he begins to see as soon as the light hits his eyes, he surely would correctly agree that he does not see before the light hits his eyes. He must, consequently, concentrate on (4).

To refute premise (4), a naive realist must counter the strong scientific reason for accepting it. There is good reason to believe that exploding stars have been seen, and that, given the scientific hypotheses about their distances from the earth and about the speed of light in outer space, they exploded light years before their explosion was seen. Because of the plentiful evidence that such explosions have been seen, a naive realist is not justified in claiming that no exploding stars have been seen. He must, then, either refute the claim that they are at such great distances, or justify that the speed of light in outer space is substantially greater than 186,000 miles per second.

The second alternative will not help him. He has the choice of arguing either that the scientific claim about the speed of light is factually false or that it is merely an inference ticket. However, neither choice is acceptable. The first choice is unreasonable because not only is the scientific claim highly confirmed by various experiments, but also some of the methods used to measure the speed are those he surely should accept for measuring more mundane speeds. Given that the distance between the Earth and Mars, Venus, or Jupiter is established by spaceship travel, the speed of light can be found by measuring the time it takes a beam of light to make the round trip. This is the same method used to measure the speed of a runner who makes one lap around a track. The second choice is even less helpful. If a naive realist construes scientific sentences about the speed of light instrumentally, then he should agree they are justified inference tickets. But then the inferences they warrant are justified, and so the calculations about the many years it takes light to get from the stars to the earth would be justified. Consequently premise (4) would be justified.

A naive realist's last hope, then, is to justify the claim that stars are very much closer to the earth than the many light years that are derivable from scientific claims. However, at present, there is at least good reason to think these stars are much farther away from the earth than are Mars, Venus, and Jupiter whose distances are known because of space travel. Consequently, because the scientific claims about the speed of light are justified, so also is the claim that some exploding stars were at least far enough away from the earth so that they no longer existed when someone saw them. That is, even if they were much closer to the earth than science claims they are, they would still not be close enough to help a naive realist. Therefore, premise (4) remains unrefuted, and, surely, quite reasonable. And because we have found all the other premises of the time-gap argument to be reasonable, we can conclude that the argument refutes naive realism.

Conclusion about Naive Realism

We have finally come to agree with the many philosophers who have claimed that naive realism should be rejected, but our reasons for this conclusion differ from those often given. In particular, they differ from those of people such as Berkeley, who attack the first thesis of naive realism. We have found no reason to reject it. As far as we have ascertained here, this thesis, which I shall later try to show is essential to the common-sense view, remains a viable candidate for one part of a justified theory of perception and the external world. We have rejected the second thesis of naive realism, or, more precisely, that part of the second thesis which states that whatever is perceived is perceptually present with a perceiver. It may seem we have also found grounds for rejecting the other part about being perceptually presented to a perceiver, because distant stars that have already exploded are not directly perceived by us approximately as they are even under conditions that are optimal for seeing sensible properties. Being nonexistent when seen, they have no properties, and thus none of those they appear to have approximate any they actually have. There is a mistake in this reasoning, however. It is clear that being light years from a star, as we are from these stars, is not being in conditions optimal for seeing their sensible properties. We should be much closer. This would result in the time-gap being so short as to be negligible. Nevertheless, because even in optimal conditions there is always some, minuscule time-gap, let us make one final amendment to the third condition. A naive realist can surely agree to replace 'appear approximately as it is at t' in (3b) with 'appear approximately as it is approximately at t.' Let us call the result (3c). As finally amended this part of the second thesis of naive realism remains unrefuted. Consequently, like the first thesis, it is still a candidate for part of a justified theory of perception and the external world.

So far we have only found reason to reject the naive realist's view that all objects perceived are present with their perceivers. This casts doubt on his acquaintance view of perception and pinpoints that the crucial question confronting us concerns what it is to perceive an external physical object. One answer, which is not required by the time-gap, but accommodates it plausibly, is that we indirectly perceive external objects. Although we have found no empirical or linguistic reasons for sensa, we have not seen whether or not the metaphysical theory of indirect realism is more plausible than other forms of realism. Historically, and for some, epistemologically, it has been the successor to naive realism. Locke and Newton turned to it for reasons derived from science that they thought refuted naive realism. Quite recently, Wilfrid Sellars has claimed that a thorough-going scientific realism requires sensa because it requires the unity of science, which in turn requires sensa. Let us, then, examine these and other metaphysical reasons for indirect realism and thus for sensa.

7 Indirect Realism

With the rejection of naive realism because of its falsified view of perception, it is natural to turn to a theory that not only fits the falsifying facts, but explains them as well. We have seen that it is the claim that we are perceptually acquainted with external physical objects that should be rejected. It is tempting, however, to try to maintain that we are perceptually acquainted with something in perception. Indeed, it might be argued that if we are not perceptually acquainted with something, we would not perceive anything even indirectly. With the rejection of naive realism, the obvious candidates for objects of perceptual acquaintance are sensa. In such a way we might find ourselves coming to embrace indirect realism.

Indirect realism, like naive realism, can be construed as consisting of two subtheses, one about the nature of the external world and the other about our relationship to it when perceiving it. As I shall interpret the minimal position, however, it does not explicitly state those properties that external objects have or lack. Thus an indirect realist need not agree with Locke about primary and secondary qualities. He might hold that sensa of secondary qualities as well as those of primary qualities resemble them. What is essential to his position about external objects is what makes him a realist in common with a Lockean, a naive realist, a modified naive realist, and a Kantian realist. This is the thesis that there are external objects—nonperceiving objects that exist independently of and unaffected by being perceived. However, unlike a Kantian realist, he holds that at least some of these external objects are perceivable physical objects. Thus we have:

> *Indirect Realism (first thesis)*: There are perceivable physical objects that are not perceivers, that exist unperceived, and that are not affected either by being perceived or, generally, by changes in the usual conditions in which they are perceived.

The second thesis centers on the claim that those external objects that are perceived are indirectly, rather than directly, perceived.

This is because in all cases of perception of a physical object, a sensum is directly perceived. Yet this is not quite precise enough because it allows for the possibility that direct perception of, for example, a red sensum consists in red-sensing as a result of some effect on the perceiver by the sensum. I believe it is clear that no indirect realist would hold this odd view. He would insist on claiming that any perceiver of an external object is perceptually acquainted with at least one sensum. Indeed, all perceptual experiences a person has of physical objects consist in the person being perceptually acquainted with sensa. But this can be even further clarified, because as stated when discussing perceptual acquantaince, we need not mention the requirements that the perceiver be normal and that conditions be optimal when considering only individual sensa. Each perceiver is normal regarding his own sensa, and he perceives them under optimal conditions. Thus, according to an indirect realist, a perceiver is not only perceptually acquainted with his own sensa, he experiences them as they are, that is, as I shall say, he senses them. Following our discussion in the preceding chapter, we can define this as follows:

> s senses sensum p at $t =$ df.
> (1) s immediately perceives sensum p at t, *and*
> (2) for any sensible phenomenal property, Q, if, at t, s has an experience of p as having Q, then at t he immediately perceives Q, which is a property of p at t.

We have, then, the following:

> *Indirect Realism (second thesis):* Whenever an external physical object is perceived by someone, he indirectly perceives it and his perceptual experience of it consists in his sensing some one or more sensa.

We can see now where an indirect realist differs from other realists. Unlike all direct realists, and thus naive realists (including modified naive realists, as I have interpreted Galileo) he claims that no external objects are directly perceived. He differs from direct realists, then, because of his second thesis. He differs from a Kantian nondirect realist and a phenomenalist regarding both theses. But even with this definition that distinguishes an indirect realist in these ways, there remains much room for disagreements among indirect realists. To see this in more detail, let us consider Locke, a classical example of an indirect realist who is also a "representative" realist, and a contemporary Sellarsian indirect realist.

A LOCKEAN REPRESENTATIVE REALISM

What is the minimum statement that would distinguish Lockean representative realism from the other versions of indirect realism? We can, I find, ignore many of Locke's claims, such as those about material substance, and so ignore many of his confusions and mistakes. I would claim, however, that there are three distinctive features of a Lockean representative realism. One concerns the causal relationship between certain (for Locke, simple) sensa and the properties or qualities of external objects, one concerns the picture-like representational function of sensa, and one is an epistemological thesis about the grounds or foundation of empirical knowledge of the external world. These three theses are adumbrated in the following three quotations. First:

> Whatsoever the mind perceives *in itself*, or is the immediate object of perception, thought, or understanding, that I call *idea*; and the power to produce any idea in our mind, I call *quality* of the subject wherein that power is.[1]

Second:

> The ideas of primary qualities of bodies are resemblances of them, and their patterns do really exist in the bodies themselves; but the ideas produced in us by these secondary qualities have no resemblance of them at all.[2]

Third:

> It is evident the mind knows not things immediately, but only by the intervention of the ideas it has of them. Our knowledge therefore, is real, only so far as there is conformity between our ideas and the reality of things. But what shall be here the criterion? How shall the mind, when it perceives nothing but

---

[1] Locke, *Essay Concerning Human Understanding*, Book II, Ch. 8, sec. 8.
[2] Ibid., Book II, Chap. 8, sec. 15.

its own ideas, know that they agree with things themselves?[3]

I believe that the two theses about the causation of sensa and the resemblance of some sensa to their causes is clear in the first two passages. However, the epistemic thesis in the third selection requires some interpretation. According to Locke, it is not merely that only sensa are directly perceived, but also that a person has immediate or noninferential knowledge solely about himself and his own ideas, including sensa. Furthermore any knowledge someone has about either the existence or properties of external physical objects is inferential knowledge derived from knowledge of certain sensa. Thus a person's basic or ultimate premises for justifying claims about the external world refer exclusively to himself as a perceiver and his own sensa. Consequently, on this view, only deduction and induction by enumeration can be used to warrant inferences. What is called "hypothetical" or "hypothetico-deductive" induction is excluded, because it allows the assumption of the hypothesis to be proved as a premise in order to justify it by its experienced consequences. Using this interpretation of Locke's epistemological thesis, we can construct the following definition:

> *Lockean Representative Realism:*
> (1) Indirect realism is true, *and*
> (2) all sensa a person senses when perceiving an external object are caused by some quality of the object, *and*
> (3) some but not all sensa so caused resemble the qualities (that is, primary qualities) that cause them, *and*
> (4) persons have knowledge of the existence and properties of some external objects, and each person's knowledge of this sort is inferred (deductively or inductively by enumeration) from knowledge solely about his own sensa and himself as perceiver.

It is widely held that the refuting objection to representative realism is that it leads to epistemological skepticism about the external physical world, and is, therefore, highly implausible. If this is true, then, as I have characterized the position with its claim that there is such knowledge, it leads to a contradiction. Nevertheless,

---

[3] Ibid., Book IV, Chap. 4, sec. 3.

although this is a standard, even textbook, objection, I do not believe it has been firmly established. Indeed, I would claim that without clearly stating the various subtheses of the theory, no refutation succeeds, and no understanding results about which subtheses it would be best to abandon in order to avoid the objection with minimal change in the theory. The objection, of course, is recognized by Locke, as is clear from the second question he asks in the third quotation above. How, indeed, given this theory, are we to know that certain of our sensa agree with, or correspond to, let alone resemble, external objects? Locke's answer is that there are two sorts of ideas which we are justified in assuming "agree with things." The first are simple ideas, which, because they are not caused by the mind but by external objects,

> represent to us things under those appearances which they are fitted to produce in us, whereby we are enabled to distinguish the sorts of particular substances, to discern the states they are in, and so to take them for our necessities, and apply them to our use.[4]

The second sort are all complex ideas, except that of substance, which are "not intended to be the copies of anything, nor referred to the existence of anything, as to their originals".[5] Thus they are not supposed to represent or "agree with" any external objects, but only with ideas "of the mind's own making."

I believe we need not worry about whether only simple ideas represent external objects, but we do have to clarify what it is for a sensum to represent, be a copy of, agree with, and conform to some property of an external object. It clearly does not require representational picture-like resemblance, because Locke says,

> The idea of whiteness, or bitterness, as it is in the mind, exactly answering that power, which is in any body to produce it there, has all the conformity it can, or ought to have, with things without us. And this conformity between our simple ideas, and the existence of things, is sufficient for real knowledge.[6]

[4] Ibid., Book IV, Chap. 4, sec. 4.
[5] Ibid., Book IV, Chap. 4, sec. 5.
[6] Ibid., Book IV, Chap. 4, sec. 4.

Thus ideas of secondary qualities, which, for Locke, surely do not pictorially resemble those qualities, do represent or conform to them. What is essential to such representation is that there is a one-to-one correspondence between each distinct (simple) sensum we have at a certain time and a distinct property of an external object that causes the sensum. We can, then, use such sensa as proxies for properties of external objects in our attempt to obtain knowledge of external objects and the relationships among them. The relationships we can discover among simple sensa correspond to relationships among external objects and their properties. Thus we can justify generalizations relating properties of external objects by means of directly perceived constant conjunctions among those sensa that are correlated with, because caused by, those properties.

The crux of this Lockean rebuttal to the objection that his theory bars knowledge of external objects can be laid out as follows:

(1) Some of my (simple) sensa are not caused by me.
(2) If a sensum is not caused by me, then it is caused by an object external to me.
(3) For each distinct (simple) sensum, there is one corresponding distinct quality of the entity that causes it.

Therefore

(4) For some distinct (simple) sensa, there are corresponding distinct qualities of objects external to me.

I believe that Locke can plausibly argue for premises (1) and (2), even given the preceding restrictive interpretation of his epistemological theory. Premise (1) could be based on his awareness of his own passivity when receiving certain sensa. Premise (2) can be construed as an instance of the general claim that every entity has a cause, which, Locke might argue, is a conceptual truth and thus is merely about relations among ideas. Thus it is somewhat plausible to construe both (1) and (2) as statements solely about sensa and their perceivers, and so they could be known non-inferentially. However, (3) is more difficult for Locke to justify. Nevertheless, I believe he might also plausibly argue that it is an instance of another conceptual truth about causation, namely, for each distinct effect there is something with a distinct capacity which, given certain initial conditions, is exactly causally sufficient for just that effect.

Surely, much of the preceding attempt to reconstruct a plausible Lockean argument is debatable, but let us grant, for present purposes, that this argument succeeds. The question, of course, is just how much we have granted. It might seem that we have granted Locke all he needs to establish that on his theory there is inferential knowledge about external physical objects and at least some of their properties, namely, those that correspond to certain of our sensa. However, he has not established this, even with what we granted him. At most he has shown that there is at least one entity of some sort which is different from and independent of himself, and that it or some other entities have properties corresponding to certain of his sensa. He has not, then, found a way to justify that there are many external objects, let alone that they are physical objects. Furthermore, he has provided no way to justify anything about what properties these external objects have, except that they have capacities of some sort that correspond to certain of our sensa. Some properties correspond to sensed whiteness and sensed bitterness, but Locke has given us no way to justify what these properties are. In brief, he has done no more than justify a claim about the structure of what is external to himself. But such a claim is compatible with a Kantian realism with its realm of unknowable things-in-themselves, and also with a phenomenalism that postulates God as the one "external" object. In the latter case, it would be the structural relationships among God's idea (perhaps archetypes) that would correspond to the structural relationships that Locke discovers among certain of his sensa.[7] But Locke claims to know more about what is external to him than this limited bit of information. The external world, he claims, consists of physical objects with certain primary qualities and certain imperceptible constituents. Can he justify this claim?

Rejection of the Lockean Theory: No Inference from Sensa to External Physical Objects

We have now reached the point at which we can make the

[7] See Berkeley, *Principles, Dialogues, and Philosophical Correspondence*, C. M. Turbayne, ed. (Indianapolis: Bobbs-Merrill, 1965), Dialogue III, 21.

decisive objection to the Lockean form of representative realism, which might be called "representational" realism. A Lockean's claim about the properties that external objects have is at best known inferentially, and his one way to justify the required inference is by means of his claim about the resemblance—seemingly representational or pictorial resemblance—between some of those properties and the sensa he is caused to sense because of those properties. Given the preceding Lockean epistemological theory, however, this resemblance claim is also at best justified inferentially, but the theory allows no way to do this. There is no way, either deductively or inductively, to infer that there are such resemblances from premises solely about oneself, one's own sensa, their sensible properties, and relationships among them. In other words, while a Lockean might be able to justify that certain sensa represent, in the sense of "stand proxy for," certain discriminable external properties, he has no way to justify any claim about what these properties resemble. It may be that our knowledge of these proxies and their relationships are suitable as a guide to life, that is, for making the predictions we need in order to know how to plan and what to expect in the future, because the lawlike structural relationships among sensa correspond to lawlike structural relationships among properties of external objects. For example, such a correspondence would obtain if substitution of sensum terms for all variables replacing physical-object terms in a Ramseyized theory should preserve truth. Nevertheless, no such structural knowledge provides grounds for knowledge of what constitutes the external world, which is one kind of knowledge a Lockean theory assumes.

Let me lay out the argument that defeats this Lockean theory. It is, incidentally, similar to Stace's argument against realism.[8] One difference between the two is that while the present argument works against this Lockean theory, neither it, nor Stace's argument succeeds against many other forms of realism. The argument is:

(1) If Lockean representative realism, that is, representational realism, is correct, then there is knowledge about what some external properties are only if some claim that some external properties (pictorially) resemble certain sensa is justified.

[8] See W. Stace, "The Refutation of Realism," *Mind* 43 (1934): 145–55.

(2) If representational realism is correct, then some such resemblance claim is justified, only if either such resemblances are directly perceived, or such resemblance claims are justified by a sound deductive or inductive argument with premises solely about sensa and their perceivers.

(3) If representational realism is correct, no case of such resemblance is directly perceived.

(4) If representational realism is correct, then such a resemblance claim is deductively justified, only if some statement solely about sensa and their perceivers entails the resemblance claim.

(5) No statement solely about sensa and their perceivers entails such a resemblance claim.

(6) If representational realism is correct, then such a resemblance claim is inductively justified, only if either it is inductively inferable from premises solely about sensa and their perceivers, or some samples of such a resemblance are directly perceived.

(7) No such resemblance claim is inductively inferable (by enumeration) from such premises.

Therefore

(8) If representational realism is correct, then there is no knowledge about what any external properties are.

(9) If representational realism is correct, then there is such knowledge.

Therefore

(10) Representational realism is incorrect.

Given our previous characterization of the Lockean theory, premises (2), (3), (4), (6), and (9) are clearly true, with the one priviso that statements solely about sensa and their perceivers include statements relating sensa to other sensa, and also statements expressing conceptual truths, that is, for a Lockean, relations among ideas. This leaves only premises (1), (5), and (7) available for him to reject.

It is easy to see that (5) is acceptable by recalling the discussion of analytical phenomenalism in Chapter 3. The same sort of considerations that counted against any sensum statements, whether probabilistic or not, entailing physical-object statements, also can be used to refute any particular claims about sensum statements entailing these resemblance sentences. As in the previous case, this would show premise (5) to be justified inductively, from counter examples to attempts to refute it. Premise (7) is seen to be correct once it is realized that as construed here, induction is restricted to induction by enumeration. This requires that the premises mention entities that are samples of the kinds of entities mentioned in the conclusion. But no premises solely about a perceiver and his sensa mention any relationships between sensa and external properties.

There may be some disagreement about (1), primarily because neither Locke nor the Lockean theory characterized above make clear whether or not justification of the resemblance claim is crucial for knowledge of the external world. Nevertheless, it seems reasonable to interpret Locke, and our Lockean, in this way. But, if objections remain, the argument can be reformulated so it involves nothing about such a resemblance. Premise (1) can be omitted, (2) replaced as below, and corresponding adjustments made in premises (3) through (7). The following is surely acceptable:

> (2a) If representational realism is correct, then there is knowledge about what some external properties are, only if either some external properties are directly perceived, or some claim about what property some external object has is justified by a sound deductive or inductive argument with premises solely about sensa and their perceivers.

What results is a sound argument, given the preceding characterization of Lockean representative realism.

The question immediately arises about what the minimal change would be that a Lockean could make in his theory to avoid this objection. He could renounce (9) and surrender to epistemological skepticism about all properties of whatever entity or entities cause our sensa. He would then have the following choice. He could embrace a Humean skepticism about the external world, which for Hume is a world of physical objects. Or he could adopt a version of Kantian realism and be skeptical about the external world, but not about physical objects. He would, in the latter case, construe physical objects as "nothing but" appearances or appearings, and refrain from any knowledge claims about any (nonrelational) properties of whatever external objects there may be. Surely, neither alternative is very appealing to an erstwhile Lockean; yet there are no others available to him if he maintains the sensum-based epistemology expressed in the fourth defining condition of his thesis. Indeed, the amended argument shows that any indirect realist, whether or not Lockean, can avoid refutation only if he rejects either (9) or this restrictive epistemological theory. Premise (3a)—that is, (3) amended to agree with (2a)—is true for any indirect realist, (5a) and (7a) are true independently of the theory, and (2a), (4a), and (6a) are implied by the epistemological theory conjoined with indirect realism. To avoid skepticism or refutation, then, an indirect realist must either adopt a less restrictive epistemological theory or avoid all such theories. In essence, yet with many differences in emphasis and detail, we can construe the adoption of such an alternative theory as the crucial change in the move from the Lockean theory to Sellarsian scientific realism.

SELLARSIAN SCIENTIFIC REALISM

Generally two obstacles have been raised for an indirect realist who wishes to replace a sensum-based epistemology with a less restrictive, yet acceptable, theory. The first is the most difficult task of specifying a form of justification other than deduction and induction by enumeration which is acceptable, not only generally, but for the indirect realist's specific needs. The second is not basically an epistemological obstacle, but one supposedly having epistemologically disastrous consequences for an indirect realist. It is the claim that the correct theories of concept formation and concept learning are empiricist theories of the sort that restrict either the meaningful or justifiable use of concepts to what is directly perceived. Indeed, if the Kantian variety of a theory of concept learning is correct, then an indirect realist has only the choice between Humean and Kantian skepticism. Under such conditions Kantian realism might well seem more reasonable.

Empiricist Theories of Concept Formation and Learning

As I interpret it, a theory of concept formation is a theory of how concepts of different sorts come to be meaningfully developed and formulated in a language. Thus it may be that the development of any language requires that the first sorts of concepts formulated are those with which a person responds to what he directly perceives. On this view, only after these basic concepts are developed might theoretical terms, including some psychological terms, come to be developed, perhaps by means of some sort of extensions or changes in the uses of the basic concepts. On the other hand, a theory of concept learning is basically a theory about the way or ways in which a human being can come to understand or acquire concepts, usually already formulated in some language. Furthermore, it is clearly possible that the required order, if there is one, in which concepts come to be formulated in a language is different from the required order, if any, in which a human being comes to understand or acquire these same concepts. I find that it is primarily theories about the order of concept learning or acquiring that have raised problems for indirect realism. In particular, there are three basically different varieties of empiricist theories which philosophers have proposed and which have bothersome epistemological consequences for indirect realism.

What makes these theories empiricist theories is that each implies that, if a person is to understand or to have acquired a nonlogical concept, then he must have had sensory experiences of a specified sort. They differ in how they specify this role of sensory experience. The first theory, which stems from Aristotle and Aquinas, I shall call "abstractionism;" the second, associated with the British empiricists, can be called "associationism;" and let us dub the third "Kantian constructionism." Let me roughly define one species of each sort as follows. First:

I. *Abstractionism:* A person acquires a nonlogical concept, C (for example, redness), if and only if:
    (a) The universal, U (for example, redness) corresponding to C is exemplified by, and thus exists in, observable particulars in such a way that the entities with which the person is perceptually acquainted in perceiving the particulars contain either U (redness) itself or something suitably similar to U (redness), and he abstracts this common universal element from these entities, *or*

(b) he constructs the concept ultimately from concepts acquired in accordance with (a).[9]

Second:

II. *Associationism:* A person acquires a nonlogical concept, *C* (for example, redness), if and only if
   (a) repeated association of a term, *T* ('red'), with instances of property *P*, (being red) with which the person is perceptually acquainted has resulted in the person understanding that *T* ('red') is to be used to express the concept *C* (redness), *or*
   (b) (as above in I)

Third:

III. *Kantian Constructionism:* A person understands a nonlogical concept (for example, redness), if and only if he has developed it in attempting to impose, in the way required by certain of the rules that govern all human understanding, some order and unity on the relevent sorts of (spatio-temporal) data with which he is perceptually acquainted.

For our purposes, there is no appreciable difference between I and II. It would seem that one of them is capable of explaining the acquisition of a concept just in case the other is also. The crucial question for both theories is to discover what additional sorts of concepts they allow us to acquire by construction, given the sorts of concepts they allow us to acquire from experience, that is, by abstraction or association. Generally, restrictive limitations have been put on our constructive ability so that a concept is acquired by construction only if it can be completely characterized by previously acquired concepts, and, thus ultimately by non-

---

[9] Compare W. Sellars' discussion of abstractionism in *SPR*, pp. 41–50. Throughout this chapter, I shall use abbreviations for Sellars' works as follows:

    IA: "The Identity Approach to the Mind-Body Problem," *Review of Metaphysics* 18 (1965); reprinted in *PP*, Chap. 15.

    PP: *Philosophical Perspectives* (Springfield, Ill.: Charles C. Thomas, 1967).

    SM: *Science and Metaphysics* (London: Routledge and Kegan Paul, 1967).

    SPR: *Science, Perception, and Reality* (New York: Humanities Press, 1963).

    SSS: "Science, Sense Impressions and Sensa: A Reply to Cornman." *Review of Metaphysics* 23 (1971): 391–447.

constructed concepts. This view of the construction of concepts corresponds to the view that any cognitively meaningful term must either be explicitly defined ultimately by terms that refer to what is directly experienced, or be such a term itself. For example, there have been attempts to show that theoretical terms, including nonsensory psychological terms such as 'believe,' are definable by physical-object observation terms, and that such observation terms are in turn definable by sensation terms. But, as is well known, all such attempts at such logical constructionism have failed.[10] Consequently, given these theories of concept learning, if indirect realism is correct, and if our constructive ability is so limited, then only sensation concepts are acquired from experience. Thus no physical-object concepts, whether observation concepts or theoretical concepts, and no nonsensory psychological concepts would be acquired at all. Even for a naive realist, however, no theoretical concepts and no nonsensory psychological concepts would ever be acquired. As a consequence, no form of scientific realism would be viable, because all its varieties are reasonable only if we are capable of understanding the world using theoretical terms and thus theoretical concepts. But if we are unable to acquire them, we are obviously unable to understand the world in terms of them. Clearly, then, the Sellarsian theory requires a different theory of concept learning.

The obstacle supposedly raised by the Kantian theory is different. As previously stated, it provides no reason to think that we do not come to understand and justifiably use theoretical concepts. Surely these are important tools we use in our attempts to organize and unify the myriads of sense impressions impinging on us. On this view, these concepts like all other empirical concepts including psychological concepts, are developed for this purpose, under the restrictions governing all human thought. The Kantian obstacle arises, however, in the further Kantian claim that nonpsychological concepts developed as conceptual responses to sense impressions can meaningfully apply at most to physical objects, and these are "nothing but" appearances (or appearings). Thus while this theory differs from I and II, as previously interpreted, because it allows

---

[10] The latter attempt is discussed in Chapter 3 and the former in my *Materialism and Sensations*, pp. 132–40.

us to understand theoretical concepts, it is importantly like both of those theories. Given indirect realism, none of these three theories allows the meaningful application of any empirical concepts of any sort to any external objects.

Neither a Lockean nor a Sellarsian can consistently maintain any of these three theories. It is clear, however, that he can justifiably reject the first two theories, because it is obvious that we do understand some theoretical concepts, contrary to these theories. The problem is that the requirements for the construction of concepts are too restrictive, and should be relaxed to allow these theories to explain our acquisition of these concepts. Once this is done, neither theory raises any obstacle for an indirect realist unless that crucial, additional Kantian stricture on the range of application of concepts is acceptable. But I find no reason to believe that concepts derived from, or developed in response to, what is directly experienced are meaningfully applicable at most to what is directly experienced. This claim is even more restrictive than the positivistic verifiability criterion of meaningfulness. That a sentence is in principle empirically verifiable does not imply that it and any concepts its terms express are meaningfully applicable only to what is directly experienced. Surely nothing more restrictive than meeting the verifiability principle should be required of empirical terms and concepts. Thus it is reasonable to hold that this Kantian obstacle to Sellarsian scientific realism can be surmounted.

A Sellarsian Theory of Concept Formation

It might seem at this point that it is incumbent on any indirect realist to propose or at least suggest plausible theories of concept formation and learning which his theory can accommodate. Sellars has partially met this challenge by sketching briefly a theory of concept formation that allows for the meaningfulness and learnability of terms that apply to theoretical entities. It is Kantian in an important respect because Sellars holds that certain empirical concepts are developed in our attempts to make conceptual responses to what is directly experienced, that is, sense impressions. One of his unique theses, however, is that only physical-object observation concepts are developed in this way (see *PP*, pp. 351–58). Thus no theoretical concepts of science and no psychological concepts, including sensation concepts, are developed in this way.

What results from this sort of conceptual response is what he calls "the manifest image," or picture, or conception of the world. It is the world so pictured, a world that does not exist according to this scientific realist, that corresponds to the Kantian intersubjective phenomenal world of physical objects.

The second unique feature of Sellars' theory is his thesis about how theoretical and psychological concepts come to be developed. He obviously must avoid that restrictive construction theory for these nonobservation concepts. He contrues both sorts of concepts, including sensation concepts, as theoretical, and claims that just as the role of models and analogies is crucial in the development of the theoretical concepts of science, so also is analogy basic in the development of our more ordinary psychological concepts (see *PP*, pp. 344–50 on models). As he says,

> The interpretation of the framework of sense impressions as a theoretical framework suggests that the analogy between the attributes of impressions and the perceptible attributes of physical objects is but another case of the role of analogy in theoretical concept formation (*SM*, p. 21).

Is Sellars' thesis reasonable? Its present rudimentary and some-what vague state makes it difficult to decide. I find this to present no problem, however, because I believe that it need not be decided in order to evaluate the Sellarsian theory, or any other version of indirect realism. My reason is this. Any adequate theory of concept formation and learning must account for our acquiring, or deve-loping, or coming to understand, theoretical concepts of science. Such a theory, when fully specified, would be a scientific theory, and the ability to explain such acquisitions would be one test of its adequacy. Thus the theory would not raise an obstacle by prohibiting our understanding of these concepts.

There is also no reason to think that such a scientific explanatory theory would require or even justify any claim that limits the range of applicability of these concepts. The problem of what they apply to, if anything, corresponds to the problem of what theoretical terms refer to, if anything. As we saw when examining the argument for scientific instrumentalism based on the theoretician's dilemma, a question about the reference or nonreference of these terms is not itself a scientific question of how to interpret the theoretical terms of a theory that explains some observed data. Because of this, successful explanation by a scientific theory generally does not, by itself, provide reason to interpret the theory or its subject matter realistically, or instrumentally, or in terms of what I call "Kantian scientific phenomenalism". This last is the theory that the theoretical terms of science refer at most to phenomena, or mere appearances. It should be noted, however, that, as will be discussed in Chapter 8, the problems that arise in attempting to interpret quantum theory realistically, do provide a strong argument for construing that theory and its subject matter instrumentally. This is primarily because of certain peculiarities in the observable effects of its purported subject matter, that is, subatomic particulars. But there is no reason to think that human learning of concepts or the development of concepts within a language have peculiarities that will force a scientific theory that explains these facts to restrict the range of applicability of certain of the concepts that are developed and learned.

Examination of Sellarsian Indirect Scientific Realism

We have found no reason to believe that some viable scientific theories of concept formation and learning will force an indirect realist to choose between Humean and Kantian skepticism. The way is clear, then, to discover whether an indirect realist with Lockean proclivities can reasonably avoid both these varieties of epistemological skepticism by devising a less restrictive epistemology than Locke's sensation-based theory. I shall approach this task by considering what is essential to a Sellarsian version of realism that is both indirect and scientific. However, one of my primary aims is to discern whether what is essential to the Sellarsian scientific realism and epistemology is as reasonable when conjoined with direct realism as it is when conjoined with indirect realism. Because of this, I shall begin by characterizing the scientific realistic theory independently of the two subtheses of indirect realism.

SCIENTIFIC REALISM

It might seem that there is just one version of scientific realism, and it is roughly captured by Sellars' claim "that in the dimension of describing and explaining the world, science is the measure of all things, of what is that it is, and of what is not that is not" (*SPR*,

p. 230). Sellars also claims that what explains best describes best, and science explains best. On this view, then, those theoretical terms of scientific theories that best explain what is observed provide the most accurate and comprehensive description of everything there is. To see that this is not the only version, nor, I believe, even Sellars' version, let us compare this thesis with one opposed to it, namely, scientific instrumentalism. As we saw in Chapter 4, this is the view that any theoretical term of science, '*T*,' for which 'There is a *T*' entails 'There is a *P*,' where '*P*' is a pure theoretical term, is merely a nonreferring symbolic device that is used to warrant inferences from observation premises to observation conclusions. It is clear that the thesis we derived from what Sellars said is much stronger than the denial of scientific instrumentalism. It is also true, however, that the mere denial is not strong enough to warrant being called even a minimal version of scientific realism. It is not enough that some theoretical terms are referring terms. Those terms, such as 'electron' and 'electron spin,' that are needed for the best scientific explanation of what is observed, must succeed in referring to particular objects and properties.

Even more is needed. It must turn out that the properties and constituents that are referred to are just those theoretical entities that the appropriate theoretical sentences would ascribe to the objects if the theoretical terms in the sentences should function referentially and descriptively. For example, if the theoretical term of psychoanalytic theory, 'repressed desire,' were needed in psychology to refer to some cause of abnormal behavior, but this cause was actually a supernatural demon that possesses people, then scientific realism would be incorrect. Also, if a Kantian scientific phenomenalism should be correct, then theoretical terms would refer to mere appearances (or appearings), and scientific realism would be false. Thus, unlike the way I have previously characterized the minimal position, we need something like the following definition:

Minimal Scientific Realism: Each nonsentient physical object and each sentient being has the constituents, properties, and relations ascribed to it by the theoretical scientific terms that are required for the best (nontranscribed) scientific explanations of its perceivable behavior and effects.[11]

Let us abbreviate this definition as stating that each nonsentient physical object and each sentient being is *at least* a scientific object.

It is clear that this position is not as strong as the one quoted from Sellars. There are two basic steps from this minimal view to the other, which I call "extreme" scientific realism. The first step is to adopt "moderate" scientific realism. This thesis, at first approximation, limits the constituents, properties, and relations of nonsentient physical objects to just those ascribed to them by science. For example, if no scientific theory that explains the behavior of such objects ascribes sensuous color to them, then none of the objects are colored. To be more accurate, however, some properties (perhaps, being aesthetically pleasing) and some relations (such as being owned by some person) should not be banned from these physical objects just because they are not necessary for scientific explanations of the behavior of the objects. Science is not the measure of *all* the properties and relations of all things. Let us say, however, that on this second species of scientific realism, science is the measure of any "*a posteriori*" property of or any relationship among nonsentient physical objects. By an "*a posteriori*" property or relationship I mean, roughly, one that it is reasonable to claim entities have or lack, only if there is some experiential evidence or theoretical scientific reason sufficient to justify the claim.

The second step is to claim that science is also the preceding sort of measure of all sentient beings, including persons. Thus if only physicalistic terms are needed to explain the perceivable behavior and effects of persons, then this extreme position, but not the more moderate position, implies that all persons are purely physical objects. We can state the moderate thesis, as follows:

> *Moderate Scientific Realism:* Minimal scientific realism is true, and each nonsentient physical object has only the constituents and *a posteriori* properties and relationships with other nonsentient physical objects that are ascribed to it by the required

[11] For my previous characterization of three species of scientific realism, see *Materialism and Sensations*, p. 230. One change here is the reference to nontranscribed theories. There are no theoretical terms in a Craigian or Ramseyan version of a theory.

theoretical scientific terms.

Let us abbreviate this as stating that all nonsentient physical objects are *merely* scientific objects, and all sentient beings are at least scientific objects. The corresponding abbreviation for the extreme view is:

> *Extreme Scientific Realism:* Each nonsentient physical object and each sentient being (including each person) is merely a scientific object.

It is clear that if we were to locate Locke in this spectrum of positions, he would qualify as at least a moderate scientific realist. This is also true of Galileo, Newton, Descartes, and, today, Sellars. However, there is doubt about whether these men would be extreme scientific realists. It is not clear that ideas for Locke and Descartes, sensations of secondary qualities for Galileo, and sensa for Sellars are either introduced or justified solely on the grounds that they are required for some explanatory function of science. Indeed, for Locke and Descartes, the existence of ideas is required primarily because of their particular sensum-based epistemological theories. That this particular reason for sensa is not one acceptable to an extreme scientific realist can be seen by realizing that no requirements of science necessitate such an epistemology. For example, based on the result of Chapter 2, a sensing-based episte-mology would seem to be at least as acceptable to an extreme scientific realist. Furthermore, the Sellarsian epistemology, which does not require sensations for a foundation, is surely compatible with what science requires. Interestingly, however, as we shall see, Sellars seems not to hold the extreme theory. And his reasons for this are, like those of Locke and Descartes, importantly epistemo-logical. Indeed, in spite of his basic epistemological disagreement with both men, these reasons lead him to agree with them that there are sensa.

SELLARSIAN SCIENTIFIC REALISM   Sellars' basic difference from extreme scientific realism is best seen by concentrating on one sort of human behavior, namely, that verbal behavior that is said to express propositional attitudes about the world. Often when such overt behavior is in response to perceptual stimulation, as when some one utters, " There is a red and triangular object here," the verbal response is said to express a perceptual propositional attitude. Such overt verbal behavior must be explained as well as nonverbal behavior (see *SSS*, p. 400), and, according to Sellars, perceptual propositional attitudes are "elements in a 'theory' designed to explain human behavior" (*SSS*, p. 398), in particular, verbal behavior. But such explanatory entities must themselves be explained. Consequently, it is not enough to explain merely observable behavior. The nonbehavioral facts that persons have perceptual propositional attitudes about their conceptual representations of the world around them, must also be explained. According to Sellars, then, a person being "under the visual impression that (visually taking it to be the case that) there is (or of there being) a red and rectangular physical object in front of one" (*SM*, p. 14) is used to explain certain overt behavior. But such "impressions that" must also be explained, says Sellars, if science is to provide a full and unified explanation and description of everything that occurs. According to him,

> It is therefore crucial to my thesis to emphasize that sense impressions or raw feels are common sense theoretical constructs introduced to explain the occurrence not of white rat type discriminative behavior, but rather of perceptual propositional attitudes, and are therefore bound up with the explanations of why human language contains families of predicates having the logical properties of words for perceptible qualities and relations (*IA*, sec. 49).

It seems, then, that Sellars disagrees with someone such as Quine about what is required to explain human behavior, that is, he disagrees with Quine's implication that "correlative physical states" will be able to take over the explanatory roles of all mental entities.[12] More specifically, he appears to claim that they will not take over the role of certain theoretical "inner" particulars, sensa, in the scientific explanation of propositional attitudes that are in turn used to explain certain verbal behavior.

It is not clear, however, why he should not agree with Quine that, although states of human beings that are *purely* physical

[12] See W. V. Quine, *Word and Object* (Cambridge, Mass.: Massachusetts Institute of Technology Press, 1960), pp. 264–65; and *The Ways of Paradox* (New York: Random House, 1966), pp. 208–14.

cannot assume the explanatory roles of propositional attitudes in the present, intermediary stage of scientific development, they can do so once neurophysiology and other physical sciences develop more fully.[13] If he did accept this, then he would slide into the "crude" physicalism he wishes to avoid (see *SM*, p. 22). But if he were an extreme scientific realist, and that theory taken with future scientific advances leads to "crude" physicalism, that is, materialism, then he should accept the materialistic consequences.

How might we best construe Sellars' resistance to a Quinean slide towards materialism? He might merely be making a prediction that science will never be able to uncover a physical correlate for each mental state, and so some mental states will always, as a matter of fact, be required (see *SSS*, pp. 397–99). His resistance, however, seems too strong to be explained in this way. A more reasonable construal is that he believes that no explanation of why someone has a particular conceptual representation of an observable object is satisfactory unless it includes reference to appropriate sensations. He says,

> Even in normal cases there is the genuine question, 'Why does the perceiver conceptually represent a red (blue, etc.) rectangular (circular, etc.) object in the presence of an object having these qualities?' The answer would seem to require that all the possible ways in which *conceptual representations* of colour and shape can resemble and differ correspond to ways in which their immediate *non-conceptual occasions*, which must surely be construed as states of the perceiver, can resemble and differ. Thus, these non-conceptual states must have characteristics which, without being colours, are sufficiently analogous to colour to enable these states to play this guiding role (*SM*, p. 18).

But, according to Sellars, sense impressions in common-sense explanations (the manifest image), and certain states involving sensa in scientific explanations, are the nonconceptual states that are appropriately analogous to color, that is, analogous regarding both their structural and nonstructural properties. Indeed, the concepts

[13] By 'purely physical' I mean something like what Sellars means by 'physical$_2$'. See *IA*, sec. 45. For my definitions of 'physical property' and 'physical object,' see *Materialism and Sensations*, pp. 12 and 14. I reject Sellars' definition on pp. 10–11.

corresponding to these entities have developed analogously from observation concepts. Nevertheless, one thing is far from clear in this account. Why is it that this guiding function is to be performed by something analogous to observable properties in nonstructural ways, as Sellars seems to think? It is true that our manifest explanations and many explanations in psychology presently rely on entities analogous in these ways. For example, red sensa are nonstructurally analogous to red physical objects. But I find no reason at this early stage of theory development to rule out the thesis that the nonconceptual states, which in future scientific explanations will have this guiding role, will be *merely* structurally isomorphic to "all the possible ways in which conceptual representations can resemble and differ." These states, then, might well be *purely* physical states of brains, which like many other sorts of guidance systems need not guide by means of nonstructural resemblances. Indeed, as was mentioned when discussing Gibson's theory, the perceptual systems he proposes seem to have no need for sensations at all. I see no reason why such systems could not also be used, again without sensations, to explain perceptual propositional attitudes, and thereby certain observable verbal behavior.

There is one more reason I believe Sellars might have for resisting materialism. He can be interpreted as believing that materialism omits certain basic features of the world that any adequate ontological theory must include in its account of what there is. These are certain of the sensuous entities we seem to experience constantly. He says, "We must find a place in the world for color in the aesthetically interesting sense with its ultimate homogeneity" (*SSS*, p. 408). It may be objected that this is inconsistent with Sellars' often enunciated opposition to "the" given, because he seems to say here that homogeneous, sensuous color is given. However, he says that he rejects "the" given in one and only one sense. According to him,

> To reject the myth of the given is not to commit oneself to the idea that empirical knowledge as it is now constituted has no rock bottom level of observation predicates proper. It is to commit oneself rather to the idea where even if it does have a rock bottom level, it is still in principle replaceably by another conceptual framework in which these predicates do

not, strictly speaking, occur (*PP*, p. 353).

Thus he can consistently maintain that color is given in some form or other, but in what form it actually occurs—whether as properties of entities (such as physical objects, light, or sensa), or as internal specifications of sensings, or as something else—is to be decided by what explains best scientifically. On this view, then, science must interpret sensuous features of the world, such as sounds, smells, and tastes; it cannot eliminate them or transform them so much that there remains nothing significantly like them. Such a Sellarsian can, then, eliminate sensuous color from the external world in a Lockean way, but if he does so he must locate something much like it in perceivers. In this respect, Sellars accepts one sort of given.[14]

While I believe the third reason for resisting materialism is the strongest because the species of "the" given on which it is based is quite reasonable, we need not decide which, if any, of these proposed reasons Sellars actually accepts. All three support the following construal of Sellarsian (and I hope Sellars' own) scientific realism:

> *Sellarsian Scientific Realism*: Minimal scientific realism is true, and each nonsentient physical object and each sentient being has only the constituents, and *a posteriori* properties and relationships that are ascribed to it by the theoretical scientific terms that are required for the (nontranscribed) scientific theory that best explains its perceivable behavior and effects in a way that also explains and interprets the sensuous features of the world and the responses of perceivers to them.

SELLARSIAN INDIRECT REALISM AND EPISTEMOLOGY   In the preceding discussion there is some hint that Sellars is an indirect realist and that his epistemological theory differs importantly from Locke's sensation-based theory. It is true that he interprets the manifest image or common-sense view of perception as a direct realism on the grounds that it understands perception as involving sense impressions construed as objectless states of perceivers, for example, red-sensings (see *SPR*, p. 100). He claims, however, that

[14] I have discussed a wide variety of givens in "Materialism and Some Myths about Some Givens", *The Monist* 56 (1972): 215–33.

the scientific image or description requires perception to involve inner, theoretical particulars, which he calls "sensa," the concepts for which are derived analogically from observation concepts. When discussing the scientific conceptual framework, he says that it is true "from the standpoint of this sophisticated framework that when a person sees that a physical object is red and triangular on the facing side, part of what is 'really' going on is that a red and tri-angular sensum exists where certain microtheoretically construed cortical processes are going on" (*SPR*, p. 103). Thus, given his scientific realism, he embraces the scientific framework as providing the best description of what there is, and so it is reasonable to interpret him to hold that indirect realism with sensa is one part of the best theory of perception and the external world. It should be noted that Sellars might claim that in the scientific image it is not correct to say that a perceiver *senses* a sensum. Rather there is some theoretical relationship between certain of the microparticles that are among the constituents of his brain and the sensum (see *SSS*, p. 428). This, however, does not imply that Sellars is not an indirect realist, because this relation is the theoretical counterpart in science of the sensing relationship. Strictly speaking, the definition of the second thesis of indirect realism should be amended to allow for such counterparts, but I shall ignore this complication because nothing essential to our discussion is lost and simplicity is gained.

Sellars' epistemological theory is not elaborated in detail, but what is essential for our purposes is captured, roughly, in his claim that what explains best describes best. This can be stated more precisely, I believe, as the principle that whatever statements are the most satisfactory as an explanation of perceivable phenomena also provide the most accurate and comprehensive description of the phenomena and of the entities explaining the phenomena. Given this somewhat plausible principle and Sellars' additional claim that a scientific explanation is the most satisfactory explanation of any perceivable phenomenon, we can justify the claim that the theoreti-cal statements of science provide the most accurate and compre-hensive description of what there is. Thus, contrary to Locke, we can justify a certain description of the external world without inferring it from premises solely about sensa and their relationships to their perceivers; and, contrary to Kant, "the real or 'noumenal' world which supports the 'world of appearances' is not a *metaphysi-*

cal world of unknowable things in themselves, but simply the world as construed by scientific theory" (*SPR*, p. 97).

I do not wish to pursue here whether it is reasonable to adopt Sellars' basic epistemological principle, and his claim that science explains best. I have argued briefly elsewhere that both claims are clearly debatable.[15] While scientific explanations are best for certain purposes, they do not seem best for other purposes. Which of these purposes, if any, is relevant to what is the best description? Indeed, why consider any sort of best explanation as sufficient for the best description? Surely the argument for scientific instrumentalism from the theoretician's dilemma opens that claim to doubt. But even if all arguments for instrumentalism are refuted, I believe that at most it is reasonable to hold the principle that the scientific theory that explains best is *at least* part of the most accurate and comprehensive description of what there is. That is, we are at most justified in accepting minimal scientific realism unless there are reasons to think, as Sellars believes, that if minimal scientific realism is correct, then minimal common-sense realism is mistaken. If this should be true, and if minimal scientific realism should be more reasonable than minimal common-sense realism, as we shall consider in Chapter 8, then there might be reason to accept at least moderate scientific realism and perhaps also the stronger Sellarsian principle.

For our purposes of discovering whether Sellarsian scientific realism combines at least as reasonably with direct as with indirect realism, we shall see that it does not matter which of the two principles a Sellarsian accepts. Let us, then, use the weaker, more reasonable principle in our final attempt to characterize Sellarsian indirect scientific realism with its accompanying epistemology made explicit. We have the following:

Sellarsian Indirect Scientific Realism (and epistemology):
(1) Indirect realism (with counterparts) is true, *and*
(2) Sellarsian scientific realism is true, *and*
(3) the statements that provide the best explanations of perceivable phenomena are part of the most accurate and comprehensive description of what there is, *and*

---

[15] See *Materialism and Sensations*, pp. 179–84.

(4) theoretical statements of science provide the best explanations of perceivable phenomena.

This theory contains everything central to Locke's theory, except the defeating sensum-based epistemology. And, on the initially quite plausible assumption that the Sellarsian epistemology is reasonable, we can draw the preliminary conclusion that Sellarsian indirect realism is more reasonable than Lockean indirect realism. Thus, if we can show that the last three defining clauses of the preceding characterization, which specify Sellarsian scientific realism and epistemology, provide no more reason to accept sensa and indirect realism than to accept some form of direct realism, we shall have some reason to conclude that there is a form of direct realism that is at least as reasonable as Lockean and Sellarsian indirect realism.

AN ARGUMENT FOR SELLARSIAN INDIRECT REALISM　　I have elsewhere examined what I had found to be the most plausible Sellarsian attempts to show that features of Sellarsian scientific realism and epistemology make indirect realism more reasonable than direct realism. I believe that I showed that all of them fail, and so I shall not reconsider them here.[16] However, Sellars replied to my first attempted refutations (see SSS), and, although I believe I adapted my arguments to avoid his replies, I would like to extract from his reply, as it illuminates other of his writings, what I now believe is the strongest argument to show that Sellarsian scientific realism provides reason to postulate sensa.

We have seen that the unique feature of Sellarsian scientific realism is its statement that there are sensuous features of the world which can be interpreted in different ways, but are not to be eliminated completely. The crucial issue is whether, given this version of scientific realism, one way of interpreting these features is more reasonable than all others. Let us make an assumption that is surely plausible: either some persons red-sense if the manifest image or description of the universe is correct, or there is some true scientific counterpart of this fact if the Sellarsian scientific image is correct. Furthermore, let us also assume that if there is to be *the* scientific image, and thus one complete scientific description of

---

[16] Ibid., Chap. 7.

what there is, then science must become unified in the sense that there is one complete scientific description of what there is which is to compete with *the* manifest or common-sense description. If no such unification occurs, then each separate scientific theory will present a partial description that will not be integrated into one overall picture. Consequently, the unified manifest image with scientific instrumentalism will prove to be more reasonable than partial scientific images with realism. According to Sellars, this unity of science requires that each description of objects that is true at some nonbasic level of science, such as the scientific counterpart in psychology of the description of a person red-sensing, must have a corresponding true description at the basic level of science. To accomodate this requirement, Sellars adopts a principle of ontological reduction, namely:

> *R.* If an object is *in a strict sense* a system of objects, then every property of the object must consist in the fact that its constituents have such and such qualities and stand in such and such relations or, roughly, every property of a system of objects consists in properties of, and relations between, its constituents (*SPR*, p. 26).

It is Sellars' claim that his reduction principle requires that the scientific counterpart of an event of a person red-sensing is reduced to, that is, consists in, an event of at least some of the scientifically basic constituents of the person individually having certain properties or relationships. And, in order that the sensuous features captured in the manifest description by 'red-sensing' not be eliminated by such reduction, some of these properties of basic entities must be scientific counterparts of sensuous manifest characteristics, such as redness (see *SSS*, pp. 413–14). Thus, according to this argument, we must, as required by the scientific image, postulate some scientifically basic entites as entities with such sensuous scientific theoretical properties. And, the most reasonable candidates for this role are sensa, rather than elementary particles of physics or scientific counterparts of Cartesian egos. Thus, given Sellarsian scientific realism, we should postulate sensa, and indirect realism is justified.

One way to lay out the details of the premises of this argument is as follows:

(1) If Sellarsian scientific realism is correct, then there is a scientific counterpart of what in the manifest image is a person red-sensing.

(2) If Sellarsian scientific realism is correct, then the scientific counterpart of a person is a system of scientifically basic entities.

Therefore

(3) If Sellarsian scientific realism is correct, then some system, *s*, of scientifically basic entities, which is the counterpart of a person, has group property, *G*, which is the scientific counterpart of the property of red-sensing.

(4) If Sellarsian scientific realism is correct, then all scientific group properties are reducible, that is, a system having a scientific group property consists in certain scientifically basic constituents of the system individually having certain properties or relations.

Therefore

(5) If Sellarsian scientific realism is correct, then *s* having *G* (the scientific counterpart of red-sensing) consists in certain scientifically basic constituents of *s* individually having certain properties or relations.

(6) If Sellarsian scientific realism is correct and system, *s*, having group property, *G*, consists in basic constituents of *s* individually having certain properties or relations, then science should postulate that there are individual basic entities with sensuous properties.

(7) Any basic entity that science postulates to have a sensuous property is either an individual elementary particle, or a counterpart of a Cartesian ego, or a sensum.

Therefore

(8) If Sellarsian scientific realism is correct, then science should postulate that there are either elementary particles with sensuous properties, or counterparts of Cartesian egos, or sensa.

(9) It is more reasonable for science to postulate that there

are sensa than that there are counterparts of Cartesian egos or that elementary particles have sensuous scientific properties.

Therefore

(10) If Sellarsian scientific realism is correct, then science should postulate that there are sensa with sensuous properties, such as "red" sensa.

Premises (1) and (2) are clearly acceptable. Premise (2) is true because persons are sentient beings, and thus if Sellarsian scientific realism is true, they have just the constituents ascribed to them by the appropriate scientific theory. It might be objected, however, that (1) should not require there to be a scientific counterpart of a person red-sensing. As we have seen, however, Sellars insists on counterparts because, I believe, he thinks that even if 'red-sensing' should appear in scientific explanations, it is likely its scientific explanatory use would differ from its manifest explanatory use. And Sellars holds that difference in use implies difference in meaning. We need not, however, debate here about a criterion for difference in meaning. We need only allow that any entity is one of its own counterparts, and then nothing essential to any of the preceding premises depends on whether or not this Sellarsian view about meaning is correct. Indeed, nothing essential depends on whether the scientific image requires different entities from those of the manifest image.

It might also seem that premise (6) is debatable, but although it is surely not an entailment, it is justified by the requirement of the Sellarsian theory that the theoretical terms that describe best must include an adequate interpretation of the sensuous features of the world. Thus unified science should somehow include in its description of basic entities some terms that in some way ascribe some such features to the basic entities. And so science should postulate that some basic entities have certain sensuous properties, if the Sellarsian theory is correct.

OBJECTION: SCIENTIFIC REALISM WITHOUT REDUCTION There remain premises (4), (7), and (9), none of which I find to be clearly acceptable. Indeed, I find (4) clearly unacceptable. The crucial problem is whether Sellarsian scientific realism can permit irreducible group properties, contrary to (4). As previously stated, the Sellarsian theory does not entail such reduction, nor does it do so when the requirement is explicitly conjoined with it that science be unified so that there is one, unified scientific description of what there is. That is, the scientific image does not require the reduction of group properties even with the reasonable assumption that it is correct only if every macro-object is identical with a system of scientifically basic entities, each of which individually has only the properties ascribed to it in the basic science (cf. *SSS*, pp. 414–15). There is no reason to think that the scientific image requires the reduction of group properties to properties that are part of the subject matter of the basic science. At most it would seem to require that the basic science can explain, by means of correspondence rules that link individual basic entities with systems, why those systems have such group properties. Nor is there any reason to think that, even if all scientific properties must be included in the basic science, it could not be done by postulating properties in the basic science that apply to groups of basic entities but not to individual basic entities. For example, temperature might be postulated in the basic science as a property that groups of basic particulars have but no individual basic particulars have. Both of these ways to accommodate group properties clearly seem to be open to the Sellarsian theory. But since neither consists in the reduction of the properties, premise (4) is mistaken.

Sellars' reply at this point would seem to be to invoke *R*, his principle of ontological reduction, but, because of a basic ambiguity in R as stated, it is not clear it supports (4). It can be construed in either of two ways. First:

> *Ra*. If an object is a system of objects, then the object having a property consists in some of the constituents of the object, *either as a group or individually*, having certain properties or relations.

Second:

> *Rb*. If an object is a system of objects, then the object having a property consists in some constituents of the object *individually* having certain properties or relations.

It is clear that the Sellarsian scientific image requires at least *Ra*, but it is also clear that Sellars needs *Rb* to justify (4). But what reason might there be to think a principle as strong as *Rb* is also required? Unfortunately, Sellars provides little to help answer this. At one point he says he accepts it without argument (*SPR*, p. 35). At another place he replies to my suggestion that he need not adopt such a strong principle for his version of scientific realism by saying that "the acceptance of the 'strong' principle of reducibility is what makes the 'version' *mine*" (*SSS*, p. 415). Surely something more is required to justify the use of *Rb*.

I think that we can uncover in Sellars' writings a better reason, but even this one does not justify *Rb*. Sellars holds ontological theses, distinct from his scientific realism, which he says "can be lumped together under the heading 'logical atomism'—thus my acceptance of a strong principle of reducibility concerning the attributes of wholes, and '*Tractarian*' approach to ontology" (*SSS*, p. 396). It is, I believe, this "*Tractarian*" approach that is crucial and requires him to adopt *Rb*, indeed, an extremely strong interpretation of *Rb*. All nonbasic objects are systems of basic objects in the sense that they are logical constructions out of basic objects. Thus all predicates, such as 'temperature,' that truly apply only to scientifically nonbasic entities, whether theoretical, observational, or phenomenal predicates, are to be contextually defined by those predicates that truly apply to individual basic entities. Thus not only is *Rb* required, but the reduction of a group property, such as temperature, expressed in *Rb*, is to be construed in terms of the definition of the corresponding predicate by predicates applicable to individual basic entities. As I have argued elsewhere, however, it is clear by now that neither scientific realism, nor any competing ontological theory, should be encumbered with what there is good reason to think are the unsatisfiable and unreasonable demands of logical constructionism.[17] Thus this, which I find to be the strongest defense of (4), fails, and so, with a Sellarsian having at least two other ways to accommodate group properties, we can reject (4) as too strong a requirement for Sellarsian (if not Sellars' own) scientific realism.

Having rejected (4), we need not consider premises (7) and (9). However, I shall examine in depth issues directly relevant to both

---

[17] Ibid., pp. 243–45.

premises when I discuss in Chapter 8 whether Eddington's scientific table consisting of discrete imperceptible particles might be identical with a common-sense table having a continuous red surface. Regarding (7), I shall say here only that it is not clear its disjunction is exhaustive. Might not the basic entities that have sensuous properties be something like fields, rather than particles, egos, or sensa? Or perhaps, contrary to (9) and Sellars' strong denial (see *SSS*, p. 437), it might be most reasonable to claim that elementary particles themselves, when—and seemingly only when—they are in certain systems, come to be sensuously colored. Again, contrary to (9), it might be no less reasonable to postulate scientific counterparts of Cartesian egos as the bearers of sensuous properties, as it is to assume sensa. I see no reason to think that the former are scientifically less respectable than the latter. Thus, even if (4) were acceptable, a direct realist might well find ways to rebut the justification of indirect realism by way of Sellarsian scientific realism.

Conclusion about Sellarsian Indirect Realism

With the rejection of (4) and the resulting different ways for a Sellarsian to accommodate sensuous qualities without postulating sensa, we can conclude that Sellarsian scientific realism *sans* sensa is at least as reasonable as Sellars' own version with sensa. This, of course, is compatible with Sellars' version being as reasonable as Sellarsian direct realism, and, in fairness to Sellars, that may be all he wishes to establish. If premise (7) were amended to include all alternatives and (9) changed to express that the postulation of sensa is at least as reasonable as the other alternatives, then both would be quite plausible. Nevertheless, the objection to (4) would still remain, and so (10) modified to reflect the change in (9) would still be unjustified. Of course, (10) further amended so it refers to what Sellars calls "his own" version of scientific realism would be justified, because (4) with its antecedent referring to this version would be true. But then we would clearly not have the most reasonable species of indirect realism. Because of the unreasonably restrictive *Tractarian* requirements that Sellars places on ontological theories, his own version is, like Locke's theory, less reasonable than what I have called the "Sellarsian" version. As the preceding discussion indicates, there is reason to think that

Sellars' *Tractarian* requirement of logical construction neither will, nor need be met. All else being equal, a theory without these restrictions is more reasonable than one with them.

PRELIMINARY CONCLUSION ABOUT INDIRECT REALISM

We have examined what I have claimed to be the most reasonable form of scientific realism that accommodates an indirect realist such as Locke. We have seen that a Lockean requires at least moderate scientific realism because of his scientific conception of the external world. Whether it is more reasonable for him to hold, in addition, the extreme or rather the Sellarsian version of scientific realism is settled, I would argue, by a claim that seems to be as close to being irrefutable as any empirical claim. This is the claim that there are sensuous features of some entities of the world, and so these features should be interpreted rather than eliminated. Thus external constraints to force interpretation, rather than elimination, should be put on any version of scientific realism which itself limits the properties entities can have. These constraints, which are included in the Sellarsian theory but not in the extreme theory, falsify the extreme theory, if science becomes and remains behavioristic in subject matter, and physicalistic in method and theoretical postulations. And it is surely plausible that science will develop in this way. Thus, I conclude that the Sellarsian theory is more plausible than the extreme theory, and that if moderate scientific realism proves to be acceptable, then the Sellarsian theory results in the most reasonable form of indirect realism when it is combined with the plausible Sellarsian epistemology and the general thesis of indirect realism. However, we have seen that Sellarsian scientific realism when conjoined with the Sellarsian epistemology does not require or even justify the postulation of sensa. It combines at least as reasonably with the view that perceivers have the nonreduced group property of red-sensing as with the thesis that they sense red sensa. Thus, we can also conclude that if moderate scientific realism is acceptable, then Sellarsian direct realism is at least as reasonable as any form of indirect realism.

Reaching this last conclusion is an important step in the attempt to discover whether some form of direct realism is at least as reasonable as any metaphysical theory of perception and the external world that requires sensa. It might seem that the one remaining step is to compare this Sellarsian version of direct realism with sensum phenomenalism on the grounds that we have found the most reasonable form of realism. This would be premature, however. There are other realistic theories we should examine first, and there are objections to all forms of scientific realism we have not refuted. We have seen that naive realism should be rejected because of its acquaintance view of perception. Common-sense realism, however, as the view of the nature of the external world contained in naive realism, might be combined with a different theory of perception to result in a more reasonable form of direct realism than the Sellarsian version. There will be extremely strong support for such a theory if, in the next chapter, we fail to find a way to neutralize the argument for scientific instrumentalism based on the theoretician's dilemma, or we find new objections to scientific realism sufficient to refute it. Another realistic theory we should also consider has so far been only mentioned. It is a form of nondirect realism which, unlike both direct and indirect realism, denies that we perceive external objects in any way. Its strongest version is Kantian realism. Let us consider it now.

Provisional Conclusion about Kantian Realism

In the Introduction, I discussed three versions of Kantian realism. One version reduces physical objects to appearances, or sensa. Two versions state that physical-object terms and concepts actually apply to nothing at all, but they are the terms and concepts that we develop, in accordance with intersubjectively applicable rules governing concept learning, to categorize the flux of our sensory experience in an understandable way. These two versions of the theory differ concerning whether these experiences are objectless sensings or include sensa. All three interpretations, however, agree that experiences are caused by external things-in-themselves, and that no physical objects are external objects. Indeed, for the last two theories, there are no physical objects at all, and thus there is nothing denoted by physical-object terms, whether they are observation terms or theoretical terms. Of course, there are noumenal objects, that is, external things-in-themselves, but, on all three versions, none of these objects are perceived in any way and none of their nonrelational properties are known.

One consequence of these three theories is what I called Kantian epistemological skepticism, which, as we have seen, receives independent support if—and, it seems, only if—it is reasonable to accept either the restrictive Kantian theory about the learning and range of applicability of concepts, or the similarly restrictive Lockean epistemology. But I have tried to indicate that such a Kantian theory of concepts is clearly overly restrictive, and I have said that the Sellarsian epistemology is at least as reasonable as the Lockean variety. It is true that I have not argued for this second claim. To do so would require a much deeper probing into epistemology than can be done here. Justification of this claim, then, must be put aside until another time. Yet, even without such justification, I believe that it is provisionally as reasonable to accept the less restrictive Sellarsian theory as to accept the Lockean theory. Consequently, on this provisionally plausible assumption that we can reject these Kantian and Lockean restrictions there is reason to reject Kantian nondirect realism with its skepticism for the Sellarsian claim that science uncovers precise information about things-in-themselves, provided, of course, that there are no reasons to reject scientific realism. We must, then, search for such reasons. We shall do so in the next chapter in the context of a discussion of reasons for and against the form of common-sense realism that I call "compatible" common-sense realism because it combines the common-sense theory with minimal scientific realism.

8   Common-Sense Realism and Science

In the discussion of minimal naive realism in Chapter 6, we found that the objection that refuted it was aimed solely at one part of the second thesis of the position. The second thesis is that to perceive a physical object is to be perceptually acquainted with it. The part which was refuted is that any object so perceived exists when perceived. We found this refuted by the time-gap between transmission of stimulus from the object and the resulting perceptual experience of the object. This left most of minimal naive realism intact. I shall claim that its first thesis is the minimal common-sense thesis about the nature of the external world, and what remains of the second thesis is a plausible candidate for the minimal common-sense theory of our perception of the external world.

I shall consider these two theses in examining the minimal common-sense view of perception and the external world. In detail, they are stated as follows. First:

> *Minimal Common-sense Realism (first thesis):* The world consists in large part of perceivable physical objects that are not perceivers, that exist unperceived, and that are not affected either by being perceived or, generally, by changes in the usual conditions in which they are perceived; many of these objects have and are perceived to have at least the minimally required sensible properties, that is, the observable, occurrent properties of size, shape, weight, solidity, texture, motion (rest), location, sensuous color, and hotness (coldness).

Second, by deletion from the second thesis of minimal naive realism, we get:

> *Minimal Common-sense Realism (second thesis):* The event of someone, s, perceiving a physical object, p, at a time, t, is identical with the event of p being minimally perceptually presented to s at t, that is:
>
> (1) s immediately perceives p at t, *and*
> (2) for any minimally required sensible physical property,

Q, if, at t, s should be a normal observer who immediately perceives p in conditions optimal for distinguishing whether or not p has Q, and in so doing he has an experience of p as having Q, *then*, at t, he would immediately perceive a property that p has approximately at t, and that is either Q or some property which is indistinguishable from Q by unaided, normal human perceivers, even in optimal conditions (*then*, let us say, at t, p would minimally appear to s approximately as it is approximately at t).

Note that the second thesis is not refuted by the time-gap argument, because neither immediately perceiving something at t, nor having p appear approximately as it is approximately at t, if certain conditions should obtain, does not justify, let alone require, that p exists at t. Thus, so far, we have found no reason of any sort to reject this common-sense realistic theory, and its intuitive appeal is some reason, perhaps quite mininal, in its favor. Justification of the theory would be significantly strengthened, if there were sound reasons to reject all forms of scientific realism. Its primary remaining competitors then would be phenomenalism and Kantian nondirect realism. But, regardless of that, if we continue to fail to uncover any problems for this common-sense theory, then it would surely have a strong claim for being the most reasonable theory of perception and the external world.

The justification of this common-sense theory would also be significantly strengthened if minimal scientific realism proves to resist all objections, and remains plausible when conjoined with minimal common-sense realism to form what I have called compatible common-sense realism. Indeed, if this combined theory is found to be viable, we will have a theory which, on the assumption that it is at least as reasonable as Sellarsian direct realism, would prove by principle P3 to be more reasonable than that theory, and also Lockean and Sellarsian indirect realism. This is because the compatible thesis is consistent with more pretheoretical, commonly accepted beliefs of mankind than are any of the other three theories. Similar reasoning would show it to be more reasonable than incompatible common-sense realism and Kantian nondirect realism, both of which reject scientific realism and thus conflict with the commonly accepted belief that science uncovers the constituents of the objects we perceive. We would then have good reason to claim that compatible common-sense realism is the most reasonable form of realism. The major remaining task would be to show it to be preferable to the various forms of phenomenalism. If this should be achieved, the goal of this book would be realized, namely, to show that compatible common-sense realism is the most reasonable theory of perception and the external world. Let us, then, consider objections to this combined theory.

It is thought by many people that the theory that results from conjoining minimal common-sense realism and minimal scientific realism is clearly implausible, indeed, perhaps even inconsistent. This problem is illustrated by the following quotation from Eddington:

> There are duplicates of every object about me—two tables, two chairs, two pens . . . One of them has been familiar to me from earliest years. It is a commonplace object of that environment which I call the world . . . It has extension; it is comparatively permanent; it is coloured; above all, it is *substantial* . . . My scientific table is mostly emptiness. Sparsely scattered in that emptiness are numerous electrical charges rushing about with great speed; but their combined bulk amounts to less than a billionth of the bulk of the table itself.[1]

One thing is clear: there are not "duplicates of every object around me." There is only one table on which I am now writing. The question is about what properties this one table has. Compatible common-sense realism states that it has properties quite like those we optimally perceive it to have and also the properties that seem to be ascribed to it in scientific theories. Let us call this thesis the "identity thesis," because it states that what Eddington called two tables are really the same table. The crucial problem for someone who holds this hypothesis is to show that it is consistent and, if consistent, that it is plausible. This requires, at minimum, that its components be shown to be individually reasonable and jointly consistent. Thus, in order to test the hypothesis we must clearly delineate its components.

[1] A. Eddington, *The Nature of the Physical World* (Ann Arbor: University of Michigan Press, 1958), pp. xi-xii.

THE IDENTITY THESIS

The identity thesis is not adequately defined merely by saying that minimal common-sense realism and minimal scientific realism are conjointly true. While the former theory is quite specific in the properties it attributes to physical objects, the latter merely states that physical objects have the properties and constituents ascribed to them in those scientific statements that best explain their perceivable behavior and effects. The crucial problem for the identity thesis arises because of the particular properties and constituents, which if scientific realism is correct, are ascribed to physical objects by the sentences that comprise scientific explanations. Thus the thesis we shall consider includes in one of its conjuncts all the consequences of a minimally realistic interpretation of science. By this I mean that one conjunct is a statement that ascribes to physical objects the properties and constituents they have *if* minimal scientific realism is true. The definition, then, is as follows:

> *Identity Thesis*: The conjunction consisting of the following statements is true: the statement of minimal common-sense realism, the statement of minimal scientific realism, and the hypothetical statement that ascribes to physical objects the properties and constituents they have on the condition that minimal scientific realism is correct.

We can also define the thesis of compatibilism, that is, the view that these two minimal theories are compatible, as the thesis that the conjunction that characterizes the identity thesis is consistent.

Because there are three conjuncts that characterize the identity thesis, the minimal requirement for showing it to be acceptable is to show that each of the conjuncts is acceptable, and their conjunction is consistent, that is, that what I have called compatibilism is correct. Beyond that, we should try to show that the conjunction is plausible. At this point in the discussion, I believe that we can provisionally assume that two of the conjuncts are plausible, namely, the statement of minimal common-sense realism and the hypothetical statement concerning theoretical properties and constituents of observable objects. We have seen that the minimal common-sense theory has escaped all the objections we have previously discussed. Furthermore, I know of only one objection that we have not examined which might be damaging. It would arise if the identity thesis should prove unreasonable, and minimal scientific realism is shown to be more reasonable than the minimal common-sense view. Because of this we are justified in not reconsidering the first conjunct unless our present examination justifies rejecting the identity thesis. The hypothetical statement is reasonable, given the quite acceptable assumption that at any time the scientific postulations made at that time are justified. For this reason I shall assume for our present purposes that the current scientific postulations are correct and will test the identity thesis using those that seem to be the most troublesome for it. Consequently, I am not interested here in speculation about whether the entities postulated by science in the future will differ in ways that will make detailed discussions of compatibilism and the identity thesis unnecessary at that time.

We are left, then, with three claims to evaluate: whether scientific realism is acceptable, whether the conjunction defining the identity thesis is consistent, and whether, if it is consistent, it is plausible. I shall first consider objections to scientific realism, and then the various objections to the acceptability of the conjunction.

OBJECTIONS TO SCIENTIFIC REALISM

In Chapter 4 we considered an argument for scientific instrumentalism which at that point seemed to provide reason to reject all forms of scientific realism. It is, furthermore, an argument which is independent of the nature of any particular scientific theories, not only at present, but at any time in the development of science. Because of this it is an extremely powerful argument. Nevertheless I hope to show that it can be at least neutralized, if not refuted. In order to justify our final evaluation of this argument, however, it is important to examine first some objections to scientific realism which are based on the present situation in particular sciences, because certain of these objections have implications for certain claims used to neutralize the argument.

Each of the objections from current science is an attempt to show that if minimal scientific realism is correct, then certain sentences that are not true, indeed, in some cases not even descriptively or factually meaningful, would have to be construed as true descriptions. Thus, it is argued, minimal scientific realism is mistaken, and all purely theoretical terms of current science should be interpreted as nonreferring calculational devices. Several objections of this sort have been previously discussed by others such as Ernest Nagel, but I wish to examine what I take to be the three most serious sorts of these objections in somewhat more detail then previously done.[2]

Objections from Contradictory Implications of Current Sciences

The first sort of objection is that if scientific realism is correct, then, because each scientific theory that best explains certain phenomena would imply certain descriptions of the world, some descriptions so derived would contradict others derived in the same way (either from the same theory or from some different theory) given certain unobjectionable statements of initial conditions. Thus at least one theory should be rejected or construed instrumentally. Nagel considers as an example of this objection that it seems we can derive from one theory that a fluid is a continuous medium and also from another theory that it is a system of discrete particles. He also considers that it seems we can derive from one theory that there are electrons, and that they are both particles and waves. But particles have discrete locations and waves do not, so nothing is both a particle and a wave. I shall consider here only the first problem, because the second, from quantum physics, involves issues so much more difficult for a realist to resolve that it requires separate treatment later.

A scientific realist can handle the first problem easily. As Nagel points out, its seeming contradiction can be resolved once it is seen that there is no need to consider fluids as composed of discrete particles for the explanatory purposes for which the theory of fluid mechanics is designed, because the observable results predicted by the theory are at worst negligibly different from those of the atomic theory of fluids. And, because the calculations are considerably simpler on the assumption of continuity, the assumption is justified methodologically. The only problem is to state how this simplifying assumption works in a way that does not ontologically commit a scientific realist to the "assumed" entities. I suggest the following schema as a way to handle all simplifying assumptions of this sort:

[2] See E. Nagel, *The Structure of Science* (New York: Harcourt, Brace and World, Inc., 1961), pp. 141–45.

(1) Given initial conditions c, if something, s, for example, a fluid, is of sort K, for example, is a continuous medium, then, given theory T_1, the results derived about the observable behavior of s are B.

(2) Given initial conditions c, and theory T_2, for example, the atomic theory of fluids, the results derived about the observable behavior of, for example, a fluid, are at most negligibly different from what would be derived using T_1 if, for example, the fluid, were a continuous medium.

Thus, on the assumption that the general claim (2) is established and that the calculations to establish (1) in individual cases are simpler than if theory T_2 is used, (1) and (2) can be conjoined to yield correct results about fluids composed of discrete particles without also permitting it to be derived that the fluids are continuous.

Objections from Ideal and Limit Entities in Current Science

The second group of objections to minimal scientific realism is that if the theory is correct, then certain statements derived from scientific theories would be clearly false because they imply the false claims that there are entities such as Newtonian point-masses, frictionless planes, instantaneous accelerations, and ideal gases. All these entities are supposedly ideal, in the sense that nothing actual is quite like them. Indeed, in some cases they are ideals that actual entities only approach, but never reach. Thus, according to this objection, scientific theories should not be realistically construed in order to avoid the derivation of sentences which, if scientific realism is correct, are false descriptive statements about what there is.

I believe the four entities cited above as examples of ideal objects are often assumed to raise the same problem for a scientific realist, and thus are often thought to require the same treatment. I find, however, that each differs from the others significantly in ways that allow different approaches by a scientific realist. We can begin to distinguish among the examples by classifying all but ideal gases as what can be called "limit" entities. Furthermore, two of them are ideal in the sense that they are limits that certain actual entities approach but never reach. Thus a point-mass is the unattainable limit of smaller and smaller volumes of mass, and a frictionless plane is a similar limit for surfaces with varying amounts of friction.

An ideal gas, however, while nonexistent, is not something that actual gases approach as a limit. An ideal gas consists of perfectly elastic, monatomic molecules that are of equal mass and size and which are in constant relative motion. It is true that perfect elasticity is a limit entity, but the other properties of an ideal gas, especially being monatomic and in constant relative motion, are not limit properties. Ideal gases function not as limits to be approached, but rather as a sort of simplifying assumption. They function differently, however, from the simplifying assumption of fluids as continuous. Except for one sort of situation, ideal gases are not assumed for ease and simplicity in devising quantitative laws governing actual gases, or in calculating accurate predictions of certain behavior of actual gases. Rather, they are used as subject matter for precise and simple laws which are then adapted, with various complications, to achieve laws that do apply to actual gases. Thus an ideal gas is ideal with respect to the simplicity and precision of the laws that apply to its behavior, rather than as an ideal limit actual gases approach.

Once we see the sense in which such a gas is ideal, it becomes clear that nothing done in science requires a scientific realist to be committed to ideal gases with their "ideal" components. The ideal gas law is not used to derive claims about actual gases, except when the molecules of the gas are far enough apart for the forces acting among them to be negligible. Thus in no other cases need the claim that there are ideal gases be derivable from any scientific claims. Of course, physicists sometimes say that gases expanded to a very large volume are ideal gases, but what is meant is that such a gas behaves as if it were ideal. In this one class of cases, then, the use of the ideal gas law can be handled the same way as the assumption of fluids as continuous. The only other way I know that a scientist might use the law, is when he assumes a certain gas to be ideal in order to discover what consequences would result. But this procedure can be construed as a conditional proof, so that the conclusion is a hypothetical and the categorical statement that there is an ideal gas is clearly not derivable.

Each of the three examples of what I called limit entities can be handled differently by a scientific realist. Newtonian point-masses can be treated as simplifying assumptions of the same sort as continuous fluids. For example, by assuming that the mass of a body is concentrated at its center of mass, it is simpler to solve problems involving vectors, such as velocity and acceleration, that affect the body. The assumption, then, is that the body's behavior as a whole is approximately the same as it would be if it were a point that is located at the center of mass of the body, that has the same mass as the body, and that is acted on by the appropriate vectors. Thus this simplifying assumption can be used without commitment to the existence of point-masses.

The example of a frictionless plane, and others such as perfect elasticity, and a rigid body, are also limit entities, but they function in the calculations of physicists like an ideal gas rather than like point-masses. Thus a scientific realist can handle them the way he does ideal gases. Derivations made assuming such entities can be handled as conditional proofs, or perhaps in some cases, as providing simple ways to obtain results that approximate correct results closely enough for certain purposes. Incidentally, absolute zero, the temperature at which, according to classical physics, there is no molecular motion, can be handled in this same way, even though it is not a simplifying assumption. Attempts to derive how something would behave at this temperature are not made for purposes of simplicity, but rather to get some indication of the effects of temperature. Here again these derivations can be construed as conditional proofs.

The last example of a limit entity is handled differently from any of the previous ways I have suggested for avoiding entities that generate objections to scientific realism. It is clear that we can derive from scientific claims that certain actual objects have certain instantaneous velocities and accelerations. And, more generally, we often do talk of the speed of a car at some instant of time. Perhaps, then, it would be better to consider these instantaneous events to constitute a third objection to minimal scientific realism. Although they are like point-masses in being limit entities, they are not ideal in the sense that implies that there are no such entities. The problem they raise for scientific realism is that it seems clearly conceptually absurd to say that something has a velocity of a certain number of feet per second at an instant of time, because it makes no sense to say that a body travels some distance at a durationless instant. In addition, there seems to be no way to compute the velocity of a body at an instant because the computation requires the distance travelled during a period of time be divided by the elapsed time.

Historically, it was proposed by Newton and Leibniz that instantaneous velocities be computed using infinitesimals. That is, the velocity of a body, B, at instant, t, is to be in terms of the infinitesimal distance, ds, that B travels in the infinitesimal duration, dt, around time t. If we compute the velocity of a falling body at t, we use the formula

$$s = 16t^2$$

where s is feet traveled. Assuming $t = 1$ second, we get

$$ds = 16 (1 + dt)^2 - 16(1)^2$$
$$= 32dt + 16dt^2.$$

Thus we get

$$ds/dt = 32 + 16dt$$

which, supposedly, is equal to 32 ft./sec. for the instantaneous velocity at 1 second. But, as Berkeley pointed out, since dt cannot be zero if the computations are to be correct, $32 + 16dt$ does not equal 32.[3] The reply is that infinitesimals differ from all real numbers in that they are greater than zero yet smaller than any real number. Indeed, unlike a real number, the sum resulting from adding an infinitesimal to itself, any number of times never is as great as any real number. Thus, supposedly, we can drop $16dt$ and get 32 ft./sec. But it can surely be objected, how can one make sense out of such "nonreal" numbers?

It is clear that a scientific realist should be most uncomfortable if he is forced to admit that there are infinitesimal distances and durations. Yet even an instrumentalist should find them most suspect as computational devises. Indeed, in the nineteenth century, the mathematical concept of a limit was developed by Weierstrass and others, and it came to be used to characterize instantaneous events without relying on infinitesimals. To say that the velocity of body B is 32 ft./sec. at the instant it has fallen for 1 second is not to say that $ds/dt = 32$ ft./sec., but it is to be interpreted as follows:

For any positive number, x, there is a positive number, y, such

---

[3] See Berkeley, *The Analyst.*

that for any duration, Δt, around instant $t = 1$ sec., where $|\Delta t| < y$, the distance, Δs, that B travels during Δt, is such that $|\Delta s/\Delta t - 32| < x$.

Roughly, this means that for all durations of time around 1 second that are less than some positive real number, the velocity of B is or closely approximates 32 ft./sec. Here we have only real numbers as values for 'x', 'y', 'Δs', 'Δt', and '32', and thus no infinitesimals. Consequently, a scientific realist can claim that bodies have instantaneous velocites without being committed to the claim that bodies travel some distance at an instant or to the claim that there are infinitesimals.[4]

While the use of the mathematical concept of a limit solves this problem, I believe it is interesting to note, briefly, that, as I understand it, infinitesimals have recently been resuscitated by Abraham Robinson in an unobjectionable way.[5] Very roughly, for first-order formal language, L, which has the real numbers as its standard model, it can be shown that L has a nonstandard model that contains in its domain objects larger than zero, but smaller than any number of the form $1/n$, where n is a real number. Such objects qualify as infinitesimals. Thus every statement in L which is true of the real numbers is also true when interpreted in terms of the nonstandard model with its objects called "pseudo-real" numbers. Therefore, certain statements true of real numbers are not expressible in L, because they are not true when applied to pseudo-real numbers, that is, infinitesimals. For example, the claim that the sum of a real number added to itself some number of times is greater than 1 is not expressible in L. On this approach the historical assumption that infinitesimals are numbers to be added to the domain of real numbers is abandoned, and with it goes its perplexing consequence that some statements that are true of real numbers are not true of all numbers. Instead, real numbers remain the standard model for a formal language, and the only change is that certain seeming truths about real numbers are not expressible in the language.

[4] Compare W. Quine on ideal objects and limit myths in W. Quine, *Word and Object* (Cambridge, Mass: The M.I.T. Press, 1967), pp. 248–51.

[5] Much of my information about infinitesimals, limits, and nonstandard models is taken from M. Davis and R. Hirsh, "Nonstandard Analysis" *Scientific American* (June, 1972): 78–86.

Regarding instantaneous velocities, the calculations are made using the nonstandard model which for the preceding example gives the result of $32 + 16dt$, where $16dt$ is an infinitesimal because dt is one. But for each pseudo-real number there corresponds exactly one real number in the standard model. In particular each pseudo-real that is infinitesimally close to a real number corresponds to that real number. Thus 32 is the real number corresponding to $32 + 16dt$, and so the instantaneous velocity is 32 ft./sec. This procedure, then, allows the use of infinitesimal distances and durations without committing a scientific realist to their existence, and without including infinitesimals in the domain of mathematical entities. Essentially, this way to resolve the problem is very similar to the one I suggested for handling simplifying assumptions such as continuous fluids and point-masses. That is, we can interpret the procedure as follows:

(1) If language L is given a nonstandard interpretation, then the infinitesimal velocity ds/dt of a falling object, B, where t is 1 sec., is $32 + 16dt$ ft./sec.
(2) The real number in the standard model corresponding to $32 + 16dt$ in the nonstandard model is 32.
(3) The magnitude of the instantaneous velocity of an object is the real number corresponding to the pseudo-real number that is derived using the nonstandard interpretation of L.

Thus far, neither of the preceding sorts of objections to scientific realism succeeds. Neither seeming contradiction between two theories, nor idealizations and limit entities have raised insurmountable obstacles. However, we have not yet considered the objection, mentioned previously, that the quantum theory implies that there are entities with the properties of particles and also with the properties of waves. But, contrary to a realistic interpretation of quantum theory, nothing has the properties of both waves and particles.

It is surely true that nothing has all the properties of a particle and all the properties of a wave at the same time, but contrary to the preceding argument, this false claim is not derivable from quantum theory and the relevant data. Given Bohr's principle of complementarity, which states that the applicability of wave concepts and the applicability of particle concepts are restricted to certain sorts of experimental situations, and given that no situation allows the joint applicability of both sorts of concepts, it is at most derivable that in some situations these entities have wave properties and in other situations they have particle properties. Thus, there is no contradiction and this problem is resolved.

Three Objections from Quantum Physics

Unfortunately, the rejection of the preceding objection does not dispose of all problems that quantum physics raises for scientific realism. There are three others that are considerably more serious. Because of this, we should do our best to estimate their damage to realism. However, before we begin, it should be noted that my ignorance of this field is vast. I attempt to indicate and evaluate these problems only because they are too serious to ignore.[6]

The first two objections argue that it is unreasonable to interpret realistically the term unique to quantum theory, that is, the term supposedly expressing the wave function or quantum mechanical state vector for particulars such as electrons. Thus this term, which we shall call 'Ψ', should be instrumentally construed. That is, 'Ψ' should be construed as merely a nonreferring inferring device that warrants statistical conclusions about observed results.[7] According to these arguments, quantum theory, atomic physics and indeed any scientific theory, such as molecular biology, which should be realistically construed only if atomic physics is, should also be interpreted instrumentally. And having gone that far, a complete instrumentalism seems justified. The third objection, which I find to be the strongest, is that even if a plausible realistic construal of 'Ψ' is found somehow, there is no plausible realistic interpretation of terms, such as 'electron,' that purportedly refer to scientifically basic particulars that are the subject matter of quantum physics. Once again, it is argued that atomic physics and its dependents should be instrumentally interpreted, and a complete instrumentalism is justified. Let us consider each objection

---

[6] I wish to thank Simon Kirby who greatly helped me to achieve whatever clarity I have reached in understanding this most difficult area.

[7] Such a view would seem to be what Bohr expresses when he says that "the appropriate physical interpretation of the symbolic quantum-mechanical formalism amounts only to predictions, of determinate or statistical character, pertaining to individual phenomena appearing under conditions defined by classical physical concepts." See N. Bohr, *Atomic Physics and Human Knowledge* (New York: John Wiley and Sons, 1958), p. 64.

separately so we can evaluate their strengths individually.

FIRST OBJECTION: 'Ψ' NEITHER REFERS TO NOR SPECIFIES ANYTHING

We can initially state the first argument quite briefly. Either the term for the state-vector, 'Ψ', refers to some property or particular, or as I shall say, it "specifies" quantitative physical properties of individual scientific basic particulars, or it "specifies" statistical properties that groups of basic particulars have even when they are not reacting observably with something, or it is merely a nonreferring mathematical inference device that warrants certain conclusions about the probabilities of making certain observations in certain experimental conditions. However, for various reasons, neither of the first three realistic alternatives is plausible, and so 'Ψ' should be construed in the fourth, instrumental way.

This argument needs much elaboration, which we can begin by attempting to characterize what I mean by saying that 'Ψ' "specifies" a quantitative property of an entity. Although it is not clear what the correct characterization should be, I shall turn for initial help to the continuing discussion about whether quantum theory is complete in the sense that by means of the term for its state vector, 'Ψ', it "completely describes" the individual particulars that are the subject matter of the theory. The highlight of this controversy was the debate between Einstein who argued that the theory is not complete, and Bohr who claimed it is. To prove his point, Einstein, with Podolsky and Rosen, produced a famous thought experiment (the EPR experiment) that Bohr countered primarily by disagreeing with Einstein's claim about a sufficient condition for an entity having a certain property.[8] Although we need not consider this

---

[8] See A. Einstein, B. Podolsky, and N. Rosen, "Can Quantum-Mechanical Description of Physical Reality be Considered Complete?" *Physical Review* 47 (1935): 777–80, esp. p. 777. N. Bohr replied in an article with the same title, in *Physical Review* 48 (1935): 696–702. Much of my information about this and related matters comes from L. Ballentine, "The Statistical Interpretation of Quantum Mechanics," *Review of Modern Physics* 42 (1970): 358–80; and M. Gardner, "Two Deviant Logics for Quantum Theory: Bohr and Reichenbach," *British Journal for the Philosophy of Science* 23 (1972): 89–109, and "Quantum-Theoretical Realism: Popper and Einstein v. Kochen and Specker," *British Journal for the Philosophy of Science, 23* (1972): 13–23. See also K. Popper, "Particle Annihilation and the Argument of Einstein, Podolsky, and Rosen," in *Perspectives in Quantum Theory: Essays in Honor of Alfred Landé*, W. Yourgrau and A. Van der Merwe, eds., (Cambridge, Mass.: MIT Press, 1971), pp. 186–94.

experiment for our purposes, we can construct a concept of a complete description based on the one used in that debate that will help unpack what it is for 'Ψ' to specify a quantitative property. Let us use the following definition:

> D1. Quantum theory completely describes entity $e = {}_{df}$. For any quantitative property P, e has P with value v *if and only if* the quantum theoretical term for the state vector for e, 'Ψ', yields that the probability that e has P with value $v = 1$ (i.e., Ψ is an eigenstate of P with eigenvalue v).

For example, if quantum theory completely describes a certain electron, then, among other properties, the electron has a certain value for its momentum just in case it is derivable, using the state vector for that electron in that situation, that the probability of its having that value for its momentum $= 1$.

On the assumption that quantum theory completely describes an entity just in case the term for the relevant state vector specifies each of the quantitative properties of the entity, we get the following definition:

> D2. The state-vector term, 'Ψ', for the entity e specifies quantitative property P of $e = {}_{df}$. For any value, v, of P, it is true that e has P with value v *if and only if* 'Ψ' yields that the probablity that e has P with value $v = 1$.

Thus although 'Ψ' does not refer to properties such as the momentum or position of an electron, any values of such quantitative properties of electrons are, according to D2, functions of 'Ψ'. Of course 'Ψ' may refer to some other property as well as specify these properties.

AN OBJECTION TO 'Ψ' SPECIFYING PROPERTIES OF INDIVIDUALS

To see problems for the view that 'Ψ' specifies properties in this sense, let us concentrate on the property of position for electrons fired from an electron gun at a single slit. The result is that the electrons form a dispersion and interference pattern after passing through the slit that closely resembles the way waves disperse and interfere in similar conditions. However, if the electrons hit a target screen beyond the slit, then, unlike waves, the electrons impinge on the screen discretely and intermittently at particular spots. If 'Ψ' for each such electron specifies its position after passing through the slit yet before hitting the screen, then, because 'Ψ' does not yield probability $= 1$ for any value for position, we can conclude the following:

> (1) It is not true that each such electron has position with a certain value after it has passed through the slit but has not yet hit the screen.

Surely (1) is initially quite implausible, and, therefore, so is the claim that 'Ψ' specifies quantitative properties. However, four general hypotheses have been offered to justify, or at least account for, statements such as (1). One of them is that it is not true (that is, false or meaningless) that a basic entity, e, has a quantitative property (such as position), when e is not being measured (that is, not interacting observably with any macro-object in a way that enables a value for the property of e to be calculated) and e does not have an eigenvalue for the property (that is, when 'Ψ' for e does not yield a probability $= 1$ for any value for the property). A second is that when e is in the preceding situation it is true that e has the quantitative property (position), but not true it has any specific (i.e., any value for) the property. The third hypothesis, suggested by some claims of Bohr and Heisenberg, is that it is meaningless to assign position and other quantitative properties to e in any situation where there is no way to calculate their values precisely from 'Ψ', or from measurement performed either on e itself, as when it hits a screen, or upon some other entity, as in the EPR experiment.[9] Reichenbach holds the fourth view, namely, that in the preceding situation the statements assigning values to the property (position) are meaningful, but are indeterminate in truth value.[10] But surely all four views are, like (1), initially quite implausible. Furthermore, an additional point makes statements like (1) and these hypotheses even more unreasonable. Therefore there is even additional reason to reject the claim that 'Ψ' specifies quantitative properties.

[9] For example, see Bohr, p. 25 where he talks of an absolute limit of speaking about the behavior of atomic objects that is independent of observation. See also W. Heisenberg, *Physics and Philosophy* (New York: Harper and Row, 1962), pp. 50–55. This view is discussed by Gardner in "Two Deviant Logics", pp. 91–92.

[10] See H. Reichenbach, *Philosophical Foundations of Quantum Mechanics* (Berkeley: University of California Press, 1944), pp. 140–45.

This point bolsters the view that basic entities have properties with definite values when not measured directly or indirectly and not specified by 'Ψ'. In the single slit experiment, no prediction of the position of an individual electron between the slit and the screen has a probability approaching 1, but after an electron hits the screen its previous path can be "retrodicted" with a very high degree of accuracy. Thus it seems reasonable to say that it occupied some specific position, and also had a certain momentum at each moment when it was unmeasured as it travelled between slit and screen.[11] But, again, because 'Ψ' for such electrons does not yield any value for position or momentum with probability $= 1$, we should conclude that (1) and the four hypotheses are false, and that 'Ψ' does not specify such quantitative properties of basic entities such as electrons.

Another objection that has been raised against all four hypotheses and the claim that 'Ψ' specifies quantitative properties is based on a modified version of the EPR experiment.[12] In a certain experimental arrangement, the total amount of spin of two entities, e_1 and e_2, is known, but 'Ψ' yields no determinate value for the spin of either entity. Consequently, if 'Ψ' specifies spin for e_1 and e_2, then we can conclude:

(2) It is not true that either e_1 or e_2 has spin with a certain value when neither is measured for spin.

And (2) also follows from all four of the preceding hypotheses but, like (1), (2) is surely initially quite implausible. Furthermore, at some later time the spin of e_1 is measured in a way that does not physically affect e_2. At that time, it is claimed that e_2 has a value for spin, because its value can be calculated using the results of the measurement on e_1. Consequently, if 'Ψ' specifies a value for spin or if the four preceding hypotheses are correct, then, in one way or another, e_2 "jumps" into a certain value for spin at the moment when e_1 is measured for spin. But it is most implausible that this change should occur to e_2 because something, which does not physically affect e_2, happens to e_1. Therefore, if it is plausible to infer the spin of e_2 from a measurement on e_1, there is additional

---

[11] This is discussed by Gardner in "Two Deviant Logics," pp. 105–07.
[12] See Ballentine, pp. 365–67.

reason to conclude that statement (2), the four hypotheses, and the claim that 'Ψ' specifies quantitative properties are false. We shall see, however, that this inference to the spin of e_2 is dubious. Thus we should reject this additional reason. Nevertheless, I believe that we have found enough reason to deny that 'Ψ' specifies quantitative properties of individual basic entities.

Someone might object to the preceding conclusion on the grounds that it is true that a basic entity has a property with a value only when the entity *itself* is being measured for that property. Thus e_2 would not obtain a value for spin when e_1 is measured, and retrodiction would be illegitimate. Aside from the fact that such a thesis is initially as implausible as the previous four views, there are two reasons why it fails as a reply to the two preceding points. One is that it would falsify the claim that 'Ψ' specifies quantitative properties. Sometimes 'Ψ' yields a probability of 1 for a value of a property of an entity when it is not measured, and so, according to D2, that property of that entity would have the value when it is not measured. The second reason is that this view runs afoul of Schrödinger's famous cat paradox.[13]

The paradox is roughly as follows. A cat is in a device such that it dies if a certain atom decays and emits a particle that hits a certain spot, but the cat remains alive if the atom does not decay. But in this case, 'Ψ' yields no one value for the position of any particle before it hits the spot. Thus when there is no measurement of the position of the emitted particles, then it follows that it is either false or meaningless to say that the atom has decayed or to say that it has not decayed. Therefore, it is also false or meaningless to say the cat is dead or to say the cat is alive. But clearly it is either true or false that the cat is dead, and consequently, false or true that it is alive. Thus we should reject the proposal that measurement is required for values. Also, because it is plausible, I believe, to assume that in the preceding situation 'Ψ' does not yield a value for position of the emitted particles, we have another reason to reject the preceding four hypotheses. On this assumption, all four also imply that it is not true that the cat is dead and not true it is alive when no emitted particle is interacting observably with anything.

---

[13] For one treatment of this problem, see J. Park, "Quantum Theoretical Concepts of Measurement," *Philosophy of Science*, 35 (1968): 225–27.

RETRODICTION AND THE UNCERTAINTY PRINCIPLE   The argument based on retrodiction might prompt another reply, namely, that the supposed fact of retrodiction violates Heisenberg's uncertainty principle. One version of the principle states that the joint imprecision of momentum and position is greater than Planck's constant. But the precision such retrodiction would provide can be less than Planck's constant, and so, according to this reply, such retrodiction should be rejected. To refute this reply, we must consider how the principle is to be interpreted. This is a principle derivable from the equations that relate the particle and wave properties of physical entities by means of Planck's constant. As a result, there is in some sense an uncertainty in the position and momentum of an entity. The more precisely it is located, the more uncertain, in some sense, is its momentum. This helps explain, for example, why electrons passing through a narrow slit that locates them relatively precisely, have a wider distribution pattern on a screen than do those passing through a wider slit. The crucial question for our concern, however, is how to interpret this uncertainty.

There are, basically, two different sorts of interpretation, epistemological and ontological. Many philosophers, I believe, take the principle to have merely epistemological consequences in a sense compatible with predictability in principle but not in practice because of the relative clumsiness of the measuring devices it is physically necessary for us to use. On this view, the uncertainty concerns merely the fact that any experiment designed to measure the position and momentum of an electron at one time will produce results conjointly imprecise in an amount at least as great as Planck's constant because of the disturbing effects of the best measuring devices. It is certainly true that such disturbances occur, but there is another epistemological consequence of the principle that this view does not capture. Even if it is assumed that, contrary to fact, the exact position and momentum of an electron is known (for example, when it is fired at a single slit), it is in principle impossible to predict, using the laws of physics, its future location (for example, where it goes after passing through the slit) with any more accuracy than allowed by the uncertainty principle. It is not, then, merely that the best measuring devices available disturb what is being measured so our measurements are inaccurate, it is also that the future behavior of an electron is not precisely predictable given precise knowledge of all the variables in the past history of the electron with which physical theories and laws are concerned. Furthermore, on the assumption, which is quite widely accepted, that there is nothing in the past history of an electron except what is available to quantum theory, there are no "hidden" variables that would provide more precise predictions than those of quantum theory. Given this, it can be seen that one ontological thesis becomes justified by means of the principle. That is, given the preceding assumption, the behavior of basic particles such as electrons is in principle not predictable, and so it is reasonable to conclude that this behavior is not causally determined.

Certainly both epistemological theses are plausible, and, although the ontological thesis is challenged by people such as Bohm,[14] it is at least plausible to accept it at present on the basis of quantum theory and the lack of predictability that follows from that theory with the uncertainty principle and no hidden variables. Incidentally, each of these three theses give some reason to claim that a realistic interpretation of quantum theory shows limitations of our knowledge about the constituents of macro-objects. Indeed, each of the theses would seem to specify a reason why our knowledge is limited. The means by which we obtain knowledge is necessarily "clumsy," and the behavior of the basic constituents is neither precisely predictable nor causally determined.

Granting all this, however, is there any reason to think that retrodicting the position and momentum of an entity more precisely than stated by the uncertainty principle violates the principle? Clearly not. Its epistemic and causal indeterminancy at most show that the behavior of something is not precisely calculable when the calculation is based on previous information only. If some macro-object should behave in a causally random way so that its behavior is at most somewhat causally influenced, then its future behavior would not be precisely predictable given total present evidence. Yet if we should observe it at two different times, we would often be able to calculate precisely its behavior between the observations. Except for one qualification to be discussed later, I know of no reason to think differently of basic entities. Epistemic and causal indeterminacy limit prediction but not retrodiction.

[14] See D. Bohm, *Causality and Chance in Modern Physics* (Phila.: University of Pennsylvania Press, 1971), chap. 4.

There is another ontological interpretation of the uncertainty principle that should be mentioned because it does imply that no precise retrodiction is possible. On this thesis, the indeterminacy is interpreted as indefiniteness. For example, at each moment between electron gun and target each electron would have momentum and position, but it would have no precise amount of momentum and would be located at no specific place. Thus these electrons would pass somewhere through the slit but would not pass over any particular point inside the slit. Note that this is not merely to say that the boundaries of electrons are not sharply defined, as would be reasonable if they were waves or wave packets; it is to say that no point clearly within the boundary of an electron coincides with any point within the slit. But we have already found reason to reject the view that electrons have merely an indefinite position. Thus, although such a thesis rules out precise retrodiction, its consequences are so unreasonable that, because there is no independent reason to adopt it, it is clear it should be rejected.

CONCLUSION ABOUT 'Ψ' AS SPECIFYING PROPERTIES OF INDIVIDUALS

We have found no way to rebut the objection to the claim that 'Ψ' specifies quantitative properties of individual basic particulars. I can think of just one other attempt. This is to reject D2 and propose a different definition. The only one I have found which is remotely plausible is a definition that someone who construes electrons as waves or wave packets might accept. It is most easily illustrated in the case of position:

> D3. The state-vector term, 'Ψ', for entity e specifies the position of $e =_{df}$. For any value, v, for position e is located (at least in part) at v *if and only if* 'Ψ' yields that the probability that e is at $v \neq 0$.

On this definition, after an electron passes through a slit it is located everywhere 'Ψ' specifies there is some probability that it is located. Thus, like a wave or wave packet, it disperses over a wide area after passing through a slit. The objection to this view is that it requires something quite implausible, namely, "the reduction of the wave packet" when an electron hits a screen beyond the slit. Just before hitting the screen it would be widely dispersed, but it hits the screen at one small spot. This seemingly instantaneous collapse of the wave is surely implausible, because the speed of the collapse would exceed the velocity of light. Thus this second and, I find, last attempt to construe 'Ψ' as specifying properties of individuals in some way or other should also be rejected, as the first argument for instrumentalism from quantum theory states.

AN OBJECTION TO 'Ψ' SPECIFYING STATISTICAL PROPERTIES OF GROUPS

Having seen it to be implausible that 'Ψ' specifies properties of individual entities, the argument for instrumentalism we are considering concludes that only three construals of 'Ψ' remain viable, namely, that it specifies a statistical property that certain groups have even when not measured, or that it refers to something or other, or that it is merely a nonreferring inferring device that warrants statistical conclusions about observed results. But, so goes the argument, both realistic interpretations are implausible, and so only the instrumental view remains. The reasons for rejecting the statistical construal can be seen by beginning with a quotation from Einstein:

> For if the statistical quantum theory does not pretend to describe the individual system (and its development in time) completely, it appears unavoidable to look elsewhere for a complete description of the individual system; in doing so it would be clear from the very beginning that the elements of such a description are not contained within the conceptual scheme of the statistical quantum theory. With this one would admit that, in principle, this scheme could not serve as the basis of theoretical physics. Assuming the success of efforts to accomplish a complete physical description, the statistical quantum theory would, within the framework of future physics, take an approximately analogous position to the statistical mechanics within the framework of classical mechanics. I am rather firmly convinced that the development of theoretical physics will be of this type; but the path will be lengthy and difficult.[15]

[15] A. Einstein, "Reply to Criticism," in *Albert Einstein: Philosopher-Scientist*, P. Schilpp, ed. (Evanston, Ill.: The Library of Living Philosophers, Inc., 1949), p. 672.

Gardner unpacks Einstein's thesis in the following way:

> The sense in which this "future physics" is to quantum theory
> as classical mechanics is to statistical mechanics is as follows.
> Our inability to predict the results of individual measurements
> arises solely from our ignorance of the values of the hidden
> variables. Dispersions in the results of measurements following
> a given preparation result solely from the impossibility of
> preparing an ensemble of systems each possessing the same
> value of [the hidden variables].[16]

According to this view, if any two electrons that are in a group
whose behavior is statistically predictable by quantum theory
behave differently in the same experimental arrangement, then they
also differ with respect to some "hidden" property, which if,
contrary to fact, it were available to us, would allow us to predict
the different behavior precisely. However, it has been shown, I
believe, that if any hidden variable theory agrees with all the
statistical measurement predictions of quantum theory, then either
it contradicts special relativity or it violates the principle, enunciated by Einstein in his debate with Bohr, that there is no action at
distance.[17] That is, either it requires that signals are transmitted
instantaneously or that values of physical properties of an entity are
causally affected by what happens to a spatially distant entity that is
not physically interacting with the first entity. But, it is unreasonable
to reject this principle and special relativity, and, at present,
experimental evidence supports the statistical measurement predictions of quantum theory. Thus, according to the first objection,
no hidden variable theory is acceptable, and, therefore, neither is
the realistic statistical interpretation.

AN OBJECTION TO 'Ψ' DENOTING WAVES OR WAVE PACKETS

Let us turn to the objection to the claim that 'Ψ' refers to something.
It is, briefly, that if 'Ψ', which expresses the wave function in the
Schrödinger equation, refers to anything, then, just as '$\mathcal{E}$' in the
Maxwell equations denotes electromagnetic fields, 'Ψ' denotes
"matter" waves or wave packets. Such waves or wave packets

---

[16] Gardner, "Quantum-Theoretical Realism," p. 14.
[17] See Einstein, pp. 85 and 682 for this principle. It also is discussed by Ballentine, pp. 363
and 377.

would be either identical with basic particulars, such as electrons, or "pilot" waves associated with basic particles.[18] The problem is that both waves and wave packets disperse after passing through a narrow slit. If, therefore, 'Ψ' denotes an electron that is a wave or wave packet, then what it denotes would disperse after passing through such a slit until it impinges observably at a small, discrete spot on a screen. At that moment there would be an instantaneous collapse of the dispersed wave. But an instantaneous collapse is surely implausible, as was noted previously.

A similar problem arises for the view that 'Ψ' denotes pilot waves of particles. This view, like the wave construal, is very helpful in explaining what is observed in the truly puzzling double slit experiment. Here the distribution pattern of electrons on a target is not the pattern that would result if each electron went through just one of the slits in a way that is independent of whether or not the other, remote slit is open. Rather it is the pattern that would result if each electron went through both slits and interfered with itself in the way a wave does. Supposedly the pilot wave passes through both slits when both are open, and this affects the behavior of the particle that passes merely through one of them. But because there is no evidence of the pilot wave at the screen, its sudden collapse or demise is required. This is implausible. Futhermore, I believe, not only has no satisfactory formalism been devised for a theory with pilot waves as hidden variables, but also, as mentioned above, such a hidden variable theory has implausible consequences. We should, therefore, reject the claim that 'Ψ' denotes waves or wave packets, and, furthermore, according to the first objection, we should conclude that 'Ψ' does not refer to anything. Consequently, with all three realistic interpretations of 'Ψ' rejected, only the fourth, instrumental construal remains.

TWO REPLIES TO THE FIRST OBJECTION AND ITS REJECTION

This completes the elaboration of the first of the three objections to scientific realism from quantum physics. There are, I believe, several places to attack it, but I shall concentrate on just two of them. The first is to deny that the viability of the realistic statistical interpretation depends on the success of an analogy between statistical mechanics and classical mechanics. That is, a statistical

[18] See, for example, Bohm, pp. 111–16 for a particle-with-wave theory.

theory about groups of individuals need not agree with Einstein's view that the behavior of each member of the group is causally determined or in any way precisely predictable in principle. At most such a theory requires that each quantitative property of each member has some one of the values which, according to the theory, there is some probability it has. But although this is consistent with causal determinism and precise prediction based on hidden variables, it does not require them, because it is also consistent with no hidden variables and causal indeterminism. Thus, I conclude, a realistic statistical interpretation of 'Ψ' remains viable, and so the first argument has not shown that only an instrumental construal is plausible.

A second way to attack the first objection is to find a plausible realistic interpretation of 'Ψ' other than the three mentioned in the objection. I believe there are at least two. It might be that, although 'Ψ' does not specify properties of individual basic entities, it does, let us say, "indeterminately indicate" them. We can define this phrase for position as follows:

> D4. The state-vector term, 'Ψ', for entity e indeterminately indicates the position of e = $_{df}$. There is a value, v, for the position of e, and 'Ψ' yields that the probability that e is at $v \neq 0$.

Unlike D2 and D3, according to this definition a nonzero probability yielded by 'Ψ' provides merely one necessary condition for an entity having a certain location. That is, 'Ψ' would function more like the predicate 'is located somewhere in the area A' than like 'is at location L.' On this realistic contrual, then, 'Ψ' would not specify any quantitative properties of either individuals or groups, but would rather roughly and imprecisely indicate properties of individuals. Because of this, the fourth realistic alternative can allow the spin and position of electrons to have precise values not yielded by 'Ψ', and so it avoids the first objection.

It might seem to some that I have overlooked an obvious fifth way to give 'Ψ' a realistic interpretation. That is, 'Ψ' could be taken to denote the wave function or quantum mechanical state. But the problem with this suggestion is that, as we have seen, it is most difficult to give any physical interpretation to such a function or state. Just as saying that ' $\sim$ ' designates negation is not sufficient for a realistic construal of the negation sign, so also saying that 'Ψ' designates a certain mathematical function is not sufficient for a realistic view of 'Ψ'. Indeed, an instrumentalist would claim that the wave function is nothing but a mathematical device for calculating probabilities of certain observable situations occurring. Realism regarding 'Ψ' requires that 'Ψ' have a physical referent or somehow indicate a physical property.

There is, however, another viable candidate for a physical referent for 'Ψ', namely, the propensity of basic particulars to behave in certain ways in certain experimental arrangements.[19] That is, the quantum mechanical state referred to by 'Ψ' is a physical dispositional property of certain particulars in certain situations. In this respect it would be something like the tendency of people to behave in various ways in certain situations. For example, when someone yells "Fire!" in a crowded theater, there is some tendency for each person to react in each of a variety of ways, although the strongest tendency may be to panic and run.

My description of the preceding realistic view of 'Ψ' is admittedly sketchy, but I know of only one minor problem with it. Surely 'Ψ' alone does not refer to propensities to have certain locations or certain momentums in certain situations, because 'Ψ' would yield figures for the various propensities only when taken with the appropriate operator for the particular property. This view, then, should not be that 'Ψ' refers to these propensities, but that it specifies them. That is, for position again we have:

D5. The state-vector term, 'Ψ', for entity e specifies the propensity of e to have property P with value v in experimental arrangement $A =_{\text{df.}}$ For any number, n, it is true that n is the value of the propensity of e to have P with value v in A if and only if 'Ψ' yields that the probability of e having P with value v in $A = n$.

Once this change is made, I believe that we have another realistic construal of 'Ψ' that avoids the first objection. Indeed, it is a view consistent with the preceding realistic view. It might be that 'Ψ' both

---

[19] See Popper, "Quantum Mechanics without 'The Observer'," in *Quantum Theory and Reality*, M. Bunge, ed. (New York: Springer-Verlag, 1967), pp. 28–40, for a propensity interpretation. I believe that Popper's view differs somewhat from the one I have sketched here.

specifies physical propensities and indeterminately indicates nondispositional physical properties. Regardless of that, however, we can conclude that there is a second reason to reject the first objection to scientific realism from quantum physics.

SECOND OBJECTION: REQUIRES ACTION AT A DISTANCE OR INSTANTANEOUS SIGNALS

I have claimed that there are at least three realistic interpretations of 'Ψ' that the first objection fails to show are implausible. There are, however, problems facing all of them, and, according to the second objection from quantum theory, these problems justify rejecting all such realistic interpretations so that only an instrumental view remains. The three realistic views imply that sometimes quantitative properties of basic entities have some value or other when those properties of those entites are not being measured themselves. This is clearly true when, without measurement, 'Ψ' yields a probability of 1 for a certain value. But, according to the second objection, this is implausible for the following reason: As I understand it, in the modified EPR experiment discussed previously, the spin found for entity e_1 by measuring it would differ for different experimental arrangements made for the measurement. But, if the spatially remote entity e_2 has some value for spin, then, without being physically affected, it would also have a different value for spin. And, according to the second objection, this is implausible because it either violates the principle that there is no action at a distance, or conflicts with the thesis of special relativity that no effects are transmitted instantaneously. Thus all three interpretations of 'Ψ', and, indeed, all realistic interpretations that assign values to properties when they are not measured, should be rejected. We are left, it seems, with only the instrumental interpretation of 'Ψ'.

I do not believe that this objection can be completely refuted, but at best somewhat weakened. This can be done by pointing out that none of the interpretations of 'Ψ' that escapes the first objection either violates a literal rendition of the principle of no *action* at a distance, or contradicts special relativity in the modified EPR case. Literally, the principle states that no value of a property of an entity is causally changed by what happens to a remote entity that is not physically interacting with the first. And, because the remaining realistic construals of 'Ψ' imply only that the entities have some value for spin before e_1 is measured, they do not imply what that value is. Thus they do not imply any *change* of value when measured, and so they are consistent with Einstein's principle and with special relativity. In *this* respect the situation is similar to one in which n balls are divided between urns u_1 and u_2 in some unknown way. But once the number in u_1 is discovered, the number in u_2 can be calculated. Furthermore, although it is true that if a different number of balls had been found in u_1, then a different number would be in u_2, this does not imply that the procedure used to discover the number of balls in u_1 would cause a change in the number in u_2.

There is, nevertheless, a disturbing difference between these two cases.[20] In the case of spin, if we had changed the experimental arrangements in certain ways, then we would have found a different spin for e_1 and, therefore, there would be a different spin for e_2. But surely no such difference in measurement arrangements would correlate with a difference in the number of balls in either u_1 or u_2. Consequently, although the three realistic interpretations of 'Ψ' do not violate the principle of no causal change at a distance, they do have the odd and seemingly implausible consequence that the values of properties of entities are somehow functionally correlated with the conditions under which certain properties of certain remote entities are measured. That is, they violate what we might call the principle of "no functional correlation at a distance."

I do not find the violation of this second version of Einstein's principle as serious as a violation of either the first version or special relativity. Nor is it as serious as a consequence of the views of Bohr·and Reichenbach that certain sentences about the spin of e_2 suddenly "jump into" truth-value upon the measurement of the spin of e_1. Yet a view with such a violation is not completely satisfactory. Indeed only an instrumental construal of 'Ψ' seems clearly to avoid all such problems.

A QUALIFIED REALISM AND REJECTION OF THE SECOND OBJECTION

Certainly, on the basis of the preceding discussion, an instrumental view of 'Ψ' is quite plausible. But is it more reasonable

---

[20]Compare Gardner, "Quantum–Theoretical Realism," p. 17.

than all of the realistic views we have been evaluating? And if it is more reasonable, should we further conclude, as both of the first two objections do, that scientific instrumentalism should be accepted because this crucial term of the basic physical science should be instrumentally construed? I shall not try to answer the first question beyond saying that it is clear, in the present state of quantum physics, that no realistic construal of 'Ψ' is more reasonable than an instrumental one, and so the latter is one, and perhaps the only acceptable view. However, regarding the second question, I find a scientific realist has at least one way to avoid the second argument for scientific instrumentalism, even if he grants 'Ψ' should be interpreted instrumentally. He could admit that all calculations involving 'Ψ' apply only to statistical predictions of measurement results, and thus 'Ψ' provides no information about basic entities —either individually or in groups—when they are not interacting with something to produce observable, measurable results. Nevertheless, he could argue that basic-entity terms need not be construed instrumentally just because 'Ψ' is. Retrodiction, perhaps, can be used to calculate values of some properties that basic entities have when they are not measured. Because of this, a realist might say that a qualified version of scientific realism for which only 'Ψ' is construed instrumentally is plausible. Consequently both of the first two objections from quantum theory, which argue from an instrumental interpretation of 'Ψ' to scientific instrumentalism are unsound.

I believe that this reply is plausible, and so the first two objections can be rejected. Unfortunately, many of the problems for realism raised in the preceding discussion can be reformulated to accommodate an instrumental interpretation of 'Ψ'. This gives rise to the third objection from quantum physics which is independent of how 'Ψ' is interpreted because it argues that certain observed facts justify an instrumental view of basic-entity terms, such as 'electron', 'proton', and 'neutron'. If this is correct, then there surely are strong grounds for instrumentalism.

THIRD OBJECTION: BASIC ENTITIES ARE NOT PARTICLES, WAVES, OR PARTICLES WITH WAVES

The objection can be stated as follows. If basic-entity terms are referring terms, then some of them refer either to particles, or waves (or wave packets), or particles with accompanying "pilot" waves. But, first, if they refer to particles, then there is instantaneous causal change or action at a distance and the phenomenon of tunneling is inexplicable. Second, if they refer to waves or wave packets, then the "reduction of the wave packet" occurs. And, third, if they refer to particles with pilot waves, then reduction of the pilot wave occurs, and there are hidden variables. But in each case at least one of these consequences is implausible. Thus it is implausible to consider such basic-entity terms as referring terms, and so they should be construed instrumentally. Furthermore, if these terms are interpreted instrumentally, then so also should be any theory that, when construed realistically, implies that macro-objects consist of entities which are denoted by these terms. Consequently scientific instrumentalism is justified.

I believe that a realist's one hope to refute this objection is by rebutting the first premise, because at least one consequence of each of the three realistic alternatives surely seems to be implausible. Let me explain my reasons for this. First, briefly reconsider waves and wave packets. Both disperse after passing through a narrow slit. Thus, whether or not 'Ψ' specifies or indicates properties of basic entities, there would be an instantaneous collapse or dis-appearance of the dispersed wave when such an entity impinges observably at a small spot on a screen. But, as we have seen, an instantaneous collapse or disappearance is surely implausible. A similar problem arises for pilot waves on the particle-with-wave interpretation. Furthermore, as mentioned previously, not only has no satisfactory formalism been devised for a hidden variable theory that postulates pilot waves, but also such a hidden variable theory either disagrees with the predictions of quantum theory, or violates some version of Einstein's principle, or conflicts with special relativity. Given present evidence, neither disagreement, nor violation, nor conflict is acceptable.

Of the three realistic alternatives, I believe that the particle interpretation is the most reasonable, although it also faces problems. One is the problem of explaining the tunnel effect, where, on this view, an alpha particle which escapes from a uranium nucleus, seems to lack sufficient energy for the escape. However, this seemingly physically impossible occurrence is shown to be possible, if not adequately explained, by means of the interpretation of the uncertainty principle that allows entities to have huge variations in energy over extremely short periods of time. Thus, for every short periods, it is physically possible that alpha particles have enough energy to "tunnel" out of the nucleus, even though the average energy of each one is insufficient. The main problem, however, is raised by the two-slit experiment. In this case, the particle interpretation violates the second version of Einstein's principle, because each particle passes through just one slit, yet the behavior of many of them is different when the remote second slit is open from when it is closed. This situation is similar to that we found in the modified EPR experiment, because in neither case is it required that a *change* in a property of an individual entity—either spin or momentum—results instantaneously from a remote change. Nevertheless, in both cases there does seem to be a functional correlation between the values of these properties and some remote situation. And both correlations, by violating the second version of Einstein's principle, seem to be implausible.

At this point a realist is left with the task either of refuting the first premise or justifying a rejection of the principle of "no functional correlation at a distance." The initial implausibility of rejecting the principle would have to be overcome by some experiment which would be more reasonably explained in terms of a realism that rejects the principle than by an instrumentalism that accepts it. This is because realism should be rejected if it is more reasonable to keep the principle and reject realism than to do the converse. But not only, I believe, have there been no such experiments, I am also not sure what sort of experiment would be decisive other than one where realism versus instrumentalism is not an issue. But this would seem to require an experiment with only observable, macro-objects, and, as far as I know, no such experiment shows the principle to have been violated.[21] A realist, then, should try to refute the first premise by producing a plausible fourth candidate for the referents of basic-entity terms. Unfortunately, he can plausibly claim little more than that a basic

---

[21] See, however, Popper, "Particle Annihilation," pp. 189–91, for the view that there could be crucial experiments at the microlevel. I believe, however, that such experiments can at most decide between realism with "action" at a distance and realism without such "action". That is, realism must be assumed if such experiments are to help decide on local versus distant "action". They will, then, not help decide the present issue.

entity, such as an electron, is, like Locke's material substance, a "something I know not what" which sometimes has particle-like characteristics, such as when the Compton effect is observed and when hitting a scintillation screen, and other times has wave-like characteristics, as when groups of them form defraction patterns. He can also claim that they have certain physical properties when measured, but he should remain quite mute about them when not measured.[22]

He must, however, be even more cautious. He must also find a way to avoid certain inferences, such as in the modified EPR experiment, and when retrodicting in the two-slit experiment. The most he can allow in the latter case are retrodictions that at least that *part* of an electron that interacts observably with a screen at some spot travelled a certain path between slits and screen. If the conclusion that the whole electron travelled the path is derivable, then he is faced either with the implausibility of a wave reduction after the electrons pass through both slits, or with the implausibility of "correlation" at a distance if each electron goes through just one slit. In the modified EPR case he must avoid the inference to the values of the spin of e_2 or any other entities remote from where the measurements are taken. He can do this by remaining mute about whether the value of the spin of e_2 varies independently of the value of the spin of e_1. By so doing he would avoid any inference to unmeasured value of the spin of e_2 from the discovered measured value for e_1. The second version of Einstein's principle provides some reason for this neutrality.

Conclusion about Quantum Physics and Scientific Realism

The preceding thesis about referents for basic-entity terms is clearly far from completely satisfactory, but it is at least somewhat supported by the preceding construal of the uncertainty principle which implies that there are important and irremedial gaps in our knowledge of any entities that, given scientific realism, would be basic. The crucial question, however, is whether this thesis is plausible enough to be at least as reasonable as an instrumental construal of all basic-entity terms. We have found that construing 'Ψ' instrumentally does not defeat scientific realism. A qualified

---

[22] This position is very similar to Gardner's in "Two Deviant Logics," p. 108.

realism that construes only 'Ψ' instrumentally is available. Yet the theory that results limits us to such meager descriptions of basic entities that we should conclude the following. Scientific realism is in such a shaky position that it should be rejected if either one of two tasks is not accomplished. The first is to counter the argument for instrumentalism from the theoretician's dilemma, which was discussed in Chapter 4, and the second is to show that the identity thesis, conjoining minimal common-sense realism and minimal scientific realism, is plausible. If one of these tasks is not successfully completed, then we should reject scientific realism for either instrumentalism or common-sense realism, neither of which we have found to face any serious problems. Consequently, we must now turn to these two tasks.

Reexamination of the Theoretician's Dilemma

When we turn to the argument for scientific instrumentalism that is based on the theoretician's dilemma, we find that, as it is stated in Chapter 4, its conclusion is not that scientific realism is false, but rather that it is reasonable to accept scientific instrumentalism, that is, it is unreasonable to accept scientific realism. Except perhaps for the present problems from quantum physics, this is the strongest argument against scientific realism that I have found, even though its conclusion is weaker than those we have already examined and rejected. Scientific realism might be correct although unreasonable. Nevertheless, if it is unreasonable it should be rejected.

What makes this instrumentalist's argument so strong is that it contains no obviously weak premise at which to aim a refutation, and it does not depend on a particular scientific theory for its soundness. Surely the first three premises are true, and, after the prolonged discussion of Craigian and Ramseyan transcriptions of theories in Chapter 4, we can see that premise (4b) is quite reasonable. That is, any epistemic systematization established by a theory, T, is preserved by either a Craigian or Ramseyan transcription of T. This leaves premises (5b), (7b), and (8), but, as stated, (8) is surely invulnerable. If there is no reason at all to postulate the existence of theoretical entities, then it is unreasonable to believe that there are any such entities. Clearly, Occam's Razor is applicable to theoretical entities. Might (5d) or (7b) be refuted? The former states that if either form of transcriptionism preserves the epistemic systematization of a theory, T, then the theoretical terms of T are not necessary to develop acceptable scientific theories and to provide acceptable scientific explanations and predictions. The latter states that if all theoretical terms are unnecessary for both these purposes, then there is no reason to postulate entities as their referents, that is, theoretical entities. A scientific realist's best hope is to attack one of these two premises. The difficult task is to find which one to attack and how to do it.

I believe we can begin to see a problem for someone who holds both premise (5d) and premise (7b) by considering a conclusion they jointly yield, namely:

(10) If either Craigian or Ramseyan transcriptionism preserves the epistemic systematization of theories, then there is no reason to postulate the existence of theoretical entities.

While none of the objections to either (5d) or (7b) which we previously examined and rejected, provide any reason to reject (10), we can, interestingly enough, use a Berkeleyan view of explanation to raise some doubt about (10) and thus the conjunction of (5d) and (7b). According to this Berkeleyan view, there are two conditions that any theoretical explanation of an event must satisfy if it is to be completely adequate. The first is that any theoretical explanation of a particular observable event is completely adequate only if it explains precisely that event, given certain precise initial conditions. The statement expressing that precisely this event occurs must be derivable, deductively or inductively, from the explaining theory and appropriate observation statements. According to Berkeley, this and this alone is the task of scientific explanation. The second condition is that a theoretical explanation is completely adequate only if it makes an event completely understandable and this requires that the causes of the event be specified. According to Berkeley, science by itself does not provide this second sort of explanation. Scientific explanations function to warrant inferences among observation statements. But these statements are only about sensa, which are inert, and so scientific explanations do not explain events in terms of their causes. Because of this, Berkeley uses the theoretical phrase 'the author of nature' to refer to an orderly and powerful mind that causes those sensa that constitute the physical objects that populate the world. And while 'the author of nature' is a theoretical term, it is one that denotes an entity because its explanatory role, unlike those of scientific theoretical terms, requires that its referent cause various sensa. Thus if such a Berkeleyan is right, there is reason to reject (10) as stated because he believes there is reason to postulate at least one theoretical entity, even though no theoretical terms are needed either to preserve epistemic systematization, or for any other scientific purpose. Indeed, if this Berkeleyan is right, premise (7b) should be rejected also.

It is easy to avoid this Berkeleyan objection as stated, however, because throughout the discussion of this instrumentalist argument it has been assumed that the argument is concerned only with *scientific* theoretical terms. And, clearly, even if an author of nature, who is perhaps God, is required for a completely adequate explanation, this does not show that any scientific theoretical terms or entities are needed. Yet, the Berkeleyan claim about two necessary conditions for a completely adequate explanation is surely relevant to whether (10) is acceptable, because, given that complete explanation requires complete understanding and complete understanding requires specifying causes, it may be that the best understanding available to us requires there to be referents of certain of the theoretical terms of the best scientific explanations available. If this is the case, then although theoretical terms are not needed to meet any requirements of an adequate *scientific* explanation, they would be needed to approach as closely as possible to the ideal of complete explanation. Thus there would be some reason to postulate scientific theoretical entities. This would falsify (10), and thus the conjunction of (5d) and (7b) also.

There are two questions to be answered in order for us to decide whether the preceding view of explanation provides the basis for a sound objection to (10) and a plausible resolution of the theoretician's dilemma. First, does the ideal of complete explanation require complete understanding in terms of the causes of what is explained?[23] Second, does the closest that we can approach this

[23] I wish to thank Boris Dirnbach for making me think about relationships between explanation and causation.

ideal at present, or, indeed, at any time, require referents for certain theoretical terms of science? In considering the first question I can do little more than emphasize two points. First, the complete understanding of a particular event requires more than deriving that it occurred from some statement of initial conditions and some complicated, quantitative inferring device that meets certain systemic conditions. When we ask why an event occurs, it is a request for the previous causes that bring about the event, or a request for a description of the mechanisms and operations that constitute the event. In each case, we are asking for more than a statement of a correct inference ticket; we are asking for information about the way the world is that results in or constitutes the phenomenon. Thus, I believe, a complete understanding of a phenomenon requires realism regarding at least some of the terms that best explain the phenomenon.

But does the ideal of a complete explanation require this kind of complete understanding? This brings us to the second point. As I have interpreted it, a completely adequate scientific explanation does not require this sort of understanding of the phenomenon explained, because, as with explanations in quantum theory, it is consistent with scientific instrumentalism. But to explain something completely is to go beyond mere successful derivation in some way. Surely, if an event has a cause, we expect its complete explanation to pick out that cause, or at least some set of causal factors that are causally sufficient for the event. Furthermore, the explanation should pick them out in a way that is available for precise prediction and is testable for purposes of verifying or falsifying competing explanations. Thus, I find it to be reasonable to answer the first question by saying that complete explanation requires complete causal understanding.

In order to answer the second question, let us first compare how a scientific realist would attempt to use scientific explanations to approach complete understanding, with what a scientific instrumentalist could do to approach the same ideal. The former would argue that complete understanding of an observable event is reached when it is quantitatively described and the occurrence of just that event is explained as the precise result of the joint or individual behavior of certain theoretical entities. Indeed, although scientific explanation does not require such causal explanations, this is the model used by many scientists when they explain observable events in terms of the effects of micro-events. For example, physicists talk of the collision of a photon with a charged particle in the Compton effect, which has the result that photons are scattered. Electrons fired from cathode ray guns are said to hit targets with observable effects. The bright lines of the emission spectrum of hydrogen are said to be caused by the emission of photons of fixed wave lengths which are created when individual electrons of excited hydrogen atoms jump from higher to lower energy states. Such explanations seem to give us understanding of certain, specific observable events because they purport to provide precise understanding of the micro-events that causally result in the observable phenomena. Surely, if this is a correct description of a realistic use of scientific explanations, then they approach quite closely that ideal of complete explanation we discussed previously.

Consider now the approaches available to a scientific instrumentalist. They are basically two: either to eschew any attempt to understand an event in terms of its causes or constituents, or to postulate causes or constituents other than those implied by a realistic construal of scientific explanations. But, clearly, it is unreasonable to claim that science provides no understanding of the constituents of observable phenomena, while proposing a wholly different set of explanatory constituents. This, of course, is not what Berkeley does in claiming that sensa are the constituents of physical objects, because they do not function as explanatory constituents for him. Furthermore, an instrumentalist who eschews any attempt at understanding beyond mere derivation, has a view of explanation quite far removed from the ideal. There remains the alternative of postulating nonconstituent causes. And here the best known available candidates are a Berkeleyan author of nature and a Malebranchean god of occasionalism. Let us, then, compare a realistic interpretation of scientific explanation in its present state with Berkeleyan explanation to discover which approaches more closely to what we have taken as the ideal for complete explanation. If scientific explanation, realistically construed, is a closer approximation, we shall have found at least some grounds for rejecting (10).

After the conclusions reached in the preceding discussion of quantum theory it certainly must be admitted that, at present at least, a realistic use of scientific explanations does not approach this ideal as closely as once had been thought. We have seen that it is reasonable to claim not only that quantum theory shows some limitations in our knowledge of the behavior of elementary entities, but also that this behavior is at most causally influenced by preceding events, and so it is not fully causally determined. Thus not only are there considerable gaps in our knowledge of micro-events, there are also significant inadequacies in any attempt to understand precisely the behavior of observable objects. Indeed, it is reasonable to conclude at present that the behavior of no entity, whether theoretical or observable, is precisely causally determined by past events. Rather its propensity for behaving in each of several different ways is increased or decreased to varying degrees by past events. Thus, for both epistemological and ontological reasons, scientific explanations presently provide an incomplete understanding of phenomena when they are realistically construed. It is clearly possible, then, to find some mode of explanation that approaches the previously stated ideal more closely than present science does when taken by itself.

Although a closer approach to the ideal than science now provides is possible, is there any reason to think any nonscientific explanatory system is now, or in the future will be, closer? The only extant competitors we have found are essentially Berkeleyan, in the sense that some theoretical entity or entities that are not capable of being investigated by science are postulated independently of science as the nonconstituent causes of observable events. Such an approach to explanation has the advantage that if it is correct, then every observable event has a specific determining cause. However, it might be objected that for the Berkeleyan schema and any similar explanatory systems, the specific nature of these causes is neither discoverable, nor testable in any way that gives a clear understanding of what occurs in terms of why one particular event, rather than any other, occurs just when it does. For a Berkeleyan, scientific explanation provides no understanding of events beyond what it supplies regarding the warranting of inferences among observation statements. Nevertheless, whatever precision is available for our understanding an event comes from science with its quantitative derivation, whether probabilistic or not. Instead of taking this to be information about constituent causes or causal influences, a

Berkeleyan explanation schema substitutes explanations in terms of
causes which, if known at all, are known only in the most general
and vague way, and do not help us understand why one particular
event occurs rather than another.

Although this objection is sound when aimed at Berkeley himself,
there is a reply available to a contemporary Berkeleyan, or, better
perhaps, a contemporary occasionalist. He could argue that in so
far as any scientific theory provides a scientifically adequate
explanation, then its Ramseyized version does equally well. But if
so, then theoretical predicates about certain sorts of willings by the
author of nature—let us say God—can be substituted for the
different Ramsey predicate variables. Furthermore, if desired,
these Ramsey structures can be simplified by using one "occasionalist" substituend for any set of Ramsey variables that functionally
relate sets of quantitative observation properties. Thus this "neo-
occasionalist" could argue that between observations involving
such quantitative observation properties, there is only one intervening theoretical event, that is, a willing by God that functionally
relates the values of the properties. Then by interpreting these
occasionalist predicates realistically, our neo-occasionalist postulates individual willings by God rather than series of micro-events.
As a result this occasionalist can use just one explanatory schema to
provide causal explanations that are as precise as any a scientific
realist can provide. Incidentally, if quantum physics provides
reason for causal indeterminism, then, contrary to Einstein, this
occasionalist would postulate that God does "play dice with the
universe."

Consider, for example, two different causal explanations of why
when the temperature of a fixed volume of gas increases a certain
amount, the gas pressure increases a corresponding amount. A
scientific realist would postulate that the gas consists of molecules
whose mean kinetic energy increases an amount that is a function of
the amount of increase in temperature. This causes a corresponding
increase in the average velocity of the molecules, which causes an
increase in the average force with which the gas molecules hit the
walls of what contains the gas. Consequently, the gas pressure
increases a certain amount. Our neo-occasionalist, however, need
only postulate that when the temperature increases a certain
amount there is just one "intervening" occurrence: God causes the

gas pressure to increase an amount that is a certain function of the temperature rise.

I can find no reason to prefer either the occasionalist or the scientific realist explanatory schema. For example, it will not help the occasionalist to argue that his schema is closer to the ideal of complete understanding because his god, unlike a scientifically basic entity, is an entity whose existence requires no explanation. An occasionalist is at most justified in postulating a being whose causal power is just adequate to produce the various observable events. It is unreasonable to think that scientifically basic entities require some explanation, but this entity requires none. Furthermore, it is no less—and no more—mysterious why God wills the functional relationships he does than that the behavior of basic micro-entities is functionally related the way it is. Both the willings and the behavior are taken as unexplained and used to explain observable behavior.

It will not help the scientific realist to argue that his schema is closer to the ideal because it uncovers the micro-constituents of observable entities and explains observable behavior in terms of the constituents. Such a view is reasonable only if there is independent reason to think that there are such micro-constituents. But the justification of the existence of micro-constituents depends on the justification of scientific realism, and so the claim that there are micro-constituents of some sort should not be used to favor scientific realism.

We have not found a reason to claim that the explanatory schema of a scientific realist most closely approaches what is reasonable to take as the ideal explanation. But we also found no other schema that approaches more closely than this one does. It is reasonable, then, to use this schema of the scientific realist to approach as closely as we can to the ideal explanation. Consequently there is *some*, albeit not much, reason to use the realistic schema. And, because this reason for scientific realism is not nullified in any way by the effectiveness of Craigian and Ramseyan procedures for preserving epistemic systematization of theories, we can also conclude that (10) should be rejected. Its antecedent is true, and its consequent is false. Therefore, the conjunction of (5d) and (7b) should also be rejected, and now we can pinpoint why this should be done. It is because (7b) is mistaken. There is *some* reason to postulate theoretical entities even if no theoretical terms are needed for acceptable *scientific* theories, explanations, and predictions. Indeed, we can go even farther and claim that there is some reason for scientific theoretical entities even if no theoretical terms are needed for the *ideal* scientific explanation. It is reasonable to think that ideal explanations require more than ideal scientific explanations, and to hold that scientific theoretical entities come as close as any postulated entities to meeting this additional requirement. It seems, then, that we have finally found a way to resolve the theoretician's dilemma by finding a use for scientific theoretical terms that provides at least some reason to postulate scientific theoretical entities, even though this use is not required for a science that is ideal for purposes of scientific explanation and prediction, and the development of theories. It should be noted, however, that there is also some reason to use the alternative realistic schema of a neo-occasionalist.

There is, however, a reply to the preceding reason for thinking we have resolved the dilemma. This reply grants that there is reason to think we have correctly identified a viable ideal of explanation, and there is reason to think that scientific explanations, given a qualified realistic interpretation, approach that ideal as closely as anything does. It also grants that these points provide *some* reason for postulating scientific theoretical entities and, therefore, that (7b) is mistaken. Craig's and Ramsey's success are not sufficient for there being no reason to postulate scientific theoretical entities. Nevertheless, according to this reply, we now have available some new information that will provide a sufficient condition, without the use of (8), for the claim that there is adequate reason for not postulating any scientific theoretical entities. The replacement for (7b) is:

> (7c) If scientific theoretical terms are unnecessary to develop acceptable scientific theories and to provide acceptable scientific explanations and predictions of empirical data, and the identity hypothesis is implausible, then it is unreasonable to believe that there are any scientific theoretical terms.

Premise (7c) is quite plausible. We found good reasons for rejecting the many objections to minimal common-sense realism that we examined in Chapter 6. Thus the theory remained quite acceptable with no qualifications and only clarifying amendments. We have just concluded, however, that in order to save minimal scientific realism from most difficult objections, we had to limit drastically the claims about basic entities that a realist is allowed to make and we had to struggle to find even some reason for scientific theoretical entities. Consequently, if the identity hypothesis is implausible, then, because there is no scientific need for scientific theoretical terms, and no need for scientific theoretical entities to approach the ideal of complete explanation as closely as possible, we should reject scientific theoretical entities and minimal scientific realism for minimal common-sense realism. Thus premise (7c) is justified.

Of course, in order to be valid the argument with (7c) needs another premise to the effect that the identity hypothesis is implausible. If that added premise is correct, then the argument succeeds. If it is mistaken, then this last attempt to revise the argument from the theoretician's dilemma fails. Furthermore, I would claim that if it is plausible to conjoin minimal common-sense realism with minimal scientific realism, then, with the addition of the preceding reason for rejecting (7b), there is sufficient reason to justify the postulations of scientific theoretical entities.

Clearly the identity hypothesis is crucial and we must examine it carefully. First, however, it should be noted that we can draw an important conclusion from the reasons that we found to justify (7c). They also justify what can be called the "supremacy" of common-sense realism over scientific realism. This means they justify the rejection of all forms of scientific realism which are implausible when conjoined with minimal common-sense realism. These include moderate, Sellarsian, and extreme scientific realism. Consequently, if any form of scientific realism is to survive our examination, it will only be the minimal version.

For many philosophers the preceding conclusion comes as no surprise, although some of them would claim that the route taken to reach it is unduly torturous and complex. It is supposedly also quite unnecessary because the point is more easily and conclusively shown in another way. If this is true, then, of course, the case for common-sense realism would be even more secure, and that for scientific realism even more precarious. It is important, therefore, to show at this point that this claim is mistaken. I shall do this by showing that one particular attempt to establish the supremacy of common sense fails. This attempt is by Stebbing, and I have chosen it because I find that it best exemplifies the sort of quick and supposedly definitive proof I wish to refute.[24]

Stebbing's Arguments for the Supremacy of Common Sense

One argument used by Stebbing is a version of the paradigm case argument, most versions of which are by now discredited. Her specific version concerns solidity and is an attempt to counter Eddington's statement that "the plank has no solidity of substance." She says:

> We can understand 'solidity' only if we can truly say that the plank is solid. For 'solid' just is the word we use to describe a certain respect in which a plank of wood resembles a block of marble, a piece of paper, and a cricket ball, and in which each of these differs from a sponge, from the interior of a soap bubble, and from the holes in a net.[25]

I agree with Stebbing's claim that Eddington is mistaken in denying that the plank is solid, but I find her reasons for this to be mistaken. Both a minimal scientific realist and a minimal common-sense realist can agree that many objects are solid, that is, firm or hard or generally resistent to pressure. But whether they can agree that some objects are *continuously* solid is far from clear. Stebbing's argument can be understood as an attempt to show that planks are solid, indeed, continuously solid regardless of anything a scientific realist claims. A similar argument would apply to things being continuously colored.

The crux of Stebbing's argument is the hypothetical statement, which can best be rephrased as stating that if 'solid' is understandable, then it is true that there are solid planks. Given this, it is easy to infer that some planks are solid, but what reason is there to accept this claim? Stebbing's reason for this is that 'solid' just is the

---

[24] Another such attempt is the one by Ryle, which I find best to construe as an argument for instrumentalism. I reject it in "Can Eddington's 'Two' Tables Be Identical," *Australasian Journal of Philosophy* (1974): 29–31.

[25] S. Stebbing, "The Furniture of the Earth," in *Philosophy of Science*, A. Danto and S. Morgenbesser, eds. (New York: Meridian Books, 1960), p. 73.

word used to describe a certain property of planks, and so if it is meaningful, or understandable, then some planks have that property. But while a word being so used does imply that it is meaningful, it does not imply that it truly describes anything. Thus 'solid' being meaningful does not imply that it truly applies to something. Furthermore, it would not help to claim that there is general agreement that 'solid' truly describes planks. This also would not show that if 'solid' is meaningful, then it follows that it truly applies to something. Although such general agreement would seem to imply that 'solid' is meaningful, it does not imply that it truly applies to anything.

A second familiar argument for the supremacy of the common-sense world can be constructed from Stebbing's statement that "the Cartesian-Newtonian philosophers seeking to account for a *seeable* world, succeed only in substituting a world that could in no sense be *seen*".[26] Of course, whether the Newtonian and also Lockean world can be seen depends on how seeing is construed. According to Locke the world is indirectly seen. However, the point of the argument is that the physical sciences function to explain the world around us, which consists of objects with sensuous, occurrent properties. Thus this familiar world is the basic subject matter or datum of these sciences, and so no results reached by these sciences can be used to show these familiar objects do not exist. But scientific realists, such as Newton, Descartes, Locke, and, today, Sellars use scientific results in just this way, and so they are mistaken.

The first point to note is that once various species of scientific realism have been delineated, we can see that this argument is primarily against moderate scientific realism. It can be directed against the minimal position only by an additional argument, such as those we shall consider, which purports to show that if minimal scientific realism is correct then minimal common-sense realism is incorrect. The second point is that a Lockean or Newtonian moderate scientific realist could reply that the subject matter that science is to explain can be taken to be whatever is directly experienced as the result of the perception of physical objects and persons. When put in this way it is possible to interpret this subject

[26] *Ibid.*, p. 78.

matter to be sensations (either sensa or sensings) which are effects of stimulus from physical objects, objects which themselves have no sensuous, occurrent properties. One reply, then, by a moderate scientific realist might be that although the results of science could not be used to eliminate everything that has sensuous, occurrent properties, there is some leeway in interpreting these entities either as physical objects or as sensations. Even if scientists continue to find it clearly convenient to talk about these entities using observational physical-object terms, and find no falsifying cases, it is nevertheless possible that what they describe are either sensa or sensings. Thus, if we were to discover that some form of indirect scientific realism is the most plausible theory of perception and the external world, then there would be at least some reason to claim that the basic data of science are indeed sensations. However, whether such a reply has much force is not relevant to our present task. Indeed, it is not one that a minimal scientific realist must consider unless there is reason to think that his thesis implies that common sense is mistaken or implausible. But that remains to be considered.

Stebbing makes one more claim that is relevant to the supremacy of common sense, but she does not defend the claim, which amounts to an assertion of scientific instrumentalism. This becomes clear, when echoing E. A. Burtt, she says, "we have allowed the physicists 'to make a metaphysics out of a method.'" Of course, the question is not whether this move has been allowed, but whether it is reasonable to claim that science not only provides a method for explaining its data, but also provides a description, perhaps the most accurate one, of what there is. If Stebbing had established the supremacy of minimal common-sense realism and had refuted the identity thesis, then she would have good reason for holding this instrumentalist view of science. But we have seen that she did neither. Consequently, we can reject her quick attempt at decisive proof of the supremacy of common sense. And since I have found no other, more plausible attempts of this sort, I shall further conclude we can do no better than rely on the long, involved, and less than conclusive argument for this supremacy which I previously defended.

We have completed our examination of the evidence for and against minimal scientific realism. We rejected certain forms of the theory, but concluded that one qualified and restricted version is acceptable if and, indeed, only if it is plausible to conjoin it with minimal common-sense realism. This is the version that requires us to interpret 'Ψ' instrumentally and to say little about basic entities. Thus, while we have rejected the more extreme forms of scientific realism, the viability of the minimal variety remains an open question, the answer to which depends upon the plausibility of conjoining the three hypotheses of the identity thesis.

Objections to Conjoining Common-Sense Realism with Scientific Realism

We have seen that the identity hypothesis consists of a conjunction of three subtheses. Two of these we have agreed are plausible, namely, minimal common-sense realism, and the hypothetical statement describing the theoretical properties and constituents that physical objects have if minimal scientific realism is correct. The fate of the third, that is, minimal scientific realism, depends on the results of our present discussion of the plausibility of the tripartite conjunction. In this discussion I shall proceed by first considering arguments for incompatibilism, that is, for the claim that the conjunction is inconsistent, and then I shall search for any additional arguments that might succeed in showing the conjunction to be implausible. I do this because the most widely accepted and strongest arguments against the thesis are two arguments for incompatibilism. Incidentally, I shall assume here an unqualified and unrestricted form of minimal scientific realism in which electrons and other such elementary entities are construed as discrete particles. I do this so we can consider the objections in their most troublesome form.

TWO ARGUMENTS FOR INCOMPATIBILISM

There are two different arguments for incompatibilism which were briefly mentioned in Chapter 6 when I discussed the sixth scientific objection to naive realism. I know of no clear statement of them, nor of anyone who has carefully distinguished between them. For example, both arguments are contained in the following passage from Aune:

Suppose that we have taken the molecular theory of matter

fully to heart and have merged it with our ordinary notions by regarding apples and billiard balls as aggregates of exotic particles. Suppose, also that we continue to speak of these familiar objects as colored. The question then arises: can we consistently use our color words in their ordinary sense? To answer this question we need only ask another: how can a gappy collection of colorless particles possibly be colored in the occurrent, continuous fashion demanded by common sense? The answer, of course, is that it cannot: essential gappiness is incompatible with ultimate continuity.[27]

One argument concerns an incompatibility between a physical object being colored and its basic constituents not being colored. The other turns on whether or not an object can be continuously colored when its basic constituents are spatially discrete particles. As I shall state it, each argument will have as its conclusion that if minimal scientific realism is correct, then minimal common-sense realism is incorrect, and thus one or the other is incorrect. For such an argument to prove incompatibilism, each of its premises must be logically necessary unless it expresses a consequence of a minimally realistic interpretation of science. If, however, some of these premises, while logically contingent, are quite reasonable, then, although the identity thesis would be consistent, it would be quite implausible. Thus we should also consider how reasonable any of these contingent premises are. This point can be put somewhat more formally as follows. The conjunction of which the identity hypothesis consists has three contingent conjuncts, and is of the form:

$$p \cdot q \cdot [q \supset (r_1 \cdot r_2 \cdots r_n)].$$

Of course, n is quite large. However, incompatibilism is correct if and only if $(q \supset \sim p)$ is derivable from $(q \supset s)$, where s is either a member or a conjunction of members of $(r_1, r_2, \ldots, r_n)$, with the addition of any other premises that are logically necessary, such as a statement expressing some entailment of minimal common-sense realism. This is the form in which I shall examine the two arguments to establish incompatibilism.

27 B. Aune, *Knowledge, Mind, and Nature* (New York: Random House, 1967), p. 172.

FIRST ARGUMENT: NO BASIC PARTICLES ARE SENSUOUSLY COLORED
The crux of the first argument, which is clearly the stronger of the
two, concerns the sensuous, occurrent color a common-sense
realist ascribes to physical objects. It states that if an object is
sensuously colored and has constituents, then at least some of its
basic constituents are colored, but if minimal scientific realism is
correct, then none of the basic constituents of physical objects are
colored. Thus, contrary to minimal common-sense realism, no
physical objects are colored if minimal scientific realism is true.[28]
Let me spell out the details of such an argument as follows:

(1) For any (sensuously) colored object x, if x has constituents (that is, x is not a basic object), then some
constituent of x is colored.

(2) If (1), then any physical object, y, is colored only if either
some basic physical object (either y or a basic constituent
of y) is colored, or some series of constituents of y goes
on *ad infinitum*.

(3) If minimal scientific realism is correct, then no series of
constituents of any physical object goes on *ad infinitum*.

(4) If minimal scientific realism is correct, then all basic
physical objects are subatomic particles.

(5) If minimal scientific realism is correct, then no subatomic particles are colored.

Therefore

(6) If minimal scientific realism is correct, then no physical
objects are colored.

(7) If minimal common-sense realism is correct, then some
physical objects are colored.

Therefore

(8) If minimal scientific realism is correct, then minimal
common-sense realism is incorrect.

We can take premises (2) and (7) to be logically necessary. The
consequent of (7) expresses one part of the statement of minimal

[28] Cf. Sellars, pp. 35–36; and also D. Armstrong, *Perception and the Physical World* (New
York: Humanities Press, 1961), p. 162.

common-sense realism, and that of (2) merely states one entailment of premise (1). The point behind (2) is that if any colored object, O_1, with constituents has at least one colored constituent, O_2, then it is entailed that O_2 also has a colored constituent, O_3, and so on, either to infinity or until a basic colored object is reached. Premise (3) states that, according to science, each series of constituents ends with a basic particle. While this is contingent, it is allowed in the argument because it expresses one consequence of a minimal realistic interpretation of science. This is also true of (4). And although it may seem that (5) should be classified in the same way, I wish to examine what I take to be the three main arguments to justify (5), in order to see whether any of them provides reason to accept it.

The premises of the first argument are the following:

(9) If minimal scientific realism is correct, then a subatomic particle has a property only if it is ascribed to the particle in particle physics.

(10) Particle physics does not ascribe color to any subatomic particles.

These two premises yield (5), but although (10) is surely acceptable, (9) is not. While (9) would be true for moderate scientific realism, minimal scientific realism only requires that objects have at least all the properties ascribed to them by science. It may be objected that we should be moderate scientific realists about the purely theoretical entities of science. However, not only is this not a requirement of the minimal position, it is not clear it is independently justified. This is because of the unsettled question of whether there are "hidden" variables. The question is whether there are properties of basic particles other than those considered by particle physics (in particular, quantum physics) which, if they were known, would allow precise predictions of certain behavior of individual particles which cannot be made given only the properties presently consider-ed. As previously mentioned, no hidden variable theories are acceptable at present, but some physicists think, as Ballantine says, that "presumably the next step must be a bold departure from the familiar [quantum] formalism."[29] If this occurs, then an acceptable

---

[29] Ballentine, p. 380.

hidden variable theory might result. Furthermore, even if, as a matter of fact, no additional kinds of properties ever come to be considered in quantum physics, and statistical predictions will always be required, the question of whether there are other properties remains open. Thus I think premise (9) is too dubious to justify some other claim.

The second attempt to justify (5) concerns certain scientific facts about the relationship between sensuous color and light:

> (11) If minimal scientific realism is correct, then a physical object is sensuously colored only if it either selectively absorbs or selectively reflects light waves.
>
> (12) If minimal scientific realism is correct, then no subatomic particles selectively absorb or selectively reflect light waves.

Once again (5) follows. We can accept (12) since the relevant reflection or absorption occurs only with certain systems of basic particles. One particle can be affected by light of multiple wave lengths, but it cannot absorb some or reflect some, whether selectively or not. However, it can be objected that we should amend (11) so that it concerns physical objects that are observably colored, that is, objects whose color is observable to perceivers. It does not seem that any scientific facts require that no physical object is sensuously colored if it is too small to be seen (if it is too small to absorb or reflect light waves selectively), or if its gravitational attraction is so great that it prohibits the reflection of light waves (if it is a "*black* hole").

The immediate answer to this objection is that no scientific facts are needed for this purpose because it is analytic that:

> (13) If something is not observable, then it is not sensuously colored.

Given (13), we can not only derive the original (11) from the amended version, we can also construct the third argument, because we can derive (5) with the clearly acceptable premise:

> (14) If minimal scientific realism is correct, then no subtomic particles are observable.

I am sure that many people believe that (13) is so obvious that it is senseless even to entertain a doubt about it. Such beliefs may help explain not only why people are convinced that no subatomic particles are colored, but also Sellars' claim that "it doesn't make sense to say of the particles of physical theory that they are coloured".[30] Nonetheless, while it is either clearly false or senseless to say about some unobservable things, such as numbers or minds, that they are colored, it is not so obvious if the reason for something being unobservable is that it is too small to reflect and absorb light waves selectively. To see this let us consider a revision of (13):

> (13a) If something is too small to be observed (to reflect light waves) then it is not sensuously colored.

Whether (13a) is more reasonable than its denial depends on how it is construed. On one construal it is clearly reasonable, but on a second construal, the one needed for the arguments for both (5) and (11), I find no reason to accept it rather than its denial. To see the difference between the two construals it is helpful to talk of the particular expanse of color that an individual object has or lacks, for example, the particular expanse of brownness a certain table has.[31] The first construal is:

> (13b) If something is too small to be observed (to reflect light waves), then no expanse of any color it has is sensuous, that is, none of its expanse of color is perceivable.

The second is:

> (13c) If something is too small to be observed (to reflect light waves), then it has no expanse of sensuous color, that is, it has no expanse of a color, some expanses of which are perceivable.

Construal (13b) is compatible with some unobservable things being colored and also with none being colored. It is thus not only weaker than (13c), but it also seems reasonable to construe it as

---

[30] Sellars, p. 35.

[31] We could also use instances of color rather than expanses to make this point. I have discussed instances briefly in "In Search of Criteria for Property Identity and Difference" (Unpublished).

logically necessary. However, the stronger claim, (13c), is not logically necessary, because it is logically possible that something is both continuously colored throughout and actually divisible until it becomes too small to be observed. Furthermore, it will not help to amend (13c) so that it is taken as a consequence of minimal scientific realism, because, as pointed out when premise (9) was examined, the minimal position does not limit the properties of basic particles. Thus the denial of (13c), which incidentally Leibniz would seem to accept, is neither a contradiction nor falsified by a minimally realistic interpretation of science.[32] I know of no other reasons that would justify (13c), and so I conclude that it is no more reasonable than its denial. Neither the second nor the third argument justifies (5).

For our purposes it is enough to show that (5), which states that a minimally realistic interpretation of science prohibits subatomic particles being colored, is no more reasonable than its denial. With the rejection of the three arguments for (5), we can conclude that this has been done. It is, nevertheless, worth considering whether premise (1) is either logically necessary or a consequence of the minimally realistic view. At most, it should be claimed that if an object with constituents is colored, then some of those constituents are colored *when* they are constituents of the object. It is possible that this is a property they have only when in certain structural relationships with other entities. It could be that isolated basic particles are colorless, but that when a group of them is structured in a certain way the resulting system has the emergent property of being colored throughout. But even this restricted version of (1) is logically contingent. It is possible, although perhaps counterintuitive, that there are relationships among colorless particles in such a system that result in something like a field spread among the particles, and that it is these "fields," rather than the particles, which are continuously colored.

It is also clear that (1) is not a consequence of a minimally realistic interpretation of science, because, again, such an interpretation leaves open the question of whether particles, individually or in groups, and "fields" have additional properties. Thus a

[32] See Leibniz on minute perceptions, for example, in *Gottfried Wilhelm Leibniz, Philosophical Papers and Letters* L. Loemker, ed. (Dordrecht, Holland: D. Reidel Publishing Co., 1956), pp. 294, 557.

minimal scientific realist could agree, for example, that a certain molecule is sensuously colored but that none of its constituents, namely, ions, electrons, protons, and neutrons, is colored in isolation. Once again we would have a premise for which there are no logical or scientific grounds. Consequently, as with (5), I find no reason to accept (1) rather than its denial.

SECOND ARGUMENT: EACH BASIC PARTICLE IS SPATIALLY DISCRETE
We have found that the preceding argument does not succeed either as an attempt to establish incompatibilism or an attempt to show that the identity thesis is implausible. There remains, however, the task of examining the second argument. Its central point is that the sensuous occurrent colors that a common-sense realist claims cover some surfaces of certain observable physical objects are continuous expanses of color, and this clearly requires that physical objects be spatially continuous. But this spatial continuity is incompatible with one consequence of a minimally realistic interpretation of science, namely, that the basic constituents of observable physical objects are spatially discrete particles.[33] We can spell out this argument in more detail as follows:

(1) If something is continuously colored, then it is (spatially) continuous throughout.

(2) If something, x, is continuous throughout, then each spatial location within x is either occupied by a basic constituent of x, or x has no basic constituents.

(3) If minimal scientific realism is correct, then all observable physical objects have basic constituents.

(4) If minimal scientific realism is correct, then each basic constituent of an observable physical object is a spatially discrete particle.

(5) If each basic constituent of something is a spatially discrete particle, then something has basic constituents only if some spatial locations within it are not occupied by any of its basic constituents.

Therefore

(6) If minimal scientific realism is correct, then no obser-

---

[33] See C. Mundle, *Perception: Facts and Theories* (Oxford: Oxford University Press, 1971), p. 56.

vable physical objects are continuously colored.

(7) If minimal common-sense realism is correct, then some observable physical objects are continuously colored.

Therefore

(8) If minimal scientific realism is correct, then minimal common-sense realism is incorrect.

We can grant that premises (1) and (5) are logically necessary, and that (3) and (4) express consequences of a minimally realistic interpretation of science. Only (2) and (7), therefore, remain to be considered.

It is easy to see that (2) is false, given the characterization of minimal common-sense realism that we adopted at the beginning of this chapter. This view requires only that the ways physical objects optimally appear are indiscernibly close for unaided, normal human perceivers to the ways they actually are. Consequently, the minimal view can accept that physical objects are not continuously colored if they are only indiscernibly different from something continuously colored. Of course if something is observably colored, as common sense entails, then it seems that some part of it is continuously colored. But there is no reason to think such a part must be observable by the naked eye. It is possible for a common-sense realist to take a "pointillist" view of all observable colored objects and to hold that each "point" of continuous color covers some area, but the area is too small to be observably discerned. Many things, of course, (such as drops of blood) would appear to be continuously colored, but the only areas actually continuously colored (such as hemoglobin in blood) would be too small to see. Furthermore, the only objection I can find to this "pointillist" thesis is that nothing is sensuously colored if it is too small to be seen, but we have already dispensed with that objection when examining the first argument. We can conclude, then, that (7) should be rejected. However, there are some people, such as Aune, Mundle, and Sellars, who seem to think that common-sense realism requires continuous, observable expanses of color. Clearly the preceding rejection of (7) will not convince them that this second argument should be rejected. Because of this, let us examine premise (2).

While premise (2) may initially seem to be logically necessary or at least highly plausible, I believe it is neither. The truth, indeed, logically necessary truth, which might lead someone to accept (2) is:

> (9) If x is continuous throughout, then each spatial location within x is occupied by some *part* of x.

While (9) is true, it differs in an important way from (2), as can be seen by noting that an inference from (9) to (2) requires at minimum:

> (10) If each spatial location within x is occupied by some part of x, then each location within x is occupied by a basic constituent of x, or x has no basic constituents.

To make (10) clearly true another disjunct must be added to the consequent, namely: each location within x is occupied by a part of x that includes no basic constituents of x. It might seem that there could be no such part, because, necessarily, any part is a constituent. However, we have been construing all basic constituents of physical objects as particles, that is objects or individuals, and some parts of physical objects are not themselves individuals. This interpretation is needed if premise (2) of the first argument and premise (4) of the second argument are to be true. If forces and fields can be taken as constituents of observable physical objects, then both premises are false. If, however, only objects are to be constituents, then while the present (4) is true, (10) requires the preceding amendment. Let us take the second alternative. We can, however, no longer derive (2), but instead:

> (2a) If x is continuous throughout, then each spatial location within x either is occupied by a basic constituent of x, or is occupied by a part of x that includes no basic constituent of x, or x has no basic constituents.

We can grant that (2a) is logically necessary, but the original argument is no longer valid, and there is no reasonable premise to add to make it valid. The same point that shows this also shows that (2) is no more reasonable than its denial, and is certainly not logically necessary. Consider the claim that a physical object is continuous throughout because all the spatial locations within it that are not occupied by discrete particles are occupied by "fields" set up by the relationship among the particles. I can find no reason to reject this claim for (2), and no reason to reject it for any additional premise to make the argument with (2a) valid. Thus, once again we can conclude the second argument fails.

Two More Problems for the Identity Hypothesis

We have examined the main arguments that are thought to establish either incompatibilism, or the implausibility of the identity thesis. We found Stebbing's arguments to be dubious and to be directed against moderate scientific realism and for common-sense realism, rather than against compatibilism or the identity thesis. The two arguments derived from Aune and Sellars are, however, attempts to justify incompatibilism, but we found neither is adequate for the task. Indeed, I concluded not only that compatibilism escapes unscathed, but also that neither argument provides reason to reject the identity thesis. I believe that there are no other reasons for rejecting compatibilism. However, there are still two important unresolved problems confronting the identity hypothesis that we must examine here.[34]

FIRST PROBLEM: PERCEPTUAL PRESENTATION AND SENSING

In the preceding discussion of the identity thesis, we considered objections that are aimed at the plausibility of conjoining the minimal common-sense description of the external world with scientific, theoretical descriptions. None of these objections considered the plausibility of conjoining scientific, theoretical descriptions of perception with the second thesis of minimal common-sense realism, which states that perceiving something is having it perceptually presented. Of course, in Chapter 6 we examined seven objections to naive realism, each of which concerns scientific statements relevant to this second thesis. But, after making three amendments and deleting the condition that what is perceived is present with its perceiver, we arrived at a version of the thesis that avoided all seven objections. I have found no other objections of these sorts, but we are faced with the fact that in Chapter 2 we used the adverbial sensing theory to help provide inductive evidence

---

[34] Another objection to the identity hypothesis is considered in the concluding chapter. It states that moral responsibility requires the rejection of minimal scientific realism.

that no scientific theory need assume sensa either to interpret its subject matter, as in psychophysics, or to explain its subject matter, as in Gibson's theory concerning seeing in perspective. Furthermore, the sensing theory was used to refute several arguments for sensa based on scientific facts. Consequently, an important part of the case for some form of direct realism has rested on the assumption of sensings rather than sensa. Somehow, therefore, we must combine the adverbial sensing theory of sense experience with the perceptual presentation view of common-sense realism, if we are to arrive at a plausible version of compatible common-sense realism. This is the crucial problem that still faces us.

One part of the problem is to fit sensing events into the account of perceiving as perceptual presentation. As discussed in Chapter 6, it is clear that a complex event beginning either with transmission or with the reception of stimulus from an object and ending with a sensing is not identical with someone immediately experiencing the object, because immediate experiencing is a simple, unanalyzable relationship. It is easy, however, to identify each event of a person having an experience of something with some sensing event. In particular, our compatibilist can postulate:

A. Each event of a person having an experience of something, E, is identical with some event of the person E-sensing.

For example, an event of someone having an experience of a table as being red (a red table) is to be taken as identical with an event of the person red-table-sensing. In this way we arrive at the following replacement for condition (2) of the second thesis of minimal common-sense realism:

(2a) For any minimally required sensible physical property, Q, if, at t, s should be a normal observer who immediately perceives p in conditions optimal for distinguishing whether or not p has Q, and in so doing he p-as-Q-senses, then he would immediately perceive a property that p has approximately at t, and that is either Q or some property which is indistinguishable from Q by unaided, normal human perceivers, even in optimal conditions.

We have not yet completely solved the problem, however, because a question remains about how to understand the relationship between immediate perception and sensing. At least the following can be said:

> B. Each event of a person immediately perceiving a physical object, *p*, occurs when and only when some event of the person sensing occurs as a result of stimulus from *p* appropriately affecting him.

That the stimulus affects a person in an appropriate way is, of course, essential for someone to immediately perceive a physical object, because stimulus from objects can cause people to have certain feelings or emotions and even to afterimage or hallucinate. Clearly such effects would not correspond to perceiving the object. However, discovering which effects are appropriate is a scientific task rather than a philosophical problem, and so I shall leave the precise specifications to scientists.[35] Nevertheless, I would like to specify somewhat further the sort of equivalence B expresses.

The equivalence is clearly not logical. It might seem plausible, however, to construe it as a causal conditional. That is, it might seem that someone sensing, when appropriately caused, in turn causes him to have a particular simple, unanalyzable relation to an external physical object. Or it might be claimed that B expresses merely a causal connection between events of two different sorts because different events of both sorts are contemporaneous effects of the same causal chain. Unfortunately, there is an objection to both of these causal construals of B. Like the combined sensing-sensum theory, both of these causal theses have the consequence that qualitatively identical proximate causes of sensing, which differ only in some remote causal ancestors, would have different effects. In some cases they would result in sensing events, and, in addition, events of immediately perceiving; in other cases they would result only in sensing events.

I believe that the relationship expressed by B is best understood in terms of two different, but related claims. The first is Ryle's thesis that perception verbs are success or achievement verbs.[36]

---

[35] Compare how Chisholm tries to handle this problem in R. Chisholm, *Perceiving* (Ithaca: Cornell University Press, 1957), pp. 142–49.

[36] See G. Ryle, *The Concept of Mind* (New York: Barnes and Noble, Inc., 1949), pp. 149–53.

The second is Chisholm's view that certain nonethical, empirical characteristics are related to the ethical characteristic of being right so as to be what he calls "right-making characteristics," that is, characteristics that are criteria for something being right.[37] I suggest that we interpret B as giving "success-making" empirical characteristics, where the success for which they are criteria is not being morally right, but rather immediately perceiving a physical object, that is, perceiving it in a simple, unanalyzable way. It is not, then, that stimulus from an object causes someone to sense in some way, and in addition, causes him to perceive it immediately, but that sensing, as the result of appropriate causes, is an "immediate-perception-making" characteristic. That is, being in such a state of sensing, appropriately caused, is a criterion for succeeding in immediately perceiving a physical object. The equivalence expressed in B, then, is neither a mere material equivalence, nor a logical equivalence, nor a causal equivalence, nor, indeed, any sort of empirical generalization to be verified or falsified by induction from observed cases. It is a criteriological equivalence, and about that I am only able to say that it is like the relationship between right-making characteristics and being right.

It is clear that what I have said above about B is not enough to justify its acceptance by a compatible common-sense realist. Consider the following objection. I have talked of events of persons immediately perceiving physical objects. Yet I have claimed they are not caused by sensing events, and are not events distinct from sensing events that are caused by whatever causes sensing events. And I have claimed that they are not identical with complex causal processes involving stimuli from objects that result in persons sensing in some way. But, surely, if there are such events, then they are causally related to such stimuli in some way. Yet the preceding discussion seems to leave no acceptable candidates for such a relationship.

There is one, and I believe only one, plausible way for a compatible common-sense realist to reply to the preceding objection. He can adopt the following:

C. Each event of a person immediately perceiving an external

---

[37] See Chisholm, Chapter 3, where he also talks of evidence-making characteristics, that is, marks of evidence.

physical object is identical with some event of the person
having an experience of something.

Whenever someone has an experience of something (and therefore
senses in some way) and he is appropriately caused to do so, then
and only then does the event of his having an experience of something succeed in being an event of his immediately perceiving an
object. Of course, not all events of having experiences are events
of immediately perceiving objects. The situation is like one where
an event of someone talking in a certain way, when, for example,
he is a minister in a marriage ceremony, is identical with his
succeeding in marrying two people. In both sorts of cases, the
person succeeds when and only when the circumstances are appropriate. It might be objected that this identification of events destroys
the analogy with the relationship between right and right-making
properties, because no state of an action being right is identical
with the state of the action having some property, P, which it
turns out is a right-making property. However, not only do many
examples (such as the event of breaking a string being identical
with winning a certain race) counter this objection by showing
how identity and a criteriological relationship can be combined,
but I believe there has been no refutation of the claim that each
state of an action being right is (contingently) identical with some
state of that action having a property P, where P is a right-making
property.
   A new objection might arise at this point, namely, that the
conjunction of A and C conflicts with my claim that immediate
experiencing is a simple relationship between a perceiver and an
object. However, A and C do not imply that it is a complex
relationship. That is, they do not imply that it is constituted of
other relationships, such as a series of causal processes, between
the perceiver and the object. And they do not imply that the
relationship involves other entities such as sensa, sense organs, and
perceptual systems. No objectless sensing and thus no event of
having an experience of something is complex in these ways. Thus
A and C are compatible with immediate-experiencing not being a
complex relationship. Nevertheless, the point of this objection is
that no objectless state of sensing involves any relationship of any
sort, and so if A and C are true, then immediate experiencing is

not a simple relationship because it is not a relationship at all.

This objection would be sound if the conjunction of A and C implied that events of someone immediately experiencing something are nothing but, that is, are reducible to, mere objectless sensing events. But this conjunction implies merely that each event of the first sort is identical with some sensing event. Therefore, given merely A and C, it is no more reasonable to claim that no event of someone immediately experiencing something includes any relationship because each is identical with some event that does not consist in any relationships, than it is to claim that some objectless sensing events include relationships between a perceiver and an object because they are identical with events that consist in such a relationship. Indeed, given B as well as A and C, we can say that some experiences of something, and thus some sensings succeed in being events in which perceivers are related to perceived objects. This is like when some event of someone talking succeeds in being an event in which the person is related to other persons, that is, an event of his marrying two people. Such events are not merely objectless states of someone talking, nor are they reducible to such states. They are that much, but they are also more. Given A, B, and C, the same is true of some events of someone sensing.

SECOND PROBLEM: SENSINGS AND STIMULUS-BASED PSYCHOLOGICAL THEORIES

Before moving on, it is worth considering one more objection to the way I have conjoined a scientific view of perception with the common-sense view. In Chapter 2, I used Gibson's stimulus-based theory as a prime example of a scientific theory of perception. But, it might be objected that my way of conjoining the two views requires that sensations are not, as Gibson claims, merely "occasional and incidental symptoms of perception." Consequently, I require a sensation-based and, more precisely, a sensing-based theory rather than Gibson's stimulus-based theory. I agree that it would surely be a serious objection if my proposal clashes with an essential part of a viable scientific theory, but there is no such clash. The only part of Gibson's thesis that is inconsistent with my proposal is that sensations occur only occasionally in perception, but, as I claimed in Chapter 2, that is implausible. At most Gibson needs to claim that sensations are only occasionally needed to explain certain perceptual facts, such as seeing in perspective. This is consistent with my proposal. I argued, moreover, that his theory does not even need sensations to explain those particular facts. Furthermore, while it is clearly plausible to conjoin the claim that sensings are effects of stimuli in all cases of perception with a sensation-based theory, it is also plausible to conjoin it with a stimulus-based theory. Sensation-based theories, such as Kant's, state that our perceptual responses, beliefs, and concepts arise as a result of our responding to sensations. Gibson's theory states that they arise as a result of our responding by means of our perceptual systems to structured stimuli, rather than to sensations. It is surely plausible that sometimes one effect of a response of a perceptual system to stimuli is a sensing event that is an event of perceiving. Its plausibility is increased, I believe, by the fact that, as I argue in *Materialism and Sensations* and will briefly argue again in the Appendix, it is plausible to identify each sensing event with some brain process that results when stimuli affect a sense organ of a perceiver.

CONCLUSION ABOUT THE IDENTITY HYPOTHESIS AND COMPATIBLE COMMON–SENSE REALISM

I have examined the most plausible objections I have been able to find that are directed against minimal common-sense realism, against minimal scientific realism, or against conjoining the two theses in a way that results in the identity hypothesis. At present only one of these objections remains unrefuted, that is, the version of the argument from the theoretician's dilemma that uses premise (7c). This argument succeeds only if it is unreasonable to conjoin the two minimal theses. But we have found reason to reject what I believe are the four major objections to such a combination. Thus we can reject this last objection to the identity hypothesis. It, and thus all three of its conjuncts, are acceptable.

During the preceding examination of the identity hypothesis, I qualified and restricted minimal scientific realism, amended the perceptual thesis of naive realism to arrive at a viable version, and postulated a criteriological relationship between each event of immediately perceiving something and that sensing event with which it is identical. I believe that what results is not only a plausible species of the identity hypothesis, but is also at least as reasonable as any version of realism. The two basic tenets of the resulting theory can be summarized as follows:

Compatible (Minimal) Common-Sense Realism:
(1) The identity hypothesis, amended to include the qualified and restricted version of minimal scientific realism, is true, *and*
(2) to perceive a physical object is to have it (minimally) perceptually presented, where:
    (a) each event of a person having an experience of something *E*, is identical with an event of the person *E*-sensing, *and*
    (b) each event of a person immediately perceiving an external physical object (i) is identical with some event of his having an experience of something, and (ii) occurs when and only when stimulus from the object appropriately affects him.

CONCLUSION ABOUT THE MOST REASONABLE FORMS OF REALISM

The last task in this chapter is to decide which versions of realism remain as competitors with compatible common-sense realism for being the most reasonable form of realism. At the end of Chapter 7 we reached two conclusions. The first was that Sellarsian direct realism is at least as plausible as Sellarsian and Lockean indirect realism. The second was the provisional conclusion that we are justified in rejecting Kantian nondirect realism. It was provisional because it depended on the plausibility of two assumptions. One is that a Sellarsian theory of knowledge and a Sellarsian theory of concept formation are at least as reasonable as restrictive Lockean and Kantian theories. The other is that science uncovers precise information about things-in-themselves. This second assumption has proven to be somewhat shaky because of the serious problems arising in quantum physics and because we found no need (although some reason) for scientific theoretical terms and entities. Consequently, because minimal common-sense realism emerged unscathed from our extensive examination, we concluded that any form of scientific realism that cannot be plausibly conjoined with this common-sense thesis should be rejected. For this reason, we rejected moderate and Sellarsian scientific realism. As a result,

Lockean and Sellarsian indirect realism as well as Sellarsian direct realism should also be rejected.

Does this rejection of the preceding three theories give us any reason to revise our previous provisional rejection of the Kantian theory? No, because our rejection depends only on the viability of the minimal version of scientific realism, and so it survives the demise of the more extreme versions. Indeed, I would claim that this reason to reject the Kantian theory has been strengthened. We have just concluded that it is plausible to conjoin a qualified minimal scientific realism with minimal common-sense realism. Consequently, we can further conclude that two theses that are inconsistent with Kantian realism are quite reasonable. The first is that some scientific theoretical sentences and some common-sense observation sentences truly describe things-in-themselves. The second is that some things-in-themselves are perceptually presented to us.

Which realistic theories are left to compete with compatible common-sense realism? There might seem to be only "incompatible" common-sense realism, which, because of its scientific instrumentalism, differs from compatible common-sense realism by rejecting scientific realism and consequently the identity hypothesis. There are, however, two others we should consider. Each accepts the modified identity hypothesis, but they disagree about the nature of perception. According to one, which I shall call "compatible sensing realism," we directly perceive physical objects, but none are perceptually presented to us because an event of a person perceiving an object is identical with the complex event that begins with the reception of stimulus from the object and ends with the person sensing.[38] The second theory, which we can call "compatible sensum realism," accepts a Lockean or Sellarsian view of perceiving, that is, it identifies perceptual experiences of something with sensing sensa that are appropriately caused by stimuli. However, it disagrees with Locke and Sellars about the external world. According to this view, which accepts only the minimal version of

[38] For a view that "perceiving consists of perceptual consciousness plus a causal relation," see R. Hirst in G. Wyburn, R. Pickford, and R. Hirst, *Human Senses and Perception* (Edinburgh and London: Oliver and Boyd, 1964), p. 328. In many other ways, however, Hirst's view of perception and perceptual experience in that book is similar to the thesis I have been defending here.

scientific realism, some secondary properties of physical objects, such as color, as well as primary properties "pictorially" resemble phenomenal properties of sensa.

It might be objected at this point that I have ignored a certain sort of metaphysical theory of perception, and thus I have over-looked an important rival of compatible common-sense realism, namely, belief theories of perception.[39] Such theories differ from the preceding four theories in that they replace the causation of perceptual experiences of something by the causation of either perceptual beliefs or inclinations to have perceptual beliefs. Thus these theories reject both sensing and sensum theories of perception. Indeed, on belief theories, perception consists of nothing more than causal processes and either certain beliefs or inclinations—often suppressed—to have such beliefs.

I find it initially quite incredible that, aside from causal processes, there is often nothing more to perceiving than being caused to have some belief. But it is even more incredible that in some cases when there is no perceptual belief, there is nothing more than a suppressed inclination to believe. This initial implausibility is even further increased by reference to examples of perception where the resulting perceptual beliefs are quite similar, but some perceptual factors other than causal processes seem, especially to the perceiver him-self, to be significantly different. For example, a person who is very familiar with the furniture in a certain room may have the same or very similar perceptual beliefs caused when he walks into the room at dusk and a short time later just after he turns on the lights in the room. But it seems quite clear that some perceptual factors, other than those beliefs and causal processes, differ significantly before and after the lights go on. The obvious candidates for what differs in this example are perceptual experiences which are caused in addition to the perceptual beliefs. Consequently a metaphysical theory of perception that ignores such factors, as belief theories do, is quite unreasonable and should be rejected, unless all its alternatives that include perceptual experiences are less reasonable. But we have found four plausible theories that accommodate these additional perceptual factors, and so we can ignore belief theories.

[39] See D. M. Armstrong, *Perception and the Physical World* (New York: The Humanities Press, 1961); and G. Pitcher, *A Theory of Perception* (Princeton: Princeton University Press, 1971).

Nothing we have examined thus far provides us with any reason to reject compatible common-sense realism or the preceding three alternatives to it. No objection to naive realism or to scientific realism affects these theories, and all four agree with plausible interpretations of scientific causal claims relevant to perception. It might be thought that an incompatible common-sense realist could plausibly construe these causal claims instrumentally and maintain an acquaintance view of perception. However, as we saw when examining the time-gap objection to naive realism, it would be implausible for any realist to reject certain very general causal claims, namely: perception of objects occurs only after stimulus from the objects first causally affects sense organs of the perceiver; and for distant objects this whole causal process requires a significant amount of time. Thus, any plausible form of common-sense realism must accommodate these causal claims, whether or not it accepts any scientific theory about the constituents of these causal processes.

We have four realistic theories to consider, and thus far we have found no clear reason to reject any of them, or to accept one of them as the most reasonable version of realism. Consequently, without appealing to the principles of reason—P1, P2a, and P3 —that were discussed in Chapter 1, we can only conclude, relative to the total evidence we have previously examined, that all four of these theories are more reasonable than any other versions of realism, and that compatible common-sense realism seems to be at least as reasonable as any realistic theory.

Summary and Concluding Remarks

SUMMARY

We have reached the point where we can return to the central argument of the book and, with the conclusions reached at the end of Parts I and II, show how the argument justifies its conclusion about compatible common-sense realism. In order to see this, first recall which premises of the argument had been justified and what remained to be done at the end of the discussion of sensa in Chapter 2.

Reasons for and Against Sensa

One crucial task in attempting to justify any sort of direct realism, is to show that it is reasonable to reject sensa. Although it is often thought that this is easily accomplished, we found that there are several different sorts of reasons for accepting sensa that should be carefully evaluated before any final conclusion is reached. Indeed, as we shall see, it was not until we finished Part II on realism that we had available what is needed to justify the rejection. This is because one important class of reasons for sensa are metaphysical reasons. Except for those reasons, however, by the end of Chapter 2 we had completed our examination and rejection of reasons for sensa. We examined empirical, nontheoretical reasons based on perceptual relativity, hallucinations, and the time-gap between transmission of stimulus and perception, and we found that none of the empirical facts involved make it more plausible to accept sensa rather than adverbial sensings. We also examined what I believe is a fair sample of scientific, theoretical reasons to postulate sensa. These included Gibson's postulation of sensa to explain seeing in perspective, his assumption of visual fields, and the claim that psychophysics requires that sensations be interpreted as phenomenal individuals with quantitative properties. Because we found no reason to postulate sensa rather than sensings in these cases, I concluded by induction that there is no reason to think scientific explanations require the postulation of sensa. Of course, such a

350

conclusion is provisional, and should be kept constantly open to review. Nevertheless, once this conclusion was reached we had justified the first two premises of the central argument. Together they imply that there are no empirical, nonlinguistic reasons for sensa. But, of course, this does not show that there are no linguistic reasons for sensa.

We examined one basic sort of linguistic reason for sensa, namely, reasons to show that the most accurate and comprehensive description of what there is requires sensum terms. It was easy to point out, however, that even if no purely physicalistic terminology is descriptively adequate so that some sort of sensation terminology is required, the sensing terminology can equally well fill these descriptive needs, that is, unless the terminology is inherently defective. Subsequently, we examined two alleged problems for the terminology and found neither one to be bothersome once we understood how the adverbial modifiers of sensing events specify the events. The adverbs are not adverbs of manner, but rather function to specify more determinately each particular sensing event. On the basic of this, we justified conclusion V of the central argument: There are neither empirical nor linguistic reasons for sensa.

There was one more task concerning sensa that we could complete without considering metaphysical theories of perception and the external world, namely, to discover whether there are fewer recalcitrant philosophical problems without sensa. Our examination of this issue consisted in showing that there are several quite puzzling and unresolved problems with sensa which are not puzzling and are also more easily resolvable for objectless sensings. This was especially true of the problem of whether or not there are sensa with an indeterminate number of stripes. Once we had shown that sensings avoid such problems, we had justified four of the five conditions that, according to the principle of reason P1, are jointly sufficient for concluding that it is more reasonable to deny than to assert that there are sensa. That is, except for considering whether there are metaphysical reasons for sensa, we had justified the antecedent of the following principle when "entities of kind K" are specified as sensa:

P1. *If* there are no empirical reasons or evidence for the

existence of any entities of kind K, no scientific theoretical
reasons and no metaphysical reasons to assume any
entities of kind K, no linguistic reasons for entities of
kind K, and fewer recalcitrant philosophical problems
without any entities of kind K, *then* it is more reasonable
to deny than to assert that there are any entities of kind K.

In short, our reason for claiming that these four conditions are
met is that it is at least as reasonable to interpret sensations as
objectless sensings, and this not only raises no linguistic problems,
but actually dissolves certain philosophical problems. Much of this
part of the case against sensa depends, therefore, on using this
sensing interpretation of sensory experience. It was for this reason
that I argued at the end of Chapter 8 that the plausibility of my
case for compatible common-sense realism depends in part on
fitting sensings into the presentation view of perception.

On Metaphysical Reasons for Sensa and Principle P1

We can apply P1 to sensa once we ascertain that there are no
metaphysical reasons for sensa. As the central argument asserts,
we can ascertain this by showing that some form of direct realism,
in particular compatible common-sense realism, is at least as
reasonable as any theory of perception and the external world
that requires sensa. We are now ready to show this. We have
already concluded at the end of Chapter 8 that compatible common-
sense realism is at least as reasonable as any form of realism.[1]
Thus, if we can also conclude that it is at least as reasonable as
any form of phenomenalism, we will have succeeded, because we
will have shown that no sensum theory is more reasonable than
compatible common-sense realism. Of course, we need only show
that some form of direct realism is as reasonable as any form of
sensum realism, and that sensing phenomenalism is as reasonable
as any form of sensum phenomenalism, to establish that there is no
metaphysical reason for sensa. We already reached these conclusions at the end of Part II and Part I, respectively. Thus we need
do no more toward this purpose. However, other steps in the

---

[1] It should be noted, however, that this conclusion is contingent on the assumption that
there are no nonmetaphysical, philosophical reasons to reject compatible common-sense
realism. This assumption is challenged and examined briefly later in this chapter.

argument require the stronger conclusion about the compatible theory and so the additional effort is clearly not superfluous.

We have uncovered no reason to prefer any of the three versions of phenomenalism to the four kinds of realism that remain in the competition. At the end of Part I, I rejected both noninstrumental versions of eliminative phenomenalism, but I declined to choose among Berkeleyan reductive phenomenalism and the two remaining versions of the eliminative theory: sensum instrumentalistic phenomenalism and sensing instrumentalistic phenomenalism. At that time, the factors weighing for and against the three theories seemed fairly evenly balanced. Our common-sense intuitions favor the Berkeleyan theory over both instrumentalisms, because of its acceptance of the existence of physical objects. Of course, our intuitions also favor the two sensum theories because they, unlike sensing phenomenalism, agree that there are always some objects experienced. However, the recalcitrant problems raised by the objects they propose, namely, sensa, but avoided by the sensing theory, at least counter-balance this factor. Furthermore, any advantage the Berkeleyan theory might have is cancelled by the problem for a Berkeleyan of fitting into his theory the statements that reductively identify physical objects with sensa, and co-ordinating them with the findings of science, even when it is construed instrumentally. We are now in a much better position than we were at the end of Part I to see just how difficult this problem is. In Chapter 6 we found that a time-gap argument refutes the thesis of the naive realist that we are perceptually acquainted with external objects. This is also the Berkeleyan view, and a time-gap objection can be raised against that version of phenomenalism, as well.

Consider the following argument. If Berkeleyan phenomenalism is true, then someone, s, sees a star at time t, if and only if at t he senses a sensum that is in the group of sensa which is identical with the star. But if at t someone senses a sensum that is in a group of sensa which is identical with a star, then the group and, therefore, the star exists at t. But just as some stars exist unseen, some stars are seen at times they do not exist. Therefore Berkeleyan phenomenalism is false. It seems that a Berkeleyan has at most two ways to counter this argument: he can either deny that some things are seen when they do not exist, or deny that every sensum sensed when an external object is perceived is in the group of sensa that is identical with the object. However, the first alternative seems to be no more viable for a Berkeleyan than it is for a naive realist. Even if all the relevant scientific claims about the distances of remote stars and the speed of light are construed instrumentally, they are nevertheless justified inference tickets, and so the conclusions they warrant are justified. And they warrant the conclusion that some stars do not exist at certain times, times at which they are seen. Because of this, a Berkeleyan might try the second alternative, and argue that the first premise of the preceding argument is mistaken because if a star does not exist at the time someone sees it, then the sensum he senses at that time is not in the group identical with the star. But such a reply also has unhappy consequences, because it forces a Berkeleyan to jetison the thesis that perception is perceptual acquaintance and also requires him to make important changes in those correspondence rules I attributed to him in Chapter 5.

I think a Berkeleyan's best hope for a plausible response is to rely on the distinction between the "loose" sense of 'exist' ('$exist_L$') and the strict sense ('$exist_S$') that I attributed to him in Chapter 5. He might then argue that although in the strict sense a star exists ($exists_S$) when and only when one of its constituent sensa is sensed, this is not true when '$exist_L$' is used. That is, just as some stars $exist_L$ when not perceived, so also some stars are seen when they do not $exist_L$. This response, then, is that the preceding argument is unsound because the premises are true only if they involve an equivocation on these two senses of 'exist.' Furthermore, this Berkeleyan might increase the plausibility of this response by arguing for the conjunction of two statements. The first is his analysis of '$exist_L$', namely:

x $exists_L$ at t = $_{df}$. If someone should perceive (be perceptually acquainted with) everything, then at t he would perceive x.

The second is the following hypothesis:

If some minimally adequate explanation of sensory experience implies that x $exists_L$ (does not $exist_L$) at t, then x $exists_L$ (does not $exist_L$) at t.

This response is somewhat plausible, yet it has some disconcerting consequences. For example, given this response, the sentence

'Some stars exist$_S$ when they do not exist$_L$.' is true. A Berkeleyan, however, could avoid such consequences if he could justify the view that the identity of each physical object with a group of sensa is what I have called elsewhere a "cross-category" identity.[2] That is, physical-object terms belong in a different logical category from sensation terms, including 'group of sensa.' He might then be able to argue that 'exist$_L$' applies meaningfully to physical-object terms but not to sensation terms, and 'exist$_S$' does not apply meaningfully to physical-object terms. Using this modified response, he could brand sentences such as 'Stars exist$_S$ when they do not exist$_L$' as meaningless rather than true, and claim that their being true is not a consequence of his theory because additional premises needed to derive them would be meaningless. One such premise is: If a physical object is identical with a group of sensa, then the physical object exists at t just in case the group exists at t.

The preceding sort of response to the time-gap objection is the best I can find for a Berkeleyan, but it is surely not completely satisfactory. Not only does it seem to be merely an *ad hoc* adjustment, it also has several quite counterintuitive consequences, unless the cross-category claim can be justified. But even if that is accomplished, some bothersome consequences remain, such as the sentence, 'A certain star does not exist$_L$ at t, yet it is nothing but a group of sensa that exists$_S$ at t.' Because of these problems, it seems, therefore, that the Berkeleyan theory is less plausible than the two remaining eliminative theories. We need not debate this point, however, because it is clear that all three theories clearly have deficiencies that compatible common-sense realism lacks. Furthermore, we have found no deficiencies unique to the compatible theory that would overturn this advantage. Consequently, compatible common-sense realism is at least as reasonable as any form of phenomenalism and, as previously claimed, as any form of realism. There is, then, no theory of perception and the external world which is more reasonable than this compatible theory, and, *a fortiori*, as premise VII of the central argument states, this theory is at least as reasonable as any theory that requires sensa. From this we can conclude that there are no metaphysical reasons

[2] See my *Materialism and Sensations* (New Haven: Yale University Press, 1971), pp. 52–53, and the Appendix.

for sensa, and, finally, by P1, that, as conclusion X states, it is more reasonable to deny than to assert that there are sensa.

FINAL CONCLUSION: COMPATIBLE COMMON-SENSE REALISM IS THE MOST REASONABLE THEORY

With VII justified and X derived, we are almost ready to infer conclusion XIII: Compatible common-sense realism is more reasonable than any metaphysical theory of perception and the external world that requires sensa. To do this we use premise XII:

> P2a. *If* (1) a theory, *T*, which does not require entities of kind *K*, is at least as reasonable as any theory that requires entities of kind *K*, (2) it is more reasonable to deny than to assert that there are entities of kind *K*, and (3) the conjunction of the reasons used to justify (1) with the denial of (2) still justifies that *T* is at least as reasonable as such theories, *then T* is more reasonable than any theory that requires entities of kind *K*.

Statements VII and X instantiate the first two conjuncts of the antecedent, and so we need only establish the appropriate instantiation of conjunct (3), namely:

> XI. The conjunction of the reasons used to justify VII with the claim that it is as reasonable to assert as to deny there are sensa, still justifies VII.

The reasons for accepting VII are those stated at the end of Chapter 8 to show compatible common-sense realism is at least as reasonable as any form of realism, and those just used to conclude the theory is at least as reasonable as any form of phenomenalism. In both cases the reasons are that compatible common-sense realism avoids all objections directed at it and avoids those that face its rivals. Then, because there is no other sort of evidence or reason that is available for such metaphysical hypotheses, except for an appeal to our intuitions, I concluded that no rival of the compatible theory is more reasonable than the theory is. Although some of the reasons I used for this conclusion depend on it being as reasonable to accept sensings as to accept sensa, none depend on it being more reasonable to reject than to accept sensa. Thus premise XI is acceptable.

With XI established we can accept conclusion XIII and as a result eliminate those of the remaining seven theories that require sensa, namely, Berkeleyan phenomenalism, sensum instrumentalistic phenomenalism, and compatible sensum realism. We are left only with the two versions of common-sense realism, compatible sensing realism, and sensing phenomenalism. The preceding discussion also shows that we have sufficient reason for accepting premise XIV: Compatible common-sense realism is more reasonable than naive realism and is at least as reasonable as any form of direct or Kantian realism, or sensing phenomenalism.

One crucial premise remains to be justified before reaching the final conclusion. It is XV: Compatible common-sense realism is consistent with more pretheoretical, commonly accepted beliefs than sensing phenomenalism, or Kantian (nondirect) realism, or any other form of direct realism except for naive realism. Using XIV, XV and another principle of reason, P3, we can derive XVII: Compatible common-sense realism is more reasonable than any form of direct realism, Kantian nondirect realism, or sensing phenomenalism. The principle is:

> P3. If a theory, T, is at least as reasonable as another theory, T', and T is consistent with more pretheoretical, commonly accepted beliefs of mankind than T', then T is more reasonable than T'.

Then using XIII and XVII it is an easy step to the final conclusion that compatible common-sense realism is the most reasonable metaphysical theory of perception and the external world.

Premise XV is easy to establish, given two plausible assumptions. First, the two theses of minimal common-sense realism express at least some of these commonly accepted beliefs. Second, another such belief certainly seems to be that science uncovers information about some of the properties and constituents of observable objects, including at least some of the causal factors relevant to perception. The one point at which compatible common-sense realism seems to diverge from commonly held beliefs is its rejection of the claim that all perceived objects are present with their perceivers. However, since none of the remaining competitors include this thesis, it will not affect the decision. Given P3 and these plausible assumptions regarding common sense, it is easy to reject both sensing phenomenalism and incompatible common-sense realism. These two theories require scientific instrumentalism and that is enough, with P3, to justify preferring compatible common-sense realism to both theories. We can, of course, similarly dismiss Kantian realism because of its rejection of scientific realism, but strictly speaking we need not consider it here because it has already been rejected. Incidentally, of the four theories that had remained before applying P3, sensing phenomenalism fares least well by P3, because it requires that there be no objects perceived, either directly or indirectly.

Two Last Competitors: Compatible Common-Sense Realism and Compatible Sensing Realism

The remaining competitor with compatible common-sense realism is compatible sensing realism. The two are remarkably similar, differing only in their view of the role sensing plays in perception. The compatible sensing theory states one causal view of perception, that is, that each event of perceiving is identical with a causal process that begins with the stimulation of a sense organ and ends with a sensing event. The common-sense theory, however, identifies each event of someone immediately perceiving with an event of his having an experience of something, and then identifies such an event with a sensing event. Thus the crucial difference is that one theory implies, but the other denies, that we immediately perceive external physical objects. The sensing theory denies this because, according to it, the relation of perceiving is not simple and unanalyzable as is the relation of immediate perception. Each event of someone perceiving something consists in a complex causal process that includes a series of events that are not identical with any sensory experience.

On the quite reasonable assumption that there is no reason to prefer one of these two theories, independently of considering our commonly accepted beliefs, we can see that compatible common-sense realism is shown to be more reasonable by P3. Of the two theories, only it accords with the common belief that perceiving is a state of sensory awareness rather than a complex series that includes many nonsensory events. That is, only the common-sense theory agrees that we immediately perceive external physical objects. This difference, then, becomes the deciding factor for these two theories, once P3 is applied. Therefore, at last, we can draw the final conclusion that compatible common-sense realism is the most reasonable metaphysical theory cf perception and the external world.

CONCLUDING REMARKS

Although we have reached the final conclusion, we are not yet finished, because two relevant concluding points are still to be made. The first can be generated by considering an objection that this last crucial advantage that compatible common-sense realism has is slim at best and hardly worthy of being the basis for such a strong conclusion. I agree that this is quite a small advantage. However, this is consistent with the conclusion which states that the one theory is more reasonable than any other. But it does not state it is significantly more reasonable. I would agree that the common-sense theory has been shown to be at most slightly more reasonable than compatible sensing realism. Indeed, I do not find that P3 and common sense show compatible common-sense realism to be appreciably more reasonable than incompatible common-sense realism. This is especially true given the very weak nature of the grounds we used to conclude that a qualified version of minimal scientific realism is acceptable. In one sense, then, this "final" conclusion is not final, but merely provisional and tentative. But it is plausible, I firmly believe, based on all the presently available evidence and reasons, and on the three plausible principles of reason. At any one time we can do no better than this, but later, of course, new evidence may arise which will force reconsideration.

My conclusion in this book, as in my last book, *Materialism and Sensations,* is tentative, provisional, and does not provide grounds for a strong preference for one theory. This, I find, is as it should be, not only because of the likelihood of new future evidence, but also because of the kind of problem considered in each book. Both the mind-body problem and the problem of perception and the external world are metaphysical problems, and I have argued elsewhere that these are problems that defy solution.[3] They are what I call "external" problems, that is, problems about what there is, whose resolutions do not depend on the rules of any linguistic

---

[3] See *Metaphysics, Reference, and Language* (New Haven: Yale University Press, 1966), esp. Part III.

framework. They are not problems about the ways we are justified in describing what there is, given, or internal to, some linguistic framework. Rather they are problems about the way things are independent of any linguistic framework. At minimum, to justify a resolution of such a problem requires considering the way different frameworks permit us to describe what there is. Ideally, for resolution, we should escape the jurisdiction of all linguistic frameworks and compare the descriptions available within each framework with the way things are, in order to discover which framework, if any, provides the best, most accurate description of what there is. But this cannot be done for reasons similar to those that show the impossibility of the Lockean task of comparing our sensa with what there is in order to discover resemblances. No empirical or logical investigation, whether linguistic or nonlinguistic, will uncover what is needed, because each is conducted from within some linguistic framework. At best, we must make some assumptions and hopefully they will allow us to conclude that one particular resolution of such a problem is more reasonable than any other. This is what I claim to have done for compatible common-sense realism.

My basic assumptions in this book have been principles P1, P2a, and P3, which I used to test various metaphysical hypotheses. Another sort of assumption that can be used to test metaphysical theses is a theory of reference that enables someone to decide which terms are referring terms, whether a referring term is a denoting term or a descriptive term, and what sorts of entities are the referents of denoting terms (such as, individuals, or sets) and descriptive terms (such as, properties, or sets, or members of sets).[4] In Chapter 1, I claimed I would try to show, by using the three principles of reason but no theory of reference, that one metaphysical hypothesis about perception and the external world is more reasonable than any other. I also said that I would test the surviving hypothesis to see whether it had any counterintuitive implications for a theory of linguistic reference. If it has no such implications, then the plausibility of the thesis is increased because it is consistent with initially credible assumptions about reference.

---

[4] Ibid., esp. Part II. See also my "On the Relevance of Linguistic Reference to Ontology," *Journal of Philosophy* (1969): 700–12; and "Reference and Ontology: Inscrutable but not Relative" *The Monist* (July, 1975).

It is easy to see that compatible common-sense realism requires nothing counterintuitive of a theory of reference. Any implications it has correspond to its common-sense descriptions of perception and the external world. On this view, not only are ordinary color terms referring terms, they also refer to properties of external physical objects. Furthermore, unlike scientific instrumentalists, such as Berkeley and Ryle, a compatible theorist takes the pure theoretical terms of science to be referring terms. The one seeming disagreement with our ordinary intuitions about reference concerns terms for mental images and apparitions. It seems intuitively that some of these terms sometimes succeed in denoting objects, but according to compatible common-sense realism there are no objects for such terms to denote. Nevertheless, a compatible theorist can agree that all sensum terms are referring terms and this is all that can be derived from a theory of reference alone. Discovering whether a referring term actually denotes something requires additional sorts of reasons, such as those we considered for sensa in Chapter 2. Of course, a compatible theorist could also agree with someone like G. A. Paul who argues against taking sensum terms as referring terms because of how they function in language.[5] But the important point for our purposes is that no compatible theorist need disagree with our ordinary intuitions about which terms are referring terms. Thus the consequences of compatible common-sense realism for a theory of reference agree with our initially credible, ordinary intuitions about referring terms. Because of this agreement, the plausibility of the compatible theory is increased somewhat. And, I believe, the independent reasons we found to accept the theory in turn increase the plausibility of any theory of reference that agrees with the consequences that compatible common-sense realism has for reference. In these two areas, in which grounds for decision are so difficult to find, such mutual reenforcement is an important addition to the other slim reasons that are available.

I have argued that any conclusion that some metaphysical thesis is acceptable should be considered to be provisional and tentative. In the particular case of compatible common-sense realism,

---

[5] See G. A. Paul, "Is there a Problem about Sense-Data?" in *Logic and Language*, A. Flew, ed., First Series (Oxford: Basil Blackwell, 1955), pp. 101–16.

however, there is another reason why caution is appropriate. This takes us to the second main concluding point I wish to make. As I remarked in a footnote in Chapter 1 when I stated principle P1, I temporarily assumed that all philosophical reasons for sensa are metaphysical reasons. It is clear, however, that there might be other philosophical reasons for sensa. Furthermore, as pointed out in a footnote in the present chapter, the conclusion that compatible common-sense realism is at least as reasonable as any form of realism is contingent on there being no nonmetaphysical philosophical objections that we have overlooked. It is important, therefore, to consider now what these various sorts of reasons might be. One obvious sort of reason for sensa is epistemological, because sensa have often been introduced on epistemological grounds. Except for such a reason for sensa and an epistemological objection to compatible common-sense realism, I have found only two arguments for sensa—one taken from aesthetics and one from ethics—and one objection to compatible common-sense realism taken from ethics. Let us consider the latter three reasons very briefly before turning to the two epistemological objections.

Properties of Aesthetic Objects and an Argument for Sensa

Certain views in aesthetics imply that there are sensa. Consider a certain landscape painting. Let us call the physical object that consists of canvas stretched over a frame and paint applied to the canvas by the artist, an "art object," and the object to which we attend when we aesthetically appreciate a painting, an "aesthetic object." We can construct the following argument for sensa. I look at this particular painting, and when aesthetically attending to the aesthetic object, I discern that it has great depth, especially where the path winds through the mountains and disappears in a blue haze in the distance. When I examine the corresponding physical art object, however, I discern that it has little depth because it is thin canvas covered with a thin layer of paint. But, of course, no object has both great and little depth. Thus the aesthetic object I perceive is different from the physical art object. But if it is not identical with this physical object, it is clearly not identical with any external physical object. Surely, then, it is most plausible to construe it as a phenomenal object, that is, a sensum or group of sensa. And, of course, this case is not unusual. Therefore, it is reasonable to conclude that the aesthetic objects we experience are sensa, and, *a fortiori*, there are sensa.

To answer this argument definitively requires an extensive excursus into aesthetic theory, which cannot be done here. However, I can roughly indicate one reply to this argument that consists in proposing an alternative construal of this example which is at least as plausible as the one leading to sensa. Thus, as with the previous arguments for sensa, this one also fails to make it more reasonable than not that there are sensa. We can begin the reply by proposing that the sense in which the aesthetic object I experience has great depth is not physical depth. And, of course, someone who argues that aesthetic objects are phenomenal objects would agree with this, because on his view aesthetic objects would have phenomenal depth. But once this is admitted, it seems no more plausible to say that I was attending to a phenomenal object with phenomenal depth than to say that I was attending to an external, physical art object, and because of my aesthetic appreciation of that object, I had a perceptual experience of great physical depth. And, given compatible common-sense realism, my experience of great depth is identical with my great-depth-sensing. But, of course, because of what caused this sensing, I did not immediately perceive great physical depth.

The suggested alternative theory would postulate that this aesthetic object is identical with the art object. It might also state that the art object has, in some sense, great depth. This property might be something like a Lockean secondary quality, that is, a capacity or power. In particular, it would be the capacity of this art object to cause someone who aesthetically attends to the art object to have an experience of great depth. Whether this view of such properties is the most plausible one, cannot be decided here. But it is surely at least as plausible as the view that they are phenomenal properties, and this is all we need to show.

I do not believe that there are any other arguments for sensa, or against compatible common-sense realism derived from aesthetics. It is true that there are special problems in the case of works of art that involve performances, such as symphonies, for determining which objects are the art objects and what their relationships are to aesthetic objects. It might be, for example, that the art objects are the scores and the aesthetic objects we aesthetically appreciate are particular performances that are not identical with the scores. But even if this is correct, I see no reason to claim these aesthetic objects are phenomenal events consisting of phenomenal sounds. It is at least as plausible to say that each aesthetic object is identical with a certain physical event that consists in a series of physical processes involving musical instruments and that results in my having, for example, an experience of great power and brilliance.

Intensity of Pain and an Ethical Reason for Sensa

The second reason for sensa I wish to consider briefly and dismiss quickly comes from ethics. Consider act utilitarianism or any theory that requires us to consider in some way the intensity of pleasure and pain in order to determine what someone ought to do in a particular situation. Following Bentham, it might be plausibly argued that we need something like an hedonic calculus for this purpose, and this requires a quantitative conception of the intensity of individual pleasures and pains. Such a calculus might be used to determine how many negative or positive (let us say) "hedons" of intensity would result from any particular action. This would allow us to determine which of the various alternative actions in a situation would be positively maximal in hedons, and, thereby, allow us to determine which action or actions in that situation maximize happiness. It is surely plausible to think that maximizing happiness is at least relevant to deciding which actions ought to be done, even if it is not the sole criterion for such decisions. Consequently, according to this argument for sensa, it is plausible that the most reasonable ethical standard for evaluating actions requires there to be feelings of pleasure and pain, that is, sensa, which have quantitative properties. And, if this is plausible, then it is also plausible to conclude that sensa are constituents of perceptual experiences.

We must await another time to debate whether quantitative properties of pleasure and pain are relevant to deciding what ought to be done. An attempt to justify an ethical standard deserves an extensive examination of its own. Nor can we debate whether intensities of pleasure and pain sensa are quantitatively measurable. Nevertheless, the science of psychophysics, which we discussed in Chapter 2, gives some reason to think that such a quality is measurable. If it is reasonable to believe that there are discoverable, quantitative psychophysical laws relating quantities of phenomenal brightness of visual sensa to measurable amounts of the physical intensity of light sources, then it is also reasonable to expect there to be discoverable laws relating quantities of phenomenal intensity of pain sensa to measurable features of certain neural events. Of course, such laws would have no practical value in almost all situations involving moral decisions, but rules of thumb relating external stimuli to certain amounts of phenomenal intensity might be helpful.

Let us grant that all the preceding claims about quantities of phenomenal intensity are reasonable, based on expected developments in psychophysics. Nevertheless, it is still no more reasonable to assert than to deny that there are sensa. As we saw in Chapter 2 when discussing psychophysical laws, it is as plausible to construe quantitative features of experience as internal specifications of objectless sensing events, as it is to construe them as properties of sensa. It is as plausible to say that John 10-pounds-senses as it is to say that John senses a 10-P-pound sensum. Similarly, it is as plausible to say that John 10-hedons-of-pain-senses as it is to say that John senses a 10-hedon sensum of pain. Once again, the sensing interpretation seems to be as plausible as the sensum interpretation.

Moral Responsibility as a Reason to Reject Scientific Realism

I know of no other argument from ethics for sensa, but there is one against compatible common-sense realism that should be mentioned. It certainly seems that people have moral obligations to perform certain actions, and, furthermore, that they are morally responsible for at least some of the actions they perform and for some they fail to perform. But, according to the present objection, moral responsibility implies free will and free will implies that those bodily actions that someone does freely are neither causally determined by some preceding event, nor at most causally influenced by and only by certain preceding events. However, if minimal scientific realism is correct, then either all bodily behavior is causally determined, or, given quantum theory, the uncertainty principle, and no hidden variables, it is at most causally influenced by and only by certain preceding events. Therefore, minimal scientific realism and, consequently, compatible common-sense realism are implausible.

This objection cannot be refuted quickly. Someone might try to accomodate it in a Kantian way by interpreting scientific terms to apply merely to phenomenal objects, which are nothing but appearances (or appearings). This allows persons, who are clearly not phenomenal objects, to be "autonomous" and morally responsible. Note, however, that the preceding objection to scientific realism is stronger than Kant's reasoning for scientific phenomenalism. The former uses the plausibility of moral responsibility to argue for the implausibility of minimal scientific realism, while Kant merely postulated scientific phenomenalism to allow for moral responsibility. Obviously, a compatible common-sense realist can accept neither of these ways to accommodate moral responsibility. Furthermore, given the problems we already have seen confronting minimal scientific realism, if the conjunction of that thesis with the claim that people are morally responsible is implausible, then it would seen that we should accept scientific instrumentalism or phenomenalism, and incompatible common-sense realism.

At present I have found only one viable means of avoiding this objection to the compatible theory. This is to argue that whatever sort of freedom is necessary for moral responsibility, it does not entail what is called "contracausal" freedom. The latter is the freedom someone has when, for example, he raises his arm in such a way that he, an individual, rather than some previous event, causes his arm to rise. Although some preceding events might causally influence what he does, none causally determine him to cause the arm to rise. In this sense, the person is an agent who causes events to occur but is not completely causally determined to do so. It certainly seems implausible that minimal scientific realism is true and also that some people have contracausal freedom. But I believe that moral responsibility does not require such freedom. If it requires any sort of freedom, then it is a freedom like that proposed by "soft" determinists, and that sort of freedom is conjointly plausible with minimal scientific realism.

Of course, my belief requires justification. The important step in this direction would be to find certain conditions that, first, clearly justify that a person is morally responsible for a certain action, and, second, do not justify either that the person is contra-causally free or that minimal scientific realism is mistaken. Once this is done, we can conclude that moral responsibility entails neither contracausal freedom, nor the denial of minimal scientific realism, because if certain evidence justifies a statement, S, and S entails P, then the evidence justifies P.[6] And, once the compatibility of moral responsibility and minimal scientific realism is established, I believe we would find no reason to deny that these two are conjointly plausible.

If the preceding series of moves is successful, then we would have avoided the continually plaguing and baffling problem about whether free will and determinism are compatible. We could even grant that human freedom is contracausal freedom, deny that there is any human freedom, yet still plausibly argue for human moral responsibility. But, of course, all this is premised on uncovering justification for moral responsibility that meets the two requirements mentioned above. And this needs its own extensive treatment. Nevertheless, I would like to indicate one approach that seems fruitful. It is like the approach many soft determinists take to attempt to establish the compatibility of free will and determinism. It seems, however, more plausible when applied to moral responsibility and determinism because those grounds for ascribing praise or blame, and reward or punishment to someone for what he does seem to be the grounds for ascribing moral responsibility to him. But clearly, utilitarian grounds for the former ascriptions are not grounds for rejecting either causal determinism or minimal scientific realism. Thus, if, as I now believe, something like utilitarian grounds justify the former ascriptions, then they justify the ascription of moral responsibility, but do not justify the rejection of minimal scientific realism. This approach may not succeed, but at present I see no reason to deny its ultimate success.[7] Consequently, I conclude, again provisionally and tentatively, that the conjunction of minimal scientific realism with the thesis that people are morally responsible is, contrary to the objection we have been considering, plausible.

[6] For an attempt to argue in this way for the compatibility of free will and determinism, see K. Lehrer, "An Empirical Disproof of Determinism?" in *Freedom and Determinism*, K. Lehrer, ed. (New York: Random House, 1966), pp. 175–202.

[7] To see where problems might arise, see the attack on Lehrer, op. cit., and his similar attempt to show the compatibility of free will and determinism, in P. V. Inwagen, "Lehrer on Determinism, Free Will, and Evidence," *Philosophical Studies* (1972): 351–57.

Epistemological Objections to Compatible Common-Sense Realism

With the rejection of reasons for sensa and against compatible common-sense realism taken from aesthetics and ethics, we are left only with the problem of whether there are epistemological reasons of either sort. As with the two reasons taken from ethics, there might be epistemological objections to compatible common-sense realism that are independent of epistemological reasons for sensa. It might be that there are no reasons for sensa, but that the most plausible theory of perceptual knowledge has implausible consequences when conjoined with compatible common-sense realism. If this is so, then it may be that a different theory, perhaps one we have rejected, will avoid these consequences and prove to be the most reasonable theory after all.

It is clear that to establish that there are no epistemological reasons for accepting sensa, or for rejecting compatible common-sense realism requires careful and separate examination of perceptual knowledge. At this time, however, I would like to indicate why I think that none of the metaphysical theories of perception we have considered have any epistemological consequences. These include theories that physical objects are directly perceived—either because perceiving is a causal process ending with sensing or because perceiving is, or implies, perceptual presentation—and the theory that physical objects are indirectly perceived because sensa are immediately perceived. I claim, then, that in an important sense, all these theories are epistemologically neutral. Of course, this alone does not show that no epistemological thesis will provide reasons to reject any of the theories, because two theories that are each plausible separately, and consistent when conjoined, may still be implausible when conjoined. Nevertheless, I hope I can in this way provide enough credibility to my claim to make it reasonable to reject provisionally all epistemological objections against compatible common-sense realism.

I shall try to show that none of the theories of perception we examined entail any claims about whether or not a perceiver either has or lacks knowledge of any sort. In particular, however, I shall concentrate on perceptual knowledge, and will begin by considering the relationships between what we have called (factual) direct perception and what we can call "direct perceptual knowledge." I believe these two concepts are often confused and conflated, perhaps because both are called "direct perception." In the Introduction we saw two examples of such conflation in the construals of 'directly perceive' taken from Russell and Malcolm. These examples illustrate the two basic conceptions of direct perceptual knowledge of an object, namely, noninferential or immediate perceptual knowledge, and perceptual knowledge that is certain. An initial problem for characterizing these concepts is that, generally, it is propositional knowledge that is said to be inferential or not, and certain or not. For example, we might say that John perceptually knows with certainty, or noninferentially, that his chair is red. The problem is how to make sense of saying that John "epistemically" perceives the red chair noninferentially or with certainty. We can get an understanding sufficient for our purposes by using the following rough definition:

> S directly perceives p epistemically at $t =$ $_{df}$. At t, S obtains (noninferential, certain) perceptual knowledge of $p =$ $_{df}$. At t, there is something that S knows (noninferentially, with certainty) about p as a result of perceiving p at t.

Here the second definiens is an attempt to tie nonpropositional epistemic perceiving to propositional knowledge. This leaves the terms 'noninferential' and 'certainty' to be defined. For the first, let us use:

> S knows that Q noninferentially $=$ $_{df}$. S knows that Q, and S would know that Q, even if he should not base it on any evidence other than Q.[8]

There are several alternative definitions of 'certainty,' but for our purposes we can consider just two. First:

> S knows that Q with certainty $=$ $_{df}$. S knows that Q and there is no reason for S to doubt that Q.[9]

[8] Cf. R. Chisholm, *Theory of Knowledge* (Englewood Cliffs, New Jersey: Prentice-Hall, 1966), pp. 26–27.
[9] See A. Quinton, "The Problem of Perception," in *Perceiving, Sensations, and Knowing*, J. Swartz, ed. (New York: Anchor Books, 1965), p. 40.

Second:

> S knows that Q with certainty $=_{df.}$ S knows that Q, and there
> is nothing more reasonable for S to believe than that Q.[10]

It is clear, I find, that (factual) direct perception of p is consistent
both with no knowledge about p, and also with there being perceptual knowledge of p that is inferential and not certain. For
example, if a particular case of someone visually perceiving a rat
that has been painted pink either includes the perceiver immediately
perceiving the pink rat, or is identical with a certain causal process
that ends with his pink-rat-sensing, then this is a case of a direct
perception of the pink rat. But both construals of this situation
are consistent with the claim that the perceiver must in part base
his justification of any of his perceptual claims about the rat on the
facts that he pink-rat-sensed and that this sensing is appropriately
caused. They are also consistent with the claim that it is more
reasonable for him to believe that he pink-rat-sensed, than that he
saw a pink rat. And it is also possible that there is some reason for
him to doubt that he saw a pink rat, if, for example, several people
in the room falsely swear to him that there is no pink rat in the room.
Furthermore, it is even possible he has no knowledge, whether
direct or indirect, about the rat. He might be a sophisticated
drunkard who has had hallucinations of pink rats before, mistakenly believes he is hallucinating again, and so has no true beliefs
about the rat at all. It seems, then, that there is no reason to think
that direct perception, whether interpreted as immediate perception
or as a causal process, has any implications for knowledge. Furthermore, it seems to have no other epistemic consequences, for
example, for what is reasonable. It seems, then, that (factual)
direct perception is a completely nonepistemic notion, and that the
thesis that physical objects are (factually) directly perceived, taken
alone, neither solves nor creates any epistemological problems.

Let us consider whether the same can be said for (factual)
indirect perception of physical objects. It has often been thought
that the way of ideas, from Descartes to Hume, is the road to
skepticism about the external world, because it allows only ideas,
or sensa, to be directly perceived. This is essentially the objection

---

[10] See Chisholm, pp. 19–21.

of Thomas Reid to those who took ideas as the immediate objects of perception. He says that "Descartes' system of the human understanding, which I shall beg leave to call *the ideal system*, and, which, is now generally received, hath some original defect; that this scepticism is inlaid in it, and reared along with it".[11] As we found when discussing Sellarsian indirect realism and epistemology, however, direct perception of sensa only—and consequently, at most indirect perception of physical objects— neither entails nor in some other way leads to skepticism. My (factually) indirectly perceiving my own hand, for example, is compatible with my perceptually knowing both noninferentially and with certainty that this is a hand. While I could try to justify my claim by inference from premises including that I am directly experiencing a hand-like sensum, this would not show I do not know it noninferentially. The important point is whether I need to justify it by inference in order to know it. If I do not need to do that, my knowledge of it is noninferential. This is clearly compatible with my seeing my hand indirectly.

On some epistemological views there are situations in which I can know that this is a hand with certainty. Knowing I am quite normal and the conditions are normal when I perceive my own hand, it is consistent and even plausible to claim that although I indirectly perceive my hand, there is no reason for me to doubt that this is a hand, and, furthermore, that there is nothing more reasonable for me to believe. It might be objected that it would be more reasonable for me to believe that I seem to see my hand and thus I do not know with certainty—in the second sense—that this is a hand. This, however, is an objection to one definition of 'certainty' rather than to my claim that indirect perception of a physical object is compatible with knowing it with certainty. There are no grounds to think that the seeming claim is more reasonable than the claim about my seeing the hand if I indirectly perceive my hand, but that it is not more reasonable if I directly see my hand. It seems, then, that certainty in the second sense should also be rejected for direct perception of my hand, if this objection is sound, and so it would not be indirect perception that precludes certainty.

[11] T. Reid, *An Inquiry into the Human Mind*, Chap. 1, sec. 7.

I think that the preceding discussion gives reason to believe that neither (factual) direct perception, nor indirect perception of something entails any claims about knowledge or lack of knowledge about it. Direct perception of only sensa does not entail skepticism or make it more plausible. Indeed, indirect perception of physical objects is at least compatible with noninferential and certain perceptual knowledge of them. And direct perception of physical objects does not guarantee or even make more plausible the claim that we have some sort of perceptual knowledge of the external world, let alone the claim that our knowledge is noninferential and certain. Of course, such direct perception adds no plausibility to skepticism. It might be objected, however, that both perceptual presentation and therefore perceptual acquaintance have implications for perceptual knowledge. Both views imply that if, in optimal conditions, someone has an experience of something having a certain sensible property, then it has a property that indiscernibly approximates that property. Thus, it might be argued, both theories imply that there are times when perceivers can know that certain objects have properties that approximate certain properties. However, as mentioned when introducing perceptual acquaintance in Chapter 6, a person would lack such knowledge, even if he immediately perceives something and believes he is experiencing it to have the property, if he is not justified in believing that he is normal and conditions are optimal. And, of course, different theories of knowledge will propose different requirements for when such a belief is justified. Thus, mere perceptual presentation and belief do not imply knowledge about external physical objects.

It seems, then, that neither the claim that only sensa are directly perceived, nor the claim that external physical objects are directly perceived in some way, has any epistemological consequences by itself. The various theories of perception are in one clear sense epistemologically neutral. This gives us at least some reason to think that there are no epistemological reasons to reject any of the theories we have considered. We have not, of course, done enough even to begin to see that there is sufficient reason to reject all epistemological objections to these theories, because some of them may yield implausible epistemological consequences when conjoined with certain epistemological theses. Consider the thesis that there is certain perceptual knowledge of something only if it is noninferentially known, and it is noninferentially known only by someone who is perceptually acquainted with it. This thesis conjoined with the claim of compatible common-sense realism that no one is perceptually acquainted with external physical objects implies that any knowledge of physical objects is inferential and uncertain. And if we also assume the Lockean thesis that all warranted inferences are either deductive or inductive by enumeration from what is noninferentially known, we can also draw the implausible conclusion that there is no knowledge of external physical objects. But because these epistemological claims are merely two from among a wide variety of alternative hypotheses, including the Sellarsian epistemological theory, this does not at present provide sufficient reason to reject all theories that do not view perception as perceptual acquaintance. Any such decision must await detailed work in epistemology. Of course, even without such an enterprise, it is clear that if the second part of the preceding thesis is plausibly amended so only perceptual presentation is necessary for noninferential perceptual knowledge, then the resulting thesis has no implausible consequences when conjoined with the compatible common-sense theory. That theory entails that perception of external physical objects is perceptual presentation.

There is also another, similar epistemological thesis that not only has implausible consequences when conjoined with compatible common-sense realism, but also might be used to argue for the acceptance sensa. According to this thesis, there is perceptual knowledge of an external physical object only if there is noninferential and certain knowledge of some object or other, and no knowledge of external objects is certain. And, since only sensa qualify as objects known with certainty, then there is perceptual knowledge, as is reasonable, only if there are sensa. Many objections have been raised about such a foundational view of perceptual knowledge, and this leaves the argument open to doubt.[12] Nevertheless, even granting that perceptual knowledge requires a noninferential and certain basis, and that only sensation statements qualify for this, there is no reason to think that the

---

[12] See W. V. Quine, *From a Logical Point of View* (New York: Harper and Row, 1963), Chap. 3; and B. Aune, *Knowledge, Mind, and Nature* (New York: Random House, 1967), *passim*.

required certain knowledge is knowledge about objects, that is, sensa. Knowledge about events of objectless sensings would fulfill this requirement at least as well. Such a foundational thesis fits plausibly with compatible common-sense realism. So also, it seems, would nonfoundational theories.

CONCLUSION

We have found some reason to think that perceptual presentation of external physical objects has no epistemological consequences, either harmful or helpful. And, based upon our very brief glimpse at epistemological theories, it seems reasonable to conclude provisionally that no viable epistemological theory will generate an objection to the thesis that we immediately perceive external physical objects. Of course, any stronger conclusion must await future detailed work in epistemology. We have, nevertheless, completed the present task. We found no reasons taken from aesthetics, ethics, or epistemology for overturning our previous provisional and tentative conclusion that compatible common-sense realism is the most plausible metaphysical theory of perception and the external world. We have, however, found reason to reaffirm the tentativeness of the conclusion. This, as I said before, is as it should be. Metaphysical problems are not solved independently of all other philosophical problems. Indeed, if my thesis that all metaphysical problems are external is correct, they are not to be solved at all. At any time, the best we can do is to meet the requirement of total available evidence, however meager it may be, and argue for the thesis that is most plausible relative to that evidence. This, and only this, is what I claim to have done here.

Appendix: Compatible Common-Sense Realism and Adverbial Materialism

At the end of *Materialism and Sensations* I concluded provisionally that, although other versions of materialism fail to resolve the problem posed by sensations, there is some reason to believe that the theory I called "adverbial" materialism is plausible. This is the theory that each sensory experience consists in an objectless sensing event that is not only identical with but also nothing but some physical event, presumably a neuronal brain event. I claimed that this conclusion is provisional because there are so many ways it might be overturned in the future. I suggested that future scientific discoveries or theories may give reason to reject the kind of lawlike relationships between sensing events and brain events that are important for justifying the identity claim. Or it might be crucial for future theories to postulate sensa with phenomenal properties instead of sensings. I also suggested that philosophical investigations of science, perception, and persons might show that some form of indirect realism or Berkeleyan phenomenalism is more reasonable than the adverbial sensing theory of sensory experience.

Now, at the end of the present book we are in a position to reevaluate that provisional conclusion about adverbial materialism. We have considerably more evidence now that is based upon our examination of certain scientific theories and upon our conclusion, and the reasons for it, that compatible common-sense realism is the most reasonable metaphysical theory of perception and the external world. We should, then, reexamine the previous conclusion about the plausibility of adverbial materialism in light of this new evidence. Does it provide reason to override the previous reasons for the theory's plausibility, or might it instead strengthen those reasons?

AN ARGUMENT FOR REJECTING EITHER THE COMPATIBLE THEORY OR ADVERBIAL MATERIALISM

Just as we saw that it is incumbent upon a compatible common-sense realist to examine whether minimal common-sense realism is plausibly conjoined with minimal scientific realism, so also it is incumbent on me to see whether this compatible theory plausibly conjoins with adverbial materialism. Initially at least, it might well seem that the resultant combination is implausible. Consider, for example, the following argument:

(1) If adverbial materialism is correct, then each event of red-table-sensing is identical with (let us say) a neuronal brain event.

(2) If compatible common-sense realism is correct, then some red-table-sensing events are identical with events of having an experience of a red table.

(3) No experiencing of a red table is a neuronal brain event.

Therefore

(4) Either adverbial materialism or compatible common-sense realism is incorrect.

Premises (1) and (2) are clearly true, but, of course, (3) is the crucial one. Is there any reason to accept it? Indeed, unless there is some relevant difference between experiencings of a red table and events of red-table-sensing, the reasons I gave (*MS*, pp. 267–76) for the identity of each sensing event with a brain event should also be sound for such experiencings.[1]

The procedure I used to justify that events, e_1 and e_2, are identical is to show that it is plausible to ascribe some extentional properties (that is, properties that are neither intentional nor intensional—see *MS*, pp. 45–46) to both e_1 and e_2, and there is no reason to claim there are properties one event has that the other lacks. To establish this for sensing events and brain events, I examined a variety of extentional properties and claimed it is plausible to ascribe each of them jointly to each sensing event and its appropriate brain event if it is plausible to ascribe it to one or the other event. I considered, for example, the properties of occurring at the same time, being at the same place, being annoying, frightening and disturbing, being an instance of someone sensing, being

---

[1] Throughout the Appendix, I shall use *MS* to refer to my *Materialism and Sensations* (New Haven: Yale University Press, 1971).

identical with a firing of nerve fibers, and being constituted of molecular events. It is true that I did not provide grounds to justify the joint ascription of many of these properties. Instead I often argued that there is no reason for denying the joint ascription, and so it is plausible to assert it. On the basis of these claims I concluded then, and still do, that the identity of sensing events with brain events is plausible. Furthermore, I find now that a similar procedure would provide equally good reasons for the plausibility of the view that each experiencing of something is identical with some brain event. Indeed, the preceding properties, and other similar ones about experiencings are equally plausibly ascribable to an experiencing of something as to its appropriate sensing event and brain event. And again I have found no reason to think there are properties that at least one of these events has and one of them lacks. For this reason, then, we are justified in rejecting (3).

A Second Argument Against Conjoining the Compatible Theory with Adverbial Materialism

The preceding objection fails. The identity claim that is required by the conjunction of adverbial materialism and compatible common-sense realism is plausible. Yet that is not the end of the matter, because adverbial materialism has two other important implications. Adverbial materialism requires not only that sense experience be construed adverbially and that each sensing event be identical with a physical (brain) event, but also that each sensing event is reduced to—is nothing but—a physical event. According to my definition of 'nothing but' in *Materialism and Sensations* (*MS*, p. 61), this third requirement is that for each extentional property of a sensing event, either it is materialistic, or each of its instances is identical with an instance of a materialistic property and this instance has only materialistic properties.[2] By 'materialistic property' I mean a property that is either a physical property or a physical-neutral property. By the latter I mean a property for which there are conditions in which it would be a property of a physical entity and also conditions in which it would be a property of something that is not physical (see *MS*, p. 8). Some examples are

---

[2] An instance of a property such as redness is not to be understood as what exemplifies redness, such as some table. Rather it is the nonrepeatable, particular bit of red color that is located where and when the red table is located.

the properties of occurring at some time, being frightening, being aesthetically pleasing, and being morally good.

Note that in unpacking this third requirement for adverbial materialism, I did not claim that a sensing event is nothing but a brain event only if all its properties are materialistic. As I shall explain when discussing the fourth requirement, reduction is not defeated when some extentional properties exemplified by sensing events are not materialistic, *if* the actual instances of those properties have, themselves, only materialistic properties.

This characterization of what it is for one event, e_1, to be nothing but an event, e_2, corresponds to what it is for one individual, o_1, to be nothing but an individual, o_2. It is this reduction of individuals that is crucial for all reductive versions of materialism—including adverbial materialism—as stated in the characterization I gave of materialism:

> Materialism = $_{df.}$ For each *a posteriori* property P of an existing individual, (a) P is materialistic (either physical or physical-neutral), or (b) each instance of P is nothing but an instance of a physical or physical-neutral property (see *MS*, p. 9).

For adverbial materialism, which rejects all phenomenal individuals such as red sensa, mental images, and pains, the crucial individuals are persons and other sentient beings who have non-materialistic properties such as the property of red-table-sensing. Consequently, the fourth requirement for adverbial materialism was stated to be that each instance of the nonmaterialistic property of sensing is identical with an instance of a materialistic property, and all the extentional properties of this instance are materialistic.

Clause (b) in the characterization of materialism is crucial for the fourth requirement. It might seem that (a) alone is required for reduction, but I find that this would be too restrictive. No logically contingent reduction of an individual is even initially plausible if all its properties must be materialistic, because each person has at least one nonmaterialistic property, such as the property of red-table-sensing. Furthermore, it also seems unreasonable to require that this property be reducible to a materialistic property M, especially if, as has been argued, this reduction requires that 'x red-table-senses' is logically equivalent to 'x has M.' For the most plausible version of adverbial materialism, this would require that each property of sensing in some way would have to be logically equivalent to some property of having certain neuronal firings. But the relationship seems clearly logically contingent. Because of this, I suggested that in such cases, if all actual instances of the property of sensing are also instances of the property of having neuronal firings and none of these instances have nonmaterialistic properties, then the fact that persons have the nonmaterialistic and nonreduced property of sensing is no obstacle to a materialistic reduction of persons. I also speculated about whether such a reduction of all instances of a property might justify, although not entail, a reduction of the property (see *MS*, pp. 116 and 255–56), but I reached no conclusion about this then and do not now.[3]

The fourth requirement, which, in some form or other, all reductive versions of materialism share, gives rise to an objection that can be directed against all reductive versions and thus against adverbial materialism. For that theory, the objection is that when a person red-table-senses, then he exemplifies the property of red-table-sensing, and so there are instances of this property if adverbial materialism is correct. But if compatible common-sense realism is correct, such instances have nonmaterialistic properties, contrary to adverbial materialism. Consequently either adverbial materialism or this compatible theory is incorrect. In more detail:

(1) If adverbial materialism is correct, then there are instances of S, the property of red-table-sensing.

(2) S is not a materialistic property.

(3) If compatible common-sense realism is correct, then some instance i, of S, has property P, the property of being an instance of perceiving a (sensuously) red table.

(4) P is extentional but not materialistic.

(5) If adverbial materialism is correct, then each extentional property exemplified by any instance of a nonmaterialistic property of a person is materialistic.

Therefore

(6) Either adverbial materialism or compatible common-

---

[3] I discuss in more detail criteria for property identity in "In Search of Criteria for Property Identity and Difference" (unpublished).

sense realism is incorrect.

Premise (1) is clearly acceptable on the justified assumption that some persons do have experiences of a red table. And, given the preceding definitions of 'materialism' and 'nothing but,' (5) merely spells out a consequence of adverbial materialism. Premise (2) is also justified because properties such as S are neither physical nor physical-neutral. S is not physical, given two assumptions I made. First, roughly, something is not a physical property of an individual if it is a property that an animate being (or undetached part of one) has only when it is alive (see MS, p. 12). Second, an animate being has the property of sensing only when it is alive. This also shows S is not physical-neutral, because it shows that there are no conditions in which it would be a property of a physical object. By definition (see MS, p. 14), no physical object has a property that an animate being has only when alive, and so, no matter under what conditions something has such a property, it is not a physical object. It was because of properties such as S that I claimed a materialistic reduction of persons would have no chance if the reduction required that all extentional properties of individuals be materialistic.

There are, however, objections to premises (3) and (4). The consequent of (3) is not entailed by compatible common-sense realism. While it entails that each event of someone having an experience of a red table is identical with an event of the person red-table-sensing, this is consistent with all such sensing events occurring without anyone perceiving a red table. Thus the theory is compatible with no instance of S having property P. But it is surely reasonable to claim that some persons occasionally perceive red tables when they red-table-sense, and so we can assume that if the compatible theory is correct, then some events of red-table-sensing are events of perceiving red tables. Nevertheless, even with this assumption, (3) does not express an entailment, because its antecedent is consistent with instance i not having property P, because i is not identical with j, the corresponding instance of the property of perceiving a red table. Again, however, it seems unreasonable to deny the identity, especially given the assumption that the corresponding events are identical. So it is reasonable to accept that the consequent of (3) is true if compatible common-

sense realism is correct. Furthermore, even if we should deny that
i is identical with j, this would not help adverbial materialism,
because j is an instance of a nonmaterialistic property, and so
adverbial materialism would require that it be identical with some
instance of a materialistic property. But i would be identical with
the only plausible candidate, namely, the corresponding instance
of some property regarding certain neuronal firings. We can
assume, then that (3) is reasonable, although not logically necessary, because it is reasonable that if compatible common-sense
realism is correct, then i is identical with j.

Examination of Premise (4) and the Definition of 'Nothing But'

Only (4) remains to be examined. It is clear that P is extentional
because no sentence resulting from substituting a singular term for
'x' in 'x is an instance of perceiving a red table' is either intensional
or intentional. That is, roughly, there is substitution *salva veritate*
in the sentence 'a is an instance of perceiving a (sensuously) red
table,' where 'a' is a singular term (see *MS*, pp. 45–46). The one
remaining question, then, is whether P is either a physical or
physical-neutral property of instances. It is not physical because
no animate being has any instance with such a property when the
being is not alive, and this is because no animate being has the
property of perceiving a red table when the being is not alive. This
also shows that P is not a physical-neutral property of instances.
If some animate being has an instance with this property only when
alive, then no physical object has an instance with this property,
and so there are no conditions in which P would be a property of
an instance that a physical object has. This, I claim, is sufficient for
P not being a physical-neutral property of instances. It would
seem, therefore, that (4) and, consequently, (6) are justified.

There is, however, an objection to (4) that can be taken from an
argument I previously used. I argued that certain properties, such
as being an instance of (or example of) an event of someone
hurting, are physical-neutral. But if this is correct, then surely the
property of being an instance of perceiving a (sensuously) red table
is physical-neutral and (4) is false. I agree that this is a correct *ad
hominem* argument against what I previously said, but I deny it
refutes (4). This is because I now find that my previous argument
is mistaken. Although it justifies that the previously mentioned

properties are *irrelevant* to the reduction of certain entities that have
them, this does not show those properties to be physical-neutral.
I stated the argument, using an analogy with the reduction of water
to H_2O molecules, as follows:

> Consider the reduction of something observable to something
> theoretical, such as the reduction of water to conglomerations
> of H_2O molecules. Given that at any one time each volume of
> water is identical with some conglomeration of H_2O molecules,
> and that we are justified in either "transferring" all the
> observation properties of water to sensa or "transforming"
> them into modes of sensing, the mere fact that this conglomera-
> tion of H_2O molecules is identical with, and is an instance
> and an example of water would not refute the reduction. If all
> the other properties of each volume of water were theoretical
> or theoretical-neutral, as is clearly possible, then having these
> three properties would not stop the reduction. Thus something
> theoretical could have these properties, and because water with
> pure observation properties could also have these properties,
> they are theoretical-neutral. It is also possible that all the other
> properties of every event that is identical with, or an instance
> or example of someone hurting are physical and physical-
> neutral. Thus, by similar reasoning, we can conclude that all
> three properties are physical-neutral (*MS*, pp. 269–70).

A parallel argument would apply to the property of being an
instance of the property of hurting (see *MS*, p. 277).

What I find correct in this argument is that it is unreasonable to
reject the claim that water is nothing but something theoretical if
the only nonreductive (neither theoretical nor theoretical-neutral)
properties of water are the three mentioned in the argument. Such
properties, I would say, are irrelevant to the reduction of water to
something theoretical. What is mistaken in the argument is the
inference from this irrelevance to the conclusion that such properties are theoretical-neutral. They clearly are not. The property of
being an instance of water is a nontheoretical, observation property,
and so nothing that has it is a theoretical entity, although, of
course, it may be reducible to a theoretical entity. Similarly, the
property of being an instance of hurting is not physical-neutral,
for the same reasons that I used to show that property P is not

physical-neutral.

My making the mistaken inference is explained, if not excused, by the previously mentioned definition of 'nothing but' that I proposed (see *MS*, p. 61). In detail, it is:

> An instance i of something S is nothing but an instance j of something else T that is ϕ or ϕ-neutral $=_{df.}$ i is identical with j and all extentional properties of i are reductive (that is, are either ϕ or ϕ-neutral).

If this definition is used, there is no way to show that any non-reductive properties are irrelevant to the reduction of water to H_2O molecules. Assume that all extentional properties of all instances of water, other than the three mentioned in the preceding argument, are either physical or physical-neutral. But the property of being an instance of water is extentional and neither theoretical nor theoretical-neutral. Therefore, by the above definition, no instance of water is reducible to anything that is theoretical, such as a group of H_2O molecules. A parallel argument would prevent the reduction of anything of one kind to something of a different kind, regardless of what other properties the entity has. This is surely an unreasonable conclusion.

We can avoid the preceding conclusions by realizing that something i is nothing but something j if all the nonreductive properties of i are irrelevant to its reduction to j. Consequently, we should revise the definition of 'nothing but' appropriately. We can do this by changing the second conjunct of the definiens to read:

> all extentional properties of i are either reductive or irrelevant to the reduction of any instance of S to an instance of T.

This amendment leaves us with the task of determining what it is for a property to be irrelevant to a reduction. Unfortunately, I have not found an adequate definition, but I believe I can state one sufficient condition and another necessary condition for cases of logically contingent identity.[4]

---

[4] In saying an identity is logically contingent, I mean only that both the corresponding identity statement and its denial are logically possible, that is, neither is a logical truth, or, more broadly, analytic. This lets the identity be metaphysically necessary in Kripke's sense, for which see S. Kripke, *Semantics of Natural Language* (N.Y.: Humanities Press, 1972), pp. 253–355.

I propose the following sufficient condition:

> If each A is identical with some B but 'Some A is not a B' is logically possible, then the property P is irrelevant to the reduction of an A to a B if 'Something is an A just in case it has P' is logically necessary.

On the assumption that 'Each instance of sensing is an instance of neuronal firing' is true but not logically necessary, this criterion allows us to say that the property of being an instance of sensing is irrelevant to the reduction of such instances to instances of neuron firing. This is because the sentence 'Something is an instance of sensing just in case it has the property of being an instance of sensing' is logically necessary. Notice, incidentally, why this sufficient condition is not also necessary. Certain instances of the property of sensing have the property of being an instance of the property of red-table-sensing. I would claim that the property of being such an instance is also irrelevant to the reduction of each instance of sensing to an instance of neuronal firing, assuming, of course, that each sensing is a neuronal firing. But it would be relevant if the preceding sufficient condition were also necessary, because the sentence 'Something is an instance of sensing and does not have the property of being an instance of red-table-sensing' is logically possible. Nevertheless, I do believe that a similar condition is necessary but not sufficient. I propose:

> If each A is identical with some B but 'Some A is not a B' is logically possible, then the property P is irrelevant to the reduction of an A to a B only if either 'All A's have the property P' or 'Everything having the property P is an A' is logically necessary.

It can be seen that this necessary condition is not sufficient by realizing that for any set of nonreductive properties, $P_1 \ldots P_n$, which an A has, that A can be described as an A with the properties $P_1 \ldots P_n$. But then, for $1 \leqslant i \leqslant n$, any sentence of the form 'All A's with the properties $P_1 \ldots P_n$ have the property P_i' is logically necessary. Consequently each A with any set of properties could be reduced to anything one chooses because each of the properties would be irrelevant to the reduction.

We have refuted the objection to premise (4) that property P

is physical-neutral and accommodated what is right in the argument I previously used to show it is physical-neutral. However, although premise (4) is acceptable, the change I made in the definition of 'nothing but' falsifies (5). We must replace it with:

> (5a) If adverbial materialism is correct, then each exten-. tional property exemplified by any instance of a nonmaterialistic property of a person is either materialistic or irrelevant to the reduction of the instance to something physical or physical-neutral.

Although (5a) is true, it requires a corresponding change in (4):

> (4a) P is extentional, not materialistic, but relevant to the reduction of instance i to something physical or physical-neutral.

Having justified (4), we have only to show that P is relevant to the reduction of i in order to justify (4a). But it is easy to see P is relevant because it instantiates the denial of the preceding necessary condition for being irrelevant. That is, the two sentences 'Some instance of sensing does not have the property of being an instance of perceiving a red table' and 'Some entity having the property of being an instance of perceiving a red table is not an instance of sensing' are logically possible. Thus (4a) is justified, and because the other premises are also justified, we should accept the conclusion and reject either adverbial materialism or compatible common-sense realism. But which one should we reject?

REASONS FOR REJECTING ADVERBIAL MATERIALISM

It might be argued that I, at least, should conclude it is more reasonable to reject adverbial materialism than the compatible theory, because I argued that the compatible theory is the most reasonable theory of perception and the external world, but I only concluded in *Materialism and Sensations* that adverbial materialism is the most reasonable form of materialism. But this is no reason for me to reject adverbial materialism, because nothing I claimed in *Materialism and Sensations* gave any reason to claim that the theory is not the most reasonable resolution of the mind-body problem. This argument can be considerably strengthened, however, by using some of the results of our present discussion of perception. If it is more reasonable to accept the adverbial theory than the compatible theory, then there should be some acceptable theory of perception that combines plausibly with adverbial materialism. But there seems to be none available. For all the perception theories we examined and found to be somewhat plausible, perceiving consists wholly or in part either in adverbial sensing or in sensing sensa. But because sensum theories are incompatible with adverbial materialism, the only alternative to the sensing thesis of the common-sense theory is one (as in compatible sensing realism) where a sensing event is merely one part of a complex causal event that is identical with a perceiving event. However, the preceding argument to show we should reject either adverbial materialism or the perceptual thesis of compatible common-sense realism, can easily be adapted to accommodate the claim that perceiving events are complex causal events that include sensing events. We need only replace the phrase referring to property P throughout the argument with: 'the property of being an instance of the property of being the sensory component in perceiving a red table.' We can conclude from this that no acceptable perceptual thesis conjoins plausibly with adverbial materialism, and so we should reject that theory in favor of compatible common-sense realism, unless we find that the latter does not conjoin plausibly with any resolution of the mind-body problem. Furthermore, barring such a finding, we should reject materialism altogether because adverbial materialism is its most plausible species.

It might be objected that this would be too quick a rejection of materialism because it ignores one sort of theory of perceiving that is designed to conjoin plausibly with materialism, that is, belief theories. If one such theory is correct, then perceptual events are nothing but certain causal processes that end with perceptual beliefs or inclinations to have perceptual beliefs. And if such beliefs and inclinations are reducible to bodily dispositions to behave in certain ways, then perceptual events are nothing but certain physical, causal processes that end with certain physical dispositions. However, I have already indicated in Chapter 8 my reasons for thinking that belief theories are implausible. Furthermore, even if it is granted that each perceptual sensory state—whether objectless, or with sensa—is identical with a state of having a perceptual belief or inclination, and that each such belief-state is identical with some disposition to behave in a certain way, it is implausible that these dispositions are nothing but physical dispositions. As I pointed out in *Materialism and Sensations* when examining analytical behaviorism (see *MS*, pp. 132–43), it is reasonable to reject any attempts to eliminate or reduce sensory states by means of analyzing sensation sentences in terms of sentences using only physical disposition terms. And a modification of the preceding argument against conjoining adverbial materialism with compatible common-sense realism will provide reason to reject a contingent materialistic reduction of beliefs that are identical with sensory states. First, it is surely plausible that, even if all sensory states are identical with beliefs or dispositions, some perceivers nevertheless have either the property of red-table-sensing or the property of sensing a red-table-like sensum. Second, it is also quite plausible that some instances of one of these properties have the property of being an instance of (the sensory component in) perceiving a red table. But because these two claims are plausible, then it is also plausible that, contrary to materialism, some instances of nonmaterialistic properties that some perceivers exemplify have extentional, relevant, nonmaterialistic properties.

AN EXAMINATION OF NONMATERIALISTIC RESOLUTIONS OF THE MIND-BODY PROBLEM

The two remaining questions are whether some mind-body theories conjoin plausibly with compatible common-sense realism, and, if some do, whether one conjunction is more reasonable than the others. It might seem that a compatibilist is forced to a dualism once he rejects adverbial materialism, and then he faces the well-known objections that refute dualism. However, I find not only that the objections to dualism do not damage it irreparably, but also that a compatibilist can plausibly avoid dualism. Consider first a nonreductive, monistic, adverbial theory. As I argued in *Materialism and Sensations* and again just now when refuting the first argument against combining adverbial materialism with compatible common-sense realism, there are no objections to nonreductively identifying each sensing event with an event of neurons firing. This is because a nonreductive identification allows sensing events and the perceivers who sense to have nonreduced instances of nonmaterialistic properties.

Let us call this nonreductive identity theory "adverbial neutral monism." On this view, each sensing event is identical with some neuronal event, but no instance of the property of red-table-sensing is reduced to any instance of the property of being a neuronal firing. Thus this neutral theory does not have the consequence of adverbial materialism that gives rise to the preceding objection. Some neuronal events have nonreduced instances of nonmaterialistic properties, such as being an event of red-table-sensing and being an event of perceiving a (sensuously) red table. And, in addition, each sensing event has nonreduced instances of physical properties, such as being a neuronal firing and being composed of microphysical events. It is because this theory states that these events have nonreduced instances of both physical and nonmaterialistic properties that I call it a "neutral" identity theory. These "neutral" events might be considered somewhat analogous to certain events that occur if the first thesis of the compatible common-sense theory is correct. Consider the event of painting something red. According to the compatible theory, this one event has the property of being an event of someone spreading sensuously red paint on the surface of something and also the property of being an event of one group of molecules being moved across another group of molecules. In both cases the very same event is a complex microphysical event and also an event involving sensuous redness. Thus in neither case are these events nothing but microevents.

On Conjoining the Compatible Theory with Adverbial Neutral Monism

We have just seen that the adverbial neutral theory is plausible, but this does not show that it conjoins plausibly with compatible common-sense realism. Indeed, there is one—and I find only one—objection to such a combination. It is basically the same objection that was raised in Chapter 8 against identifying each event of immediately perceiving a physical object with some sensing event. The problem is that for someone to perceive immediately an object is for him to have a certain simple and unanalyzable relationship to the object. But neuronal brain events are constituted of complex systems of microphysical events. Thus, according to the objection, no such complex events are identical with events that consist in one entity having a simple relationship to another. So, assuming there are events of both sorts, as the compatible theory states, what results is a dualism of mental and physical events.

The reply to this objection uses two premises. The first, which was justified in Chapter 8, is that each relational event of immediately perceiving something is nonreductively identical with some sensing event. I likened such identities to those where an event of someone talking is identical with a relational event for which the event of talking, under certain conditions, is a criterion, namely, an event of the person marrying two people. Similarly, I argued, a certain event of my red-table-sensing is both identical with and, under certain conditions, a criterion for a relational event of my immediately perceiving a red table.

I have just argued for the plausibility of the second premise: each event of red-table-sensing is nonreductively identical with some neuronal event. This identity claim, conjoined with the first premise, entails that each event of immediately perceiving something is nonreductively identical with some neuronal event. And because I see no objection to conjoining the two premises, I conclude that it is plausible to accept what they entail. The view that results is that certain complex microevents are not only neuronal brain events, they are also more, because they are red-table-sensings and also experiencings of a red table. And under appropriate conditions they are even more, because they succeed in being events of immediately perceiving a red table. This is something like what we saw in the example of how an event of painting something red could be more than a complex series of molecular motions because it could also be an event of spreading sensuously red paint on the object. Indeed, in some cases it could be even more, namely, when it succeeds in being an event of an artist creating a certain work of art.

Reasons for Rejecting Dualistic Theories

I find the preceding reply sufficient to reject the previous objection, but it is not completely satisfactory because it does not fully dispel the mystery of how one event can be a neuronal event, a sensing event, and also an event of immediately perceiving an external object. This obscurity results in part because of my dependence on the unclear concept of a criterion and my claim that certain events are identical with the events for which they are criteria. It might well seem, then, that although it is somewhat plausible to combine the compatible theory with adverbial neutral monism, it would be clearly more plausible to conjoin it with some form of dualism. If this were done, the criteriological mystery would be avoided, because for a dualist there would be two distinct events, one a complex physical event and one involving the simple relationship of perceiving. There are, however, objections to the two most plausible versions of dualism—dualistic interactionism and epiphenomenalism—that show neither of them to be more plausible than adverbial neutral monism.[5]

If sensing events causally interact with brain events but are distinct from all physical events, then it is especially puzzling how such events can causally affect the body. It seems most plausible to postulate that they affect nerve impulses in the brain and thereby affect bodily responses to what is perceived. However, not only is such an effect puzzling, there also seems to be good reason to think there is no need to postulate it in order to explain perceptual responses. As indicated in Chapter 2 when considering a modification of Gibson's theory of perceptual systems, there seems to be no explanatory need for sensings or sensa in addition to brain entities. However, the most serious problem is that the most plausible accounts of how such sensings would affect the brain seem clearly to violate two basic conservation principles of science. For example, if a phenomenal event of my red-sensing affects my brain by causing a series of neuronal firings to begin, then not only is it quite mysterious how this phenomenal event excites neurons to fire, but also such a stimulation of neurons would seem to violate the principle of the conservation of energy. For a phenomenal event to cause neurons to fire is to change the total energy of the affected neurons without any corresponding change of energy in the cause, which because it has no mass, has no energy.

Another possibility is that this phenomenal sensing event affects my brain merely by changing the relative distribution of resistance at certain synapses so the paths of certain nerve impulses through

---

[5] I have discussed these problems at a somewhat elementary level in *Philosophical Problems and Arguments: An Introduction*, 2nd edition (New York: Macmillan Publishing Co., 1974), pp. 243–79.

the brain is changed.[6] If this is what occurs, there is no change in the overall energy in the brain so the principle of the conservation of energy is not violated. Nevertheless a change in the total momentum of the affected nerve impulses would not only be brought about in a quite puzzling manner, but it would also violate the principle of the conservation of momentum. To change the direction that something is traveling is to change its momentum and, according to this principle, such a change requires a corresponding change in the momentum of the cause of the change. But lacking mass, a phenomenal event has no momentum, and so this would be a case where momentum is not conserved.

It is clear that adverbial neutral monism avoids these problems. Consequently, although it is somewhat mysterious how one event is a complex of microevents and also an event of my immediately perceiving something, the corresponding mysteries and additional problems confronting interactionism are sufficient to show that it is more reasonable to conjoin compatible common-sense realism with the neutral theory than with interactionism.

Epiphenomenalism remains to be considered. It avoids the preceding crucial objection to interactionism by viewing sensing events as phenomenal by-products of brain activity that causally affect nothing at all. Nevertheless, one objection is that it is somewhat mysterious why some activities of certain molecular structures result in such emergent nonmaterialistic events. Indeed, such emergent events seem no less puzzling than the corresponding emergent, nonmaterialistic properties of events that confront the neutral theory when it is conjoined with compatible common-sense realism. Furthermore, epiphenomenalism, unlike the neutral theory, is also faced with Feigl's objection that it requires nomological danglers; that is, it requires effects that are not part of any continuing causal chain of events and are not needed for either explanation or prediction of any human behavior. I agree that, all else being equal, a theory that avoids such danglers is to be preferred, but I find that neither this nor the first objection is fatal. Nor, by itself, is the objection that epiphenomenalism has consequences that conflict with our strongly felt beliefs that our

[6] C. D. Broad considers this thesis in *The Mind and Its Place in Nature* (London: Routledge and Kegan Paul, 1962), pp. 107–08.

sensory experiences often affect our bodily responses in significant ways. Nevertheless, because the first two objections have some force, they warrant the conclusion that it is at least as reasonable to conjoin the compatible theory with the neutral theory as with epiphenomenalism. Then we can use this conclusion with the third objection to epiphenomenalism and with principle of reason, P3, that favors common sense, to conclude that the combination of the compatible theory with the neutral theory—which agrees with our belief that sensory experience affects behavior—is more reasonable than the combination of the compatible theory with epiphenomenalism.

CONCLUSION: ACCEPTANCE OF THE NEUTRAL VERSION OF COMPATIBLE COMMON-SENSE REALISM

I have argued that it is unreasonable to adopt any form of materialism if one accepts compatible common-sense realism and that it is more reasonable to reject the former than to reject the latter. I have also argued that adverbial neutral monism plausibly conjoins with the compatible theory and that no dualistic theory combines with it as plausibly. Consequently, with its most plausible competitors defeated, I conclude that what we can call the "neutral version" of compatible common-sense realism is the most reasonable metaphysical theory of mind, perception, and the external world. Of course, for reasons that I indicated previously in this book and in *Materialism and Sensations,* this conclusion is tentative and provisional.

Bibliography

(Compiled by Steven A. Kaufman)

This is a selective bibliography. References are classified according to the topics to which they are germane. The topics are listed roughly in the order in which they are taken up in the text. For a very helpful review article with extensive bibliography, see P. Machamer, "Recent Work on Perception," *American Philosophical Quarterly* 7 (1970): 1–22.

ON SENSA

Arguments for the Existence of Sensa

EMPIRICAL NON-THEORETICAL ARGUMENTS

An extensive bibliography on this topic can be found in J. Cornman, *Materialism and Sensations* (New Haven: Yale University Press, 1971), pp. 339–342 under the heading "Arguments for the Existence of Sensa." Chapter 6 of *Materialism and Sensations* includes a detailed discussion, and subsequent rejection of these arguments.

These arguments are discussed at great length, and then rejected, in C. W. K. Mundle, *Perception: Facts and Theories* (Oxford: Oxford University Press, 1971), Chaps. 2 and 5.

A recent defense of the argument from illusion is presented in M. Kiteley, "The Argument from Illusion: Objects and Objections," *Mind* 81 (1972): 191–207. Another recent argument for the existence of sensa is presented in O. R. Jones, "After Images," *American Philosophical Quarterly* 9 (1972): 150–158.

SCIENCE-BASED ARGUMENTS

Arguments for the existence of sensa based upon theories of the psychology of perception are presented by J. Eccles in *The Brain and the Unity of Conscious Experience* (Cambridge: Cambridge University Press, 1965); W. R. Brain in *The Nature of Experience* (Oxford: Oxford University Press, 1959); and "Space and Sense-Data," *British Journal for the Philosophy of Science* 11 (1960): 177–191; J. R. Smythies in *Analysis of Perception* (London: Routledge and Kegan Paul, 1956); and "The Representative Theory of Perception", in J. R. Smythies, ed., *Brain and Mind* (London: Routledge and Kegan Paul, 1965), pp. 241–256; J. J.

Gibson in *The Senses Considered as Perceptual Systems* (Boston: Houghton, Mifflin, 1966), Chap. 14; and "New Reasons for Realism," *Syntheses* 17 (1967): 162–172; and G. M. Wyburn, R. W. Pickford and R. J. Hirst in *Human Senses and Perception* (Toronto: University of Toronto Press, 1964), Part II.

Arguments based on the physiology of perception are presented by W. R. Brain in *Mind, Perception, and Science* (Oxford: Blackwell, 1951), Chap. 1; R. L. Gregory in *Eye and Brain* (London: Winfield and Nicolom, 1966); and G. M. Wyburn, R. W. Pickford and R. J. Hirst in *Human Senses and Perception,* Part I.

J. J. Gibson assumes sensa (pictorial images) to explain "seeing in perspective" in "Pictures, Perspective, and Perception," *Daedalus* 89 (1960): 216–227; and *The Senses Considered as Perceptual Systems,* Chap. 14. Explanations of seeing in perspective which do not invoke sensa can be found in E. H. Gombrich, *Art and Illusion* (London: Phaedon, 1962), Chap. 8; M. Luckiesh, *Visual Illusion* (N. Y.: Dover, 1965), Chap. 7; N. Goodman, *Languages of Art* (N. Y.: Bobbs-Merrill, 1968), pp. 10–19; and M. H. Pirenne, "The Scientific Basis of Leonardo Da Vinci's Theory of Perspective," *British Journal for the Philosophy of Science* 3 (1952): 169–216.

Berkeley argues for the existence of sensa from considerations of the visual field in *Essay Towards a New Theory of Vision* in A. A. Luce and T. E. Jessop, eds., *The Works of George Berkeley,* vol. I (Edinburgh: Thomas Nelson and Sons, 1948–1957). Berkeley's account is criticised in D. M. Armstrong, *Berkeley's Theory of Vision* (Parkville: Melbourne University Press, 1960). More recent arguments based on considerations of the visual field are presented by J. J. Gibson in *The Perception of the Visible World* (London: Allen and Unwin, 1950). Gibson's account is criticised by E. G. Boring in "Visual Perception as Invariance," *Psychological Review* 59 (1952): 141–148. Gibson responds to this criticism in "The Visual Field and the Visual World: A Reply to Professor Boring," *Psychological Review* 59 (1952): 149–151. A later statement of Gibson's views can be found in *The Senses Considered as Perceptual Systems,* Chap. 14. Other arguments based on consideration of the visual field are discussed in D. W. Hamlyn, "The Visual Field and Perception," *Aristotelian Society,* Supplementary Volume 31 (1957): 107–124; and A. C. Lloyd, "The Visual Field and Perception," *Aristotelian Society,* Supplementary Volume 31 (1957): 125–144.

Much of the work in the science of psychophysics seems to presuppose the existence of sensa. For example, see L. Hurvich and D. Jameson, *The Perception of Brightness and Darkness* (Boston: Allen and Unwin, 1966), Chap. 1; T. W. Reese, "The Application of the Theory of Physical

Measurement to the Measurement of Psychological Magnitudes," *Psychological Monographs* 55 (1943); and S. S. Stevens and E. H. Galanter, "Ratio Scales and Category Scales for a Dozen Perceptual Continua," *Journal of Experimental Psychology* 54 (1957): 377–411.

S. S. Stevens and H. Davis, *Hearing: Its Psychology and Physiology* (N.Y.: John Wiley and Sons, 1938), Chapter 1, contains an argument that sounds, etc. are not properties of physical objects. In A. L. Comrey, "Mental Testing and the Logic of Measurement," *Educational and Psychological Measurement* 11 (1951): 323–334, an argument is given that psychophysics is involved with the measurement of nonphysical dimensions.

There are, however, psychophysicists who take the position that psychophysics does not require the existence of sensa. Most notable among the early workers in the field are E. G. Boring in "Did Fechner Measure Sensations?" *Psychological Review* 35 (1928): 443–445; and "Fechner: Inadvertent Founder of Psychophysics," *Psychometrika* 26 (1961): 3–8; and G. Bergman and K. W. Spence in "The Logic of Psychophysical Measurement" in H. Feigl and M. Brodbeck, eds., *Readings in the Philosophy of Science* (N.Y.: Appleton-Century-Crofts, 1953), pp. 103–119. A modern proponent of this view is C. W. Savage in *The Measurement of Sensation* (Berkeley, California: University of California Press, 1970), esp. Chap. 10 and 11.

Reasons to Reject Sensa

THE 'SENSATION' ELIMINATION THEORY

The theory is presented by R. Rorty in "Mind-Body Identity, Privacy, and Categories," *Review of Metaphysics* 19 (1965): 24–54. J. Cornman criticises the theory in "On the elimination of 'Sensations' and Sensations," *Review of Metaphysics* 22 (1968): 15–35; and *Materialism and Sensations,* Chap. 5. R. Bernstein criticises the theory in "The Challenge of Scientific Materialism," *International Philosophical Quarterly* 8 (1968): 252–275. Rorty responds to these criticisms in "In Defense of Eliminative Materialism," *Review of Metaphysics* 24 (1970): 112–121.

THE CASE OF THE STRIPED TIGER

This issue is discussed by H. H. Price, "Review of *The Foundations of Empirical Knowledge,*" *Mind* 50: 280–93; and by R. M. Chisholm in "The Problem of the Speckled Hen," *Mind* 51 (1942): 368–373. Chisholm raises it again in *Perceiving* (Ithaca, N. Y.: Cornell University Press, 1957), p. 118. Ayer answers Chisholm's objections in *Philosophical Essays* (N. Y.: St. Martin's Press, 1965), pp. 90–98.

PHENOMENALISM

Berkeley's Theory

ON MINDS AND NOTIONS

Berkeley presents an early version of a theory of mind in *Philosophical Commentaries* which is contained in Volume I of A. A. Luce and T. E. Jessop, eds., *The Works of George Berkeley*, 9 Volumes (Edinburgh: Thomas Nelson and Sons, 1948–1957). Berkeley discusses notions in *Alciphron* and *Three Dialogues Between Hylas and Philonous*, both of which are contained in Volume III of the Luce and Jessop collection. Berkeley's most elaborate treatment of notions is in *Principles of Human Knowledge*, reprinted in C. M. Turbayne, ed., *Berkeley: Principles of Human Knowledge, Text and Critical Essays* (N. Y.: Bobbs-Merrill, 1970), especially Sections 135–145.

Berkeley is interpreted to be proposing a nondenoting theory of mind-terms by C. M. Turbayne in "Berkeley's Two Concepts of Mind" in *Berkeley: Principles of Human Knowledge, Text and Critical Essays*, pp. 145–160. A similar interpretation is given by J. Murphy in "Berkeley and the Metaphor of Mental Substance," *Ratio* 7 (1965): 170–179.

J. Cornman constructs a Berkeleyan theory of notions in which mind-terms function as theoretico-reporting terms, and so as denoting terms, in "Theoretical Terms, Berkeleian Notions, and Minds" in the Turbayne collection of essays on the *Principles*, pp. 161–181; and in "A Reconstruction of Berkeley: Minds and Physical Objects as Theoretical Entities," *Ratio* 13 (1971): 76–87.

Berkeley's theory of mind is also discussed in A. A. Luce, *The Dialectic of Immaterialism* (London: Hodder and Stoughton, 1963), Chap. 10; G. Pitcher, "Minds and Ideas in Berkeley," *American Philosophical Quarterly* 63 (1969): 198–207; S. A. Grave, "The Mind and Its Ideas: Some Problems in the Interpretation of Berkeley," in G. W. Engle and G. Taylor, eds., *Berkeley's Principles of Human Knowledge* (Belmont, California: Wadsworth Publishing Company, 1968), pp. 10–23; I. C. Tipton, "Berkeley's View of Spirit" in W. E. Steinkraus, ed., *New Studies in Berkeley's Philosophy* (N. Y.: Holt, Rinehart and Winston, 1966), pp. 59–71; R. Grossman, "Digby and Berkeley on Notions", *Theoria* 26 (1960): 17–30; and J. W. Davis, "Berkeley's Doctrine of the Notion," *Review of Metaphysics* 13 (1959): 378–389.

ON PHYSICAL OBJECTS

Berkeley's theory of physical objects is presented primarily in *Principles of Human Knowledge*, especially Sections 1–33; and throughout *Three Dialogues Between Hylas and Philonous*.

C. M. Turbayne's collection of essays on the *Principles* contains several papers dealing with Berkeley's theory of physical objects: W. H. Hay, "Berkeley's Argument from Nominalism," pp. 37–46; R. J. Van Iten, "Berkeley's Alleged Solipsism," pp. 47–56. The classic paper by G. E. Moore, "The Refutation of Idealism" is also reprinted, pp. 57–84; as is W. T. Stace's reply, "The Refutation of Realism," pp. 85–99.

J. Cornman, "A Reconstruction of Berkeley: Minds and Physical Objects as Theoretical Entities," answers many of the classical objections to a variety of Berkeley's claims. A quite different interpretation can be found in G. J. Warnock, *Berkeley* (Baltimore: Penguin Books, 1953). Berkeley's theory is also discussed by K. Marc-Wogau in "Berkeley's Sensationalism and the *Esse Est Pircipi* Principle" in *Berkeley's Principles of Human Knowledge*, pp. 57–74; A. Guzzo in "Berkeley and 'Things'" in *New Studies in Berkeley's Philosophy*, pp. 72–84; and H. M. Bracken in "Berkeley's Realism", *Philosophical Quarterly* 8 (1958): 41–53.

ON MATHEMATICS AND SCIENCE

Berkeley's view of mathematics is contained primarily in *The Analyst*, Volume IV of the Luce and Jessop collection; and *Principles of Human Knowledge*, Sections 119–134. His view of science can be found in *DeMotu*, Volume IV of the Luce and Jessop collection; and in *Principles of Human Knowledge*, Sections 97–117.

An interesting and illuminating discussion of Berkeley's views on science is presented in K. R. Popper, "A Note on Berkeley as Precursor of Mach and Einstein," reprinted in Turbayne's collection of essays on the *Principles*, pp. 129–144. Berkeley's philosophy of mathematics is also discussed by C. B. Boyer in *The Concepts of the Calculus* (N. Y.: Columbia University Press, 1939), Chap. 6; F. Cajou in *History of the Conceptions of Limits and Fluxions in Great Britain From Newton to Woodhouse* (Chicago: Open Court, 1919), Chap. 3; J. O. Wisdom in "The Analyst Controversy: Berkeley's Influence on the Development of Mathematics," *Hermathena* 29 (1939): 3–29; "The Compensation of Errors in the Method of Fluxions," *Hermathena* 57 (1941): 49–81; and "The Analyst Controversy: Berkeley as a Mathematician," *Hermathena* 59 (1942): 111–128; and G. J. Withrow in "Berkeley's Critique of the Newtonian Analysis of Motion," *Hermathena* 82 (1953): 90–112. T. E. Jessop discusses Berkeley's philosophy of science in "Berkeley's Philosophy of Science" in *Berkeley's Principles of Human Knowledge*, pp. 101–111.

ON EXPLANATION

Berkeley's views about explanation are stated in *Philosophical Commentaries*, and *Principles of Human Knowledge*, Sections 1–33. J. D.

Mabbot, "The Place of God in Berkeley's Philosophy," reprinted in the Turbayne collection of essays on the *Principles*, pp. 201–219, contains a discussion of some of the issues raised by Berkeley's views on explanation. A fairly detailed discussion of Berkeley's theory of explanation and causality is presented in G. Buchdahl, *Metaphysics and the Philosophy of Science, The Classical Origins: Descartes to Kant* (Cambridge, Mass.: MIT Press, 1969), Chap. 5, sec. 7 and 8.

Analytical Phenomenalism

G. E. Moore argues for a version of analytical phenomenalism in several of the papers which are collected in *Philosophical Studies* (N. Y.: Harcourt, Brace, 1922); *Some Main Problems of Philosophy* (N. Y.: Macmillan, 1953); and *Philosophical Papers* (N. Y.: Humanities Press, 1959).

B. Russell proposes or defends such a theory in "The Philosophy of Logical Atomism," reprinted in R. C. March, ed., *Essays in Logic and Knowledge* (London: Allen and Unwin, 1956), pp. 175–282; *An Inquiry into Meaning and Truth* (London: Allen and Unwin, 1956), sec. 4, 6, 8, 9 and 10; *The Problems of Philosophy* (N. Y.: Oxford University Press, 1959), Chap. 5; and *Our Knowledge of the External World* (London: Allen and Unwin, 1961).

R. Carnap's enterprise in *The Logical Structure of the World*, reprinted in *The Logical Structure of the World and Pseudoproblems in Philosophy* (Berkeley, California: University of California Press, 1967) can be seen as an attempt to carry out the "construction" of the sensible world within the guidelines of analytical phenomenalism. Similarly, for N. Goodman's enterprise in *The Structure of Appearance* (N. Y.: Bobbs-Merrill, 1966).

Analytical phenomenalism is criticised in Arthur Pap, *Elements of Analytical Philosophy* (N. Y.: Macmillan, 1949), Chap. 2; R. Chisholm, *Perceiving* (Ithaca, N. Y.: Cornell University Press, 1957), pp. 189–197; H. Feigl, "Existential Hypotheses: Realistic vs. Phenomenalistic Interpretations," *Philosophy of Science* 17 (1950): 35–62; W. Sellars, "Phenomenalism" reprinted in *Science, Perception and Reality* (London: Routledge and Kegan Paul, 1963), Chap. 3; D. M. Armstrong, *Perception and the Physical World* (London: Routledge and Kegan Paul, 1961), Chaps. 5 and 6.

SUBJUNCTIVE ANALYSIS

This theory has been proposed by A. J. Ayer in *Language, Truth, and Logic* (London: V. Golancz, 1936), Chaps. 7 and 8; in a somewhat weakened version in *The Foundation of Empirical Knowledge* (London: Macmillan, 1955), Chap. 5; and "Phenomenalism," reprinted in A. J.

Ayer, *Philosophical Essays* (N. Y.: St. Martin's Press, 1965), Chap. 3.
Ayer finally rejects the theory in *The Problem of Knowledge* (Baltimore:
Penguin Books, 1956), Chap. 3, sec. (vi) and (vii).

PROBABILISTIC ANALYSIS

The theory is presented by C. I. Lewis in *An Analysis of Knowledge and
Valuation* (La Salle, Ill.: Open Court, 1946), Chaps. 7 and 8, sec. 16 and
17. It is criticised in R. M. Chisholm, "The Problem of Empiricism,"
Journal of Philosophy 45 (1948): 512–517. Lewis replies in "Professor
Chisholm and Empiricism," *Journal of Philosophy* 45 (1948): 517–524. G.
Chatalian criticises the theory in "Probability: Inductive versus Deductive," *Philosophical Studies* 3 (1952): 49–56. Chisholm again objects to
the theory in "Lewis' Ethics of Belief," reprinted in P. A. Schilpp, ed.,
The Philosophy of C. I. Lewis (La Salle, Ill.: Open Court, 1968), pp.
223–242. Lewis replies in "Reply to Chisholm" in Schilpp volume, pp.
660–661. Also in the Schilpp volume is a critical article by W. H. Hay,
"Lewis' Relation to Logical Empiricism," pp. 309–327. Lewis' reply is
found on pp. 663–664.

Theoretical Phenomenalism

This theory has been developed by Cornman in "Theoretical Terms,
Berkeleyan Notions, and Minds"; "A Reconstruction of Berkeley: Minds
and Physical Objects as Theoretical Entities"; and most definitively in
"Theoretical Phenomenalism," *Nous* 7 (1973): 120–138, which contains
the bulk of the material of Chap. 5 in this text.

Sellars discusses a theory similar to the one developed by Cornman
which he calls "the new phenomenalism" in *Science, Perception and
Reality* (London: Routledge and Kegan Paul, 1963), Chap. 3.

SCIENTIFIC INSTRUMENTALISM—CRAIGIAN ELIMINATION PROGRAM:
STATEMENT OF THE PROGRAM

Craig's theorem is proved, and its implications for the philosophy of
science are discussed by W. Craig in *A Theorem About First-Order
Functional Calculus With Identity, and Two Applications* (Ph. D. thesis,
Harvard University, 1951); "On Axiomatizability Within A System,"
Journal of Symbolic Logic 18 (1953): 30–32; "Replacement of Auxiliary
Expressions," *Philosophical Review* 65 (1956): 38–55; and "Bases for
First-Order Theories and Subtheories," *Journal of Symbolic Logic* 25
(1960): 97–142.

Craig's elimination program is outlined, in less technical jargon, in H.
Putnam, "Craig's Theorem," *Journal of Philosophy* 62 (1965): 251–260;
and J. Cornman, "Craig's Theorem, Ramsey Sentences, and Scientific

Instrumentalism." *Synthese* 25 (1972): 82–128, sec. III.

OBJECTIONS TO THE CRAIGIAN PROGRAM

THEORETICAL TERMS AND OBSERVATION TERMS   Several philosophers have presented criteria for drawing the distinction between theoretical terms and observation terms. Among the most influential of these are R. Carnap in "Testability and Meaning," *Philosophy of Science* 3 (1936): 419–471; and "The Methodological Character of Theoretical Concepts", in H. Feigl and M. Scriven, eds., *Minnesota Studies in the Philosophy of Science* I (Minneapolis: University of Minnesota Press, 1966), pp. 38–76; R. B. Braithwaite in *Scientific Explanation* (Cambridge: Cambridge University Press, 1959), Chap. 3; E. Nagel in *The Structure of Science* (N. Y.: Harcourt, Brace and World, 1961), Chap. 5; and "The Meaning of Reduction in the Natural Sciences" in P. Weiner, ed., *Readings in the Philosophy of Science* (N. Y.: Scribners, 1953), pp. 531–559; G. Maxwell in "The Ontological Status of Theoretical Entities" in H. Feigl and G. Maxwell, eds., *Minnesota Studies in the Philosophy of Science* III, (Minneapolis: University of Minnesota Press, 1962), pp. 3–27; C. Hempel in "The Theoretician's Dilemma" in H. Feigl, M. Scriven, and G. Maxwell, eds., *Minnesota Studies in the Philosophy of Science* II (Minneapolis: University of Minnesota Press, 1958), pp. 37–98; and J. Winnie in "The Implicit Definition of Theoretical Terms," *British Journal for the Philosophy of Science* 18 (1967): 223–229.

An attempt to draw the distinction in a somewhat different way can be found in J. Cornman, *Materialism and Sensations*, Chap. 2.

Objections to the proposed dichotomy between theoretical terms and observation terms are given by P. Achenstein in "The Problem of Theoretical Terms," *American Philosophical Quarterly* 2 (1965): 193–203; and "Theoretical Terms and Partial Interpretation," *British Journal for the Philosophy of Science* 14 (1964): 89–105; M. Spector in "Theory and Observation," *British Journal for the Philosophy of Science* 17 (1966): 1–20, 89–104; M. B. Hesse in "Is There an Independent Observation Language?" in R. G. Colodny, ed., *The Nature and Function of Scientific Theories* (Pittsburgh: University of Pittsburgh Press, 1970), pp. 35–77; C. R. Kerdig in "The Theory-Ladenness of Observation," *Review of Metaphysics* 24 (1971): 448–484; W. V. O. Quine in "Grades of Theoreticity" in L. Foster and J. W. Swanson, eds., *Experience and Theory* (Amherst: University of Massachusetts Press, 1970), pp. 1–18; F. Dretske in "Observation Terms", *Philosophical Review* 73 (1964): 25–42; A. Pap in *An Introduction to the Philosophy of Science*, Chaps. 1–4; C. Hempel in *Philosophy of Natural Science* (Englewood Cliffs, N. J.: Prentice-Hall, 1966), pp. 80–85; and "On the Standard Conception of

Scientific Theories" in M. Rudnor and S. Winokur, eds., *Minnesota Studies in the Philosophy of Science* IV (Minneapolis: University of Minnesota Press, 1970), pp. 142–163.

INDUCTIVE SYSTEMATIZATION   Objection to the Craigian elimination program on the grounds that it does not guarantee the preservation of inductive systematization are presented by C. Hempel in "The Theoretician's Dilemma"; and "Implications of Carnap's Work for the Philosophy of Science" in P. A. Schilpp, ed., *The Philosophy of Rudolf Carnap* (La Salle, Ill.: Open Court, 1963), pp. 685–710; I. Scheffler in *The Anatomy of Inquiry* (N. Y.: Alfred A. Knopf, 1963), pp. 193–203; K. Lehrer in "Theoretical Terms and Inductive Inference," *American Philosophical Quarterly Monograph Series, Studies in the Philosophy of Science* 3 (1969): 30–41; and I. Niiniluoto in "Inductive Systematization: Definition and Critical Survey," *Synthese* 25 (1972): 25–81, sec. VIII. S. Kaufman replies to Niiniluoto in "The Preservation of Epistemic Systematization Within the Extended Craigian Program," *Synthese*, 27 (1974): 215–222.

RELEVANCE TO SCIENTIFIC INSTRUMENTALISM   Objections to the program on the grounds that it is irrelevant to the issue of scientific instrumentalism are presented by C. A. Hooker in "Craigian Transcriptionism," *American Philosophical Quarterly* 5 (1968): 151–163; H. Putnam in "Craig's Theorem"; E. Nagel in *The Structure of Science*, pp. 134–137; and J. J. C. Smart in *Philosophy and Scientific Realism* (London: Routledge and Kegan Paul, 1963), pp. 27–32.

SCIENCE AND SIMPLICITY   N. Goodman criticises the program on the grounds that it does not preserve the simplicity of the theories to which it is applied in "Review of Craig," *Journal of Symbolic Logic* 22 (1957): 317–318. Goodman expresses his views about the importance of simplicity for scientific theorizing in "Science and Simplicity" reprinted in *Problems and Projects* (N. Y.: Bobbs-Merrill, 1972), pp. 337–346; "The Test of Simplicity" in *Problems and Projects*, pp. 275–294; and *The Structure of Appearance*. Among the other philosophers who have stressed the importance of simplicity for scientific theorizing are P. Duhem in *The Aim and Structure of Physical Theory* (Princeton: Princeton University Press, 1954), Chaps. 2 and 7; W. V. O. Quine in *Word and Object* (Cambridge, Mass.: MIT Press, 1960), Chap. 1; M. Bunge in *The Myth of Simplicity* (Englewood Cliffs, N. J.: Prentice-Hall, 1963); and K. R. Popper in *The Logic of Scientific Discovery* (N. Y.: Harper and Row, 1968), Chap. 7 and Appendix VIII.

   C. A. Hooker argues that Goodman's objection to the program carries no force in "Five Arguments Against Craigian Transcriptionism," *Australasian Journal of Philosophy* 46 (1968): 265–276.

SCIENTIFIC INSTRUMENTALISM—RAMSEYIAN TRANSCRIPTION: STATEMENT OF THE PROCEDURE AND FAVORABLE COMMENTS

The procedure is introduced by F. Ramsey in "Theories" reprinted in R. B. Braithwaite, ed., *The Foundations of Mathematics and Other Logical Essays* (N. Y.: Humanities Press, 1931), Chap. 9. Braithwaite discusses the procedure and its implication for the philosophy of science sympathetically in *Scientific Explanation*, Chap. 3. A staunch advocate of the importance of the procedure is H. Bohnert in *The Interpretation of Theory* (Ph. D. thesis, University of Pennsylvania, 1961); "Communication by Ramsey-Sentence Clause," *Philosophy of Science* 34 (1967): 341–347; and "In Defense of Ramsey's Elimination Method", *Journal of Philosophy* 65 (1968): 275–281. R. Carnap comments favorably on the relevance of the procedure to the philosophy of science in *Philosophical Foundations of Physics* (N. Y.: Basic Books, 1966), Chap. 28. R. M. Martin presents a modified version of the procedure in "On Theoretical Constructs and Ramsey Constants," *Philosophy of Science* 33 (1966): 1–13. The importance of the procedure for the issue of scientific instrumentalism is discussed by J. Cornman in "Craig's Theorem, Ramsey Sentences, and Scientific Instrumentalism." D. Lewis employs the Ramsey method in defining theoretical terms in "How to Define Theoretical Terms," *Journal of Philosophy* 67 (1970): 427–445.

OBJECTIONS TO THE RAMSEYAN PROCEDURE

FAILS TO PRESERVE INDUCTIVE SYSTEMATIZATION Objections to the Ramsey procedure on the grounds that it does not preserve the inductive systematization of the theories to which it is applied are presented by I. Scheffler in *The Anatomy of Inquiry*, pp. 203–222; and "Reflections on the Ramsey Method," *Journal of Philosophy* 65 (1968): 269–274; E. Nagel in *The Structure of Science*, 141–142; and I. Niiniluoto in "Inductive Systematization: Definition and Critical Survey".

C. A. Hooker responds to Scheffler's objections in "Craigian Transcriptionism," *American Philosophical Quarterly* 5 (1968): 152–163. Cornman attempts to show that none of these objections are conclusive in "Craig's Theorem, Ramsey Sentences, and Scientific Instrumentalism", sec. 7.

UNNECESSARILY EXPANDS ONTOLOGY I. Scheffler objects in "Reflections on the Ramsey Method" to the use of the Ramsey method on the grounds that it needlessly expands the ontological commitment of the theories to which it is applied, because the Ramseyan transcribed theory contains predicate variables and thus is ontologically committed to the existence of properties. H. Bohnert responds to Scheffler's criticism in "In Defense of Ramsey's Elimination Method." Bohnert is supported in his response by J. Cornman in "Craig's Theorem, Ramsey Sentences, and Scientific Instrumentalism", sec. VII.

NAIVE REALISM

Phenomenological Objections

[See references on sensa listed under *Empirical Non-Theoretical Arguments*.]

Science-Based Objections

Many philosophers and scientists have proposed arguments against naive realism which are based on the science of color vision. Among the most prominent are R. L. Gregory in *Eye and Brain*, Chaps. 9 and 11; H. von Helmholtz in "Colours and Light Waves" reprinted in R. J. Hirst, ed., *Perception and the External World* (N. Y.: Macmillan, 1965), pp. 61–75; Y. LeGrand in *Light, Color, and Vision* (London: Chapman and Hall, 1957), Chap. 19; F. Birren in *Color in Your World* (N. Y.: Collier, 1962); I. Newton in *Optiks* (N. Y.: Dover, 1952); and W. C. K. Mundle in *Perception: Facts and Theories*, Chaps. 3, 6, and 9.

Other science-inspired arguments against naive realism are presented in K. Koffka, "Why Do Things Look As They Do?" reprinted in R. J. Hirst, ed., *Perception and the External World*, pp. 78–94; W. Penfield and A. T. Rasmussen, *The Cerebral Cortex of Man* (N. Y.: Macmillan, 1950); and W. Penfield and L. Roberts, *Speech and Brain Mechanism* (Princeton: Princeton University Press, 1959). [See also references on sensa listed under "Science-Based Arguments"]

NONDIRECT REALISM

Locke's Indirect Realism

ON IDEAS

Locke's discussion of ideas is presented in *Essay Concerning Human Understanding*, A. C. Fraser, ed. (Oxford: Clarendon Press, 1894), Book II. Locke's theory of perception is discussed in detail by J. W. Yolton in *John Locke and the Way of Ideas* (London: Oxford University Press, 1956); and *Locke and the Compass of Human Understanding* (Cambridge: Cambridge University Press, 1970), Chap. 4; J. Bennett in *Locke, Berkeley and Hume* (Oxford: Clarendon Press, 1971), Chaps. 1, 3, and 4; and

D. O'Connor in *John Locke* (Baltimore: Penguin Books, 1952). R. Jackson discusses Locke's theory of ideas in "Locke's Distinction Between Primary and Secondary Qualities," in C. B. Martin and D. M. Armstrong, eds., *Locke and Berkeley* (N. Y.: Anchor Books, 1968), pp. 53–77; and "Locke's Version of the Doctrine of Representative Perception" in *Locke and Berkeley*, pp. 125–154. J. W. Yolton also discusses Locke's theory of ideas in "Locke's Concept of Experience" in *Locke and Berkeley*, pp. 40–52; and "The Science of Nature" in J. Yolton, ed., *John Locke: Problems and Perspectives* (London: Cambridge University Press, 1969), pp. 183–193. Also of interest are J. Bennett, "Substance, Reality, and Primary Qualities," in *Locke and Berkeley*, pp. 86–124; D. Lewis, "The Existence of Substance and Locke's Way of Ideas," *Theoria* 35 (1969): 124–146; M. Mandelbaum, *Philosophy, Science, and Sense-Perception* (Baltimore: Johns Hopkins University Press, 1964), Chap. 1; G. Aspelin, "Idea and Perception in Locke's Essay," *Theoria* 33 (1967): 278–283; D. Greenlee, "Locke's Idea of Idea," *Theoria* 33 (1967): 98–106; G. G. Brittan "Measurability, Commonsensibility, and Primary Qualities," *Australasian Journal of Philosophy* 47 (1969): 15–24; D. M. Armstrong, "The Secondary Qualities," *Australasian Journal of Philosophy* 46 (1968): 225–241; and K. Campbell, "Primary and Secondary Qualities," *Canadian Journal of Philosophy* 2 (1972): 219–232.

ON KNOWLEDGE OF THE EXTERNAL WORLD

Locke's theory of knowledge is presented in *Essay Concerning Human Understanding*, Book IV. It is discussed in R. S. Woolhouse, *Locke's Philosophy of Science and Knowledge* (N. Y.: Barnes and Noble, 1971); J. Gibson, *Locke's Theory of Knowledge and Its Historical Connections* (Cambridge: Cambridge University Press, 1960), Part I; M. V. C. Jeffreys, *John Locke* (London: Methuen, 1967), Chap. 4; A. Hostader, *Locke and Skepticism* (Ph. D. Thesis, Columbia University, 1955), Chap. 4; D. Perry, "Locke on Mixed Modes, Relations and Knowledge," *Journal of the History of Philosophy* 5 (1967): 219–235; J. Margolis, "Locke and Scientific Realism," *Review of Metaphysics* 22 (1968): 359–370; M. J. Osler, "John Locke and the Changing Ideal of Scientific Knowledge," *Journal of the History of Ideas* 3 (1970): 3–16; R. E. A. Shanab, "Locke on Knowledge and Perception," *Journal of Critical Analysis* 2 (1971): 16–23; and A. D. Woozley "Some Remarks on Locke's Account of Knowledge," *The Locke Newsletter* (1972): 7–17.

Sellars' Scientific Realism

Aspects of Sellars' theory of perception are presented in *Philosophical Perspectives* (Springfield, Ill.: Charles C. Thomas, 1959), Chaps. 7, 12,

14, and 15; *Science, Perception, and Reality* (London: Routledge and Kegan Paul, 1963), Chaps. 2 and 3; and *Science and Metaphysics* (London: Routledge and Kegan Paul, 1968), Chaps. 1 and 2. The theory is discussed by R. J. Bernstein in "Sellars' Vision of Man-In-The-Universe," *Review of Metaphysics* 20 (1966): 113–143, 290–316, esp. sec. I and III; B. Aune in "Comments (on Sellars' "Phenomenalism")," H. N. Castañeda, ed., *Intentionality, Minds, and Perception* (Detroit: Wayne State University Press, 1967), pp. 215–285; and *Knowledge, Mind, and Nature* (N.Y.: Random House, 1967), Chap. 4; K. Lehrer in "Review of *Science, Perception, and Reality*," *Journal of Philosophy* 62 (1966): 266–277; G. H. Harman in "Review of *Philosophical Perspectives*," *Journal of Philosophy* 66 (1969): 133–144; J. Cornman in "Sellars, Scientific Realism, and Sensa," *Review of Metaphysics* 23 (1970): 417–451; and R. Ackermann, "Sellars and the Scientific Image," *Nous* 7, 1973: 138–151.

Sellars responds to Aune's remarks on "Phenomenalism" in "Reply (to Aune's "Comments")," *Intentionality, Minds, and Perception*, pp. 286–300. Sellars responds to Cornman in "Science, Sense Impressions, and Sensa: A Reply to Cornman," *Review of Metaphysics* 24 (1971): 391–447. Cornman discusses Sellars' theory again, in the light of Sellars' response, in *Materialism and Sensations,* Chap. 7.

Kant: Appearances and Things-in-Themselves

Kant's theory of perception is presented in *Critique of Pure Reason*. Kant's theory of physical objects as appearances, and his view of the role of things-in-themselves in perception are discussed in P. F. Strawson, *The Bounds of Sense* (London: Methuen, 1966), Part IV; W. Sellars, *Science and Metaphysics,* Chaps. 2 and 6; H. J. Paton, *Kant's Metaphysic of Experience* (London: Allen and Unwin, 1936); H. A. Pritchard, *Kant's Theory of Knowledge* (London: Oxford University Press, 1909); R. P. Wolff, *Kant's Theory of Mental Activity* (Cambridge, Mass.: Harvard University Press, 1963); J. Kemp, *The Philosophy of Kant* (London: Oxford University Press, 1968), Chaps. 1 and 2; N. Rotenstreich, *Experience and Its Systematization* (The Hague: M. Nijhoff, 1965), Appendix; F. Grayeff, *Kant's Theoretical Philosophy* (Manchester: Manchester University Press, 1970); D. R. Cousin, "Kant's Concept of Appearance," *Philosophy* 16 (1941): 169–184; S. F. Barker, "Appearing and Appearances in Kant," *The Monist* 51 (1967): 426–441; G. Schrader, "The Thing In Itself in Kantian Philosophy" in R. P. Wolff, ed., *Kant: A Collection of Critical Essays* (N.Y.: Anchor Books, 1967), pp. 172–188; C. M. Turbayne, "Kant's Refutation of Dogmatic Idealism," *Philosophical Quarterly* 5 (1955): 225–244; M. D. Wilson, "Kant and 'the Dogmatic Idealism of Berkeley'," *Journal of the History of Philosophy* IX (1971): 459–475;

and J. Hoagland, "The Thing in Itself in English Interpretations of Kant,"
American Philosophical Quarterly 10 (1973): 1–14.

COMPATIBLE COMMON-SENSE REALISM

Scientific Realism

SPECTRUM OF POSITIONS

MINIMAL SCIENTIFIC REALISM   Minimal scientific realism and three other
species of scientific realism listed below are characterized by J. Cornman
in "Sellars, Scientific Realism, and Sensa," and in *Materialism and
Sensations*, pp. 229–234. A different characterization is given in J.
Cornman, "Can Eddington's 'Two' Tables be Identical?" *Australasian
Journal of Philosophy* 52 (1974): 23–24.

MODERATE SCIENTIFIC REALISM   Contemporary proponents of moderate
scientific realism include B. Russell in *An Inquiry into Meaning and Truth;*
and *Our Knowledge of the External World;* C. D. Broad in *Perception,
Physics, and Reality* (Cambridge: Cambridge University Press, 1914);
and *Scientific Thought* (N.Y.: Harcourt, Brace, 1923); B. Aune in
Knowledge, Mind, and Nature (N.Y.: Random House, 1967); D. M.
Armstrong in *Perception and the Physical World* (London: Routledge
and Kegan Paul, 1961); R. J. Hirst in *The Problem of Perception* (London:
Allen and Unwin, 1959); J. R. Smythies in *Analysis of Perception*; and
M. Mandelbaum in *Philosophy, Science, and Sense-Perception.*

EXTREME SCIENTIFIC REALISM   Advocates of extreme scientific realism
include W. V. O. Quine in *Word and Object,* pp. 260–266; *The Ways of
Paradox* (N.Y.: Random House, 1966), Chaps. 18 and 19; and *Ontological
Relativity and Other Essays* (N.Y.: Columbia University Press, 1969),
Chap. 3; J. J. C. Smart in *Philosophy and Scientific Realism* (London:
Routledge and Kegan Paul, 1963), Chaps. 4 and 5; A. S. Eddington in
The Nature of the Physical World (N.Y.: Macmillan, 1929), Chap. 13;
R. W. Sellars in *The Philosophy of Physical Realism* (N.Y.: Macmillan,
1932); and D. C. Williams in "Naturalism and the Nature of Things,"
Philosophical Review 53 (1944): 417–443.

OBJECTIONS TO MINIMAL SCIENTIFIC REALISM

IDEAL AND LIMIT ENTITIES   Accounts for dealing with idealizations in
scientific theories in a way compatible with scientific realism are given
in E. Nagel, *The Structure of Science*, Chap. 6; W. V. O. Quine, *Word
and Object*, pp. 248–251; S. Toulmin, *The Philosophy of Science* (London:
Hutchinson and Company, 1967), pp. 116–120; S. Toulmin, "Ideals of
Natural Order," in D. Shapere, ed., *Philosophical Problems of Natural*

Science (N.Y.: Macmillan, 1965), pp. 110–123; W. C. Humphreys, *Anomalies and Scientific Theories* (San Francisco: Freeman, Cooper, and Company, 1968), pp. 138–147; P. Duhem, *The Aim and Structure of Physical Theory*, pp. 168–172; C. D. Broad, *Scientific Thought*, Chaps. 1, 2, and 12; K. R. Popper, *The Logic of Scientific Discovery*, Appendix XI; A. N. Whitehead, *Interpretation of Science* (N.Y.: Bobbs-Merrill, 1961), Chap. 5; and N. Lawrence, "Whitehead's Method of Extensive Abstraction," *Philosophy of Science* 17 (1950): 142–163.

QUANTUM PHYSICS An instrumental construal of quantum physics is presented by W. Heisenberg in *Physics and Philosophy* (N.Y.: Harper and Row, 1962); and by N. Bohr in *Atomic Theory and the Description of Nature* (Cambridge: Cambridge University Press, 1934); *Atomic Physics and Human Knowledge* (N.Y.: John Wiley and Sons, 1958); *Essays 1958–1962 on Atomic Physics and Human Knowledge* (N.Y.: Interscience, 1963); and "Discussions With Einstein on Epistemological Problems in Atomic Physics" in P. A. Schilpp, ed., *Albert Einstein: Philosopher-Scientist* (La Salle, Ill: Open Court, 1949), pp. 199–242. Bohr's views are discussed critically by M. R. Gardner in "Two Deviant Logics for Quantum Theory: Bohr and Reichenbach," *British Journal for the Philosophy of Science* 23 (1972): 89–109.

A statistical interpretation is presented by H. Margenau in "Quantum-Mechanical Description," *Physical Review* 49 (1936): 240–242; and "Measurements and Quantum States (Part II)," *Philosophy of Science* 30 (1963): 138–151; J. Park in "Quantum Theoretical Concept of Measurement (Part I)," *Philosophy of Science* 35 (1968): 205–231; and L. E. Ballantine in "The Statistical Interpretation of Quantum Mechanics," *Review of Modern Physics* 42 (1970): 358–380. A. Einstein seems to hold this view in "Reply to Critics" in *Albert Einstein: Philosopher-Scientist*, pp. 665–688.

K. R. Popper advocates a propensity interpretation in *The Logic of Scientific Discovery*, Chap. 9; "The Propensity Interpretation of Probability," *British Journal for the Philosophy of Science* 10 (1959): 25–42; "The Propensity Interpretation of the Calculus of Probability, and the Quantum Theory," in S. Körner, ed., *Observation and Interpretation in the Philosophy of Physics* (N.Y.: Academic Press, 1957), 65–70; "Quantum Mechanics Without 'The Observer'" in M. Bunge, ed., *Quantum Theory and Reality* (N.Y.: Springer Verlag, 1967), pp. 7–44; and "Particle Annihilation and the Argument of Einstein, Podolsky, and Rosen," in *Perspectives in Quantum Theory: Essays in Honor of Alfred Landé*, W. Yourgrau and A. Van der Merwe, eds. (Cambridge, Mass.: MIT Press, 1971), pp. 192–193.

The statistical and propensity interpretations are discussed critically in N. Grossman, "Quantum Mechanics and Interpretations of Probability Theory," *Philosophy of Science* 39 (1972): 451–460; and M. R. Gardner, "Quantum-Theoretical Realism: Popper and Einstein v. Kochen and Specker," *British Journal for the Philosophy of Science* 23 (1972): 13–23.

A "hidden variable" view is proposed by D. Bohm in *Causality and Chance in Modern Physics* (Philadelphia: University of Pennsylvania Press, 1971), esp. Chap. 4; "A Proposed Explanation of Quantum Theory in Terms of Hidden Variables at a Sub-Quantum-Mechanical Level" in *Observation and Interpretation in the Philosophy of Physics*, pp. 33–40; D. Bohm and J. Bub, "A Proposed Solution of the Measurement Problem in Quantum Mechanics by a Hidden Variable Theory," *Review of Modern Physics* 38 (1966): 453–469; and L. DeBroglie in *The Current Interpretation of Wave Mechanics* (N.Y.: Elsevier, 1964). Also relevant are A. Einstein, B. Podolsky and N. Rosen, "Can Quantum Mechanical Discription of Reality be Considered Complete?" *Physical Review* 47 (1935): 777–780; S. Kochen and E. P. Specker, "The Problem of Hidden Variables in Quantum Mechanics," *Journal of Mathematics and Mechanics* 17 (1967): 59–87; J. S. Bell, "On the Einstein Podolsky Rosen Paradox," *Physics* 1 (1964): 195–200; and "On the Problem of Hidden Variables in Quantum Mechanics," *Review of Modern Physics* 38 (1966): 447–452.

A. Petersen gives a historical survey of various interpretations of quantum physics in *Quantum Physics and the Philosophical Tradition* (Cambridge, Mass.: MIT Press, 1968). N. R. Hanson discusses the "Copenhagen Interpretation" critically in *The Concepts of Positron* (Cambridge: Cambridge University Press, 1963). Another discussion of the prominent views is contained in C. A. Hooker, "The Nature of Quantum Mechanical Reality: Einstein versus Bohr" in R. G. Colodny, ed., *Paradigms and Paradoxes* (Pittsburgh: University of Pittsburgh Press, 1972), pp. 67–302.

Recent Work on the interpretation of quantum physics includes A. Fine, "Some Conceptual Problems of Quantum Theory" in *Paradigms and Paradoxes*, pp. 3–32; W. B. Gallie, "The Limits of Prediction" in *Observation and Interpretation*, pp. 160–164; and H. Mehlberg, "The Problem of Physical Reality in Contemporary Science" in *Quantum Theory and Reality*, pp. 45–65.

COMPLETELY ADEQUATE EXPLANATIONS

The "covering-law model" of scientific explanation is presented and developed in detail by C. Hempel and P. Oppenheim in "Studies in The Logic of Explanation" reprinted in C. Hempel, *Aspects of Scientific*

Explanation (N.Y.: Macmillan, 1966), Chap. 10. Hempel develops his views further in "Deductive-Nomological vs. Statistical Explanation," *Minnesota Studies in the Philosophy of Science* III, pp. 98–169; and *Philosophy of Natural Science,* Chaps. 5 and 6.

Hempel's views on explanation are discussed critically in M. Scriven, "Explanations, Predictions, and Laws" in *Minnesota Studies* III, pp. 170–230; M. Brodbeck, "Explanation, Prediction, and 'Imperfect' Knowledge" in *Minnesota Studies* III, pp. 231–272; and P. K. Feyerabend, "Explanation, Reduction, and Empiricism" in *Minnesota Studies* III, pp. 28–97.

Alternatives to the covering-law model are presented in I. Scheffler, *Conditions of Knowledge* (Chicago: Scott, Foresman, 1965); S. Toulmin, *Foresight and Understanding* (N.Y.: Harper and Row, 1963); L. K. Nash, *The Nature of the Natural Sciences* (Boston: Little, Brown, 1963), Chap. 11; N. R. Hansen, *Patterns of Discovery* (Cambridge: Cambridge University Press, 1961); T. S. Kuhn, *The Structure of Scientific Revolution* (Chicago: Chicago University Press, 1962); P. K. Feyerabend, "Problems of Empiricism"; and R. B. Braithwaite, *Scientific Explanation.*

The Identity Hypothesis

SUPREMACY OF COMMON SENSE

L. S. Stebbing argues for the supremacy of common sense in *Philosophy and the Physicists* (N.Y.: Dover, 1958), Part II; "The Furniture of the Earth" reprinted in A. Danto and S. Morgenbesser, eds., *Philosophy of Science*, pp. 69–81; and "Realism and Modern Physics," *Aristotelian Society,* Supplementary Volume 9 (1929): 146–161. E. F. Caldin advocates a similar view in *The Power and Limits of Science* (London: Chapman and Hall, 1949), Chaps. 2 and 3. Other proponents include J. Laird in "Realism and Modern Physics," *Aristotelian Society,* Supplementary Volume 9 (1929): 112–125; and C. E. M. Joad in "Realism and Modern Physics," *Aristotelian Society,* Supplementary Volume 9 (1929): 126–145.

Stebbing's arguments are criticised in B. Aune, *Knowledge, Mind, and Nature.* Chaps. 3 and 7; D. M. Armstrong, *Perception and the Physical World*, pp. 167–171; C. W. K. Mundle, *Perception: Facts and Theories,* Chap. 10; and J. Cornman, "Can Eddington's 'Two' Tables be Identical?" pp. 27–29.

INCOMPATIBILISM

The view that common-sense realism is incompatible with scientific realism is put forth by B. Russell in *An Inquiry into Meaning and Truth,* pp. 9–20; J. Smythies in *Analysis of Perception*; A. S. Eddington in *The Nature of the Physical World*, Chaps. 4 and 5; C. W. K. Mundle in *Perception: Facts and Theories,* Chaps. 3 and 9; W. Sellars in *Science, Perception and Reality*, Chap. 1; and J. J. C. Smart in *Philosophy and Scientific Realism*.

N. Maxwell argues against Smart's reasons for incompatibilism in *Physics and Common Sense, A Critique of Physicalism* (M.A. thesis, Manchester University, 1965); and "Physics and Common Sense," *British Journal for the Philosophy of Science* 16 (1966): 295–311. P. L. McKee argues against Smythies' reasons in "Perception and Physiology," *Mind* 80 (1971): 594–596. Cornman argues against incompatibilism in "Can Eddington's 'Two' Tables be Identical?"

IMMEDIATELY PERCEIVING AS SUCCESSFUL SENSING

PERCEPTION TERMS AS SUCCESS TERMS   G. Ryle presents this view in *Concept of Mind*, pp. 149–153; and *Dilemmas*, Chap. 7. It is discussed in F. N. Sibley, "Seeking, Scrutinizing, and Seeing," *Mind* 64 (1955): 455–478; H. Hudson, "Achievement Expressions," *Analysis* 16 (1955): 127–130; Z. Vendler, "Verbs and Times," *Philosophical Review* 66 (1957): 143–160; S. Malinovich, "Perception: An Experience or an Achievement?" *Philosophy and Phenomenological Research* 25 (1964): 161–168; and B. Rundle, *Perception, Sensation, and Verification* (Oxford: Clarendon Press, 1972), Chap. 5.

RIGHT-MAKING CHARACTERISTICS   Chisholm discusses the criteriological approach to evidential and moral judgements in *Perceiving*, Chap. 3; and *Theory of Knowledge*, Chap. 4. It is also discussed in C. D. Broad, "Some Main Problems of Ethics," *Philosophy* 21 (1946): 99–117; A. Duncan-Jones, *Butler's Moral Philosophy* (Harmondsworth, England: Penguin Books, 1952), Chap. 8, sec. 1 and 2; and R. M. Hare, *The Language of Morals* (Oxford: Oxford University Press, 1952), pp. 80–85.

Index of Definitions

Accounts of theories, correct, 201*n*;
Sellarsian, 201*n*; standard, 201*n*

Compatibilism, 287
Concept theories, abstractionism, 260;
associationism, 260; Kantian
constructionism, 260

Epistemic theorem, 161
Exist$_L$ (Berkeley), 205
External object, 21

Identity thesis, 287
Inductive derivability, 155

Materialism, 378

Nothing but, 383

Perceivable, directly, 15
Perceiving, experiencing, sensing:
appear as it is, 222; be perceptually
acquainted with, 223, 235–36; be
perceptually presented, 223; directly
perceive an object, 7, 14; directly
perceive a property, 41–42; directly
perceive (epistemically), 369;
immediately perceive, 221;
indirectly perceive, 15
Property, *a posteriori*, 266;
extentional, 376; materialistic, 377;

phenomenal, 6; physical, 380;
physical-neutral, 377
'Ψ' indeterminately indicates position,
308
'Ψ' specifies propensity to have property
P, 309
'Ψ' specifies quantitative property *P*, 298

Realism, compatible (minimal)
common-sense, 346; indirect—first
thesis, 248, second thesis, 249;
Lockean (representational), 251;
minimal common-sense—first thesis,
284, second thesis, 284–85; naive
(minimal)—first thesis, 219; second
thesis, 224; scientific, *see* Scientific
realism, Sellarsian indirect (and
epistemology), 273–74

Scientific realism, minimal, 265–66;
moderate, 266–67; extreme, 267;
Sellarsian, 271
Sensum, 5
Sensum generalization, 197–98
Systematization, deductive, 137;
epistemic, 161; inductive, 155

Term, empirical, 141; observation,
147; pure observation (Berkeleyan),
127; pure theoretical, 141;
reporting, 111; theoretical, 112;
theoretico-reporting, 112

411

General Index

Achinstein, P., 142n, 143n, 144n
Acquaintance, 3; perceptual, 49, 221, 223, 228, 235–36, 244, 246–47, 284, 349, 354, 374. *See also* Direct perception
Action at a distance, 306, 310–11, 314, 315. *See also* Functional correlation
Adverbial materialism, xi–xii, 375–87
Adverbial neutral monism, 388–92
Adverbial sensing theory, xi, chapter 2, appendix. *See also* Sensings
Adverbial terminology. *See* Sensing terminology
Aesthetics, 362–64
Analytic phenomenalism, 2, 119–25, 130, 204, 257; subjunctive analysis, 121–23; probabilistic analysis, 123–25
Apparitions, 14, 47, 51–52. *See also* Hallucination
'Appear': intensional sense, 40; epistemic sense, 64; nonepistemic sense, 64
Aquinas, 259
Aristotle, 259
Armstrong, D., 331, 348n
Aune, B., 329–30, 337, 339, 373n
Austin, J., 2–3, 7
Author of nature, 99, 101, 116, 317, 318, 320. *See also* Berkeley, G.; Gods
Ayer, A., 2, 6, 28, 39, 125–26; analytic phenomenalism, 119–22, 187; striped tiger, 79–82

Ballentine, L., 297n, 300n, 332
Belief theories, 348, 386–87
Berkeley, G., 2, 3–4, 6, 39, 53, 89, 133, 187, 220, 235, 246, 293; direct perception, 5–10; phenomenalism, 15–18, 19, chapter 3, 184–86, 198, 202, 211–13; objections to realism, 94–99, 224–25; perceptual relativity, 96, 97–98, 225, 227; defense of phenomenalism, 99–131; and explanatory schema, 99, 116–18, 183–84, 317–18, 320–22; and

notions, 100, 101–18; bundle theory, 100, 125–29, 130–31, 187, 201–07; and mind-terms, 102–06; theory of mind, 102–18, 192; on language, 106–07; and observation terms, 107–10, 126–29; and theoretical terms, 107, 115–18, 126–29; and reporting terms, 111–12, 115–18, 128; and instrumentalism, 114–18, 129–30, 361; and 'exist,' 204–05, 207, 354–55; and time-gap, 353–55. *See also* Correspondence rules; Ideas; Phenomenalism; Sensa
Black holes, 333
Blood: color of, 236–39; hemoglobin in, 238, 239
Bohm, D., 303n, 307n
Bohnert, H., 149, 164n, 166, 167
Bohr, N., 295–99 passim, 306
Brain, W., 42n, 47, 48, 51n
Braithwaite, R., 144
Brightness: apparent, 62–65; sensation, 62, 64, 66
Broad, C., 391n
Burtt, E., 328

C-rules. *See* Correspondence rules
Campbell, K., 230, 242n, 243n
Carnap, R., 25, 86n, 108n, 109, 144
Cartesian ego, 275, 280
Causal ancestors, 44–46, 341
Causal: indeterminism, 303, 321, 365; determinism, 365–67
Causal intermediaries, 5, 8–9
Central argument of book: stated, 29–30, 31, 33–34; discussed, chapter 1, 50, 69, 77–78, 88, 349, 351–62
Certainty, 369–71
Characteristics: right-making, 342–43; success-making, 342–43
Chisholm, R., 11–13, 14n, 64, 341n, 342, 369n 370n; adverbial theory, 5n, 17n; adverbial terminology, 73–77; on analytic phenomenalism, 119–25, 187. *See also* Sensing terminology

413

DATE DUE